The Ancient Indus

The ancient Indus civilization was erased from human memory until 1924, when it was rediscovered and announced in the *Illustrated London News*. Our understanding of the Indus has been partially advanced by textual sources from Mesopotamia that contain references to Meluhha, a land identified by cuneiform specialists as the Indus, with which the ancient Mesopotamians traded and engaged in other forms of interaction. In this volume, Rita P. Wright uses both Mesopotamian texts and, principally, the results of archaeological excavations and surveys to draw a rich account of the Indus civilization's well-planned cities, its sophisticated alterations to the landscape, and the complexities of its agropastoral and craft-producing economy. She focuses principally on the social networks established between city and rural communities; farmers, pastoralists, and craft producers; and Indus merchants and traders and the symbolic imagery that the civilization shared with contemporary cultures in Iran, Mesopotamia, Central Asia, and the Persian Gulf region. Broadly comparative, her study emphasizes the interconnected nature of early societies.

Rita P. Wright is associate professor of anthropology at New York University. A John D. and Catherine T. MacArthur Fellow, she has conducted archaeological field research in Afghanistan, Iran, and Pakistan. She is the editor of *Gender and Archaeology* and coeditor, with Cathy L. Costin, of *Craft and Social Identity*.

Case Studies in Early Societies

Series Editor
Rita P. Wright, *New York University*

This series aims to introduce students to early societies that have been the subject of sustained archaeological research. Each study is also designed to demonstrate a contemporary method of archaeological analysis in action, and the authors are all specialists currently engaged in field research.

The books have been planned to cover many of the same fundamental issues. Tracing long-term developments and describing and analyzing a discrete segment in the prehistory or history of a region, they represent an invaluable tool for comparative analysis. Clear, well-organized, authoritative, and succinct, the case studies are an important resource for students and for scholars in related fields, such as anthropology, ethnohistory, history, and political science. They also offer the general reader accessible introductions to important archaeological sites.

Other titles in the series include:

Ancient Mesopotamia
Susan Pollock

Ancient Oaxaca
Richard E. Blanton, Gray M. Feinman, Stephen A. Kowalewski, Linda M. Nicholas

Ancient Maya
Arthur Demarest

Ancient Cahokia and the Mississippians
Timothy R. Pauketat

Ancient Puebloan Southwest
John Kantor

Ancient Middle Niger
Roderick J. McIntosh

Ancient Jomon of Japan
Junko Habu

Ancient Tiwanaku
John Janusek

The Ancient Egyptian State
Robert J. Wenke

THE ANCIENT INDUS

Urbanism, Economy, and Society

Rita P. Wright
New York University

CAMBRIDGE
UNIVERSITY PRESS

CAMBRIDGE UNIVERSITY PRESS
Cambridge, New York, Melbourne, Madrid, Cape Town, Singapore,
São Paulo, Delhi, Dubai, Tokyo

Cambridge University Press
32 Avenue of the Americas, New York, NY 10013-2473, USA

www.cambridge.org
Information on this title: www.cambridge.org/9780521576529

© Cambridge University Press 2010

First published 2010

Printed in the United States of America

A catalog record for this publication is available from the British Library.

Library of Congress Cataloging in Publication data
Wright, Rita P.
    The ancient Indus : urbanism, economy, and society / Rita P. Wright.
        p.   cm. – (Case studies in early societies)
    Includes bibliographical references and index.
    ISBN 978-0-521-57219-4 (hardback) – ISBN 978-0-521-57652-9 (pbk.)
    1. Indus civilization.   I. Title.   II. Series.
    DS425 W75 2009
    934–dc22   2008020090

ISBN 978-0-521-57219-4 Hardback
ISBN 978-0-521-57652-9 Paperback

Contents

List of Figures, Tables, and Boxes

Figures

Tables

Boxes

Acknowledgments

I especially acknowledge how fortunate I have been to conduct research in South Asia. After twenty-five years, I still consider this region one of the most beautiful in both its landscape and its people. I have been privileged to work with an extraordinary group of archaeologists and to have met and befriended countless local people in villages and towns. Their generosity, hospitality, and sense of history have changed the way I think about the world. I hope I have conveyed in some small measure the historical riches of the region.

This book could not have been written without the benefit of the earlier research of many colleagues. I am especially grateful to Jean-François and Catherine Jarrige for inviting me to participate in the excavations at the site of Mehrgarh. During several field seasons, the Jarriges and other members of their team, Gonzaque Quivron, Marielle Santoni, and Anaick Samzun, generously shared with me their broad knowledge of the archaeology of Baluchistan. My research at Mehrgarh was followed by a longer-term commitment to the Indus site of Harappa. I owe a great debt to members of the Harappa Archaeological Research Project (HARP), first and foremost among them George Dales who initially invited me to join the Harappa team and to Mark Kenoyer and Richard Meadow for continued collaboration. Other Harappa colleagues–Harriet "Rae" Beaubien, Barbara Dales, Brian Hemphill, Kenneth Kennedy, Nancy Lovell, John Lukacs, Marco Madella, Donna Strahan, and Steve Weber–always provided much food for thought and insights into Indus "things." I also conducted a survey centered around Harappa, and I thank my collaborators on the Beas Regional Survey, Afzal Kahn and Joe Schuldenrein, along with Susan Malin-Boyce, Laura Miller, Mark Smith, and Suanna Selby, for their contributions to the success of the research. Rafique Mughal encouraged me to conduct the survey and was a collaborator in the early stages of the project. Late in the project, I was especially fortunate to work with Reid Bryson, whose knowledge of the climatology of the region gave me a new set of eyes. My path crossed in the field with many students from New York University, the University of

Wisconsin, and Harvard University – Bill Belcher, Sharri Clark, Randall Law, Heather Miller, and Laura Miller – who conducted their dissertation research at Harappa and now are professional colleagues. Their stimulating conversations and world-class projects have added substantially to my understanding of the Indus civilization.

Many friends and colleagues took the time to read chapters and sections of the book at different stages in its preparation. I appreciate their taking the time from their own work to provide me with perceptive comments. My sincere thanks to Norman Crowe, Dale Curran, Louis Flam, Jean Freebern, Dorian Fuller, Kenneth Kennedy, Virginia Kerns, Andrew Lawler, Susan Malin-Boyce, Heather Miller, Heidi Miller, Laura Miller, Kathleen Morrison, Gregory Possehl, Karen Rubinson, Joe Schuldenrein, Matthew Spigelman, Bruce Trigger, Steve Weber, Wilma Wetterstrom, and especially Holly Pittman who gave generously of her time and expertise to walk me through the intricacies of the art of seals and sealings. Kathleen Ehrhardt has my unending gratitude for having read the entire manuscript and made extensive comments on its organization and content. She helped me bring into better focus the themes advanced throughout my book. Four anonymous reviewers of the book proposal and the prepared manuscript provided me with useful commentary. I appreciate the experience and insight they brought to their reviews.

Several colleagues were generous in granting me access to data and permission to use illustrations from their published works. Nilofer Shaikh was most generous in providing me with her unpublished evidence from regional surveys of the Lower Indus conducted by her team from Shah Abdul Latif University. Randall Law aided me immeasurably in preparation of a map identifying raw material sources during a time when he was in the final stages of his dissertation. Ute Franke-Vogt, Gonzague Quivron, Catherine Jarrige, Michael Jansen, Gregory Possehl, the Harappa Archaeological Project, the British Museum, and the American Museum of Natural History provided me with permission for several of the illustrations. The photograph on the book cover was taken in the early 1960s by Munir Khan at Harappa.com.

I am especially appreciative of several research assistants who worked with me on the book. Lia Tsesmeli prepared the majority of the illustrations, creating several original maps, with great skill. Danette Newcomb worked on the figures in their final stages. Jillian Swift was in the unfortunate position of taking on the job of research assistant in the final stages of the book's copyediting, bibliography, and index preparation, and last-minute figure creation and revision. I remain appreciative of her assistance and excellent research skills.

This book is the tenth to be published in the series Case Studies in Early Societies, which I founded with Cambridge University Press. Seven other books currently are in the works. I am forever grateful for the support and guidance of Jessica Kuper in the United Kingdom who steered me through a successful review process for the series and the first books that were published before her retirement. Her successor, Simon Whitmore, brought strong editorial skills and perceptive understandings of the field of archaeology. More recently, Beatrice Rehl, commissioning editor in the New York office, took on many of the archaeology projects, to which she brings a broad vision of our field and its place in the wider world of scholarship. Finally, I am most grateful for the assistance of Ernie Haim and Sara Black, whose patience and forbearance in spite of the countless deadlines missed gave me the support I needed during the final stages of production.

I could not have written this book without the support of several institutions. New York University provided me with two semester-long sabbaticals during which I completed most of the writing. A grant from NYU made it possible to hire research assistants. I especially owe a debt of gratitude to the Government of the Islamic Republic of Pakistan, Ministry of Culture, Sports, Tourism and Youth Affairs and the Department of Archaeology and Museums for granting me permission to participate in excavations and surveys.

My ability to see this book to fruition is in no small measure due to the support of my parents as I ventured into archaeology and later as I began writing this book. They both passed away before I was able to complete the book, but since they always knew that I could do it, they would not be surprised to see it bound and on shelves today. My family, Dale, Susan, Kara, Dave, Mike, Pat, and Jack are at the core of my being. Their confidence and love mean everything.

1   A Long-Forgotten Civilization

This book is about a civilization that was erased from human memory until the early part of the twentieth century and the discoveries made by the explorers, travelers, and archaeologists whose accounts and research brought to light the civilization's significance in world history.

The Indus civilization is one of three in the "Ancient East" that, along with Mesopotamia and Pharonic Egypt, was a cradle of early civilization in the Old World (Childe 1950). Mesopotamia and Egypt were longer lived but coexisted with the Indus civilization during its florescence between 2600 and 1900 B.C. (see Figure 1.1 for locations of the three civilizations). Of the three, the Indus was the most expansive, extending from today's northeast Afghanistan to Pakistan and India. Its major centers lie within major river systems, the Indus and the Ghaggar-Hakra Rivers. The Indus, one of the great rivers of Asia, flows through the valley, passing under the shadow of the Himalayas and coursing through a vast dry zone before emptying into the Arabian Sea. Its waters have sustained the people of the Indus Valley for thousands of years. The Ghaggar-Hakra straddles the two countries of Pakistan and India. It once flowed with great strength through what is today northwest India (the Ghaggar) and eastern Pakistan (the Hakra).

Scholarship on the Indus civilization has lagged behind that of Mesopotamia and Egypt for several reasons. First, Mesopotamia and Egypt figure in biblical accounts, and their links to the west have long excited the interest of Western scholars. In the late 1700s, Napoleon's military expedition to Egypt included 167 specialists who documented and studied the history and monuments of ancient Egypt. They published their findings in illustrated works that became well-known throughout Europe. Similarly, ancient Mesopotamia was the subject of many early travelers' accounts that romanticized its fabulous ruins. The western explorers who investigated these ruins sought to document places and events known from biblical accounts.

A second reason for the lag in scholarship is that the writing system of the Indus civilization has not been deciphered. Each of the three

1

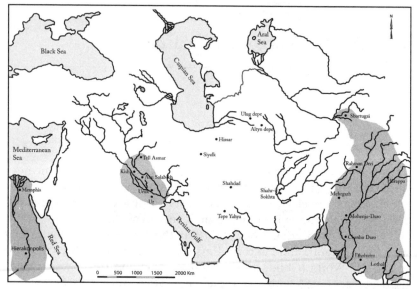

Figure 1.1. Ancient states in the Near East and South Asia. Left to right: Egypt, Mesopotamia, and the Indus. © R. P. Wright.

ancient civilizations possessed a system of writing, and more than a hundred years ago scholars deciphered the Egyptian hieroglyphic and Mesopotamian cuneiform writing systems. The Indus script still remains a mystery.

In this book, I emphasize the ways in which archaeologists have met the challenge of reconstructing – without the aid of written records – the (pre)history of the Harappans, a name used for the people of the Indus, whose remains were first discovered at the site of Harappa (see Figure 1.2 for sites referred to in the text). They have based their interpretations mainly on the objects and buildings that the Harappans produced and used and have made great strides in piecing together the less accessible aspects of the civilization's past.

As a way of introducing the rich database available to archaeological reconstructions of the region's past, I begin by discussing the earliest references to the lands the Indus people occupied and the events leading up to discovery of the civilization. The establishment of the Archaeological Survey of India under British colonial authorities in 1861 marks the true beginning of official archaeological research in the region and the final naming of the civilization in the early twentieth century. From there, I go on to recount the work that continues to this day.

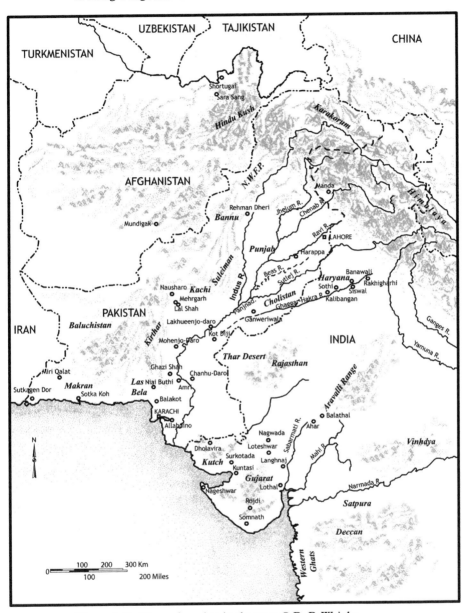

Figure 1.2. Sites referred to in the text. © R. P. Wright.

My own research in this region began in the mid-1970s when I joined a research project seeking evidence for settlement in a remote valley of Afghanistan and trade with far-off Mesopotamia. Later, I was invited to join the excavations at Mehrgarh, an archaeological site in Pakistan located at the foot of a major mountain pass that climbs westward to Afghanistan. Mehrgarh was settled at around 7000 B.C. and was the first agricultural settlement in this region. My interest in both of these projects was on the interaction spheres that tied South Asia to the greater Near East and other neighboring areas. Later, I joined a team at Harappa, one of the first Indus cities, where my research continues to focus on exchange systems and has expanded to include the development of urbanism, the region's agropastoral and craft-producing economy, and the emergence of this complex society.

A Civilization Rediscovered

Our first accounts of the Indus civilization come from written texts in southern Mesopotamia at about 2400 B.C., long before it was named by Western scholars. Frequent references in Mesopotamian texts are to a place called Meluhha, a distant land to the east, where peacocks could be heard and treasures like gold, tin, and carnelian procured. The texts speak of battles, acquisition of booty, diplomacy, and other ventures as well as the maritime and overland routes by which they were obtained. Seaworthy boats from Mesopotamia sailed the Persian Gulf, scheduling travel in accordance with annual monsoons and the prevailing winds and stopping at ports where sweet water was available. Overland travel involved traversing through vast arid regions and mountainous zones either on foot or by animal-drawn carts. These references are rather short-lived, however, and they disappear from the Mesopotamian documents by 1700 B.C. In later periods, references to Meluhha (see Figure 8.1) are to a different region altogether, thus putting an end to these early glimpses of the Indus.

Western scholarship on the history of the region began in the seventeenth century when European merchants incorporated the East India Company for purposes of trade in east Indian spices. The company had gained permission from the Mughal Emperor, Jahangir, to establish a mercantile "factory," and trading posts were built along the east and west coasts of India. Europeans were attracted to the region for its economic opportunities, but many also had scholarly interests. Various voluntary associations were founded based on their historical and literary pursuits. Although closely connected to the British colonial administration, these associations were not part of the government. Founded in 1784, the

Asiatic Society was the earliest. It was followed by the Bombay Literary Society (1804) and the Literary Society of Madras (1812). Most members were East India Company employees, and their overall purpose was to make "India legible" (Trautmann and Sinopoli 2002:494). Studies initiated by members of the societies differed from the works of travel writers and earlier histories that were based on firsthand observations. Instead, their focus was on reading and interpreting works written in Sanskrit and other South Asian languages. Their scholarly works "claimed a superior authority... [because they] did not merely see the outer person but had access to the mind and intentionality of the Asian, the inner person" (Trautmann 1997:30–7; Trautmann and Sinopoli 2002:495). Viewed from that perspective, archaeological remains (material culture) were secondary and useful primarily as complements to textual studies.

Exploration that led to archaeological discoveries was left to the patronage of civil authorities and military officers. A major effort during the early nineteenth century involved survey work designed to document the extent of "Indian" territory and to collect a variety of data useful to the colonial enterprise. Surveyors produced maps that showed geographical features and documented river systems and geodetic observations. They also collected botanical and geological specimens and measured distances between locations for mapping purposes, and recorded local customs. Surveyors often followed other interests and accumulated large collections of manuscripts, drawings, and antiquities, subsequently publishing detailed "plans and measurements of monuments and sites" (Singh 2004:5).

Other forms of intelligence and "diplomatic" efforts resulted in important archaeological discoveries. Charles Masson (originally James Lewis) was a deserter from the Bengal European Artillery who had assumed an American identity, a fairly common practice of the time (Lahiri 2005:4). As part of an arrangement to gain an official pardon, he was assigned to an intelligence-gathering network that included an agreement to turn over any collections of antiquities that resulted from his travels for the East India Company (Lahiri 2005:19). Masson was conversant with classical sources and Alexander's campaigns, a factor that most likely drew him to explore certain areas. In 326 B.C., Alexander had marched his Macedonian troops into the northern parts of what today are Afghanistan and Pakistan and sent small contingents to sail the Indus River and march across the Punjab. He often noted the presence of archaeological sites and speculated on their identity based on the then known textual sources. In 1829, Masson journeyed on horseback through the Punjab recording the presence of archaeological sites and monuments. He later published his findings in three volumes, which included detailed illustrations and descriptions of the ancient settlements. In the context of this book, Masson's most important discovery was Harappa, a major city of the Indus civilization. He made detailed records describing the site as it existed in the early 1800s. Masson was impressed with Harappa's massive size and its several high mounds resulting from hundreds of years of the accumulation of deteriorating architecture and human activities. He commented on (and in some instances illustrated) the thousands of artifacts still visible on the surface of the site. Masson mistakenly believed the site dated to an historical period and one that had been mentioned by Alexander's troops. However, according to local residents, whose views Masson recorded, the mounds were remnants of an ancient city ruled by a king named Hara Pala whose "lust and crimes" (he had committed incest with a family member) had led to the demise of the city (C. Masson 1842; Lahiri 2005:10).[1]

Also under the employ of the East India Company, Alexander Burnes followed Masson two years later, sailing up the Indus River to assess the "viability for future movements" of the company's army. He arrived at Harappa in 1831 (Lahiri 2005:14) and provided additional details to Masson's observations. He noted that parts of the ancient city had been built of baked brick, and he commented on the ongoing destruction of the site brought about by local residents. Removing baked bricks from the site to construct and repair their homes was a local village practice that had created a situation that Burnes referred to as "perfect chaos" (Burnes 1834; Lahiri 2005:12).

Later, brick robbing on an even grander scale would prove to be a catalyst for continuing interest in Harappa. In spite of the visits of Masson and Burnes and their documentation of the site, engineers entrusted with the construction of a major railway system designed to link parts of the region failed to recognize the site's significance with disastrous consequences for its preservation. Railway engineers carted away sufficient brick from Harappa's buildings to provide 100 miles of ballast for tracks between Multan and Lahore. General Alexander Cunningham, who later became the head of a newly created Archaeological Survey of India, visited Harappa in 1853 and 1854 before railway construction. Like others before him, he was impressed by its size, especially the massive walls of what he incorrectly thought had been a Buddhist monastery, and planned to return to conduct excavations. When he returned many years later, the bricks from the original construction had been removed (Lahiri 2005:18) and were nowhere to be seen.

In 1858, the East India Company was dissolved, and the region came under the responsibility of the British Crown, a condition that prevailed until 1947. The "formalization" of archaeology as an official focus of the colonial government took place in 1861. Alexander Cunningham, now retired from military service, led these efforts (Trautmann and Sinopol, 2002). As noted previously, Cunningham had a strong interest in the region's past, and although he was trained in Sanskrit, unlike many of his contemporaries whose focus lay in the study of texts, his primary interests were in numismatics and archaeological fieldwork, which he considered a more reliable basis with which to reconstruct the history of the Indian past than the literary scholarship that dominated historical studies. By the time he took on the directorship of the Archaeological Survey, Cunningham was "widely acknowledged as the subcontinent's foremost expert in archaeology" (Lahiri 2005:498), having conducted excavations and surveys in numerous areas.

Later, Cunningham returned to Harappa to conduct a proper survey and to map the site. He published a brief account of his investigations and provided illustrations of a selection of artifacts, including stone tools, pottery, and small objects that resembled "chess pawns." His most spectacular discovery was a seal that belonged to a Major Clark (later donated to the British Museum), which he described as follows (it is illustrated in Figure 1.3):

The seal is a smooth black stone without polish. On it is engraved very deeply a bull, without a hump, looking to the right, with two stars under the neck. Above the bull there is an inscription in six characters, which are quite unknown to me. They are certainly not Indian letters; and as the bull which accompanies them is without a hump [like the traditional zebu cattle], I conclude that the seal is foreign to India. (1875:108)

Figure 1.3. Major Clark's seal from Harappa reported by Alexander Cunningham. Courtesy of the British Museum.

The seal could be held with two fingers by gripping a small knob on the back. When pressed against soft clay or other pliable material, it left a distinctive image, presumed to identify an individual or a group just as a signature or corporate seal does today. Of all the finds discovered at Harappa during this period, the stamp seal excited the most scholarly interest, because it implied that the people who left it behind were literate, a feature associated with complex societies and cultures then known only from later periods in the history of India. The fact that it displayed an unknown script was a clear indication that Harappa may have been the site of a culture not recorded in textual sources, though this possibility went unnoticed at the time.

The seal and others subsequently discovered were suggestive of a "half-glimpsed world" (Lahiri 2005:27) that remained unknown until the 1920s. Cunningham retired in 1885, after which the archaeological survey went through restructuring, decentralization, division into regional circles, and finally recentralization under the leadership of John Marshall in 1902 (Trautmann and Sinopoli 2002:501). As the head of a state-sponsored institution, Marshall's position at the archaeological survey came under the close supervision of the viceroy of India, Lord (G. N.) Curzon who selected him for the position.

Under tight budgetary constraints, but under Lord Curzon's instructions, Marshall launched a campaign to oversee architectural conservation and inspections of sites around the country. Marshall and his survey officers conducted only limited excavations during his early years as director general. They excavated several Buddhist sites and monuments, although Marshall seems to have recognized the possibility that a more ancient past existed (Lahiri 2005:58). Marshall did not conduct any excavations at these sites until much later. Instead, he deployed colleagues to conduct work at non-Buddhist sites. In 1909, Hirananda Sastri was sent to Harappa to oversee a survey in connection with the site's preservation. The brick robbing there had continued, and Sastri was commissioned to determine whether the site could be protected or purchased from the landowners. Sastri's report was never published, and from what is known, he was not impressed with the site's importance; nevertheless, he did note that the proportion of the standard bricks used in buildings at Harappa was different from bricks found at Buddhist and other early historic cities (Lahiri 2005:79). This indicated that the site was not of Buddhist origin.

Several years later, Daya Ram Sahni returned to conduct an excavation on two of the mounds at Harappa which was paid for and brought under the Ancient Monuments Preservation Act (Lahiri 2005:171). Meanwhile, other officers from the archaeological survey were deployed to Mohenjo-daro: D. R. Bhandarkar in 1911, R. D. Banerji in 1919 and

1922–3, M. S. Vats in 1924, K. N. Dikshit in 1924–5, H. Harqreaves in 1925–6, and E. H. Mackay in 1927–1931.

Exploration also took place in areas beyond the Indus plain. At the same time artifacts were being unearthed in non text-related locales in the core area, similar kinds of enigmatic discoveries were also being made in the remote region of Baluchistan. In 1876, Major E. Mockler excavated at the site of Sutkagen-dor near the coast and to the west of the Indus Valley (see Figure 1.2), at a site now known to have been an Indus port of trade. Twenty-five years later an explorer, Hughes Buller, discovered the site of Nal in the Las Bela area (see also Figure 1.2). The pottery produced at Nal is decorated in complex geometric patterns and in a variety of colors. This type of polychrome pottery was previously unknown and given its distinctive qualities made for easy comparisons when found elsewhere. Later, artifacts of greater antiquity than the cities themselves suggested an early period of growth before full florescence of the civilization.

Returning to Mohenjo-daro, it was Banerji and Vats who may have been catalysts for the startling revelations that were soon to be known concerning this forgotten civilization. Banerji had been sent back to Mohenjo-daro in December of 1922. He had visited the site previously, found distinctive stone implements, and conducted surveys nearby. By the time of his return, he was convinced that Mohenjo-daro was of "remote antiquity" (Lahiri 2005:219). This idea was partially confirmed by the discovery of inscribed seals, of a type that had been found in Harappa. In correspondence with Marshall in 1923, Banerji described the seals as "identical" to those found at Harappa. Later, he also compared some of the ceramics from Mohenjo-daro with those at Nal that Mockler and others had discovered. Even though we know now that the Nal ceramics predated Mohenjo-daro, they did contribute to the early stages of settlement that led up to Indus cities. Clearly he was on the right track. He also used the term "prehistoric" to signify a culture (presumably unknown) in his descriptions of Mohenjo-daro. Though he had identified writing on the seals, it was undecipherable, therefore, preliterate. Banerji's attempts to link up the artifacts at Mohenjo-daro with others that had been discovered was a key point. In the same year, M. S. Vats, one of the principal excavators at Harappa, who had worked at Mohenjo-daro, made similar comparisons. In correspondence with Marshall, he noted the similarities of the seals and script. He also compared various ceramics, brick sizes, terracotta figurines, clay bangles, and sling balls at Mohenjo-daro to others he had seen at Harappa.

Determined to get to the bottom of this riddle, Marshall called for a meeting with Banerji and D. R. Sahni, who also had excavated at Harappa and arranged to ship excavation plans, drawings, and artifacts to a central place for their joint discussion. The body of data they examined included representative artifacts from Harappa (contributed by Sahni from his excavations) (Lahiri 2005:254). A meeting of this sort is an archaeologist's dream, sorting through materials and drawing on the knowledge of several experts, especially in this case because what was being discovered was emerging as an entirely new and unknown culture. The size of the sites and strong similarities among them suggested they were dealing with something as yet largely unknown but of great significance.

In the end, Marshall was convinced. Writing for the *Illustrated London News* some days later, he boldly stated:

Not often has it been given to archaeologists, as it was given to Schliemann at Tiryns and Mycenae, or to Stein in the deserts of Turkestan, to light upon the remains of a long-forgotten civilization. It looks, however, at this moment, as if we were on the threshold of such a discovery in the plains of the Indus.

Unable to state the age of the civilization, he went on to observe that the Indus (which he named after the river system) artifacts differed from any known other civilizations in the region, though he drew ecological parallels with Pharaonic Egypt and Mesopotamia. All were positioned on great river tracts with fertile soils, unfailing water supplies, and water transport for ease of communication (Lahiri 2005:264). This article appeared in the *Illustrated London News* on September 20, 1924.

Large numbers of photographs accompanied Marshall's article. Soon after its appearance, scholars responded to the news. In a return note to the *News*, Archibald Henry Sayce who was conversant in ancient languages and archaeology wrote that the remarkable discoveries that Marshall wrote about were

even more remarkable and startling than he supposes. The inscribed "seals" or plaques found at Harappa and Mohenjo-daro are practically identical with the Proto-Elamite tablettes de compatibilité discovered by DeMorgan at Susa [in Mesopotamia]. The form and size of the plaques are the same, the "unicorns" are the same, and the pictographs and numerals are also the same. The identity is such that the "seals" and tablets might have come from the same hand. (Sayce 1924)

Later two other scholars, C. J. Gadd and S. Smith, concurred with what Sayce had written and offered a chart comparing certain signs from the Indus with those of Mesopotamia. Although neither Sayce nor Gadd and Smith were implying that the Indus was derived from these other cultures, they agreed that their symbolic system was indicative of contemporaneity. The effect was dramatic: "At one stroke the history of

India had been pushed back by 2,000 years and placed on a par with the histories of Egypt and Mesopotamia" (Franke-Vogt 1991b:181).

Reconstructing a Long-Forgotten Civilization

In 1947, following decades of anticolonial resistance, Britain partitioned India into two self-governing nations, India and Pakistan, and withdrew from the region. The area of eastern Bengal became East Pakistan; in 1971, it gained independence and is now Bangladesh. Obviously, these political divisions did not prevail during the early history of the region. The territory of the Indus civilization cut across the borders of today's India and Pakistan and even extended into parts of Afghanistan. Archaeologists now have carried out explorations in India under the auspices of the Archaeological Survey of India and in Pakistan under the Department of Archaeology of the Government of Pakistan, both formed after partition. Indian and Pakistani archaeologists have been joined by many foreign scholars from Europe, North America, and Asia.

The goals of archaeologists have changed dramatically since the brick-robbing days of the nineteenth century and the earliest research in the twentieth century. In this brief account of the major trends after Cunningham's discoveries in the mid-nineteenth century, I provide an overview of the questions that have guided archaelogical research.

As discussed, the East India Company and the British government funded much of the early research. During the colonial period, archaeological exploration focused on mapping the territory and plotting the location of archaeological sites. This included recording the architecture and city plans of its major sites and retrieving antiquities. As a colonial power, the British government sought to demonstrate the brilliance of an early and forgotten civilization that had once occupied territory that, millennia later, they had conquered. The research thus had a political dimension. It served to create an image of a common heritage for the vast territory encompassed by British India, thus justifying the existing political boundaries by looking to the past.

Many of the British scholars who engaged in this research – from Sir John Marshall to the others who followed him such as Stuart Piggott and Sir Mortimer Wheeler – were influenced by their training as classical archaeologists. One exception was Ernest Mackay, who worked closely with Marshall on the earliest excavations, and who had previously conducted research at archaeological sites in Mesopotamia. Marshall and Mackay painted a peaceful picture of the civilization. Finding no evidence of conflict and warfare, and unable to locate temples or royal tombs, they concluded that the Indus civilization had been ruled by "literati, priests, craftsmen and traders" (Shaffer and Lichtenstein 1999). In contrast, Wheeler and Piggott, based on interpretations likely colored by their own World War II experiences and their training in classical archaeology, led them to stress "militaristic imperialism" (Shaffer and Lichtenstein 1999). Their evidence came from site plans reminiscent of those found in Roman archaeology, including features they referred to as "citadels," "bastions," "defences," and "gateways." They also identified copper and bronze objects as implements of war.

Wheeler attributed the origins of this fully developed civilization to stimulus diffusion because there seemed to be no antecedent developments to explain its "sudden" emergence. He believed that new ideas had diffused from a more culturally advanced group (Mesopotamia) to one less developed (the Indus), resulting in Mesopotamian stylistic elements and artifacts found at Indus sites. The presence of a small number of Indus seals in Mesopotamia and objects of a Mesopotamian style at Mohenjo-daro (e.g., the pattern on the garment of the small statue shown in Figure 1.4) seemed to indicate the spread of ideas from Mesopotamia. In the 1968 edition of his much acclaimed book, *The Indus Civilization*, Wheeler described the Mesopotamian impact:

It is legitimate to affirm that the idea of civilization came to the Indus from the land of the Twin Rivers, whilst recognizing that the essential self-sufficiency of each of the two civilizations induced a strongly localized and specialized cultural expression of that idea in each region. (1968:25)

Recent discoveries, including written documents from Mesopotamia and artifactual evidence from the Indus, have discredited Wheeler's view of the Indus. As discussed earlier, Indus people were in contact with Mesopotamia and a wider world based on interaction among equals. While the Mesopotamian texts attest to contact with the Indus by the middle of the third millennium B.C., more recent discoveries of Indus artifacts at sites in Iran, Central Asia, and the Arabian peninsula indicate that its contacts (discussed in detail in Chapter 8) took place throughout a vast region that took a very different form from what Wheeler had suggested.

Other twentieth-century research has filled in some of the gaps in understanding the roots of the Indus civilization. The explorations of Sir Aurel Stein (1928, 1931, 1937, 1943a,b), Walter Fairservis (1956, 1959), and Beatrice de Cardi (1983) in Baluchistan uncovered settlements that predate the Indus civilization. Mehrgarh, later discovered and excavated by the French Archaeological Mission to Pakistan, is the oldest of these sites (J. -F. Jarrige and Lechevallier 1979). Together,

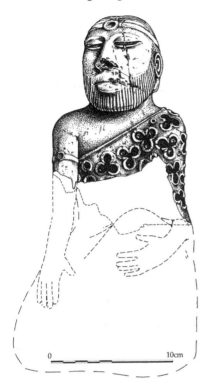

Figure 1.4. The "Priest King" statue from Mohenjo-daro. Redrawn from a reconstruction by Ardeleanu-Jansen (1991).

the results of these projects demonstrate that many antecedent developments had taken place before people established settlements in the Indus Valley.

More general scholarship on questions about the development of civilizations is of equal interest. By the middle of the twentieth century, discoveries in the Indus began to attract the attention of scholars with broad interests in the comparative analysis of civilizations. The question arose, whether study of the Indus could contribute to an understanding of early civilizations more generally. In the late 1940s, American anthropologist Julian Steward (1949) drew attention to the similar environments in which several early civilizations developed, pointing out that the cradles of early civilization in Egypt, Mesopotamia, and the Indus shared common ecological adaptations. According to Steward, their locations along major river systems were keys to the development of civilization, and he suggested that their arid environments fostered a dependence on state-controlled irrigation systems that were essential to crop cultivation. The control of major water works by centralized leadership, Steward argued, led to social divisions within societies. While the results of subsequent research in the Indus and elsewhere lent little support to his ideas, many archaeologists remain interested in how the environments of early civilizations affected their development, a question discussed in more detail in later chapters.

Today archaeologists are conducting many new excavations and surveys throughout South Asia. Some projects build on longstanding questions but bring fresh perspectives and the application of modern technologies to their study, while others raise new questions. For example, at Mohenjo-daro a team of architectural historians and archaeologists from the Aachen Research Project Mohenjo-daro (Jansen 1993a,b) have redrawn the settlement plan of the city and reevaluated its chronological development. Other scholars from the Italian Mission to Mohenjodaro (Tosi, Bondioli, and Vidale 1983) have discovered new evidence for craft workshops. Restoration projects funded by UNESCO have also produced noteworthy results. Archaeologists have found important new evidence along the now-dry riverbed of the Ghaggar-Hakra Rivers, where two major cities, Ganweriwala and Raghigarhi, have been discovered. A third city, Dholavira, is located to the south in the Rann of Kutch.

These discoveries greatly alter our conception of the extent of city development, while discoveries of smaller village and town settlements help us understand the relations between urban and rural communities. Researchers now have a better understanding of the environmental conditions at the onset of settlement as well as changes that occurred during the florescence of the civilization and the eventual abandonment of Indus cities. The evidence comes from deep sea coring, pollen analyses, and geomorphological studies. Currently, the number of settlements with material related to the Indus civilization numbers in the thousands and includes sites in Afghanistan, Pakistan, and India (Figure 1.2).

As I noted earlier in this chapter, since 1987 I have been involved in a major research effort at the Indus city of Harappa, led by a team from the United States in collaboration with local and foreign scholars.[2] The Harappa Archaeological Research Project (HARP) was founded by Dr. George Dales of the University of California Berkeley (Figure 1.5) and has involved extensive excavations focused on establishing site layout, craft-producing areas, and a well-defined stratigraphic sequence. Radiocarbon analyses at Harappa have contributed to developing an absolute chronology. In addition, I have directed a landscape and settlement survey of the now-dry bed of the Beas River near Harappa. Evidence from the Beas survey has rounded out our understanding of

Figure 1.5. George Dales, director of the Harappa Archaeological Research Project (1986–1991) and Donna Strahan, site conservator, examining a ceramic found at Harappa. Photograph by Harappa Archaeological Research Project © HARP.

urbanism, that is, the onset and florescence of regional settlement and Harappa's relationship to its rural communities. In spite of the destruction caused by the nineteenth-century brick robbing, our work has yielded important new findings, many of which form the core of later chapters in this book.

In the remainder of this chapter, I introduce some concepts that are recurrent points of reference in the text, and also explain the theoretical perspective that I adopt in this book. By presenting these ideas at the outset, I hope to provide a framework for understanding the Indus civilization.

Perspectives on Civilizations

Up to this point I have used the terms "civilization," "city," and "state" without defining them, appealing to the reader's general understanding of their meaning. In everyday discourse, these terms may be used loosely and interchangeably, but here I outline some specific meanings that signal different types of social phenomena.

The word "civilization" is problematic, often misunderstood, and subject to changes in definition. The French historian, Fernand Braudel, devoted an entire chapter in his *A History of Civilizations* to tracing out its various meanings. He suggested that the differences in meaning turn on the degree to which the term implies moral, as distinct from material, values. For example, in eighteenth-century France, it had a decidedly moral meaning. Civilization is contrasted with barbarism and referred to as "the process of being civilized" (Braudel 1993:3). By the first quarter of the nineteenth century, the sense of the word had changed dramatically. It had come to mean "the characteristics common to the collective life of a period or a group" (Braudel 1993:6). Unlike the eighteenth-century meaning, it did not necessarily connote a specific level of cultural achievement. The term could be applied to a broader range of groups, without value judgments about appropriate moral behavior and degree of civility.

In defining the Indus civilization, I focus on features that define its style, as manifest in its material culture, the objects that people made and used, and the landscapes and architectural features they created. There is no prior judgment about its superiority to previous periods or other cultures. I will say more about the various components of the style of the Indus civilization in this and subsequent chapters.

Another term I have used repeatedly in this book is "city." Cities of the past, like those in the present, were centers of population, but they never reached the scale of today's major cities such as New York or Paris. At its peak, classical Rome had a population of a million people, but in the Middle Ages the city's population declined to 100,000. In France, medieval walled cities had only 2,000 or 3,000 residents (Rybczynski 1995). In the Indus civilization, the population of any one city probably never rose above 50,000.

A distinguishing feature of cities is that they are homes to diverse social groups that are drawn to them as major centers of economic, political, and ceremonial life. We know from excavations that Harappans lived in densely packed neighborhoods (Figure 1.6) and engaged in diverse occupations. Although Harappan society was largely agrarian, based on agriculture and animal husbandry, many specialist craft producers lived in the city. The diversity in cities had social, as well as economic and political, dimensions.

The concept of urbanism refers to cities and the surrounding villages and towns that form a sustaining network. Although scholars have identified isolated cities that do not interact with the surrounding countryside, these are rare. In the more typical pattern, the city exists as a seat of authority, an attraction to the rural population, and a potential

Figure 1.6. Houses and streets at Mohenjo-daro. Courtesy
M. Jansen, Aachen Research project Mohenjo-daro.

source of refuge and services. Cities, in turn, depend on the hinterlands
for products and an inflow of people.

This pattern of city and countryside has been documented for several
Indus cities. Based primarily on studies of regional settlement patterns,
the results reveal the presence of settlements of varying sizes, ranging
from small villages to medium-sized towns. Limited studies from
excavations and documentation of activities visible on site surfaces indicate that many small settlements in the Indus carried out activities that
contributed to the urban economy. In that sense, the regional studies
document an expanded urban landscape and mutual dependencies of
cities and their hinterlands.

These terms – "civilization," "city," and "urbanism" – differ from the
concept of a state. Much like civilization, the term "state" can be interpreted in various ways. A conception of states that has dominated archaeology is what McIntosh refers to as the "Ex-astra" model (2005:19). At
the top of this model is a ruler (his/her head in the stars' a claim to divine
status) and below in rigidly hierarchical order are successive ranks of
producers, their status defined by their proximity to the ruler. Under
such a system all decisions are made by the ruler, and people in its lower
ranks are "state-dependent."

Archaeological interpretations of early states have moved away from the state-dependent model as new evidence has come to light that has altered our understanding of the authority structures of early states. For example, McIntosh describes the city of Jenne-Jeno in the Middle Niger (400 A.D. to 1100 A.D.) as a self-organized, corporate community in which multiple authorities existed, none of which monopolized power. Under different circumstances, the Maya civilization (300 A.D. to 900 A.D.) was less centralized than once thought. While the great Maya Lords did control the acquisition of status-enhancing goods such as jade, shell, magnetite, and quetzal feathers, their vast and varied agricultural system was maintained by local groups (Demarest 2004).

Studies of other early states reveal similar patterns of variability of rule (Nichols and Charlton 1997). For example, new interpretations of textual sources from southern Mesopotamian, once the iconic exemplar of a rigidly centralized state, indicate that even though rulers dominated aspects of the political economy, many other segments of the society received land grants, carried out independent production and consumption, and owned "date orchards and sometimes grain fields" (Stone 2007:219; Wright 2008). Urban spaces in Mesopotamian cities were not segregated by wealth. Large, well-appointed "houses were nestled alongside small, poor structures [and] an important official could live beside a humble fisherman" (Stone 1997:20). These data provide a picture "of urban residents who were both independent and connected to the public sector" (Stone 2007:219). J. N. Postgate (1992) suggests that the administration of Mesopotamian cities was by consensus of the local councils. The latter comprised males of the town who served as elders in local institutions.

Other examples come from closer to home in South Asia. After the Indus civilization was long gone, historical states, reveal similar patterns. In research at the fourteenth-through seventeenth-century A.D. state of Vijayanagara, Sinopoli (2003) has documented (through archaeological and textual sources) a vibrant economy comprised of people engaged in many different occupational activities in a political economy that was independently organized under the auspices of kinship, guild, and other nongovernmental groups. Finally, some states in historic South Asia were administrated by monarchs, whereas others are described as "republican" (Kenoyer 1997a). Republican states were ruled by a council in which leaders were drawn from among the leading families in the city. People in the city belonging to merchant and ritual specialist groups, and leading families participated in daily meetings of the council.

Finally, this pattern of independently organized groups, in distinction to centralized rule, is further documented by a recent comparative study. Bruce Trigger (2003) compared seven early states, in which there had been sustained archaeological research and written documentation, either in the form of scribal texts or ethno-historic accounts. They included Mesopotamia, Egypt, China, Maya, Aztec, Inka, and Yoruba. In them, he found that many types of authority were present in the form of self-government or councils comprised of important lineages, merchant associations, temple organizations and various other influential groups (Trigger 2003:269).

Theoretical Perspective

My focus here draws on this broadened picture of early states from the perspective of the Harappan political economy. By political economy, I mean the intertwined nature of political and economic organization, social differences, and ideological frameworks. To that end, my interests are in reconstructing, the infrastructural arrangements behind Indus agriculture, pastoralism, and craft production, its landscape construction and urban forms, and its human-landscape interrelations. I place a strong emphasis on understanding the Indus agropastoral and craft-producing economy as a basis for drawing out the diversity of occupations, organizations, and people who lived in Harappan cities. Through the analysis of these core elements of Indus society – its urban and rural communities and agropastoral and craft-producing economies – I try to show the unique ways in which its many specialist producers engaged in social and economic networks with consumers and other producers.

   In many discussions of agriculture, pastoralism, and craft production in early states, these three aspects of the economy are dealt with separately. This seems an artificial separation, since, at least in the Indus case, there are elements in each that overlap. For example, the use of fiber from animals is inseparable from the production of wool cloth, although the tasks may be engaged in by different specialists. Thus, each involves the dedication of labor resources and, in the case of fiber, of land for pasturage and management of specialized breeds. During the Urban period, as the civilization expanded into an ever-widening territory, there was an increased intensification, diversification, and specialization of the agropastoral and craft-producing economy. Individuals with specialized technical knowledge created previously unknown products and broadened their relations with those who consumed them, altering forms of production, organization, distribution, and exchange. In addition to the development of new specialized breeds for fiber, traction, and possibly dairying, multi-cropping strategies were employed, along with plough agriculture, new crop processing techniques, arboriculture, and cotton production. Crafts kept pace with these changes, creating products from some of the newly developed agrarian products and raw materials by applying innovative ways of producing craft products.

Many of the new products were made possible by applying innovative methods of production in which materials were transformed through the application of heat or a chemical process (H. M. L. Miller 2007:44). For the Indus, I view this "transformative" mindset as a particular technological style adopted by Indus artisans. Two examples are the grinding down of stone to create malleable pastes for the production of ornaments and inscribed devices and enhancing the color of stone by subjecting it to heat to bring out its latent minerals. This same mindset, though, can be seen in Indus landscapes in which the builders of their cities manipulated particular elements in nature much like the artisans who produced smaller, mobile objects. Such transformations are most apparent in Indus cities where engineering works were constructed of a kind unprecedented for their time, evincing the same mindset to transform the natural landscape to one totally humanized by altering and rearranging normal flows of water and a conscious plan to reclaim material processes for human use. It was a technological style in which Indus artisans appropriated the natural metamorphic processes that took millennia to accomplish in nature and transformed them in a matter of weeks, as though they had discovered the Earth's most intimate secrets long before geologists had done so in the modern era.

One of the ways in which we can gain access to the social differences within Indus society is through the new products and landscape alterations visible in their material world. New objects and places were created in cities and access to them marked certain people as the same or different from others. It is with that in mind that I place a strong emphasis on landscapes as layered, physical, and social settings and as cognitive or "practiced places" in which Harappan perceptions of their place in society were made visible. In that sense, I have steered away from over emphasizing the centralized nature of urban settings in favor of bringing to light the different social groups in which goods and services circulated. To enhance this view I focus on Indus cities as places of memory and social and community identity, not as passive backdrops to everyday practices but places that mold and recast human perceptions of identity and social status.

Another way in which I deviate from some recent Indus scholarship is by using references in various chapters to the interconnected nature of the Greater Near East and the Indus. Namely, I refer to southern Mesopotamia, Iran (proto-Elamite cultures), and Central Asia. I have placed a great deal of emphasis on trade (discussed in some detail here), and at various points in the book I explore the effect of these exchanges, beyond the trade of things to that of "ideas." Perhaps Indus scholars have shied away from such views, once described as "diffusionary" and universally rejected in anthropology. Indus scholarship has especially been burdened with a legacy based on Wheeler's now rejected notion that the "idea of civilization came to the Indus from the land of the Twin Rivers." I am especially interested in exploring these connections in the context of discoveries throughout this intercultural space and in light of recent debates on Indus religious ideologies.

Investigation of the political economy is especially appropriate given the forms of evidence found in the material record of the Indus civilization. Given the absence of a deciphered written record, my approach necessarily concentrates on the rich material record that archaeologists have brought to light in Indus cities and in their regional studies. Each of these bodies of accumulated data is an important resource with which to offer a new synthesis using the perspective of anthropological archaeology that I adopt here. In formulating these interpretations, I draw from what I consider the best of processual archaeology in its empirical grounding, but am also mindful of many of the caveats expressed in postprocessual debates.

Understanding how the Indus civilization emerged, and its political economy, requires taking a long-term perspective and tracing out developments that led to the settlement of cities. Although I focus mainly on the civilization at its peak of urbanism, I devote several chapters to settlements that preceded urbanism. These early settlements, and more generally the origins of agriculture and sedentary life, were important precursors to urbanism in the Greater Indus Valley. Interim periods, drawn on as needed, help establish the links between the origins of agriculture and urbanism. In the next section, I outline the key transformative points in the development of the Indus civilization, providing a foundation for more detailed discussion in later chapters.

The Indus Civilization: Chronologies of Indus Antecedents, Coalescence, Decline, and Transformations

The explorations and excavations undertaken by Indus scholars in the past fifty years have revolutionized our understanding of this great civilization. When first discovered, and for years afterward, archaeologists such as Wheeler and Piggott puzzled over its "sudden" emergence. They could not have known that many new discoveries would securely document a long sequence of development, preceding the appearance of Indus cities. Settlements that predate the emergence of the Indus civilization possess many elements critical to initial settlement on the Indus and Ghaggar-Hakra plains. Investigating them is essential if we hope to understand the circumstances in which the civilization developed.

In this book, I have simplified several chronological schemes (Shaffer 1992; Kenoyer 1998; Possehl 2003), emphasizing the important transformations that led to urbanism, to the gradual breakdown of urbanism, and to the disappearance of key stylistic elements of the civilization itself. I also take a broad geographic perspective, encompassing the Indus and Ghaggar-Hakra plains and settlements in surrounding zones. Following Shaffer (1992:442), this region "extends from the Himalayan Mountains in the north to the Arabian Sea in the south ... [and] is bordered by the Baluchistan mountains [to the west] and on the east by the Thar Desert and the Ganges-Yamuna Divide." It includes two major river systems – the Indus and the Ghakkar-Hakra (Figure 1.2) – and evidence of Indus settlement beyond the mountains of Baluchistan and in northern Afghanistan. The several thousand years of prehistory that are most relevant span the period from 7000 to 1500 B.C.[3] as shown in Table 1.1. Box 4.1 in Chapter 4 provides additional chronological details.

During the Early Food Producing period, some of the basic domesticates such as wheat and barley appear for the first time in South Asia. The Harappans continued to exploit these crops after settling on the Indus plain. However, domestication actually occurred in areas outside the Indus proper, and several thousand years before the development of urban settlements. Our best evidence is from Mehrgarh, which is situated in an ideal environment for the domestication of plants and animals because it lies in a natural habitat zone for many of the plants and animals domesticated. Mehrgarh is the only site for which we have evidence of a long span of settlement in this early era of domestication. Settlements elsewhere also contributed to the food resources of the

Table 1.1. Generalized Chronology

Phase	Dates
Early Food Producing	6300–4000 B.C.
Pre-urban period	4000–2600 B.C.
Urban period	2600–1900 B.C.
Post-urban/Late Harappan period	1900–1300 B.C.

More detailed breakdowns of the internal chronology for each phase will be presented in the relevent chapters.

Harappans and, along with Mehrgarh, are discussed in more detail in Chapter 3 and other chapters.

By the Pre-urban period agriculture had spread throughout most of the Greater Indus Region, and the number of settlements had grown. The major settlements occupied during this time were Mehrgarh, Nausharo, Kot Diji, Amri, Kalibangan, Balathal, Loteshwar, the earliest phases of Harappa and Dholavira, and several settlements in the Cholistan region.

The major florescence of the civilization occurred during the Urban period between 2600 and 1900 B.C. During this period certain aspects of material culture showed a marked uniformity in the adoption and use of seals and written script mentioned earlier, a system of standardized weights, distinctive pottery styles, and terracotta human and animal figurines. New architectural features included planned cities and extensive public works. In addition, there was an expansion of settlements throughout the Greater Indus Region and neighboring areas. At this point, the five major centers – Harappa, Mohenjo-daro, Dholavira, Ganweriwala, and Rakhigarhi – are known to have achieved full development.

During the Post-urban/Late Harappan period, from 1900 to 1300 B.C., occupation of Indus cities declined. As people abandoned cities and dispersed into the countryside, settlements shifted toward the northeast to the Ghaggar plain, away from the Indus Valley toward northwest India and Gujarat. The population occupied a more limited region, and their material culture grew less uniform and more localized. The circumstances under which the civilization came to an end remain matters of debate in Indus studies and are discussed in detail in Chapter 11.

Rethinking Perspectives on the Indus Civilization

The Indus civilization encompassed a region greater than any of its contemporaries. Although the Mesopotamians made references to the distant land of Meluhha believed to be the Indus over 4,400 years ago and its physical remains were known in the nineteenth century, it was not "named" until the 1920s, when archaeologists undertook excavations in its major cities. In this chapter, I have emphasized the history of its discovery, the different approaches scholars have taken in reconstructing the Indus civilization, and its general chronology. I also included a discussion of the theoretical perspective adopted in this book. A basic premise, reflecting the perspective of anthropology, is that social, economic, and political activities are integrated phenomena and must be viewed in the context of the environmental constraints and opportunities of the natural world the Harappans occupied.

I have divided this book into eleven chapters. I begin with a description of the environmental settings encountered by the first settlers in the region and present evidence for an Harappan presence. Chapter 3 describes the very beginnings of agriculture and settlement. In Chapter 4, I cover the expansion of settlement in the Pre-urban period, when many new settlements appear on the Indus and Ghaggar-Hakra plains. In Chapters 5 through 10, my focus is on the civilization at the peak of its expansion, Indus urbanism, and its regional networks. Chapters 6 and 7 focus on the intensification and specialization of its agropastoral and craft-producing economy (Chapter 6) and the organization of production, distribution, and exchange (Chapter 7). I devote Chapter 8 to external trade and interaction with cultures beyond the Indus civilization. In Chapter 9, I discuss Indus architectural forms, material culture, and the notion of cultural landscape features as windows into the social and economic divisions within Indus society. For the Indus civilization, one of our best windows into the effects of the constructed environment on social perceptions is its cities. In this context, our goal is to envision how the Harappans experienced the constructed landscape as they went about their daily lives and to see how their social positions were actualized within it.

My focus in Chapter 10 is on the different interpretative frameworks employed by Indus scholars in their attempts to reconstruct the spiritual side of Indus life and their religious institutions. Among other things, I discuss the similarities among the motifs and themes employed on Mesopotamian, Iranian, and Indus seals. I then place the messages conveyed on the seal narrative imagery in the context of comparative studies of early civilizations and religious systems of thought. In Chapter 11, I bring together the final days of the Indus and the causes and consequences of the abandonment of its major settlements.

2   Geographical and Environmental Settings

The varied and diverse landscapes of the regions in which the Harappans and their predecessors settled have been subject to several types of environmental changes over the millennia. These changes occurred as a result of natural processes (tectonic activity, disruptions in river systems, and climate change) and human activities (alterations to the landscape and human manipulation of natural resources). In this chapter, I focus on the former. Although I discuss long-term dynamics both past and present, I wish to concentrate on the Harappan landscape, identifying and describing some of the kinds of environmental dynamics that were underway during Harappan times. Importantly, I relate some of the ways in which archaeologists have attempted to reveal these processes. I will describe recent projects in which archaeologists have collaborated with experts in geology, climatology, and ecology to reconstruct past environments. Results of these collaborative studies not only provide new views of stability and change in the region's geographical and environmental settings but are becoming the basis for developing some fresh ideas about the impact of these changes on Harappan lives and settlement history.

My discussion in this chapter first previews some of the factors to consider in assessing the impacts of differences in landscape and climate between the present and the past. This is followed by a section entitled, Geography and Climate Today, and provides a basic orientation to the principal physical features visible on present-day maps of the region, current rainfall patterns, and general environmental conditions. The last sections of the chapter describe changes that occurred between 10,000 and 3,000 years ago, the periods most relevant to the settlement in the region and to the Indus civilization. A final section presents a case study drawn from my own research, New Solutions and Perspectives, that places climate and environmental changes in a broader framework inclusive of the Harappan's responses to these changes.

Factors to Consider in Assessing Differences between Past and Present

As discussed in Chapter 1, the Indus and Ghaggar-Hakra Rivers, were the loci of many Indus settlements. Like people in many other early civilizations, the Harappans were dependent on rivers for a productive agrarian economy, that included dependence on the natural floodwaters of the river systems.

As an illustration of differences between past and present, we can consider the Indus River and contrast its current productivity to its productive potential in the past. Today, the Indus plain is the bread basket of Pakistan, providing most of its stable food resources based on an economy involving agriculture and animal husbandry. The Indus River and its tributaries produce annual flows of water that are, for example, twice that of the Nile in Egypt and ten times that of the Colorado in the southwestern United States (Revelle 1964). The total area of cultivable land is more than 30 million acres (Revelle 1964:3) and a variety of plants and animals provide the population with basic foods, including wheat, barley, rice, beef, and lamb. Of additional importance are secondary products such as plant (cotton) and animal (wool) fiber, dairy products and animals for traction. In a study conducted in the mid-twentieth century, it was estimated that the food and fiber produced on the Indus plain could meet the needs of over 100 million people (Revelle 1964:11).

But to assess the significance of these land and water resources to the people of the Indus civilization, we need to adjust our thinking and reflect back to populations living in the region in the past. Today's estimates of production, acreage yield, and population capacity depend on the use of modern technologies, such as tractors, pesticides, and massive irrigation systems, to name a few. A strong centralized government also aids farmers in plant and animal production. The scale of production possible today is beyond the scope of the administration or technologies available during Indus times. Yet, as we will see in the following chapters, the people of the ancient Indus managed to exploit quite successfully a wide variety of local resources, showing remarkable ingenuity harnessing and maximizing production in a much less well-controlled natural environment.

The construction of massive dams and sophisticated water-holding devices that control the timing of flow of water are relatively recent innovations. But these human-induced changes are not the only means by which landscapes have been modified. Natural occurrences have dramatically altered the location and flow of river systems. South Asia lies in a zone of intense tectonic activity, affecting the region on both large and small scales. The most dramatic change occurred over fifty million years ago when two continental plates – the Indian and Eurasian – collided, causing a violent crumbling of the earth's crust. This collision of plates created the Himalayan Mountains. Significantly, earth processes, such as earthquakes and minor geological forces of a less dramatic sort (discussed later in this chapter in more detail) continue to alter the topography.

Climate changes also have had significant effects on the environment of the region. Scientists who specialize in reconstructing long-term climate change have documented the presence of extensive ice sheets and periods of glacial advance and retreat that occurred in the higher altitudes of South Asia, more or less coincident with those in northern Europe. The most intensive periods of glacial retreat occurred before 10,000 years ago, but ice melting from the Himalayas continues to influence climate, rainfall patterns, and changes in sea level. Air current circulation patterns from annual monsoons and westerly winds also exert a major influence. These factors will be discussed in some detail in following sections of the chapter.

Geography and Climate Today

A brief tour of the overall Indus region, which covers a vast area inclusive of the northeastern edge of Afghanistan, all of Pakistan, and parts of India (Figure 1.2), provides a framework for the following discussion of the geography, climate, and major river systems.

Geographical Setting

The region can be divided into five major zones: (1) peninsular India, (2) the vast interior of the alluvial plains, (3) mountain chains to the north, (4) western mountains and valley border zones, and (5) the eastern border zone and the Thar Desert.

Peninsular India (portions of which are shown in southern India on Figure 1.2) includes several physiographic features. The Deccan plateau covers a large portion of the peninsula. Its northern boundary is marked by the Satpura, Vindhya, and Aravalli mountain chains. The western Ghats run along the western edge of the peninsula, separating the plateau from the sea. They average 900 meters above sea level and rise as high as 2,200 meters in elevation.

The region's interior is the heartland of the Indo-Gangetic plain. It includes three major river systems – the Indus, the Ghaggar-Hakra, and the Ganges-Jamuna. (Figure 1.2) – although the latter is of less importance to Indus settlement. Several major tributaries are part of the Indus system. Moving from west to east, they are the Jhelum, Chenab, Ravi, Beas, and Sutlej. These five rivers meet at the Panjnad and today flow into a single channel of the Indus. To the east of the Indus system lies the ancient Ghaggar-Hakra. The Ghaggar in India still flows seasonally, but the Hakra in Pakistan is now only visible as a relict channel in the deserts of Cholistan. The Indus and Ghaggar-Hakra were once the location of four of the five major cities of the Indus civilization. Finally, the Ganges-Jamuna forms the northeastern boundary of the region.

Massive mountain chains border the plains to their north. The most dramatic are the Hindu Kush, the Karakorum, and the Himalayas. The second highest peak in the world, K-2 at an elevation of around 8,611 meters, is located in the Karakorums in Pakistan; Mt. Everest, the highest peak at over 8,850 meters, is in the Himalayas in Nepal.

The western border zone includes two major mountain chains. The Kirthar and Suleiman Mountains form a border between the frontiers of the province of Baluchistan and the western edge of the Indus alluvial plain. On the western side of the Kirthars and Suleiman, there are several landscape features of relevance. They include mountain chains and valleys that extend from northeastern Baluchistan and bend toward the southwest. These valleys provide natural corridors between the Indus plain, Baluchistan and regions farther west in Iran (Scholz 1983:14). The remainder of Baluchistan consists of extensive rocky deserts in the north and northwest and a coastal belt that borders the sea. Finally, the Northwest Frontier Province (NWFP) includes rugged mountainous zones and valleys, such as the Gomal plain where the archaeological site of Rehman Dheri is located.

The eastern border of the region is formed by the Thar Desert, an extensive area that is approximately 805 kilometers long by 403 kilometers wide, with sparse vegetation. The Thar's western boundary encroaches upon the lower Indus plain in Pakistan and its northwest margin in Cholistan. Its eastern boundary extends to the Aravalli Mountains and to the Rann of Kutch on its south, where the fifth major Indus city is located.

Climate

The present climate of South Asia is variable due to differences in topography, air circulation patterns, and cyclic shifts in monsoon and winter rainfall. Coordinating subsistence activities with the timing of these environmental factors is critical to the successful cultivation of plants and raising of animals. Under current conditions, with the exception of most of Baluchistan, the entire region is affected to some degree by seasonal temperatures and precipitation brought about by summer monsoons and winter westerlies. Monsoons are the result of the buildup of low pressure during winter that continues as the landmass begins to heat up, especially during April, May, and June. The thermal contrast between ocean waters and land area draws in trade winds from the sea that blow in a northeasterly direction. Moisture-filled winds release heavy rains along the peninsular coast, the Western Ghats, and as far north as the slopes of the Himalayas, where they are deflected westward to the northern Punjab. Rains continue from mid-June to September. Their most dramatic effects depend upon the intensity of the monsoons. In Gujarat, for example, 250 to 500 millimeters of rainfall can occur in a single day. At other times, when the monsoons are less intense, the same region can be subjected to severe drought (Weber 1991, 1990). After monsoon season, cooler weather continues until March. On the Gangetic plains, summer monsoon rains provide an abundance of precipitation, whereas in the Upper and Lower Indus rainfall is much lower (less than 200 to 700 millimeters, and 100 to 300 millimeters respectively). In Baluchistan, the monsoon precipitation belt is confined to parts of Kachi and the Las Bela area.

A separate and distinct source of rainfall is the westerly winter rains associated with storms originating in the Mediterranean that pass through the Middle East and along the southern coasts of Baluchistan. They terminate in the northwest of the Indian subcontinent. Most of the winter precipitation from westerly storms falls in the north of the Indus area, in the foothills, and western Himalayas.

Climate Change Before, During and After Peak Periods of Settlement

There are vigorous debates concerning the paleo-climatic conditions and climate change before, during, and after the peak periods of the Indus civilization. Some scientists argue that until 6,000 years ago (roughly 4000 B.C.) vegetation in the region was more abundant than today due to wetter conditions. The major settlements at that time were not on the alluvial plain but at its margins in the mountain valleys and their foothills of Baluchistan at places like Mehrgarh, to be discussed in Chapter 3. After 4000 B.C., wet phases continued as a result of "higher precipitation efficiency" involving winter rains. It was under these conditions that larger numbers of people began to move to the alluvial plains of the Indus Valley and the Ghaggar-Hakra plains

(Bryson and Swain 1981:138). This period was followed by a decrease of precipitation that occurred due to a shift of westerly circulation patterns to the south and a weak monsoon (Bryson and Swain 1981; Singh et al. 1990). For example, Phadtre (2000) analyzed pollen from alpine peat collected in the Himalayas and noted a greater abundance of evergreen oak compared to pine between 5400 B.C. and 4100 B.C. This difference suggested that the climate was cold and the monsoon moderate. The higher abundance of pine between 4000 and 2500 B.C. suggested that monsoons were at their highest intensity during that period. Between 2000 and 1500 B.C., there was progressive cooling and decrease in monsoon-intensity which Phadtre (2000) describes as perhaps "the weakest monsoon event" during the last 10,000 years (Phadtre 2000:122). In partial support of these data is evidence from marine cores taken off the coast of southern Pakistan (von Rad et al. 1999). Analysis of this evidence (based on the relative thickness of continentally derived monsoon deposits) shows fluctuations in precipitation with peaks of monsoon intensity until ca. 2000–1750 B.C. when there was a period of instability in which precipitation was at its minimum. Von Rad believes this aridification affected a broad region that included the Middle East and North Africa, which led to the reduction of Nile River discharge and abandonment of sites in Syria.

While there is general agreement that there were fluctuations in precipitation and drying trends, interpretations differ on the timing of these changes. A study based on sediment samples from different micro-environments from the Ghaggar River in northwest India from riverbeds, floodplains, depressions, dunes and dune fields documented oscillations in precipitation (Courty 1989, 1990, 1995). These oscillations began 10,500 years ago when precipitation was abundant. A change occurred around 5,000 years ago when there was decreased precipitation and increased aridity. The arid phase began during the peak urban period of Indus settlement, at ca. 4000 B.C. until 2500 B.C. Another study of sediments, but from a lake bed (Enzel et al. 1999) identified a drying phase at 2894 to 2643 B.C., similarly suggesting that the peak periods of Indus settlement took place during a dry period.

What makes the studies problematic when taken together are the disagreements in the timing of the fluctuations (Morrison 2008). These problems have been partially resolved in a recent synthesis of the current evidence. Based on a recalibration of many of the chronological dates, Marco Madella and Dorian Fuller (2006) reconstructed the following pattern: Sometime around 12500 and 8500 B.C. there was a period of higher rainfall, but one marked by fluctuating arid spells. By 8500 to 7000 B.C. rainfall levels were high but were interspersed with arid periods.

The pattern continued until 5200 B.C. but with more frequent and severe periods of aridity. Beginning sometime around 3950–3700 B.C., there was an increased drying trend. Although monsoon rains were reduced, there were consistently high levels of winter rains. After 2800 B.C., rainfall levels declined bringing about "modern levels of aridity" (2006:1289). According to this reconstruction, the periods of high precipitation occurred before full-scale urbanism, which Madella and Fuller (2006) suggest would have resulted in increasing agricultural surpluses among communities in the pre-urban period. These surpluses may have influenced the spread of settlements onto the alluvial plain (2006:1297). By 2200 cal B.C., they followed others in suggesting that a significant drying trend had occurred.

For the moment, all that can be said based on the evidence reviewed in this section is that conditions most likely were wetter as settlers moved into the mountainous regions of Baluchistan, a situation that may have persisted until the onset of accelerated settlement onto the alluvial plains. There was a trend toward warmer and less moist conditions sometime before the Pre-urban period and during Urban periods. By the Post-urban period there was a severe drying trend. See Box 2.1 for other evidence relevant to climate change.

Box 2.1 Climate Change and Archaeological Methods

The various "proxy" measures described in this chapter are just some of the ways in which to reconstruct the climate. Other evidence includes a variety of archaeological methods based on site and regionally specific research essential to reconstructing paleo-climates and environmental conditions.

One type of evidence includes features of the cultural landscape. Gabarbands are stone-built dam constructions designed to control and store water (Stein 1931; Raikes and Dyson 1961; Flam 1993a; Harvey and Flam 1993). Their discovery at archaeological settlements in areas of Baluchistan and Kohistan that are not agriculturally productive today due to lack of rainfall suggests there was greater precipitation in the past. Other landscape/architectural features suggestive of wetter climates include the elaborate drainage systems that the Harappans built in their cities to be discussed in Chapters 5 and 9 (Marshall 1931). In addition, the use of baked brick as a major building material would have required abundant fuel to produce bricks and thus a more thickly forested area that might indicate higher degrees of rainfall in the past than there is

Box 2.1 (*Cont.*)

at present. Raikes and Dyson (1961) calculated that 400 acres of forest would be needed to supply the fuel required to rebuild Mohenjo-daro.

Of additional importance are charcoal remains found in archaeological deposits. Vegetation identified from northern Baluchistan for periods between 4000 and 2500 B.C. (at Mehrgarh and the nearby sites of Lal Shah and Nausharo) included plant varieties (prosopis, acacia, tamarix, and the sissoo tree) from two local ecosystems, a riverine forest and shrub or woodland (Thiebault 1988a, 1988b, 1989, 1992; Tengberg and Thiebault 2003). These same two ecosystems were exploited on the Indus plain in Pre-urban and Urban periods at Kot Diji (Tengberg and Thiebault 2003:28) and in southern Baluchistan at interior sites in the Makran along the Kech River. In both cases, wood from riverine forests and shrubs or woodlands also were exploited. They included some of the same varieties (tamarix, prosopis, and sissoo tree). Studies of pollen from approximately the same time period undertaken by McKean (1983) at Balakot in Las Bela also identified the same species in that region (McKean 1983). Her data were dated between 4300 and 4100 cal B.C. and ca. 1900 cal B.C. Both analyses present a potential argument for a "denser and floristically richer" environment than today (Tengberg and Thiebault 2003:51). However, as McKean noted, these same plants are present under the semi-arid conditions of the present.

Finally, representations of plants and animals depicted on Indus artifacts provide information on local environments. One of the most distinctive images on Harappan seals is the tiger (Piggott 1950; Wheeler 1968). The image on Figure 10.5a is one example. If the climate was the same as it is today, then where was the jungle habitat that the tiger prefers? Was the tiger imported and kept in a zoo? We know that in contemporary societies, in Mesopotamia and Egypt, rulers kept exotic animals. Although the absence of tigers in the Indus today might suggest the environment was substantially wetter during Indus times, the effects of massive irrigation on the Indus plain has dramatically altered the landscape, perhaps as recently as the last two hundred years (Possehl 2003). In addition, the tiger may have become extinct as the result of wild game hunting. Descriptions of hunting expeditions during the British colonial period speak of abundant game in much the same way as the wild game on the African savannah are spoken of today. Another factor to consider is the intrusion of domestic animals, such as sheep and goat, and grazing activities. Grasslands may have been destroyed by processes similar to those occurring in Africa today that are threatening to eliminate the elephant (Possehl 2003).

The Indus in the Past – Documenting Landscape and River System Dynamics

One of the major lifelines of the Indus civilization was its river systems. The Harappans did not construct irrigation networks, as was the case among their contemporaries in Mesopotamia; instead, they depended on the annual flooding cycles of its major rivers. The timing and velocity of water flowing into the region varied seasonally, but the most dramatic changes in the landscape were the result of long-term processes, involving shifts in the locations of the rivers themselves and the amount of water they discharged. A new picture of the location of the river systems is emerging through the use of aerial photography, remote sensing imagery, regional surveys, and geoarchaeological research. Our best documentation of these changes is from the Upper and Lower Indus and the Ghaggar-Hakra in Cholistan and northwest India.

The Upper and Lower Indus

The complexities of the Indus river system have been documented at several locations on the Upper and Lower Indus. They include the Ravi River where Harappa is located, and the now dry-bed of the Beas River near Harappa in the Upper Indus. Extensive studies have also been conducted in the Lower Indus basin.

The division between the Upper and Lower Indus is at the Panjnad, where the five rivers currently converge with the Indus (Figure 1.2). With the exception of the Ravi, the upper channel courses of the Indus are mildly entrenched and allow for channel migration over an extensive terrain. Water sources in Harappan times were most plentiful along the active floodplain such that the selection of settlement locations were dependent upon the extent of lateral migration of the rivers across the plain. An additional feature is the buildup of "bars," or raised land areas, accompanying channel shifts, displacements, and the creation of a low-grade meander and scroll topography within the broader alluvial plain. These alluvial changes created surfaces that were sufficiently high to have been unaffected by floods (Belcher and Belcher 2000). The city of Harappa was settled on an elevated terraced area and may have been surrounded by a river meander and an oxbow lake at the northern edge of the city (Pendall and Amundsen 1990; Amundsen and Pendall 1991; Belcher and Belcher 2000). Small ponds also may have formed in slackwater, depressions, or overflow chutes where floodwaters collected. These would have been reliable sources of water after flooding subsided, creating microenvironments from which floral and faunal resources could be exploited. This pattern continued until dams were built in the nineteenth century. Prior to dam construction, fields were watered by direct overflow of the main river channels. Seasonal impoundments and channels probably formed along the margins of the main drainage lines and their duration would have been dependent on longer term precipitation trends.

Research on the Beas is based on a regional settlement survey and geo-archaeological research (Wright et al. 2002, 2005a and b; Schuldenrein et al. 2004, 2007). The Beas (see Figure 1.2) once flowed in a direction that parallels the present-day location of the Ravi River. The dried-up channel of the Beas is still visible on remote sensing imagery (Figure 2.1, a declassified Corona Satellite image from 1965). The image shows a section of the Beas (the white wavy line) and relict channels (marked with arrows) not visible on the ground. The mounded areas (the black dots) are archaeological sites, some of which have not yet been dated. The Harappan settlements are aligned on terraces flanking the Beas channel, suggesting that the river was active during the periods of Indus settlement. As will be discussed later in New Solutions and Perspectives, the Harappan sites were sufficiently large and alluviation was of a correspondingly more limited magnitude that it was possible to develop a chronological sequence with which to correlate cultural and floodplain deposits. The results demonstrated that within a relatively contained region of the Upper Indus, the varied but dependent flow regimes of the subjacent Beas and Ravi channels created a complex alluvial basin with variable topographies and microenvironments (Schuldenrein et al. 2007: Table 2). Collectively, the catchment created extensive tracts of productive land for cultivation and pasturage.

Below the confluence at the Panjnad, the Lower Indus flows a distance of 800 kilometers. The Lower Indus has been the subject of extensive study by members of the Sindh Archaeological Research Project, led by Louis Flam. Currently, the course of the Lower Indus has remained relatively stable due to flood protection embankments along the river that shield it from the western mountain streams and the piedmont region (Flam 1993a:272; Jorgenson et al. 1993; Schroder 1993). Importantly, the Sindh project has documented major changes in the Lower Indus that involved significant differences between its present course and those prevailing in Harappan times.

During the period preceding settlement of the region by the Harappans and in its urban phase of development, several different river channels of the Lower Indus existed, changed their courses, and disappeared over time. These reconstructions are based on historical

Relict Meanders

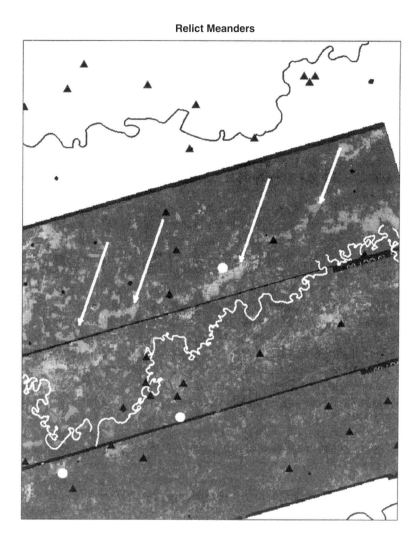

Beas Survey Sites
Punjab Survey Sites
Old Beas River
Detect sites

0   5   10   20   30
                            Kilometers

Figure 2.1. Declassified corona satellite image showing traces of the now dry Beas River and relief channels. Photograph by R. P. Wright and C. Hritz.

sources, ground observations of geomorphic processes, landform reconstructions, and the use of aerial photographs (Flam 1993a). Ancient river courses have been identified by meander (ridge and swale) topography. Each new channel produced its own natural levee, forming interconnected topographic ridges where shallow flood basins or ponding occurred. The maps on Figures 2.2 and 2.3 show the Lower Indus at two key time periods. Figure 2.2 represents the period from 8000 to 4000 B.C., when several courses flowed through the Lower Indus. The two primary courses were the Jacobabad on the western edge of the plain and the Nara Nadi to the east. Initially, the Indus followed the Jacobabad course as it flowed into the region from the north. The Nara Nadi, a parallel river system, followed a course directly to its east. The Nara Nadi was the southern extension of the Ghaggar-Hakra system that flowed in from the northeast. A second observable change in the Lower Indus occurred between 4000 and 2000 B.C. Figure 2.3 shows the shift eastward away from the Jacobabad course to a "prior" course,

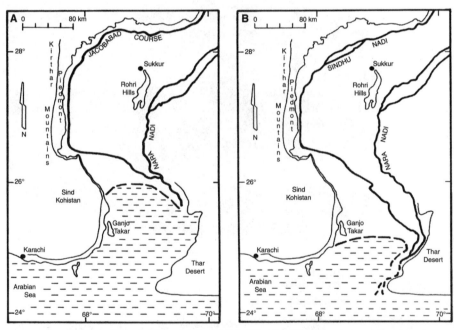

Figure 2.2. (left) and 2.3. (right) The Jacobabad course and approximate coastline ~10,000 to 4,000 year B.P.; The Sindhu Nadi and Nara Nadi and approximate coastline ~4000 to 2000 year B.C. (~6000 to 4000 year B.P.). Redrawn from Flam (1993a)

the Sindhu Nadi, that flowed on the western portion of the Lower basin (Flam 1993a, 1999). The course of the Nara Nadi remained the same, but its confluence with the western branch, the Sindhu Nadi, occurred farther to the south, just to the north of the coastline.

As Flam has noted, these configurations of the Lower Indus are significantly different from the current, single course of the Indus visible on modern-day maps (Flam 1993a, 1999). Unlike today, Mohenjo-daro was strategically located between the two systems but conceivably in a vulnerable situation. Twenty-five kilometers southeast of the Sindhu Nadi course, the city may eventually have been abandoned as the result of episodic and abrupt channel displacements that placed the city "in a hazardous position close to the brunt of the annual flood" (Flam 1993a:287).

The river adjustments evident when the two Lower Indus maps are compared may have been the result of tectonic forces and/or environmental changes. According to Flam (1999), the drying of the Ghaggar-Hakra system affected the flow of the Nara Nadi. In the Lower Indus, major changes in the flow of the Sindhu Nadi and Nara Nadi "would have brought widespread abandonment of many sites and a movement of population out of the Lower Indus basin into adjacent and more "stable areas" (1999:317).

One final difference shown when Figures 2.2 and 2.3 are compared is the location of the coastline. Changes in the coastline were the result of the gradual buildup of deposition of the alluvium as the Jacobabad and Nara Nadi moved southward between 8000 and 4000 B.C. and the Sindhu Nadi and Nara Nadi did likewise from 4000 to 2000 B.C. Provisional studies of the coastline suggest that during the Indus Urban period it was situated 95 miles north of its present location (Flam 1993a:283).

The Ghaggar-Hakra

The second major river system and the location of a large number of Indus settlements is the Ghaggar-Hakra to be discussed in chapters 4 and 5. Like the Upper and Lower Indus, significant alteration in the channel and flow of this system has occurred since the area was occupied by the Harappans. The Ghaggar rises in the foothills of the Himalayas. In Harappan times, it flowed south where it joined the Hakra in the Cholistan region, now a desert. From there most likely the Ghaggar-Hakra flowed south into the Nara Nadi. According to H.-P. Francfort, the floodplain of the Ghaggar may have been six to eight kilometers wide (1986) before Harappan occupation of the region. Other research in this region by Rafique Mughal has involved extensive settlement surveys in the Cholistan region. The location of sites preserved adjacent to the Ghaggar-Hakra suggests that there was less danger from flooding than along the Indus. Eventual abandonment of settlements was due to changes in river courses that may have been attributable to tectonic forces (1997:108).

Today, the relict channel of the Ghaggar-Hakra disappears into the semi-arid regions to its south (the modern districts of Haryana and Rajasthan) (Courty 1995:108). These changes in the present position of the Ghaggar-Hakra occurred over a period of several thousand years. The study of paleosols conducted by Marie-Agnes Courty (1995) referred to earlier indicates that between 4000 and 2500 B.P. (ca. 2000–500 B.C.), during the period of drier conditions, there was reduced seasonal flooding and concommitant retreat of the primary drainage arteries 100 to 150 kilometers northward. It is unclear from the study when a predictable seasonal flooding cycle ceased.

Although questions remain concerning the specific circumstances that initiated these drastic changes in the Ghaggar-Hakra, changes in the drainage net were most likely the result of two interacting factors involving the Yamuna River that runs east of the Ghaggar-Hakra and is part of the Ganges River system. In this tectonically active area, the slope and topography of the plain may have been altered. In addition, the natural aggradation of the upstream bed of the younger Yamuna River system may have caused periodic floods that deflected the river across the watershed between the Indus and Ganges systems. During a period of deflection to the west, the Yamuna may have flowed into the Ghaggar and captured its waters.

The Ganges-Yamuna

The Ganges-Yamuna system is located in a region less central to the major urban centers of the Indus civilization. However, the presence of Indus settlements and the changes in the flow of the Ghaggar-Hakra make this system particularly relevant, since a shift of settlement toward the Ganges-Yamuna occurred during the last phases of the Indus civilization.

New Solutions and Perspectives on Climate Change

The results of paleo-climate studies provide a framework from which to generalize on the effects of climate change at Harappan settlements. However, climate-based reconstructions can fall short, when the evidence is brought to bear on the environmental repercussions generally and in local settings specifically. Moreover, too often climatic changes are considered in simplistic terms as causal or "catastrophic" phenomena that signal the birth or death of a civilization. Are there ways to discern how climatic fluctuations affected the environment as a whole? Can we determine whether the Harappans were "fine-tuned to the environment" and can we identify the full range of changes and adjustments made in response to the climatic fluctuations (Rosen and Rosen 2001:546)? Can we document elements of social choice in response to these changes?

With these factors in mind, I discuss new evidence that documents the effects of environmental changes in the context of a localized case study. My focus is on a collaborative project I initiated with a team of archaeologists (in collaboration with Mr. Afzal Khan) a geoarchaeologist (Joseph Schuldenrein), and a climatologist (Reid Bryson) to model changes in the climate and the river system along the Beas in the Upper Indus. The study was the first in this region to establish a regional stratigraphic framework for rural settlements near a major Harappan center and to reconstruct aspects of the region's environmental history, i.e., climate and river regimes during the Pre-urban, Urban and Post-urban periods. Although not part of the original conception of the survey, we have also incorporated archaeobotanical evidence from excavated stratified contexts at Harappa analyzed by Steven Weber (2003).

Our major focus was a landscape survey and mapping project conducted over several field seasons (Wright et al. 2005a,b, 2008; Schuldenrein et al 2004, 2007). One aspect of the research was to document all archaeological settlements contemporary with Harappa and to record their material culture. This aspect of the project will be discussed in more detail in Chapters 4 and 5. A second focus was the investigation of present and past courses of the Beas in order to correlate settlements with their locations with respect to river channels. A guiding principle was to integrate available soil stratigraphies from Harappa (Amundson and Pendall 1991; Pendall and Amundson 1990) and to probe and date the interface between the natural surface of Beas mounds and the initial intact occupation horizon. We used a hand-driven coring device that reached a depth of more than three meters into the soils and the alluvium. We also collected soil sediments from site surfaces and limited test trenching at selected sites. The data from the soil horizons documented periods of landform stability and the timing of stabilization of the floodplain and initial settlement. From these data we were able to date changes in river regimes and floodplain transformations as follows.

The soil stratigraphies indicate that in this region of the Upper Indus moister climates prevailed at around 8000 to 5000 B.C., followed by a period of diminished precipitation and drier conditions (ca. 5000–3000 B.C.). The latter occurred at around the time increasing numbers of settlements are present on the alluvial plains. Our data for the period from ca. 3300 to 1500/1300 B.C., and the peak period of occupation for settlement at Harappa and along the Beas (ca. 3300–1900 B.C.) indicate that there were frequent fluctuations in climate and larger scale stream migrations and precipitation levels than at other times. After that period, there was a surge in precipitation but by then the region had been abandoned.

Bryson's Archaeoclimate model (see Box 2.2) complemented our on-the-ground data as it is fully consistent with our geoarchaeological results. It also fills in some important gaps in river discharge patterns and ratios of monsoon to winter rainfalls. Key to understanding these fluctuations is the ratio of monsoon (summer) to winter rainfall distributions (see Box 2.2).

Box 2.2 The Past Climate of Harappa and Beas River Discharge: An Archaeoclimatic Model

The homeland of the Indus culture has two sources of moisture: the summer monsoon from the tropical waters from the south, largely in high summer, and winter rains associated with westerly storms. These two sources are in turn modulated by the local topography, which ranges from some of the highest mountains to quite featureless plains.

The westerly storms of winter move along the boundary between colder air to the north and warmer air to the south. This boundary is marked by the location of the jet stream aloft. The storms generally start in the eastern Mediterranean, move across the "Fertile Crescent," down the Persian Gulf, and along the Makran Coast to wind up in Pakistan and northwest India.

The monsoon of high summer is associated with the northward advance of the Inter-Tropical Convergence (ITC), which separates northern hemisphere from southern hemisphere air, which is laden with moisture from its long passage over tropical seas.

We can reconstruct the history of the positions of these features and others from the astronomically calculable radiation from the sun at the top of the atmosphere (the Milankovitch cycles) and its modulation by volcanic aerosols in passing through the atmosphere. The volcanic aerosol record is obtained from the radiocarbon-dated sequence of global eruptions calibrated against the measured

Box 2.2 (*Cont.*)

modern record. Then using synoptic climatology, we can calibrate the resulting model to fit the local climate.

Figure 2.4 shows the result for the locale of Harappa. Other places in which archaeologists have discovered Indus materials show this same abrupt drought event but with more or less intensity depending on the location and topography. Indus agriculture must have suffered grievously with the sudden decrease in rain ca. 2000 B.C., although as Rita Wright discusses in the text, Harappan farmers appear to have made various adjustments in the adoption of multicropping patterns. If the two-century averages decreased about 15%, the decadal values could have decreased by 50%. The precipitation in the last 2,000 years, though changeable, never returned to values of Indus culture times.

For a more complete description of the modeling method, see Bryson, R. A. 2005. "Archaeoclimatology." In *The Encyclopedia of World Climatology*, edited by J. E. Oliver, p. 68. Springer, Dordrecht.

Brson, R. A. and K. M. DeWall, ed. 2007. *A Paleor-Climate Workbook: High Resolution Site Specific Macrophysical Climate Modeling and CD*. Mammoth Springs publication, Hot Springs, S.D.

– Reid. A Bryson

During the periods of dramatic fluctuations in river discharge between 10,000 and 7,000 years ago, there were steady increases in precipitation with monsoon levels at 220 millimeters and winter rains at 100 millimeters (320 millimeters of rainfall annually) (see Figure 2.4). Between 5000 and 4000 B.C., precipitation levels stabilized until 3500 B.C. when the monsoon diminished and winter rains increased. Between 3000 and 2000 B.C., the total rainfall recorded is 300 millimeters primarily from winter rains. Precipitation was at its lowest after 2000 B.C. but recovered a few hundred years later.

In summary, even though there are certain disparities between our local evidence and the more general reconstructions (based on data from a broad region) of the paleo-climate described earlier, our working hypothesis for the Beas/Harappa region is that there were frequent climatic shifts that were linked to variations in stream discharge (Figure 2.5). These linked transitions occurred during a period of several thousand years, when strong seasonal rains were followed by

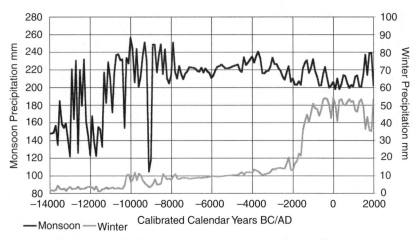

Figure 2.4. Modeled seasonal precipitation history, Sahiwal, Pakistan (near Harappa). Photograph by R. P. Wright.

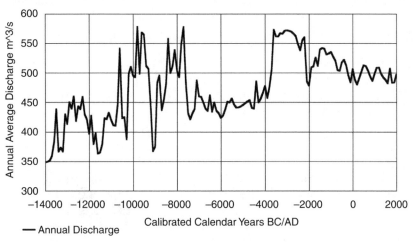

Figure 2.5. Modeled annual discharge history, Beas River at Mandi Plain. Photograph by R. P. Wright.

more uniform moisture distributions. At around the time that the Beas sites and Harappa were settled, river discharge was relatively stable along the Beas, but this changed at around 2000 B.C. when discharge diminished.

This interpretation is wholly consistent with the Beas settlement geography and the onset, duration, and final abandonment of Beas settlement. There are fifteen settlements in the Pre-Urban period, eighteen in the Urban period, and all but four remained in the Post-urban/Late Harappan (for details, see Chapters 4 and 5). The latter coincides with diminished size of Harappa, though settlement there continues for several hundred years beyond the onset of the period of reduced rainfall.

Can we explain the extended period of settlement at Harappa after 2000 B.C. to perhaps as late as 1300 B.C. by human responses and fine-tuned observations of the fluctuating environmental conditions? Our best evidence is from the archaeobotanical record at Harappa that suggests this was the case. Throughout the periods of settlement at Harappa, and we assume on the Beas, farmers continually made adjustments to changing conditions by experimenting with different crops. While wheat and barley were the "mainstays of the agriculture system" (Weber 2003:180), the Harappans adopted a multicropping system that took advantage of changing conditions throughout the year. Wheat and barley were cultivated in the winter months, and millets, a drought resistant crop, and some fruits in the summer. Thus far, increasing proportions of summer crops have been documented during certain periods, attesting to very specific strategies adopted by farmers in response to shifting environmental conditions. Our future research is directed toward more precise correlations between the environmental changes and adjustments to the cropping system.

While the conclusions presented here are preliminary, we have been able to fine-tune some of the effects of the kinds of fluctuations the Harappans faced. First, our model establishes the conditions and timing of climatic changes specific to the Harappa/Beas region. Second, our results project changing precipitation regimes to quantifiable discharge rates of the Beas. Finally, Harappan farmers appear to have responded to ecological challenges by implementing a multicropping system and adopting drought-resistant crops. By combining these data with soils collected at Harappa and the Beas (Pendall and Amundson 1991; Schuldenrein et al. 2007), geoarchaeological and archaeo-climate modeling, and archaeobotanical studies of cropping patterns at Harappa (Weber 2003), we have begun to monitor human responses to changes in climate and river regimes.

When the Indus civilization did come to an end, the process was not uniform. Although the long-term trend at Harappa and Beas – and perhaps for the Upper Beas generally – was reduced settlement in the Post-urban/Late Harappan period, regional occupation may have persisted until 1700 B.C. and possibly later. The adjustments made by the Harappans in this region are suggestive of puposeful and, at least for a time, successful responses to changing landscape and environmental conditions. The timing of the abandonment of settlements in other parts of the Indus varied and will be discussed in Chapter 11.

Conclusions

The Indus civilization occupied a region of enormous potential. This potential included an expansive floodplain and an agricultural regime based on floodwater farming and the cultivation of a diversity of plants and animals. Still, settlement involved risks. Although debates on climate change, fluctuations in rainfall patterns, changes in river discharge rates, and tectonic activity remain an open question, they do suggest that in some instances the Harappans adapted successfully to uncertain conditions. Our evidence from the Beas indicates that the collection of environmental and archaeological data based on regional surveys holds considerable promise for understanding the complex dynamic linking climate and landscape change. Taken a step further, understanding of this dynamic eventually filtered into the adaptive strategies adopted by Late Harappan societies. People and their polities made choices that hedged against potential risks in specific locations.

In the next chapter, I turn the discussion to 7000 B.C. when we have the earliest evidence for settled life in South Asia. Our attention focuses on the site of Mehrgarh on the Kachi Plain in northern Baluchistan, where we can witness the development of many traits that are antecedent to the Indus civilization (J.-F. Jarrige and Meadow 1980). Among the most significant advances are the first steps toward the domestication of many of the plants and animals that became the staple foods in the Indus civilization.

3   From Foraging to Farming and Pastoralism

In order to sustain a large civilization under the environmental conditions described in Chapter 2, a number of technologies had to be in place. Of primary importance was the development of subsistence strategies adapted to life specific to the environmental conditions of the Greater Indus region. Although some aspects of subsistence practices were developed on the Indus plain, a basic foundation was established during several thousand years of experimentation before the development of urban centers and settlement on the plain. Other changes that went hand in hand with these experiments were social and economic, involving the establishment of permanent village settlements and ways of life that were new to this region.

There are a number of ongoing debates among archaeologists on the question of agricultural and pastoral origins in South Asia and its implications. (1) Is South Asia an original hearth of domestication (i.e., were the plants and animals domesticated from local flora and fauna)? If not, where they did come from? (2) Can we pinpoint when specific plants and animals made their first appearance? (3) Did domestication of plants and animals occur all-at-once or over a period of time? (4) What types of social and economic changes occurred as people adopted domesticated plants and animals? Why did people forego their hunting and gathering way of life for farming and animal husbandry?

This chapter has two purposes. The first is to review the current evidence for early domestication in the region. In doing so, I discuss the archaeobotanical and zooarchaeological evidence used to answer some of the questions raised in the preceding paragraph. The review takes us to Mehrgarh and Baluchistan (Figure 3.1) and to Loteshwar and Balathal in western India. In Box 3.1, I summarize some of the methods employed by archaeobotanists and zooarchaeologists investigating early domestication. The second is to explore the implications of the adoption of domesticates to the development of a sedentary village life. For this I turn to the site of Mehrgarh. This important site is situated at the foot of a major pass (see Figure 3.1 for the location of the Bolan Pass) on the

Figure 3.1. Map of Baluchistan and neighboring regions showing trade routes (dashed lines). © R. P. Wright.

western margins of the Indus alluvium. Throughout history, this pass has served as a major artery between regions to the west of Quetta at its head, the Kachi Plain at its base, and the Indus. I briefly refer to evidence from settlements in regions neighboring Mehrgarh.

Box 3.1 How Did Humans Domesticate Plants and Animals and How do Archaeologists Distinguish Domestic from Wild Forms?

The domestication of plants necessarily included periods of experimentation when certain cereal grasses were preferentially selected. Not all domesticates are grains, but most of the world's staples are. In the Near East and in Baluchistan during this period, the predominant plants were wheat and barley, which when processed could be used to make a porridge-like food, bread, and possibly beer (see Miller and Wetterstrom 2000:1123–39). Mehrgarh lies near the Irano-Anatolian

Box 3.1 (*Cont.*)

region, encompassing an area stretching from eastern Turkey, most of Iran and Afghanistan (Tengberg and Thiebault 2003:24). Therefore, many of the cereals found as domesticates at Mehrgarh lie within the normal distribution zone of plants that had been domesticated much earlier in the Near East.

Archaeobotanists are archaeologists with a specialty in the study of ancient plant remains. One of the keys archaeobotanists use in assessing whether a plant could plausibly have been domesticated in a particular area is whether the site on which the plant remains were found are in its normal distribution zone. They also examine size and other morphological characteristics that undergo changes with domestication. In determining whether a cereal has been domesticated, archaeobotanists examine the stem or rachis. A brittle rachis is a key to the annual growth cycle of wild cereals, since its structure is optimal for natural seed dispersal. Cereal grasses are propagated when seeds held in the rachis are released to the ground where they lie dormant during the winter. With the spring rains and warmer temperatures, the seeds sprout and new plant life begins. When people began to collect wheat and barley, they selected grasses with a tough rachis to avoid the loss of grains while harvesting, thereby reducing the natural seed dispersal mechanisms and making them dependent on humans to artificially separate the seeds and plant them. A tough rachis is an indication of domestication.

A similar type of experimentation occurred with the selection for animals. The domestication of animals involves a process of management that differs from plant care but that is equally dependent on manipulation by humans. This process may have begun with the herding of animals, most likely with the aid of dogs. Dogs have been domesticated for longer than any other animals, perhaps as long as 14,000 years ago. *Zooarchaeologists* are archaeologists who specialize in studies of animal bones and use similar criteria employed by archaeobotanists. For example, they asess whether the animals were within their normal distribution zone. Are there changes in size and other morphological characteristics? Another important clue is the sex of the animal and age at death. The actual keeping of animals probably occurred as they were raised and kept from a very young age. For example, if a number of sheep of different sexes were raised together, selective breeding could then be practiced. The criteria applied and the complexities of these determinations remain controversial issues. For a more complete discussion, see Pringle (1998) and Meadow (1996), for specifics of northwestern South Asia.

I focus on Mehrgarh for several reasons. First, it is the earliest settlement in South Asia for which there is a well-documented sequence of domestication. Second, it was occupied for a 3,000-year period preceding the Indus civilization, thus providing a long-term view of early settlement in South Asia. Third, many of the subsistence strategies developed at Mehrgarh were essential to settlement on the Indus plain; and fourth, there are aspects of the material culture at Mehrgarh that later became widespread throughout the Indus civilization. My purpose is not to show that the Indus civilization developed out of Baluchistan or Mehrgarh; it is simply the best example of an early village settlement in South Asia (C. Jarrige et al. 1995; J.-F. Jarrige et al. 2005; J.-F. Jarrige 2000).

From Hunting and Gathering to Farming

For most of human history, people have obtained their food by hunting wild animals, fishing in lakes and coastal waters, and gathering wild plants. This form of hunting and gathering has continued into the twenty-first century, and anthropologists have documented its viability as a means of subsistence. Hunters and gatherers procure their food by moving on a seasonal basis to the places where wild plants can be collected at specific times of the year and where animals seek grazing lands.

The first region in world prehistory for which we have extensive evidence for a shift from a hunting and gathering way of life to farming and animal keeping is from the Near East between 8,000 and 10,000 years ago. The main domesticated plants were cereal grasses (rye, wheat, and barley) documented over an area that extends from the eastern Mediterranean to southern Turkey, Syria, Iraq, and western Iran. Domestication of sheep, goats, and cattle followed closely on the heels of the adoption of domesticated plants in the same region. Since plant and animal domestication in South Asia began slightly later, sometime between 7000 and 6000 B.C., the question raised is whether the plants and animals were imported or domesticated from local forms, since they included some of the cereal grasses and sheep, goats, and cattle found in the Near East. In other parts of the world, foods like rice, yams, and millets found in Southeast and East Asia were the basic staples. Rice and millets were also important foods in South Asia and have been discovered at Harappa by 3200 B.C., to be discussed in Chapter 6.

The most important plants at Merhgarh included a mix of wild and domesticated species and wheat and barley.[1] Mehrgarh is located within the natural distribution zone for wild barley, and its grains have a distinctive morphology – short compact spikes, shortened internodes (nodes are part of the stem of the plant where leaves are attached and internodes are the spaces in between), and small rounded seeds – that is characteristic of grains cultivated but not completely domesticated (Costantini 1984:29,31). Based upon these factors, a strong case can be made for local domestication of barley. On the other hand, the presence of einkorn and emmer, wheat forms that lie east of the distribution of their wild ancestors, suggests they were brought from the Near East (Meadow 1993:301).

The earliest evidence for animal remains at Mehrgarh is approximately 7,000 B.C., when only wild species are found. The shift to a mixed exploitation pattern dominated by domesticated species and lesser quantities of wild animals was gradual. Replacement of local wild forms with domesticates was a more lengthy and variable process than plant domestication, making it difficult to pinpoint a specific time period when animal domestication occurred.

Two factors considered in evaluating whether animal species such as goats, sheep, and cattle present at Merhgarh were locally domesticated or imported are their increased representation over time and their decreasing body size (Meadow 1998). Based on these criteria, the argument for local domestication of goats is compelling. Goats may have been kept in the earliest settlement at Mehrgarh, considering the presence of young goats in several early burials. Cattle, like goats, increase in number and individual body size diminishes over time. The predominant domesticated cattle species is the zebu (*Bos indicus*), a type indigenous to South Asia. Studies have demonstrated the presence of genetic differences between South Asian cattle (the *Bos indicus*) and Near Eastern forms (*Bos taurus*) (Meadow and Patel 2003:71), providing strong evidence for local domestication of the zebu by 4800 B.C. Whether sheep were domesticated locally or brought to the region is less clear. Although their size diminutions are suggestive of local domestication, genetic studies indicate that all modern forms are descended from a single Near Eastern ancestor (*Ovis orientalis*) (Meadow and Patel 2003:71).

Other areas of Baluchistan have not been subjected to the intensive research carried out at Mehrgarh, but surveys and limited excavations suggest that experimentation with plants and animals was widespread by 4300 B.C. For example, at Kili Ghul Mohammad (Figure 3.1), located north of Mehrgarh near Quetta, there are house structures and evidence of domesticated sheep/goats and cattle (Fairservis 1956:382) in deposits dated to 4300 B.C. Also present in the same levels are sickle blades and grinding tools (Figure 3.2) used

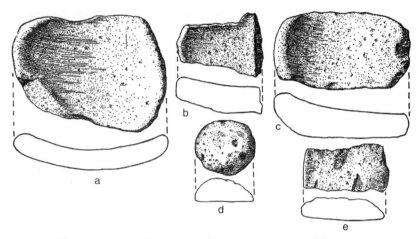

Figure 3.2. Grinding slabs from the Quetta Valley, Damb Sadaat, one-quarter natural size. Courtesy of American Museum of Natural History.

for processing grains (Fairservis 1956). Therefore, it seems likely that with additional excavations at sites like Kili Ghul Mohammad that include proper collections of faunal and floral materials, more evidence for domestication will come to light.

Outside Baluchistan, the evidence for early domestication is less robust. With respect to animal domestication, there are controversies regarding species identifications and determinations concerning whether skeletal remains are from wild or domestic animals. Richard Meadow and Ajita Patel (2003:74) have identified domesticated cattle at the site of Loteshwar in northern Gujarat (see Figure 1.2 for the site's location). To obtain a secure date, they subjected charred zebu cattle bone to radiocarbon analyses. The results showed a time range from 3657 cal. B.C. to 2250 cal. B.C. Based upon these results, Meadow and Patel have suggested there may have been "multiple centers of cattle domestication in South Asia" (2003:74) (i.e., an early domestication of zebu in Baluchistan and a later, independent development in India).

The agropastoral economy at Loteshwar differed from that of Mehrgarh. At Mehrgarh, the economy was based on farming and pastoralism, suggesting that the villagers were relatively self-sufficient, since diverse food resources were available within a single community. In contrast, the economy at Loteshwar may have been based solely on animal keeping, presenting something of a dilemma. As Meadow and Patel note "no pastoral system exists, or is likely to have existed for very long, without agricultural products being available through one means or another, whether this be tillage, trade, or raid" (2003:75). The closest known settlements for which plant domestication has been documented is at Balathal in Rajasthan, where wheat and barley are present by 3000 B.C. These crops are not native to the region, so they most likely diffused from regions to the west (Fuller 2003:373). Possibly there were agriculturalists with whom the pastoralists at Loteshwar interacted; alternatively, the people at Loteshwar supplemented their diets by collecting wild plants.

In summary, our best evidence thus far suggests that, for some plants and animals, South Asia was an original hearth of domestication, while others diffused from the Near East. We can now document the presence of domesticated plants and animals in Baluchistan between 7000 and 6000 B.C., beginning first with wheat and barley, followed closely by sheep, goats, and cattle. By 4500 B.C., domestication in the region was widespread. Elsewhere, now documented at Loteshwar and Balathal, the domestication of cattle and wheat and barley, respectively, occurred much later.

Focus on Mehrgarh – The Choice of a Site and the Establishment of a Chronology

Jean-Francois Jarrige, Director of the French Archaeological Mission to Pakistan and of excavations at Mehrgarh, and Richard Meadow (Jarrige and Meadow 1980) have characterized developments at Mehrgarh as "antecedent" to the Indus civilization. Specifically, they have in mind the plants and animals first domesticated at Mehrgarh and the sophisticated technologies invented there and later adopted and refined by craft producers in the Indus valley and elsewhere.

Mehrgarh is an ideal site on which to conduct archaeological research. It is large, covering over 200 hectares (a hectare is a metric unit equal to 2.471 acres) and has been continuously occupied for over 3,000 years. (See Box 3.2 on mound development.) Settlement at Mehrgarh shifted during the years of occupation due to changes in the course of the Bolan River. Therefore, specific areas were inhabited during different periods. While organizing the excavations at Mehrgarh, Jarrige assigned individual excavators to specific sectors labeled MR1-7 on the site plan so that information about the entire sequence of the settlement could be collected almost simultaneously (see Figure 3.3).

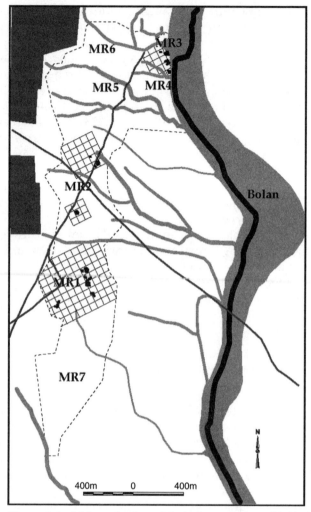

Figure 3.3. Mehrgarh plan with designated site grid. Redrawn from
C. Jarrige et al. 1995.

Table 3.1 breaks down habitation areas found at the site into three clusters. Each cluster has a period designation – Periods I/II, III, and IV–VII
and an approximate time period associated with it. The Period I/II
living area cluster (designated MR3/MR4) is located at the northeast
corner of the site and represents a relatively small settled community.
During this early phase, the settlement grew from two hectares to 12
hectares in area. Over the following Period III (MR2), it expanded

Box 3.2 Mounds and Tells

Many South Asian archaeological sites are mounds (tells or kots) built up over years of settlement. Mounds develop as a result of the construction materials used and local building techniques. Mudbricks, a locally available building material, have been used in the region for centuries for all sorts of structures. They are produced by placing clay or mud in a mold and allowing it to dry in the sun to harden. These mudbricks make durable houses, but over time the mudbricks break down and the building is leveled. These building remnants are used as foundations for new buildings and the accumulation of broken-down mudbricks and other debris gradually results in artificial mounds. Like a time capsule, the new building seals earlier construction and human activity.

Digging mounded sites can be difficult, especially if archaeologists are interested in uncovering long periods of occupation, since there may be a significant overburden of mudbricks before the earliest levels of occupation can be reached. Large horizontal exposures of early occupations can be difficult to achieve. Mounded sites do have advantages, however, because the layers of rubble, pottery sherds, and broken-down mudbricks preserve a record of the relative order (the oldest at the bottom and the most recent at the top) in which materials were abandoned and accumulated over time.

At Mehrgarh, the expansion of the settlement across a large plain (see Figure 3.2) made excavation of all periods simultaneously possible; this strategy was adopted by J.-F. Jarrige, the team's director. He assigned members of his team different sectors of the site for excavation so that at one and the same time, they were uncovering occupational levels for the entire sequence. A disadvantage of a site like Mehrgarh, however, is that it lacks a single stratigraphic section for all periods of occupation. However, as discussed in this chapter, Periods I and II can be linked through a massive section cut by the Bolan River. Another well-preserved stratigraphic unit is the mound occupied between Periods VI and VII.

over a larger area of 75–100 hectares in which activities were dispersed. The densely clustered settlement represented in Periods IV–VII (MR1/MR7) covers approximately sixty hectares. An additional period, Period VIII, extends beyond the time segment discussed in this chapter and will be discussed in Chapter 11.

Table 3.1. Summary of Chronology and Occupation at Merhgarh

Period Chronology	Area Occupied	Extent of Occupation
A First Village		
I 7000–4800 B.C.	MR3/4/6	2–3 hectares
IIA 4800–4300 B.C.	MR3/4	
IIB 4300–4000 B.C.	MR3/4	12 hectares
Villages at the Crossroads		
III 4000–3200 B.C.	MR2	75–100 hectares
A Mosaic of Villages and Towns		
IV–VII 3200–2500 B.C.	MR1/7	60 hectares

The social and economic developments apparent at Mehrgarh are visible in the archaeological record beginning with first settlement in Period I through its eventual abandonment in Period VII. Next, I discuss each period of settlement at Mehrgarh using five categories of archaeological evidence – subsistence, architecture, burial practices, material culture and technology, and external contact – to demonstrate similarities and differences among the designated periods (see Figure 3.4 for examples of house forms, compartmented buildings, burials, and other structures in the different periods).

A First Village (7000–4000 B.C.)

The sedentary lifestyle of an agriculturalist, in contrast to the more mobile existence of hunters and gatherers, has a profound impact on virtually all aspects of social life. It signals a shift in mindset from consideration of more immediate planning for a distant future and reflects on concepts of ownership in which possession of agricultural fields or animal stock provided a "foundation for social differentiation based on the accumulation of material wealth" (Meadow 1989, 1993:296).

The first signs of village life at Mehrgarh are from areas MR3 and MR4. At this early time, the village was positioned very near the Bolan River and sometime during Periods I and II, the river shifted its course and cut through the settlement. Individual layers (or strata) resulting from human occupation are visible in a twelve-meter-deep section that documents over thirty architectural phases of rebuilding. This extensive architecture is consistent with the 2,300 years of habitation reflected in radiocarbon dates.

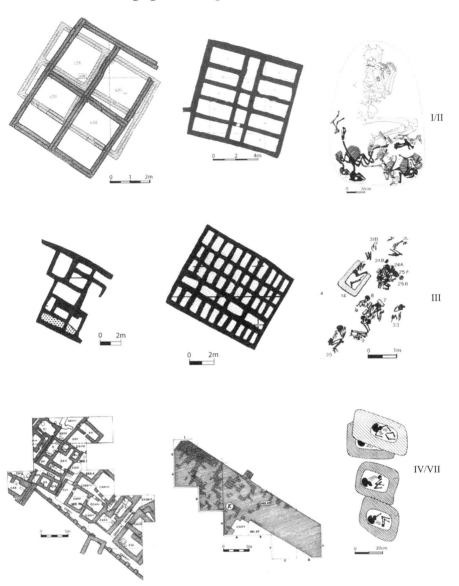

Figure 3.4. Architectural structures and burials at Mehrgarh in designated periods. Left to right: Period I/II: house forms, compartmented building, and burials; Period III: house form, compartmented building, and burials; Period IV–VII: house forms, platform, infant burials. Redrawn from C. Jarrige et al 1995

Subsistence

As discussed earlier in "From Hunting and Gathering to Farming," soon after people settled at Mehrgarh several species of plants were either domesticated there or adopted from the Near East. The domestication of animals followed.

There are several reasons for the success of domestication at Merhgarh. Environmental conditions are favorable because there is good access to water and arable soils. In addition, its location within a short distance of mountains (rising 1,500–1,800 meters), foothills, and alluvial plain provides abundant and diverse vegetation (Tengberg and Thiebault 2003:27). In low-lying areas, vegetation consists of small trees and shrubs (acacia, tamarisk, and willow), while in upland zones there are subtropical evergreen and temperate forests (pistachio, almond, juniper, and pine). Within these several different ecological zones, a variety of wild progenitors of domesticable plants and animals are present. On a single day, the climate can vary from the comfortably warm on the plain to moister and colder conditions at higher elevations. In the early 1980s, I worked for several seasons at Mehrgarh. Vivid in my memory is a day in February when I admired a sunflower in full bloom in the dig courtyard. At the same time, the mountains in the distance were snow covered.

Of additional importance are rainfall patterns. In the region around Kachi where Merhgarh is located, rainfall is low and plant growth and pasturage are dependent upon the presence of seasonal streams and springs. Our understanding of past climates there is limited (Meadow 1987). Plant and animal communities most likely were clustered in restricted zones, where water sources were available.

At present, agriculture and pastoralism are most successful on the plain and basin areas, and on a more limited basis within the mountain valleys. Pasturage for animals is available along the narrow slopes and in the lower elevations of the mountains (Scholz 1983). The Kachi Plain is a productive area for crops such as wheat and barley. While some villagers remain on the plain and in the intermediate zones throughout the year, others engage in a pattern referred to as transhumance in which segments of the population move their animals to cooler pasture lands at higher elevations, abandoning their homes during hot summer months. Still others are nomadic pastoralists who migrate between mountain and plain throughout the year, escaping the extreme heat and torrential monsoon rains (Scholz 1983).

Architecture

The structures at Mehrgarh during Periods I/II comprise four types. With the exception of temporary structures built of animal skins supported by wooden poles, the basic building material was sun-dried mud.

1. The most popular dwellings consist of four rooms of equal size, measuring 5.5 × 3.75 meters (J.-F. Jarrige et al. 2005:137). (See Figure 3.4 for examples.) Other dwellings consist of two, six, or even ten rooms. On the whole, the buildings are not decorated, but a few have floors or walls decorated with red ochre and geometrical patterns in red, black, and white (J.-F. Jarrige et al. 2005:135); two others were paved with burnt pebbles and carbonized animal bones (C. Jarrige et al. 1995:454). Considering the absence of doors at ground level, entrance to dwellings apparently was through the roof.

2. A second type of building is made up of a number of compartments too small for habitation. These compartmented buildings appear in the upper levels of Period I and throughout Period II. The example shown in Figure 3.3 consists of twelve rectangular rooms and four square ones. Typically, compartmented buildings measure approximately five/eight meters and consist of small, individual rooms measuring 3 by 1.5 or 1.5 by 1.25 meters, about the size of a modern closet. The largest compartmented building has fifteen rooms (Quivron 1987). Judging by their size, the buildings most likely were used communally for storage. The artifacts and debris left behind included ash, grinding and mulling stones, charred seeds, and nine unbaked cylinders placed on a platform outside one of the compartmented buildings. These artifacts suggest that people were engaged in food processing, such as parching cereal grains, baking bread, or storing food and that the buildings were used as granaries (Jarrige et al. 2005:136). One exception is a partially worked elephant tusk indicative of craft production. These subterranean compartments would have been hidden from outsiders if covered with brush or other materials and would have provided secure storage areas.

3. There also were separate walls associated with some compartmented buildings, found either attached or free standing, perhaps to prevent erosion.

4. Platforms (not illustrated) appear to have been working areas in view of their association with circular firepits and trash consisting of burnt pebbles, ashes, and bone (perhaps from a domestic activity); the flint

artifacts consisting of blades, cores, and borers were used for butchering, preparing hides, and working bone and antler.

Burial Patterns

Thus far, more than 320 burials have been discovered in Period I. Over a period of years, as the walls of houses deteriorated, they were broken down and abandoned, and new structures were built. This process was repeated so that as dwellings were abandoned, they were reused as graveyards (J.-F. Jarrige et al. 2005:132).

An extensive study of 150 burials from Period II was carried out by the physical anthropologist, Pascal Sellier (1991). Sellier calculated life expectancy at 31 years and estimated a birth rate of 4.5 children per female, a rate consistent with present-day hunting and gathering populations (1991:78). Of the burials examined, 35% were children, 68 percent of whom were younger than five years of age.

Burial types and grave goods varied during Periods I and II.

The most common form of burial was a burial chamber, accessed through a long shaft and sealed by a mudbrick wall. Some chambers contained several individuals, who lay in flexed positions, oriented in an east–west direction (see Figure 3.4) and turned south toward specially constructed walls (Cucina et al. 2005:81). Bodies were bandaged or wrapped in leather shrouds impregnated with red ocher, a mineral used for processing leather (Sellier 1991).[2]

Others were placed in a simple pit approximately 1 or 1.5 meters deep (Cucina et al. 2005).

A few of the burials were disarticulated, indicating that the bones were placed in the burial chamber long after the individual's death. These secondary burials may indicate that the interred died while away from home. At death their bodies may have been placed in a temporary burial or exposed to the elements until their remains could be brought back to their ancestral home for final burial.

Funerary goods consisted of personal items such as ornaments (necklaces, anklets, bracelets, belts, and pendants), tools made of stone and bone, clay and stone vessels, and baskets. In one exceptional burial, a polished stone ax and three flint cores were placed in a basket and lay near the skull of the deceased (Figure 3.5). Sixteen blades from the same core were set in parallel rows along the spinal column (C. Jarrige et al. 1995:246). Another exceptional burial included stone and shell necklaces (a male), a flat shell disc pendant, and stone ankle beads. Five goats under the age of three months were found at the individual's feet. Several

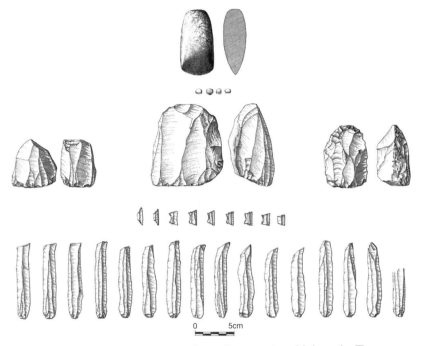

Figure 3.5. Grave goods from Grave 114 at Mehrgarh. Top row to bottom: polished stone axe, four turquoise beads, three flint cores, nine geometric flint microliths, sixteen flint blades from a single nucleus. © Gonzague Quivron.

graves of young females also contained goats that had been placed in baskets in a semicircle "around the legs of the deceased" (C. Jarrige et al. 1995:137). The presence of flint cores, blades, and polished stone axes in adult male burials and bone spindles with females suggests a sexual division of labor. Finally, one of the most surprising recent findings at Mehrgarh is the discovery of "the drilling of human teeth *in vivo*" with stone tools.[3] They included four females, two males, and three sex unknown, the first instance of "proto-dentistry in an early farming culture" (Coppa et al. 2006:755).

Material Culture and Technology

Artifacts provide insights into the lifestyle of a population. At Mehrgarh, they are consistent with a transition from a hunting and gathering way of life to that of farming and herding. Evidence for cooking and food processing, includes mortars and millers for grinding grain into flour. At first, food was cooked by stone boiling in baskets lined with bitumen, a tar-like substance to make the basket impermeable. By the end of the period (beginning in Period II), pottery was being produced at Mehrgarh. Pots provided an improved and more efficient method of cooking because new types of food could be added to the diet and their digestibility and palatability enhanced. Pottery containers have heating qualities that make it possible to maintain a boiling point and cook food at temperatures with sustained heat. Food can be left unattended for longer periods than in other containers, and toxins within certain foods can be reduced (Arnold 1985:128). (See Box 3.3.) Stone tools were used both for hunting and butchering meat and for collecting soft grasses. Sickles, for example, were used for harvesting grains. They were composed of small blade fragments "set into bitumen that had been placed in a groove in a wooden haft" (Vaughan 1995:614).

Box 3.3 Pots to Cook and New Foods to Eat

The use of clay as a construction material occurred as a two-stage process at Mehrgarh. Initially clay objects were formed by hand and were unfired. For example, there are unfired clay pots in burials; animal and human figurines are found in other contexts; mudbrick was used as a building material (see Box 3.2) or as linings for circular ovens (J.-F. Jarrige and Lechevallier 1979:469). In a second stage, straw-tempered, low-fired ceramic vessels appeared. Within a few centuries finer and higher-fired pots, terracotta nails, bangles, figurines, clay rattles, seals, and pendants were produced. A similar sequence from unbaked to kiln-fired clay occurred in the Near East, where unbaked clay objects precede fired ones by several centuries. In both instances, the obvious experimentation with hand-formed, unfired clay objects as a precursor to fired ones suggests local innovation rather than the spread of the idea from one region to another.

Fired clay objects also made possible a variety of vessel forms, beyond what had been possible with basketry, leather skins, or stone. Specific shapes and sizes were developed for distinctive tasks, some utilitarian and others more decorative. Two decorative types – Togau and Faiz Mohammad – are discussed in Box 3.5.

Pottery vessels go hand in hand with the adoption of new foods and cooking technologies. Some vessels were used to cook foods at a sustained rate without constant attention to boiling as was the case with the baskets or stone bowls used for stone boiling before ceramic vessels were produced. Ceramic vessels can be placed over a hearth,

Box 3.3 (*Cont.*)

and their food contents can be cooked at a sustained heat. Foods prepared in this manner are more palatable, and the toxins in certain grains (wheat, barley) can be reduced, improving digestibility.

Finally, tall, fired pots make ideal vessels for storing water because baked clay retains its coolness. Special manufacturing techniques can be used to make vessels nonporous. At Mehrgarh, dishes were used as covers for vessels, making their contents secure from intruders.

Figure 3.6. Human figurines from the site of Mehrgarh. Courtesy C. Jarrige.

Other activities included woodworking, spinning, weaving, sewing, and hide processing. Both males and females, judging by the graves at Mehrgarh, wore ornaments, including necklaces, anklets, rings, belts, and headbands made of shell, turquoise, lapis lazuli, copper, and steatite. Also present were animal and human figurines. (See Box 3.4 and Figure 3.6.) Finally, cotton fibers and seeds also were discovered in these early levels at Mehrgarh (J.-F. Jarrige et al. 2005:139) and were most likely used to produce cloth.

Box 3.4 Human Figurines at Mehrgarh

At Mehrgarh human figurines are miniature works of art in clay. Although modeled by hand and pieced together in segments, they are rendered with extreme care. The style and manufacturing techniques of the figurines changed over time and, therefore, are good chronological indicators.

The earliest human figurines in Periods I and II are seated or standing and schematically represented (Figure 3.6). They were formed from a single piece of clay, with minimal representation of arms and legs; a few were adorned with necklaces and belts applied to the basic figure. Some were decorated with red ochre. In general, they range in size from 1.5 to 10 centimeters. A very few are larger, and most are made of unbaked clay. Many of the figurines have feminine characteristics (realistic breasts); one standing figure bears the hint of genitalia and is obviously male (C. Jarrige 2005:30,31). Only one human figurine from Period III has been found (C. Jarrige 2005:28).

The style of representation and production technique changes between Periods II and IV. From Periods IV to VII, the figurines are composites of elements consisting of a principal shape onto which pieces are sculpted or added. Features include pierced eyes encircled with a coil, bulbous breasts, and hairstyles worthy of any of the most fanciful coutures, including coiled hair or exotic curls that cascade down the figure's upper torso. Figurines are represented with elaborate ornaments. All figurines are female during Periods IV–VI, but males are represented in Period VII. Some changes in aspects of technology and style throughout Period VII are best illustrated by them. Male figurines are identifiable by their genitals and a special "phallic" pendant ornament. By the middle of Period VII, they have broad shoulders and lack jewelry. They wear magnificent headdresses and generally are standing, in some cases holding an infant; in fact, by the end of the period, the only example of an individual holding an infant is a male. Males also underwent hairstyle changes from braids or knots early in Period VII to long flowing strands pulled to the top of their heads and held with a band knotted at the back.

It is difficult to assign function to these figures. Were they toys like Barbie and G.I. Joe dolls of the twentieth century? We can presume the figurines encoded certain behaviors, prescribing appropriate roles for males and females. At the same time, did they have ritual significance? Catherine Jarrige (1991, 2005) conducted an extensive study of

Box 3.4 (*Cont.*)

the Mehrgarh figurines. As she points out, their frequent presence in trash deposits gives the impression they were discarded haphazardly. However, there are several clues that may lead to an understanding of their significance to the people at Mehrgarh. One is reflected in the *locations* of trash deposits. Since many of the deposits are found in household areas, they may represent a "domestic cult," perhaps associated with "representations of tutelary deities for the family, the clan or...[a]...relevant profession" (C. Jarrige 1991:92). Another possibility is their use for "magical practices, as is frequently the case in agrarian societies" (C. Jarrige 1991:92).

While cleaning early standing and seated figurines, Jarrige noted the presence of "holes running through the figurines. ... Small twigs cut straight through...going to and fro several times when the clay was still soft...[that]...could either represent an attempt for a magical treatment or pain, be it moral, psychological or physical – or a way to harm someone through an image" (C. Jarrige 2005:34).

Finally, the recent discovery of one of the pierced human figurines in a grave from Period I, in which the figurine was held to the dead woman's face in clasped hands, may indicate something about the role she played in society (2005:34).

External Contacts

Many of the raw materials needed to produce tools at Mehrgarh were accessible locally, but others have been identified from more distant sources. Nearby materials included clay, reeds, leather, bone, antler, bitumen, and flint. In contrast, the lapis lazuli and marine shell were from distant sources. Lapis lazuli comes from northeastern Afghanistan, and the marine shells, from the coastal waters to the south.

Summary – Period I/II

The people at Mehrgarh had developed viable farming and animal husbandry strategies and the requisite tools and technologies of agriculturalists, such as storage and food preparation. The evidence for secondary burials suggests that some members of the community left the village for periods of time, possibly moving their animals to mountain pasturage during summer months.

They also invented new technologies beyond farming and animal keeping, developing innovative ways of handling and procuring materials. New technologies in this region, such as firing clay to make pots, are a first at Mehrgarh, as are new ornamental styles and ways of handling raw materials. Villagers also took advantage of the site's location at the foot of the Bolan Pass to gain access to precious raw materials. Finally, there is a hint of emerging social differences, suggested by the contents of some of the burials.

Even though we are able to formulate a picture of the first village at Mehrgarh, we remain virtually in the dark and can only speculate about the presence of other culture groups in the region. On the one hand, Mehrgarh was isolated, although it is possible that other villages existed nearby and have not been discovered. Very likely, hunters and gatherers who chose not to settle down were nearby, and a traveler walking through the hills and plains of the region 8,000 years ago would have encountered groups employing a variety of subsistence patterns. On the other hand, there were contemporary agricultural villages in eastern Iran to the west and Central Asia to the north with which they may have been in some contact.

Villages at the Crossroads (4000–3200 B.C.)

The transformations at Mehrgarh during Period III are part of larger developments throughout this area of Baluchistan and beyond. The most dramatic was in the increased number of settlements. On the Kachi Plain, we know of at least one other large settlement at Pathani Damb (Figure 3.1), positioned like Mehrgarh at the foot of a major mountain pass (the Mula) leading from the north and west to the Indus Plain (de Cardi 1983). Other villages were located to its west serving as "feeder routes leading into the Mula" (de Cardi 1983:4). They also were strategically positioned along mountain valleys for travel south and west. Several sites were located at the head of the Bolan Pass near Quetta (e.g., Damb Sadaat and Kili Ghul Mohammad) well positioned for procuring nonlocal materials such as lapis lazuli. In addition, there are numerous sites to the north of Kachi in Zhob and Loralai, providing alternate routes onto the Indus Plain.

Several factors may account for this increase in settlements. According to Sellier (1991), the birthrate at Mehrgarh was higher (see discussion that follows), indicating a population increase, possibly due to a settled way of life. In addition, new people, attracted by the agricultural villages, may have migrated to the region. Some formerly mobile populations also may have established more permanent or semipermanent settlements.

Returning to Mehrgarh, the village shifted its location in Period III to MR2 (Figure 3.3), and the settlement pattern at Mehrgarh changed. In contrast to the tightly clustered village in Periods I and II, activities were spread over 75+ hectares in which there were specialized zones for storage (the compartmented buildings), habitation (dwelling units), burial, and craft-producing activities. In spite of these changes, there is a continuity in the material culture.

Subsistence

The pace of domestication and diversity of foods produced accelerated from previous periods. In addition to wheat and barley, oats and goats-face grass (a naturally occurring cereal) have been identified. The morphology of the wheat and barley changed to rounded forms, a possible indication that they were grown in artificially watered fields (Costantini 1984). This process likely involved use of simple structures to collect receding floodwaters. People continued to exploit a mixture of domesticated and wild animals, a consistent pattern throughout the occupation of Mehrgarh. However, by Period III, the decrease in size of goats and cattle typical of the transition from wild to domesticated species ended (Meadow 1998), indicating that the domestication of these animals was complete.

Architecture

The dwelling units, compartmented buildings, walls and platforms continued to be the main architectural forms.

Dwelling units had a number of rooms, ranging from three to eight. The house shown on Figure 3.4 consisted of seven rooms. Like others, it was basically rectangular. Judging by their "organic" structure, they may have been added to over time. House walls were substantial. In some instances, their walls were built with two rows of mudbricks; the back walls had three rows, suggesting that exterior walls served as protective barriers against outsiders. In addition, the thicker mudbrick walls may have provided support for a second story. Access to rooms was limited; the largest were accessible through small openings, but smaller ones were without doors, suggesting they were used for storage. As before, houses probably were entered from the roof.

Compartmented buildings were built with a larger number of divisions than in Periods I and II. The example in Figure 3.4 has an unusually high number of rooms, but all of them were too small for habitation, suggesting that they continued to be used for storage. Although many compartmented buildings were empty, tools were found just outside the building. They included stone mortars, pestles, and slabs used for food

processing. Domestic hearths were in open spaces near the compartmented buildings.

Not shown are platforms and walls of several types. Some are associated with compartmented buildings, whereas others comprise a system
of terraces and retaining walls used to stabilize and protect buildings
from the high water flooding of the Bolan.

Burial Patterns

Ninety-nine complete burials have been discovered in the MR2 sector.
Seventy-three are adults older than twenty years of age, and twenty six
are juveniles and children. There were no infants buried in this area.
Of the identifiable adult burials, half are male, and half are female.
The average age at death was 24 years. Estimates of birthrates are 5.8
per adult female (Sellier 1991:81). The vast majority of burials are primary, but a few are secondary, having been reopened on several occasions to insert more bodies. Most people were buried in simple pits
but a few had mudbrick walls on one side. Rarely, a kind of mudbrick
coffin was used. As in Period I, bodies were placed in a flexed position, "bandaged" with a nonleather material and oriented as earlier in
Period I/II.

The types and amounts of grave goods varied (Sellier 1991:77).

They include burials devoid of any artifacts.

Other burials contain a *Standard* set of ornaments (necklaces, bangles,
and anklets made of turquoise, steatite, calcite, shell, copper, and lapis
lazuli). Steatite beads were produced using an elaborate technique that
was developed at Mehrgarh and continued to be used and modified in
the later periods (Samzun and Sellier 1985). The details of manufacture
are described in Chapters 6 and 7.

Some burials contained *exceptional* goods. They included Standard
ornaments plus pottery, stone vessels, basketry, bronze, or semiprecious
stone. Percentages recorded by sex and age are shown in Table 3.2.

Table 3.2. Percentages of Types of Grave Goods in Period III by Age and Sex

Type	Adult Female (%)	Adult Male (%)	Juveniles and Children (%)
Absent	25	60	73
Standard	39	20	5.5
Exceptional	36	20	11.5

Age Differences. The lowest percentages of artifacts were found in the burials of children and juveniles. We can only speculate on why these variations occurred. It may not have been culturally appropriate for juveniles and children to wear them. Conceivably, children did not achieve full "personhood" until puberty, when they officially joined the adult world. Grave goods may have had a religious significance tied to concepts of the afterlife from which younger individuals were excluded. Exceptional artifacts in adult burials may have been personal possessions that a prepubescent individual did not have.

Sex Differences. The most dramatic differences are between males and females. Questions of style or cultural taboos on the wearing of ornaments for males can be ruled out because standard ornaments were present in some male burials. Higher percentages of standard and exceptional grave goods in women's burials might reflect values accorded to their reproductive capacities, their productive labor, or their kinship affiliations. For example, if marriage patterns at Mehrgarh were matrilocal (the couple lives in a woman's home village), grave goods brought for females as offerings by mourners may have been more numerous.

Finally, the homogeneity of burial practices when age and sex differences are taken into account, demonstrates that there were agreed-upon rules or prescribed "codes" of appropriate behavior in the construction of burials, distribution of grave goods, and orientation and preparation of the body. Immature individuals were conceived of as being different from adults; similarly, males were treated differently than females. In other words, biological differences (age or sex) had taken on cultural significance.

Material Culture and Technology

Consistent with other aspects of Period III, there is a diversity of materials and finished products, demonstrating new specializations, forms of skilled knowledge, and access to raw material sources. New terracotta (low-fired clay) objects included bangles, small balls, and rattles. Animal figurines continued to be produced, but only one human figurine has been found. Stone tool types increased and included axes, stone hammers, maceheads, weights and counterweights, and copper implements and ornaments (e.g., hooks, amulets, double spiral-headed pins). Bone tools included awls, points, and needles. Another innovation is the use of a specific stone (green phatanite) for bow drills, a tradition known later in the Indus and in eastern Iran as well (Samzun and Sellier 1985).

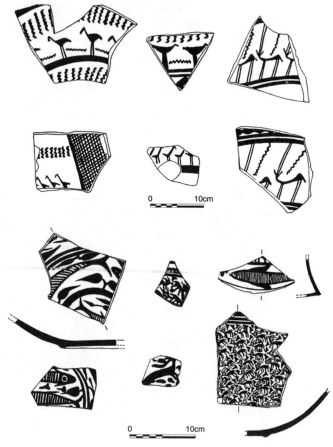

Figure 3.7. Togau and Faiz Mohammad ceramics from the site of Mehrgarh. © R. P. Wright

Most tools were discovered in household contexts, suggesting that both domestic tasks and craft production took place in some residential areas. For example, in one room, there were grinding stones and pestles used in cooking, along with bone needles for basketry or weaving, and bone points and awls for leatherworking (Russell 1995:583).

Other crafts were produced in areas separate from households. Exceptionally fine pottery was produced in a large-scale workshop isolated from dwellings or compartmented buildings. The workshop contained the remnants of three kilns and a six-meter-deep deposit of layers of kiln, walls, ash, charcoal, and pottery. The style of pottery in the deposit was fairly uniform, suggesting that thousands of vessels had been produced within a relatively short period. (See Box 3.5 and Figure 3.7 for examples of Togau motifs.) Objects associated with production included bone tools for polishing or burnishing pottery and grinding stones and pestles for preparing clay and pigments used for decorating the pots. Other artifacts in the ceramic production area included terracotta animal figurines, beads, or spindle whorls, and perhaps the possessions of the potters. Materials found at various other locations on the surface

Box 3.5 A New Aesthetic

The pottery produced at Mehrgarh is among the most beautiful and technically sophisticated in any early society. The earliest ceramics produced in Period I/II consisted of simple vessel forms, which were first produced from a clay tempered with the chaff from grain. Later the ware produced was finer, free of chaff, and with lustrous red surfaces. By Period III, potters produced fancier types using decorative motifs that enhanced the aesthetic qualities of their pots. The first pottery decorated with painted motifs is called Togau. Potters used geometric motifs, probably borrowed from basketry patterns and more figurative ones such as stylized gazelles (see Figure 3.6) and plants familiar in their surroundings. Mehrgarh potters were masterful innovators, engaging in experimentation by manipulating atmospheres in kilns and utilizing iron oxide pigments to produce designs in black and red set in registers over the natural red-orange surface of their pots (Wright 1985, 1989, 1995). Later, potters created other types in increasingly exotic colors. They produced the colors by experimenting with new pigments and applying them after the vessels were fired. Finally, they were able to change the overall color of the pottery itself from the natural reddish color of the clay to gray. To accomplish that, they fired the pottery at high temperatures and controlled the atmosphere (the amount of oxygen) in the kiln. This period of experimentation culminated in one of the most technically sophisticated pottery types – called Faiz Mohammad (named for the site on which it first was found) – ever produced in prehistory. Faiz Mohammad pottery was widely sought after for its unusual gray color and extraordinary painted designs. Examples of the gray pottery produced at Mehrgarh have been found as far away as eastern Iran (Wright 1984). It is easy to imagine someone proudly displaying these vessels in one of the niches found in Mehrgarh houses during Periods VI and VII.

were quantities of lapis lazuli, turquoise, carnelian, and marine shell associated with stone and copper tools used in the manufacture of beads and other ornaments. For the first time, there is evidence for metal working in the form of crucibles containing traces of copper.

External Contacts

As the raw materials listed in this section indicate, Mehrgarh had become part of a larger circle of interacting communities engaged in farming and herding economies drawing on local and nonlocal raw materials. Although a larger segment of the population lived in the village throughout the year, some villagers may have moved to higher elevations in warmer months.

Summary – Period III

As part of the general trend toward an intensified agricultural and pastoral economy, villagers at Mehrgarh became increasingly involved in trade and craft production. Many new technologies were invented, reflecting ways of handling materials that continued to be the standard in the Indus civilization even after Mehrgarh was abandoned. These long-standing crafting practices are especially evident in both reductive (stone and bone working) and pyrotechnological crafts (metallurgy and ceramics). Artisans developed a particular "style" of working in which objects were produced by first breaking down raw materials and reconstituting them through heating. This technique is typical of pyrotechnological crafts such as pottery production but unusual with stone and bone. Steatite bead making (reconstructed in Chapter 6) is one example of a pyrotechnological craft, but the same methods were applied in the manufacture of faience, for which there are a few examples in Period III. The presence of fourteen crucibles with traces of copper is the earliest evidence for metallurgy in this region.

On the basis of this impressive evidence, J.-F. Jarrige (1995) proposed that Merhgarh served as a kind of "marketplace" for the exchange of raw materials and craft and agricultural products. The marketplace he has in mind is less formally organized than those in today's large cities; nonetheless, it served as a distribution center for goods and services. Clearly, the variety of crafts and the large numbers of items produced (e.g., the six-meter-deep deposit containing the fragments of thousands of pots) supports his proposal, since materials produced at Mehrgarh were well beyond the needs of local consumption. One possibility is that seasonally migrating groups traveling between the highlands and lowlands and even beyond into

Afghanistan, as they do today when borders between these regions are opened, could have brought back raw materials and traded them to settled villagers in exchange for finished products made with the specialized technologies developed at Mehrgarh. Today, villagers and their more mobile cousins engage in a kind of reciprocal exchange in which agricultural products are swapped for animal products and exotic raw materials from farther afield (Scholz 1983). Although we cannot demonstrate kinship ties of this kind for ancient Mehrgarh, the close resemblance of the material culture found at Merhgarh to other villages on the Kachi Plain and in the highlands suggests that contact was carried out at a sustained level.

A Mosaic of Villages and Towns (3200–2500 B.C.)

Since Mehrgarh's initial settlement at around 7000 B.C., between Period IV and Period VII, the overall size and number of nearby settlements and those beyond Baluchistan increased (see Chapter 4). For example, by 3300 B.C., there was a small settlement at Harappa on the Indus Plain, which would later grow to one of the major Indus cities. Mehrgarh engaged in an ever more widening sphere of interaction with groups within and outside of Baluchistan to its west and east. Six kilometers from Mehrgarh, a new village, Naushoro, was founded in Period VII. Also in Period VII, a pottery type known as Kot Diji (or Early Harappan) was discovered at Mehrgarh (see Chapter 4 Chronology). The distribution of this pottery style marked a connection with emerging settlements on the Indus Plain. On the west, there is evidence for the exchange of pottery produced at Mehrgarh as far distant as settlements in eastern Iran (Wright 1984, 1989, 2002b).

Sometime after Period III, the settlement plan at Mehrgarh changed dramatically. There is a shift to the area labeled MR1 and MR7 (Figure 3.3). Trends initially developed during Period III continue to intensify through Periods IV–VII.

Subsistence

One possible explanation for the shift in settlement is that the Bolan River had now maintained a stable course. This inference is based on the discovery of ditches filled with a rusty-colored sediment characteristic of the bottom of canals. It has been suggested that the canals were used to divert water from the floodplain to land at its margins in order to increase the area of potentially cultivable land (J.-F. Jarrige 1995:76) and agricultural yields.

Another innovation and new use for available resources included the fermentation of grapes and barley for wine and beer. One house floor, for example, included a circular cavity covered with imprints of grape seeds, thought to be "the bottom of a press." In other dwellings, grape seeds and vine segments were found in hearths (J.-F. Jarrige 1995:76). Although there is no direct proof, barley also may have been processed in the preparation of beer (J.-F. Jarrige 1995:76–7).

There is both change and continuity in animal keeping and meat consumption. These changes are reflected principally in the greater exploitation of sheep and goats in distinction to cattle. This shift had environmental implications. Given that sheep and goats are more comfortable in highland zones in the hot summer months, their selective exploitation is an indication of continuation of the transhumance pattern (J.-F. Jarrige 1995:76,77). Finally, there is a differential distribution of animal bones in various rooms, courtyards and trash deposits, a pattern first noted in Period III (Meadow 1989b; J.-F. Jarrige 1995:77). These may be the result of cultural food preferences or broad social and political patterns in people's ability to gain access to particular foods.

Architecture

The evidence from Periods IV and V is limited but consistent with discoveries in Periods VI and VII. The principal form of architecture during these periods is tightly clustered dwelling units.

Dwellings are larger than those in Period III and the compartmented buildings disappear. House forms are built in a random fashion without an apparent plan (Figure 3.4) and rooms contain many architectural details suggestive of their functions. Most houses had small storage rooms. Marielle Santoni, the archaeologist who excavated some of the storage rooms describes the contents of one of them as follows:

Pottery and other artefacts were piled on wooden shelves and in niches or stored in large pots and baskets, traces of the last preserved as imprints ... [In one] ... the original shape of one of the six baskets was preserved. This basket contained two miniature pots, a laurel-shaped flint arrow-head, a bone tool ... [and] ... a large jar was also used to store twelve pots. (Santoni 1989:181)

Judging by this description, the pots had been placed on wooden shelves that collapsed sometime in antiquity causing them to come crashing down to the floor where Santoni found them.

Another new architectural feature was the use of niches cut into interior walls. One house containing a large block of rooms had a total of six niches cut into three of the interior walls. Niches of this type are places for visible storage of items in more constant use than those in the less accessible storerooms.

For the first time we see a system of lanes separating buildings. Entrances into the houses led from the lanes into their interiors, where there were large courtyards. In many houses, other rooms, most likely sleeping quarters, were built around them.

The presence of hearths in the courtyards and large storage jars in houses is new. Storing food and other household items in individual houses rather than the larger, communal compartmented buildings represents a shift to more family-oriented, individualized living quarters in which residential groups maintained their own food resources and other materials.

A single mudbrick platform much larger than others in previous periods was constructed in Period VI/VII. It was underlain with regularly spaced square pillars or buttresses and is adjacent to the complex of buildings just described, though separated from them by a narrow lane (Figure 3.4). Mudbrick for platforms is part of a long architectural tradition at Mehrgarh observed in Periods I–III. However, the platform in this period is immediately adjacent to residential structures and is associated with a plastered wall. The platform, which has not been entirely excavated, measures 300 square meters. J.-F. Jarrige (1995) believes it functioned as a "system of leveling and terracing ... [reflecting a concern for] ... the arrangement of space" (J.-F. Jarrige 1995:83). It may be a prototype for similar platforms used for leveling and terracing in the urban periods of the Indus civilization (see Chapters 5 and 9).

Burial Patterns

Approximately seventy graves were found at a cemetery near the residential areas. All interments are infants or newborns. Their bodies were placed in mudbrick-lined pits in flexed positions and in an east-west orientation as practiced in preceding periods. With the exception of a single small bead found at the neck of some of the infants, consistent with child burials in Period III, no grave goods accompanied these burials.

The only adult burial contemporary with the infant burials was discovered in a clay box buried between two walls (J.-F. Jarrige 1995:85). The body is in a flexed position and oriented east-west, its head turned north. Two plates were placed below the hands of the deceased. The sex of this individual is undetermined but he or she wore a necklace of alternating carnelian and lapis lazuli beads and bracelets of white (steatite?) beads.

Material Culture and Technology

There continued to be innovations in styles and technologies during this time. Familiar objects in dwellings include mortars and pestles for food processing and sickles for harvesting grain. Terracotta animal figurines include zebus and dogs. Human figurines, built of a different style from those in Periods I through III, are of males and females (Box 3.4 and Figure 3.6). Other terracotta objects include small rattles, most likely children's toys.

Craft producers possessed a diversity of skills and engaged in some large-scale production. Most pottery production is found in courtyards or other open spaces in residential areas. Catherine Jarrige, the principal excavator of the MR1 area, found a large pit kiln (see Figure 6.6 for kiln types) estimated to have held 200 pots. In Period V, she identified a "potters' quarter" containing approximately 150 vessels, interpreted as the activity of one or two families (J.-F. Jarrige 1995:78), producing pottery quantities beyond their own requirements. In another area, the potters kept many pots that were distorted or cracked from overfiring, the types of pottery that one might find as a sale item or "second," and not quite up to the standard of the potters' intentions. Santoni believes the potters saved them "as a kind of reference collection of 'seconds'" (Santoni 1989:181), providing models for shape and size of future vessels.

The most spectacular advance in pottery production was the invention of a two-chambered kiln, which I excavated at the site of Lal Shah, near Mehrgarh. It was in use at the very end of occupation at Mehrgarh (J.-F. Jarrige 1995:87).

One of the most distinctive pottery types produced at Mehrgarh was Faiz Mohammad grayware, named for a site located midway along the Bolan Pass. It was produced in a limited number of forms and decorated with distinctive design motifs (see Box 3.5). Production techniques required a high level of technical skill because in order to produce its characteristic gray color and red or black designs, potters developed a sophisticated knowledge of kilns and firing procedures. A study I conducted employing neutron activation analysis, a technique that produces a chemical fingerprint of ceramic clays, confirmed that Mehrgarh was a production site for Faiz Mohammad ceramics and that some pottery produced there was exchanged to the far distant settlement of Shahr-I Sokhta in eastern Iran (Figure 3.1) (Wright 1984, 1989, 1995).

There are a wide variety of objects made from raw materials not previously found at Mehrgarh, but we have not as yet located production areas to determine whether they were produced there or imported. They include ivory and bone "button" seals, a variety of metal tools, and the general replacement of bone for metal in leather processing and woodworking. Specialized microdrills and other drilling tools were used to produce beads and ornaments of semiprecious stone. A lapis lazuli bead was found with a copper rod inside, possibly a drill left behind during manufacture (J.-F. Jarrige 1995:81). Finally, small seals produced with geometric designs were discovered in residential areas. Stamps of this kind most likely were used, as they were later, to signify an individual or social group (see Box 7.2).

External Contacts

Mehrgarh was one among many villages and towns in Baluchistan and in other regions including those to the north in the present-day Northwest Frontier Province (NWFP), the Greater Indus Valley to its east, and Afghanistan and eastern Iran to its west (Figure 1.2). From this point on, villagers at the site participated in a complex of interactions with cultures that were widely distributed. Many new settlements developed in parts of India as well, but people at Mehrgarh appear not to have been in contact with them.

Nearer to home in Baluchistan, Mehrgarh continued its close ties with villages and towns to its north along the Bolan Pass, in the Quetta region at the apex of the pass, to the north in modern districts of Zhob and Loralai, and to the south in Kalat and the Makran. (See Figure 3.1 for potential routes.) These contacts attest to extensive trade networks. Items traded include marine resources from the south (evidence for shell artifacts) and lapis lazuli, gold, and copper from Afghanistan and possibly eastern Iran. Perhaps most important was trade with settlements on the Indus. Along with Pathani Damb, and possibly others in Zhob and Loralai, Mehrgarh served as a gateway to and from northern, western, and coastal areas and the Indus.

Finally, as I mentioned in the introduction to this chapter, Periods IV–VII at Mehrgarh overlap with developments outside of Baluchistan. Of special importance are villages and towns within the Indus Valley, on the Ghaggar-Hakra Plain, and in central and southern India. The presence of Early Harappan/Kot Diji pottery associated with the Pre-urban period on the Indus and Ghaggar-Hakra Plains (see Chapter 4) at Mehrgarh are indicative of possible contact (the specifics as yet unknown) with settlements there.

Summary – Period IV/VII

By Periods VI and VII, Mehrgarh had clearly entered a new phase in its development. In Periods VI and VII, Mehrgarh took on the configuration of a large village or town with streets and lanes and clustered residential areas. The communal storage in compartmented buildings of former periods was replaced by storage rooms, now securely located within individual houses. Many storage areas contained large quantities of expertly crafted pottery produced in numerous craft-producing areas, and may have become a symbol of wealth. In many houses large quantities of pots were carefully stored, some possibly containing food reserves, while others were empty and left for future use as a form of accumulated wealth. A related development is the construction of niches within houses used to display favored and useful objects, a visible form of wealth and aesthetic pleasure to residents and others entering households.

These changes reflect on new conceptions of ownership. Given that craft-producing areas were located in courtyards or adjacent to residential areas, craft production was carried in household contexts. Most likely nuclear or extended families engaged in production on a part-time basis during off-season periods when agriculture and pastoralism required less attention (Wright 1991).

Settling Down: The Domestication of Plants
and Animals, the Development of a Village Farming
Community into a Sizable Town,
and Expanded Interaction

I described the sequence at Mehrgarh in some detail as an illustration of how one village farming community developed into a sizable town before the onset of urbanism on the Indus and Ghaggar-Hakra plains. For several thousand years preceding the emergence of cities, basic technologies were developed, including animal and plant domestication, water control systems, ceramics, metallurgy, and stone manufacturing. This combination of technologies was necessary to settlement in the harsh environment of the Indus Plain and was a basis for subsequent innovations there.

Changes in subsistence, society, and the economy were profound. A major transition from the lives of hunters and gathers to a gradual shift to an agropastoral and craft-producing economy is documented at Mehrgarh over a period of some several thousand years (7000–2600 B.C.).

Earlier in this chapter, I raised several questions about the introduction of agriculture and pastoralism. The evidence is clear that South Asia is an original hearth of domestication for some animals (goats, cattle), but research continues on the question of sheep. Transitional forms of barley suggest at least some species were domesticated at Mehrgarh, although the weight of the evidence for wheat is more suggestive of diffusion from the Near East, though species modifications may have occurred locally. Our best estimates of the timing of these changes are that the process began soon after 7000 B.C. However, this date is only approximate, since the entire process appears more gradual than sudden. Perhaps most significant are the social and economic changes involving shifts to more individualized, family-centered residential patterns, specialization of craft technologies, and elaboration of exchange networks that linked Mehrgarh in a vast interaction sphere.

Some archaeologists refer to the domestication of plants and animals as a "revolution" because people were able to settle in one environmental zone on a permanent basis rather than continue the more mobile pattern of hunters and gatherers. In the case of Mehrgarh and later settlements that grew up around it, changes in subsistence set in motion a totally new way of life, one enabling the establishment of villages and towns with fairly large population clusters.

The evidence from Mehrgarh has even greater significance to our overall understanding of the developments leading to the Indus civilization. Before the excavations at Mehrgarh, the archaeological record for South Asian settlements extended back to approximately 4500 B.C. Based on the presence of ceramic styles similar to types known from Central Asia in southern Turkmenistan, some archaeologists believed that developments in South Asia were the result of external influences. The evidence from Mehrgarh has changed all of that, since the site predates the Central Asian settlements, demonstrating that it was a center of innovation with a long and extended sequence of development. As J.-F. Jarrige (1995) has pointed out, we now consider similarities of material culture with those in Central Asia to be the result of cultural interaction not diffusion.

Other archaeologists considered Baluchistan irrelevant to the developments of the Indus civilization. For example, in 1968, the British archaeologist, Sir Mortimer Wheeler, in the third edition of his influential book, *The Indus Civilization*, based on the evidence available at the time, declared that whatever events had occurred in the "hill towns and villages" of Baluchistan, they were of little interest to the extensive and elaborate civilization that grew on the Indus Plain. For Wheeler, as impressive as Baluchistan might be, it was simply a cultural backwater, in his words a "back curtain to the main scene" (Wheeler 1968:9) and of little importance to the growth of the Indus civilization. His statements are based on the evidence available at the time, and the most that Wheeler could envision was that the Baluchistan sites provided a link, ambiguously defined, between better-known settlements to the west and others on the Indus Plain. He further asserted that the towns and villages of Baluchistan represented an "experimental and adventurous phase" best characterized as "communal life, on a small scale" (Wheeler 1968:9).

Wheeler, of course, could not have known about the unique discoveries waiting among the extensive remains at Mehrgarh. In fact, Mehrgarh presents us with an exceptional set of evidence and an understanding of important innovations and changes occurring at the frontier of many developments in South Asia that preceded developments on the alluvial plains of the Indus and Ghaggar-Hakra. In Chapter 4, I contextualize these events within the wider sphere of developments beyond Baluchistan.

4   An Era of Expansion and Transformation

My focus in this chapter shifts to the Greater Indus and Ghaggar-Hakra Plains to settlement histories that lead up to the great cities of the Indus civilization. As discussed in Chapter 3, archaeologists no longer accept Wheeler's early impression that settlements in Baluchistan, like Mehrgarh, were a "back-curtain to the main scene" (Wheeler 1968:9). The settlements to which Wheeler did accord importance for this Pre-urban period were Amri, Kot Diji, and Kalibangan. They are contemporaneous with the last stages of occupation at Mehrgarh and can now be placed in a broadened context that considers the results of new excavations and surveys throughout the region. These new discoveries provide a more complex understanding of the Pre-urban period. For example, recent excavations at Harappa have shown that the site was settled by 3300 B.C. (possibly 3500 B.C.), whereas in Wheeler's time, its initial settlement was thought to have occurred around 2400 B.C. (Wheeler 1968:125). In Cholistan, newly published data (Mughal 1981, 1982, 1992a,b, 2001) have documented initial settlement there at the same time that Harappa was settled.

Wheeler viewed the environmental conditions in riverine locations as motivating factors in the development of social complexity. He emphasized those aspects that could be linked to a process of urbanization emanating from the plain itself. He put it this way:

If an intermittently fertile upland [Baluchistan] provides the optimum conditions for the earlier assays in communal life within the boundaries of an easy rural self-sufficiency, the riverine plains on the other hand throw out a challenge ... The river itself and its flanking lowlands facilitate and stimulate traffic, commercial or military, and at once enlarge human relations far beyond the precedent of the upland valley. The opportunities and difficulties implicit in civilization are present and insistent. (Wheeler 1968:24)

The expansion of settlement during the Pre-urban period involved movement of people to the alluvial plains of the Upper and Lower Indus and the Ghaggar-Hakra region. In the Upper Indus (see Figure 1.2 for general locations and maps below for specifics), the best known sites include Harappa, located in the Upper Indus on the Ravi River, those in Cholistan, and Kalibangan to its east and south where the Ghaggar-Hakra River once flowed. On the Lower Indus, primary settlements were at Kot Diji and at Amri to its south on the western margins of the alluvial plain.

Expansion also included settlements on the margins of these alluvial plains and in previously occupied mountain zones. As discussed in Chapter 3, the later levels at Mehrgarh (its Periods IV–VII) were contemporaneous with the pre-urban sites on the alluvial plains, and some artifacts indicating contact (the Kot Diji pottery referred to in Chapter 3) have been documented with settlements there. In addition, the number of settlements in the Quetta, Zhob, and Loralai areas discussed in Chapter 3 continued to expand at the same time that new villages and towns were settled in the mountains and valleys of Baluchistan and elsewhere.

When taken together with settlements like Mehrgarh and others discussed in Chapter 3, we can envision a mosaic of large and small settlements covering an area of some 300,000 square kilometers. As will be discussed, artifactual evidence suggests that raw materials and finished products were transported over significant distances. These well-established linkages constitute just one of the factors that contributed to the rise of the great cities of the Indus.

An Age of Emerging Polities

I have used the term "emerging politics" to characterize these pre-urban settlements based on several factors. First, they are emerging polities in the sense that they are coexisting political units in which no single group dominates any of the others. Second, there is evidence for active exchange networks based on the presence of nonlocal raw materials and overlapping types of material culture. Much like peer polities known in other regions, settlements in this period are now spread over an expanded area, and although each possesses a distinctive material culture, they derive some of their growth from interaction among peers. Third, the villages and towns that developed during this period are increasingly complex, both economically and socially. Changes are visible in the increased numbers and sizes of settlements, adoption of new technologies and production of objects, and exchanges of raw materials and finished products. Finally, there is an increased level of uniformity in material culture and site planning. Unlike Baluchistan and the hill countries that have been our primary focus to this point, these communities are situated in less circumscribed environments, where larger tracts of land are available for cultivation and pasturage.

Although we cannot identify by name the political or social units that coordinated these impressive changes, they are suggestive of actions taken among people who participated in increasingly complex societies. The following list provides an outline of the development of these patterns:

1. Presence of diverse communities, ranging in size from small villages to major towns
2. Presence of settlements having different functions
3. Increase in population density
4. Economies based upon agriculture, pastoralism, raw material exchange, and craft specialization
5. Settlements with planned layouts oriented to the cardinal points
6. Settlements showing significant community building projects, including architectural structures, such as fortifications, revetment walls, and massive platforms
7. Division of communities into sectors (perhaps neighborhoods is a better word)
8. Creation of communication systems
   a. Written symbols that are apparent precursors to the Indus script, documented at Harappa and surrounding rural settlements
   b. Seals to identify individuals or groups
   c. Precursors to a measurement system that became the standard for the Indus civilization (the discovery of a weight)
9. Establishment of exchange systems for acquisition of nonlocal raw materials
10. Production of a variety of new objects
11. Employment of many different and innovative production techniques
12. Fabrication of the same object using different materials and production techniques

In the sections that follow, I describe the settlements on the alluvial plains of the Indus and Ghaggar-Hakra as well as the outlying regions. The sections are divided geographically and according to the phases described in Box 4.1 that define the chronology for the Pre-urban period.

Upper Indus – Harappa Excavations and the Pre-urban Period

The excavations at Harappa are excellent starting points from which to observe some of the changes that occurred during the Pre-urban period that preceded the development of the first cities of the Indus civilization.[1] New discoveries of Pre-urban occupations at the site have resulted

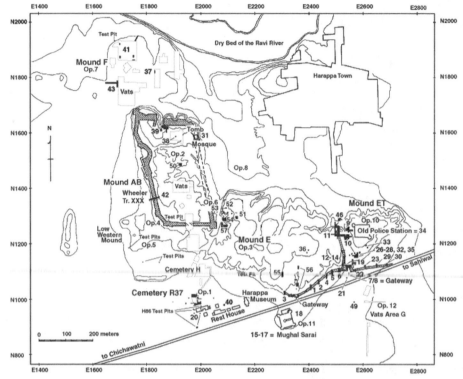

Figure 4.1. Site plan of Harappa (2001). © HARP.

in a reformulation of the importance of Harappa in the development of urbanism. In the past little was known of early occupations. However, settlement is now known to have extended back to 3300 (perhaps 3500) B.C. This evidence is complemented by a regional settlement pattern study along the Beas River (see Figure 1.2 for location) because it places the city into the wider regional context within which this major city developed (Wright et al. 2005a,b).

Harappa's long history of occupation is reflected in the physical topography of the site. Mound designations also are labeled on Figure 4.1. The settlement consists of a cluster of mounds with different chronological histories. Parts of Mound AB and E were occupied during all periods at Harappa. They include the Ravi phase, when the settled area was between seven and ten hectares, and the Kot Diji phase discovered on Mounds AB and E, when the town expanded over an area approximating twenty-six hectares. At its peak, Harappa was spread over all of the areas shown, some 150+ hectares. During the latest occupation at Harappa, the Post-urban/Late Harappan (to be discussed in Chapter 11), the city was diminished in size to approximately twenty-four hectares.

The site of Harappa is the only major Indus site for which we have an excavated sequence from the early Pre-urban period through the subsequent Urban and Post-urban periods, making it one of the most important sites in the Indus civilization.

Upper Indus – Ravi Phase

The Ravi phase represents the earliest Pre-urban occupations at Harappa. It is named for a distinctive pottery type found in those earliest levels.

Ravi wares had not been noticed until the mid-1990s when Heather Miller (1999b) discovered them while conducting a systematic surface survey that included the north side of Mound AB. Fragments of Ravi pottery (sherds) were discovered partially hidden in gullies, having been deposited there through processes of natural erosion and human and animal traffic. Since then, excavations of Ravi materials have focused on the northern edge of Mound AB, although there now is evidence for Ravi occupation on the northwest corner of Mound E.

As discussed in Box 4.1, designation of this phase is based on the presence of a pottery type classified as Ravi. Although the Ravi ceramics bear close similarities to the Hakra wares found at contemporary sites in Cholistan and elsewhere, they are sufficiently different to warrant a typological distinction. Naming the pottery Ravi, after the river on which Harappa is situated, emphasizes its local characteristics.

The examples in Figure 4.2 illustrate the similarities and differences between the Ravi and Hakra ceramics. Both were produced from clays that fired to a red color and were decorated with black paint/slip;[2] many have burnished surfaces, a process that results in a polished or shiny exterior. Other slips used were brown and white. Many Hakra and Ravi ceramics have textured surfaces. The differences between them, then, are in the shapes of vessels and/or the ways in which their decorations are combined. For example, in Figure 4.2 the two vessels (a, b) have similar shapes; both have rounded bases and are painted. However, their upper bodies differ, one (Figure 4.2a) has a simple rim and gradually tapers to a carination, whereas the other (the Hakra, Figure 4.2b) has an out-turned rim and a more abrupt and angular carination. Other differences are illustrated by comparing the Ravi pot (Figure 4.2c) with the other examples illustrated. The Ravi pot has a flat base. Its textured surface is similar to that of the Hakra vessels (Figure 4.2d,e), but the composition of the slurry (sandy materials mixed with clay) and rim shapes differ (Kenoyer and Meadow 2000:62). Finally, both of the Ravi vessels shown in Figure 4.2 are hand-built (Kenoyer and Meadow 2000:64) while the Hakra example (Figure 4.2b) is wheel made; others illustrated are hand-built (Mughal 1997:66).

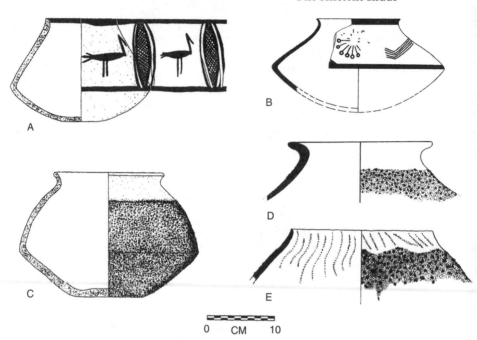

Figure 4.2. Comparison of pottery styles from Harappa and Cholistan. Redrawn from Harappa Archaeological Research Project and M. R. Mughal (1997: Figures 8 and 9).

Box 4.1 Periods, Phases, and Other Schemes – Amri, Kot Diji, Hakra and Ravi, Sothi-Siswal – What's It All About?

In order to present the materials we excavate in a systematic manner, archaeologists have developed terminologies and categorizations with which to describe them. At Mehrgarh, a periodization scheme was used by the excavators based on the stratified contexts in which materials and features were discovered. For example, in Period III at Mehrgarh, specific sets of materials were consistently found together in stratified contexts. They included compartmented buildings, types of burials, and ceramic styles, such as the Togau wares.

A different scheme was used by Jim Shaffer (1992) when he was asked to update the chronology for South Asia. He framed his categories based on the terms – tradition, era, and phase. *Tradition* referred to a stylistic analytical unit, for example, Baluchistan; a subdivision of that tradition was labeled as an *era*, such as Early Food Producing.

This designation differs from my use of this term in Chapter 3, since for Shaffer the Early Food Producing Era is confined to Period I at Merhgarh. *Phase* designations were Shaffer's smallest analytical unit and were based upon "a diagnostic ceramic style located at one or more sites during a particular time" (Shaffer:1992:442); for example, the Amri phase is based upon a distinctive ceramic type. Other phases in Shaffer's scheme are Hakra and Koj Diji with their characteristic ceramic types. Categorization of ceramic types is based upon a variety of stylistic criteria, such as color of the clay body, form of vessels, decorative motifs, application of slips and paints, and so forth.

I employ some of the distinctions developed by Shaffer but have simplified his scheme. First, I have discarded the terms tradition and era and used the category, Early Food Producing to describe early farming and pastoralism at Mehrgarh and contemporary/neighboring settlements. Second, I have divided the culture history of settlements on the alluvial plains into three periods and named them Pre-urban, Urban, and Late Harappan/Post-urban to reflect the major transitions that occurred. Chronological histories during the Pre-urban period are subsumed under Shaffer's phase categories. Their regional equivalences are based upon geographical distinctions as shown on Table 4.1

Table 4.1. Pre-urban Ceramics and Regional Equivalences

Upper Indus	
Ravi	3300–2800 B.C.
Early Harappan/Kot Diji	2800–2600 B.C.
Lower Indus	
Amri	3300–2600 B.C.
Hakra	3500–3000 B.C.
Early Harappan/Kot Diji	3200–2600 B.C.
Ghaggar-Hakra in Cholistan	
Hakra	3500–3000 B.C.
Early Harappan/Kot Diji	3000–2600 B.C.
Ghaggar-Hakra in Northwest India	
Early Harappan/Kot Diji	3200–2600 B.C.
Sothi-Siswal	3200–2600 B.C.

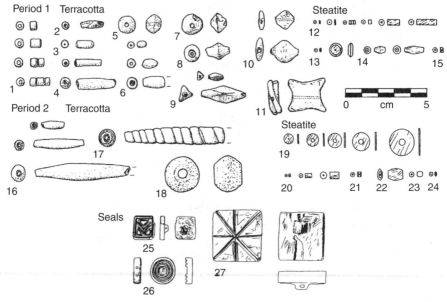

Figure 4.3. Small finds from Ravi and Kot Diji levels at Harappa. Redrawn from Harappa Archaeological Research Project.

In spite of significant erosion in the deposits, the evidence for the Ravi phase at Harappa includes a well-defined stratigraphic profile with many *in situ* features and activity areas. Structures were built of wooden posts and walls were constructed of plastered reeds. Many different living floors were superimposed one above the other, representing successive rebuilding. They were associated with domestic use and craft production, and feature kitchen areas where cook pots were found in association with a hearth and pits used for storing grain.

Many different crafts were being produced from local and nonlocal materials (Figure 4.3). These included terracotta beads, bangles painted with bands or fired to a gray color and decorated with incised designs, and a distinctive terracotta bangle with pinched exterior ridges. Also present were terracotta human (seated females) and animal (bulls) figurines. Bone artifacts included points that may have been projectiles, awls, and spatulas for basketry or leather working and a spindle whorl for spinning fiber.

Other crafts included ornaments in various stages of production (Kenoyer and Meadow 2000). Several varieties of nonlocal stone were used and different production techniques applied. For example, steatite blanks were being prepared with a toothed copper saw and perforated with a copper drill, while beads – short cylindrical lapis and carnelian – were made using a different technique. While the lapis beads were perforated by pecking, carnelian was drilled with a cylindrical stone drill. In addition, there are quantities of finished and unfinished marine shell bangles produced in different styles. The presence of lapis, carnelian, and marine shell in the context of unfinished objects attests to the presence of contact over long distances for their procurement, making them especially valuable due to their rarity. Also discovered among the Ravi materials were miniature terracotta carts that may be copies of actual vehicles, perhaps made of wood, used for transport.

Upper Indus – Early Harappan/Kot Diji Phase

Kot Diji pottery is widely distributed throughout the Indus Plain. The most typical forms are short-necked jars decorated with a variety of exteriors, including banded (with black, brown, white or red paint/slip) rims; surfaces textured with a sandy, red slip; and/or painted with wide and narrow bands (Figure 4.4). Other forms include flanged vessels, bowls, jars, and a dish-on-stand. Geometric and floral designs were painted on the exteriors of some vessels. A "sunburst," pipal leaves, fishscales, and intersecting circles occur on others. These designs and slight variations in some forms continue into the Urban period. In general, Kot Diji ceramics were produced on the potter's wheel.

There is a continuous stratigraphic sequence between the Ravi and Kot Diji phases at Harappa, although there is an expansion of settlement and many structural features are new in the latter. The occupation of Mounds AB and E, already noted for the Ravi phase, continues, but settlement expands to over 26 hectares. Bricks became the principal building material and were produced in uniform sizes with a ratio of 1:2:4. New in the Kot Diji phase is the construction of massive mudbrick perimeter walls, separating Mound AB from Mound E. Also new are massive mudbrick platforms and what appears to be early city planning in the layout of streets in a north–south/east–west orientation (Kenoyer 1993). The evidence for walls and platforms suggest fairly large-scale community efforts, standardized ratios of mudbrick indicative of a shared system of measurement, and possible presence of masonry specialists.

Along with the expansion of settlement and the diversity of building projects, there is an increased number of areas devoted to craft

Figure 4.4. Examples of Kot Diji pottery. Courtesy of G. L. Possehl.

production, the complexity of technologies employed, the production of new products, and the use of nonlocal materials. Beads produced from glazed steatite were already evident in the Ravi phase; however, during the Kot Dijian phase, the production process experienced refinements of the technique, and new objects such as glazed button seals were produced (Figure 4.3). Other objects providing continuity with later periods are numerous terracotta objects, such as human and animal figurines and cart models. Nonlocal materials include lapis lazuli, carnelian, chert, marine shell, copper, and gold. A very significant find for this phase is a cubical stone weight that conforms to weight categories used as a standard of measurement in the Urban period.

Craft production is evident in several areas. One, on the northwest side of Mound AB, was associated with mudbrick walls and hearths, possibly a residential area, where two pottery kilns were discovered, along with evidence for weaving (a spindle whorl for spinning yarn) (see Figure 4.1 for location of Mound AB). In another, on the northwest side of Mound E, a potter's workshop was discovered that consisted of a small pit kiln and production debris. The majority of pottery found there was produced on a potter's wheel. To the south of the potter's workshop, but separate from it, several other crafts were being produced. They included seals with graffiti and signs that appear to be precursors to the Indus script. Signs of this type also were scratched onto pottery either before or after the individual pieces were fired. Although some may represent marks made by potters to identify their wares, others appear to represent an early form of script. Some seals were produced with narrative scenes and images of animals. Of particular interest is a sealing depicting a so-called unicorn, a common motif found on seals in the Urban period. (See Figure 6.10 for examples from the Urban period.)

A well-documented feature of the Kot Diji phase at Harappa is the adoption of an agropastoral economy. Wheat and barley are traditional winter crops, most likely diffused from sites like Mehrgarh in Baluchistan. The presence of millet, a drought-resistant crop, usually grown in the summer months, suggests that farmers were also experimenting with a year-round cropping system. The pastoral component is defined by the exploitation of domestic cattle, sheep, and goats for meat and their secondary products. Evidence for a fishing "industry" involving the procurement of local and marine species, will be discussed in more detail in Chapters 6 and 7.

Upper Indus Regional Surveys Near Harappa

Of additional significance is evidence for settlements in areas near Harappa in the Upper Indus (Figure 4.5). The discovery of Pre-urban period settlements near the Chenab, Ravi, and the Beas Rivers were one result of a major reconnaissance survey conducted by the Punjab Archaeological Survey under the auspices of the Department of Archaeology, Government of Pakistan. The survey team discovered over 1,000 prehistoric and historic archaeological sites and monuments

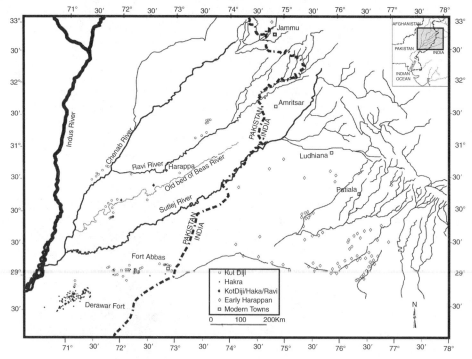

Figure 4.5. Upper Indus settlement patterns in Pre-urban period. Left to right – Chenab, Ravi, and Beas sites; Cholistan and Northwest Indian sites. © R. P. Wright

(Mughal et al. 1997; Rasool 1996), thirty-four of which were occupied during periods related to the Indus civilization.

Of these, thirty were occupied during the Pre-urban period. They include eight sites on the west bank of the Ravi, five of which are less than five hectares, two between five and ten hectares, and two others at fifteen and sixteen hectares. Jalilpur, the site on the southeast bank of the Ravi, was discovered by Mughal (1972) and is less than two hectares. Five of the sites on the west bank of the Chenab are less than five hectares, and two others are between five and ten hectares. It should be noted, however, that since the two large settlements on the west bank of the Ravi were continuously occupied between the Pre-urban and Urban, these measurements may exceed the actual area occupied during the earlier period.

Indus settlements on the Beas were more intensively studied than was possible in the Punjab survey. The Beas project involved a systematic mapping and application of a collection strategy not previously applied to settlement studies in this region. Eighteen settlements occupied between the Pre-urban, Urban, and Post-urban periods were investigated. This sparse number of settlements on the Beas, and on others recorded by the Punjab survey, very likely do not represent a true picture of the number of settlements occupied in the past. These regions experienced major transformations during the late nineteenth and early twentieth centuries, when extensive infrastructural projects were implemented, including a railroad system, major irrigation project and extensive cultivation that very likely resulted in the destruction of archaeological sites.

On Figure 4.5, the three areas shown from left to right are the Chenab, Ravi, and Beas sites in the Upper Indus near Harappa; the Ghaggar-Hakra Plain in Cholistan in the regions of Derawar Fort and Fort Abbas; and to its east, settlements in northwest India. Pre-urban settlements along the Beas are distributed in a uniform and linear fashion along its former bed. An exception is the small cluster located at the river's southern extension, along a tributary of the Beas that is no longer visible. However, as the settlements were clustered in an environment that varied from those along the river, it opens the possibility that settlers were exploiting different microenvironments. Perhaps those living along the river practiced agriculture, while others at its margins engaged in pastoralism. In that event, this distribution could represent interaction among groups of specialist producers.[3]

Combining evidence from surface materials and stratigraphic sequences, based on test-trench excavations, we identified both Ravi/Hakra and Kot Diji phase occupations along the Beas. Ravi/Hakra wares were present at the site of Vainiwal, located midway along the stretch of settlements and the two others identified as Kot Diji/Hakra/Ravi sites. These sites continued to be occupied during the Kot Dijian phase along with eleven other sites (Wright et al. 2005a,b; Schuldenrein et al. 2004 and 2007). Similarities in material culture and the occurrence of a number of sherds inscribed with Indus script led us to conclude that there was significant interaction between these smaller settlements and Harappa.

The Ghaggar-Hakra – Cholistan Survey

The evidence for Pre-urban period occupation in this region is exclusively from surface surveys. Although the surveys were extensive, they did not involve site mapping. Ceramics and other objects were collected based on selective sampling (in distinction to a random sample) in which only diagnostic materials were collected.

Unlike the high degree of cultivation in and around Harappa today, the Cholistan Desert is sparsely inhabited. The area is excessively arid with summer temperatures above 38 degrees centigrade and rainfall is too low to carry out extensive cultivation. It is a forbidding landscape where agricultural yields are minimal. The principal subsistence economy is based on cattle herding and nomadic pastoralism.

During both the Pre-urban and Urban periods, the environmental potential of this region was significantly different from the present, since the Hakra River flowed through it and served as a major lifeline for agriculture and pastoralism. What makes Cholistan of special interest to archaeologists is that a large number of settlements were abandoned due to an outflow of population that began during the Indus period and continues to the present. Many of these sites are preserved today. According to Rafique Mughal (1992b:106, 1997, 2001), the archaeologist who directed the survey,[4] hydrographic changes have resulted in a shift in settlement patterns. One of the first documented shifts occurred sometime around 2500 B.C. when the Yamuna River, which lies to the east of the Ghaggar-Hakra, captured one of its tributaries, the Chautang River, thereby reducing the water at its north and east where the Hakra now meets the Indian border. A second change took place sometime around 1500 B.C. when the Sutlej River, which originally joined the Hakra, was captured by the Beas, rendering the Hakra totally dry (Mughal 1997:26).

One hundred thirty-eight pre-urban settlements have been discovered along the now dry bed of the Ghaggar-Hakra River in the Cholistan region of Pakistan (Figure 4.5). Mughal divided the Pre-urban period into two groups, the Hakra (comparable to the Ravi), followed by the Early Harappan (Kot Diji regional phase). By comparing the sizes and locations of settlements and associated artifacts, we can observe population shifts reflective of changes through time.

The Ghaggar-Hakra Plains – Hakra Phase

The distinguishing chronological marker for this period in Cholistan is the Hakra pottery, which Mughal dated to 3500–3000 B.C. based on comparisons to similar types at excavated sites. The characteristics of the Hakra phase were discussed in my comparison of the Hakra and Ravi wares and are shown in Figure 4.2. They are hand-made and wheel-made globular jars and bowls with geometric motifs and textured surfaces.

Hakra (the part of the Ghaggar-Hakra system surveyed by Mughal) settlements are distributed along both banks of the river as was the case with the Beas settlements. However, a major difference is the large number (likely due to the area's early abandonment and absence of large-scale cultivation) of settlements and their short-term occupations. For example,

Table 4.2. Site Size Categories – Hakra Phase[a], Cholistan Survey

	Small Village	Large Village	Small Town	Large Town	Total No. of Sites
Hectares[b]	0.1–5	5.1–10	10.1–20	20.1–30	
	21	5	7	4	= 37

[a] A hectare is equal to 2.47 acres.

very few sites are continuously occupied during the Pre-urban (Hakra and Kot Diji) and Urban periods. Figure 4.5 shows the distribution of Hakra and Early Harappan/Kot Diji settlements.[5]

Mughal broke down the Hakra settlements based upon their size (Table 4.2). Site size distribution broke down as follows: Site size variation shows a pattern in which a small number of towns (those in the 10+ category) coexisted with a larger number of small villages. The largest large town settlement was twenty-six hectares.

The large size of some settlements suggests that a substantial portion of the population was engaged in agriculture and other forms of pastoralism. Since the Cholistan settlements have not been excavated, we do not have archaeobotanical or zooarchaeological remains with which to piece together subsistence practices.

Artifacts associated with the Hakra phase are typical of domestic and craft-producing contexts. They include grinding stones and pestles, shell and terracotta bangles, small terracotta balls, humped bull figurines, and stone tools for utilitarian purposes. Others, such as bone points and punches, were associated with leatherworking and basket making; spatulas with pottery production; and kilns, with pottery firing. Production debris includes bits of copper, unworked carnelian, and agate (Mughal 1997:68). The presence of these materials, such as stones, shell, and copper attests that long-range contacts were in place that allowed for their acquisition.

Ghaggar-Hakra Plains – Early Harappan/Kot Diji Phase

The Kot Diji ceramics are similar to those in the Upper Indus. Like the Ravi at Harappa, some Hakra pottery shares characteristics with the later Kot Dijian wares, especially globular jars and pedestaled vessels, though the fabrics and treatment of their exteriors differ.

With respect to the alignments of settlements, Figure 4.5 shows a significant shift toward Fort Abbas during the Kot Diji phase, though a few remain near the Derawar Fort. When we review site size categories (see Table 4.3), however, the major differences are in the more balanced representation of all site categories in terms of total area occupied. The two largest settlements were 27.3 hectares (Gamanwalla) and 22.5 hectares (Jalwali). Neither of these sites was occupied during the Hakra phase.

Table 4.3. Site Size Categories – Kot Diji Phase[a], Cholistan Survey

	Small Village	Large Village	Small Town	Large Town	Total
Hectares	0.1–5	5.1–10	10.1–20	20.1–30	
Total number of sites	19	8	3	2	= 32

[a] Mughal (1997) lists fifty-nine.

Other important changes occur in the site function category. Mughal was able to determine site function based upon site size, surface features, and artifacts. Table 4.4 compares the number of settlements and kiln and camp sites in the Hakra phase with those from the Kot Diji phase: Based on these numbers, we can posit a dramatic shift between the Kot Diji and Hakra phases. A significant population of nomadic pastoralists inhabited this area during Hakra times (Mughal 1997:40). Many had visible "living floors" and traces of preserved mud walls. Remarkably, some pots remained standing where they were left when the camp site was abandoned as many as 5,000 years ago. In the Kot Diji phase, the number of camp sites is greatly reduced, suggesting that the nomadic pastoral component, though still present, virtually disappeared from the region. The most reasonable explanation for this is that pastoralists settled into the villages and towns that came to dominate the area. In addition, there is a rise from 2% to 14% of single function settlements devoted to pottery or metal production suggestive of increased craft specialization.

Table 4.4. Functional Categories – Kot Diji and Hakra Phases, Cholistan Survey

	Number of Sites	
	Hakra	Kot Diji
Sites with kilns	2	14
Settlements	45	23
Camp sites	52	3

Like the material culture associated with the Hakra phase, many Kot Diji artifacts are typical of domestic and craft-producing activities. Along with grinding stones and pestles, stone tools include blades and arrowheads. Also present are copper bits, terracotta animal figurines, beads, and spindle whorls. At two sites, Mughal found remains of unworked lapis lazuli (Mughal 1997:71), a nonlocal resource, procured from Afghanistan. Also present in Cholistan are various nonlocal ceramics linking Cholistan to Baluchistan.

Ghaggar-Hakra Settlements in Northwest India

After the partition of India in 1947, Indian archaeologists conducted extensive surveys and excavations, bringing to light large numbers of sites in northwest India and elsewhere (Bisht 2000a:27). Unfortunately, the division of scholarship between the modern borders of Pakistan and India has inhibited the coordination of research projects so that there currently is no clear synthesis concerning the relationship of patterns identified on the Ghaggar (in India) and its extension in Pakistan (the Hakra).

The ceramics in northwest India in this Pre-urban period bear strong similarities to the Kot Diji types in the Upper Indus and Cholistan. Still, there is sufficient variation in forms and surface features that archaeologists have established an additional category, the Sothi-Siswal. Resemblances between the Kot Diji ceramics in Cholistan and the Sothi-Siswal materials are not surprising given the contiguous nature of the two regions. Interestingly, there are occasional pottery links to northern Baluchistan,[6] as was the case in Cholistan, Harappa, and some of the Beas settlements. These data complement the evidence for technologies (for example, faience) known at other contemporary settlements and nonlocal raw materials, such as copper, gold, steatite, marine shells, and lapis lazuli that are suggestive of interaction among Pre-urban settlements.

Although Sothi and Siswal are two sites on which these ceramics were discovered, Kalibangan and Banawali (Figure 4.5) are the best documented sites during the Pre-urban period of settlement in the Ghaggar region. The materials at Banawali and Kalibangan are "identical in respect of ceramics, architecture, and antiquities" (Bisht 1987:142).

According to Possehl (2003), there are 165 sites associated with this phase. Their general distribution is shown in Figure 4.5, where the sites are labeled as Early Harappan based on the best available information and published maps. Settlements were clustered in and around the ancient rivers outlined. What is most interesting about the pattern of settlement is that in the Pre-urban (Early Harappan/Sothi-Siswal phase), most sites were discovered within the southern extension of the rivers, suggesting the region was a major center of pre-urban development. Rakhigarhi, for example, has been reported to be 100 hectares in size, though no definitive publication is available at present.

Expansion of Settlements in the Upper Indus and Ghaggar-Hakra Plains

The results of research on the Pre-urban Upper Indus (Ravi/Hakra, Kot Diji/Early Harappan and Sothi-Siswal) at Harappa and Ghaggar-Hakra Plains in Cholistan and northwest India provide us with an unexpected set of evidence, forcing reevaluation of the significance of Pre-urban developments. In Chapter 1, I stated that to understand the Indus civilization and its political economy, it is necessary to adopt a long-range/temporal perspective in which developments leading up to the settlement of its cities are traced. Based on the present evidence from excavation and survey, it seems clear that large numbers of people began migrating to the plain by 3300 B.C. and that a continuous expansion of settlement led to the urbanism that began at around 2,600 B.C.

As the evidence demonstrates, people engaged in a number of innovations, resulting in new social and economic patterns. As will be shown in subsequent chapters, many of these advances, involving developments in agriculture and pastoralism, community layout, craft production, and exchange systems for procurement of raw and finished materials were important components of the Urban period, albeit on a smaller scale. Finally, the production of stylistically similar goods using different raw materials may represent emerging social differentiation involving limitations on consumer access to products of differing value (see H.M.L. Miller 1999a, 2008 and Chapters 6 and 7 in this book). I address the implications of these changes and the types of inferences that can be drawn with respect to the emerging social differentiation leading up to the Urban period in a concluding section of this chapter.

The Lower Indus Valley

Evidence for occupation of the Lower Indus alluvial plain comes from excavations and surveys. Sites shown in Figure 4.6 are based on recent surveys conducted by a Shah Abdul Latif University in Khairpur team led by Nilofer Shaikh and the Sindh Archaeological Research Project (Flam 1981) and excavations conducted throughout the twentieth century. As in the Upper Indus, the phases of occupation in the Lower Indus are based on the occurrence of particular ceramic types and also variation in overall assemblages. The river alignments shown in Figure 4.6 were discussed in Chapter 2.

Lower Indus Valley – Hakra and Kot Diji Phases

The Khairpur survey team identified two pre-urban phases, the Hakra and Kot Diji. The environmental conditions of the area have not been studied extensively, but there is some indication that they differed in the past, since all of the sites identified are located near small backwater lakes (Shar et al. 1996). For the Hakra phase, the team identified eight workshops at the Dubi complex and nine settlements in the Thar Desert.

These sites are located in what would be considered a fairly inhospitable region today. At present, the Dubi area is occupied principally by nomadic pastoralists during periods of monsoon rains. The Dubi Sites are distributed in separate clusters each identified as an archaeological site by the presence of diagnostic pottery and stone tools. Although sizes for the Thar sites have not been published, they do not appear to be small workshops.

In the Kot Diji phase, there is an expansion of settlement with twenty workshops recorded in the Dubi area, a new site at Kandharki, and eight Thar settlements. The site of Kot Diji is the first settlement in which Kot Diji ceramics were found, and all of the forms described under this phase at other sites are variations on the basic characteristics as outlined previously and as shown in Figure 4.4. Also many decorations associated with the type (e.g., the fishscale pattern, pendant loops, and other naturalistic designs) were emulated on different ceramic forms of the Amrian type, which is discussed later.

Kot Diji was discovered in 1935 and excavated in the 1960s (Khan 1965; Mughal 1970). It was occupied in two broad phases. The first predates the urbanization of the Indus Plain (ca. 2800 B.C.) and corresponds to the Kot Diji phase at Harappa. During this phase Kot Diji was 2.6 hectares in size. Structures, including house dwellings, are made of mudbrick. As at Harappa, there is a massive defensive or retaining wall dividing the site. Parts of the wall are produced from undressed limestone, very likely from a nearby source, with extensions made of mudbrick. The wall also was built up with a revetment (that presumably served to buttress the wall) on its exterior and bastions at its corners. One of the bastions was 6.1 meters wide and 4–5 meters high. Within the walled enclosure, there were large buildings whose function are uncertain.

The material assemblage consists of typical artifact types found on most pre-urban sites throughout the plain. These include terracotta

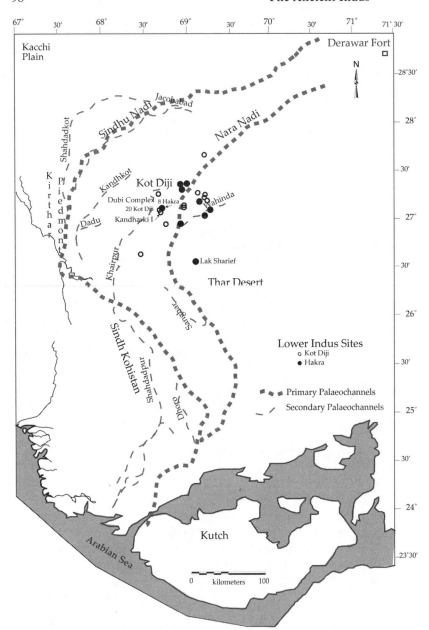

Figure 4.6. Lower Indus settlement Patterns in Pre-urban period.
© R. P. Wright.

triangle-shaped cakes, beads, bangles, cone shapes (either gaming pieces or spindle whorls), animal and female figurines, and cart frames with wheels. Objects of bone and shell (bangles and beads), stone (slingballs and chert blades and cores, most likely from the Rohri hills to its north), grinding stones, pestles, gaming pieces, sickle blades, knives, arrow-heads, and seals and metal (bangle, beads, and rings) also are found at Kot Diji.

Lower Indus Valley – Amri Phase

The site of Amri (see Figure 1.2) is located on the margins of the Lower Indus alluvial plain (or basin) in Sindh Kohistan (Figure 4.6).[7] The principal basis for this phase is a distinctive pottery type first discovered at Amri. The Amri pottery bears several motifs, such as looped designs, sigmas, and gazelle horns comparable to the designs on Togau type pottery at Mehrgarh III (see Box 3.5), suggesting some interaction between this region and Baluchistan (Shaffer 1992). But other vessels bear stylistic elements associated with Kot Diji and Hakra. These pottery styles are indicative of interregional contact as well as continuity between the Amrian phase and the later Urban period.

Amri was occupied by at least 3500 B.C., possibly several hundred years earlier. It continued to be inhabited throughout the Pre-urban and Urban periods. The site is less than eight hectares and was contemporary with Mehrgarh for at least 1,000 years. In its earliest levels, there were no structures, but mudbrick buildings were found in later pre-urban levels. Houses were rectangular and built on stone footings or gravel. They consisted of several rooms that probably were roofed in much the same way as those at Mehrgarh (J. F. Jarrige 1995:76). Also, as at Mehrgarh, there was a second type of mudbrick structure reminiscent of the multiple cellular compartments but without a central corridor between cells as is the case with most compartmented structures at Mehrgarh. The compartments at Amri are of varying size, some as small as 1 by 1 meters. Since they did not contain artifacts or other debris, it is impossible to determine their specific function. Hearths and other materials suggestive of domestic activities are found in spaces between the compartmented buildings. This arrangement is similar to what was found at Mehrgarh. It is unclear whether the compartmented buildings functioned as storage units, but this seems the most likely explanation.

Amri was not an isolated site but coexisted with numerous others in neighboring regions. At least twenty-nine settlements were located at the margins of the Lower Indus Basin in the Kirthar Mountains, the Piedmont, and Sindh Kohistan where assemblages similar to those at

Amri and Kot Diji have been discovered. One of the better known settlements, Ghazi Shah was excavated by Flam (1993b). It has a varied ceramic assemblage. They include Amri wares, along with other types suggestive of interaction with settlements in the mountainous zones, such as Mehrgarh.

Unlike the settlements in the alluvial plain, those in the Kirthar, Piedmont, and Sindh Kohistan did not have an extensive land area or reliable water source for crop growing or pasturage for animals. In some locations, waters from springs could be channeled to fields, and several sites are located either near springs or along the routes of seasonal torrents (Flam 1981:54). In the Kot Dijian phase in Sindh Kohistan, Flam also documented numerous gabarbands, or check dams, consisting of single or multiple walls fortified with stone. Three gabarbands associated with two Kot Dijian settlements were constructed to close off or control the flow of water; in other instances, they were used to remove coarse sediment or to distribute flow from a perennial spring on to the cover floodplain. These water management strategies very likely were precursors to similar small-scale landscape modifications on the alluvial plain.

Expansion of Settlement in the Lower Indus

Although we can identify distinctive local traditions in each area there are broad similarities among the regions discussed here. Affinities in material culture, principally in the form of raw materials, possibly ceramics and/ or other finished objects, suggest sustained, long-distance contact. While regional cultural features predominated, individual regions became links in a chain of polities devoted to agropastoral economies. Flam (1981), refers to these links as a "vast interaction sphere" (1981:66) involving the procurement of resources over long distances.

We know little about settlements in the regions lying between these settled areas. Conceivably they were inhabited by mobile, nomadic populations if we can assume the Cholistan data are representative. The mechanisms of exchanges facilitating these distributions reflect a larger system of relationships that surely blurred homogeneity in other aspects of the individual regional polities discussed.

Beyond the Indus and Ghaggar-Hakra Plains – Baluchistan

The settlements discussed in the following section lie outside of the Indus Plain in a region "in-between" the sites described in this chapter and the areas to the west in southeastern Iran and beyond. They are contemporary with the Pre-urban period but have mixed assemblages, leading to the idea that they interacted with groups on the Indus Plain, Iran, and the Arabian Peninsula. These lands in-between provide an important contrast to the more uniform developments on the Indus and Ghaggar-Hakra Plains and demonstrate links to far-flung regions.

Even in the twenty-first century, this region lies at a borderland between South Asia and Iran, a position that mirrors that of the third millennium B.C. during the Pre-urban period. Settlements in southern Baluchistan at that time appear to have been closely aligned with southeastern Iranian cultures and others across the Persian Gulf in present-day Oman and the United Arab Emirates. In this section, I provide a brief account of the influence of several different cultures in this region. In Chapter 8, I will return to these several influences in the context of long-distance trade.

There is great geographical variability in southern Baluchistan and in the locations of Pre-urban period settlements there. I have divided the region into two zones, the Las Bela and the Makran (see Figure 1.2). The Las Bela area includes mountain chains that run along its eastern margins from the Arabian Sea to the Hindu Kush, providing an effective barrier to the Indus Plain. Areas of settlement include highland basins, deserts, river valleys, and plains. The Makran lies to the west of the mountains as noted on Figure 1.2, and bordering eastern Iran.

In the Pre-urban period, several sites of interest are in Las Bela. Balakot is 2.7 hectares and located on the Las Bela Plain and the Sonmiani Bay. The pottery at Balakot has affinities with northern Baluchistan and Amri, but also includes a different type, designated as Nal. Nal pottery refers to a distinctive canister-shaped vessel with painted motifs in floral and zoomorphic designs, including polychromes. Other artifacts are made of lapis lazuli and other semiprecious stones, shell, and copper/bronze objects (Dales 1979). Subsistence at Balakot was based on cattle, sheep, and goat pastoralism with limited hunting and shell fishing, while plant foods were predominantly barley and jujube. Approximately 50% of the fauna at Balakot is from fish remains (Belcher 2003:122), suggesting that the economy had a strong marine component. Nal pottery also dominates at a second site, Niai Buthi, but other vessels found there are more typical of northern Baluchistan; one chlorite fragment from a distinctive type of vessel with engraved designs of a southeastern Iranian style also was discovered. Finally, a single site in the Karnach Valley, Murda Sang, was occupied for two periods. Its earliest levels correspond to those at Balakot, while a later level is associated with the following period. The cultural affinities in the later levels at Balakot are with the Indus civilization (Franke-Vogt 2005b). In contrast, Niai Buthi is abandoned. A new settlement at Murda Sang, though containing elements typical of the Urban period, has yielded assemblages characteristic of materials associated with the Kulli, a culture that coexisted with the Indus in this region.

Turning to the Makran, the evidence is equally mixed culturally. Today, and likely in the past, this region presents a forbidding landscape characterized by isolated areas of occupation, mainly in valleys and oases settlements. The site of Miri Qalat (Besenval 1997) is dated to the first half of the fourth millennium B.C. (3900–3500 B.C.). Pottery types are mixed, some typical of pre-urban sites discussed in this chapter and others showing strong affinities with the Iranian Plateau. There are craft areas where shell bangles were being produced, along with terracotta bangles. In levels dated to approximately 3500–2900 B.C., there is an absence of artifacts or features related to the pre-urban Indus, and all finds point to southeastern Iran. This situation continues until the second half of the third millennium (ca. 2500 B.C.), when all of the material culture is related to the Urban period, including a steatite seal with a "unicorn" image and Indus script and pottery styles.

Pre-urban Ecological and Settlement Diversity

This chapter set out some of the major transformations taking place at the onset of alluvial settlement in the greater Indus Valley. As discussed in Chapter 2, the timing of movement on to the plain was dependent to some degree upon environmental factors, involving the stabilization of river systems; however, other factors entered into the mix including the potential for expanded agricultural and pastoral economies. The Cholistan data from the Ghaggar-Hakra survey documents the presence of specialized groups involved in nomadic pastoralism, a livelihood that very likely extended on to the Ghaggar Plain in northwest India. At Harappa the possible experimentation with cattle or sheep and goat breeds for traction (as indicated by the presence of cart models) was another type of specialized pastoralism. In the Lower Indus, the presence of temporary workshop scatters may also suggest pastoral movements. Of particular interest is the evidence for water control systems on the margins of the alluvial plain. The evidence for the construction of gabarbands and the locations of settlements near perennial springs on the Lower Indus suggests that before intensive settlement occurred on the alluvial plain, people experimented with water-retaining devices. These processes began some time around 3500 B.C.

Early in this chapter, I described the Pre-urban period as an age of emerging polities. We regard them as separate polities because of the distinctive nature of their material culture. Still a key factor is their active engagement in exchange networks and interaction that stimulated growth within and among them.

My discussion has focused on changes in settlement patterns, economic advances, the creation of new technologies and products and specialization of crafts. Specific developments were listed at the beginning of the chapter. These provide a picture of life on the plain and included innovations in the agropastoral economy and the emergence of social differentiation in many aspects of society. They include an explosion in the number of settlements known from small numbers at first and increasing with time and space to eventually encircle the plain. Taking into consideration the settlements in the entire loop encompassing the greater Indus and those along the Ghaggar-Hakra, there appears to have been a gradual migration to the alluvial plains. An additional factor is the regionally differentiated settlement types described for Harappa and the Beas, and well-documented by the better preserved settlements along the Hakra and Ghaggar Rivers. Taken together, these two regions provide evidence for a hierarchy of settlements in which there is a variation of site sizes, so that some people lived in large towns, while others settled in tiny villages. At some of the settlements described and others not discussed, there were sizable community efforts in massive wall constructions either for water control or for defensive measures. At Harappa, and at a number of sites streets oriented to the cardinal points and the presence of massive mudbrick platforms attest to shared community principles and active engagement in planning at least by some segments of the society.

Even though there is a clear connection between the objects and production technologies present as early as Mehrgarh Period III (see Chapter 3) with the material culture on the alluvial plains, technologies were elaborated upon, and new objects were produced. Our best evidence for these changes is from Harappa where a range of technologies and the specialized knowledge required in their production has been documented, suggesting the presence of a variety of specialists engaged in significant innovations. Although it may be that Harappa was a single center of innovation at this time, it seems most likely that other centers existed, such as in Cholistan, where so many settlements have been discovered.

The evidence for the creation of new technologies, along with the isolation of production areas at locations on the margins of settlements (at Harappa and Cholistan) and at special function sites, is a major indicator of changes in the organization of production. While the potentially noxious and unpleasant odors emanating from new kinds of manufacturing may have precipitated crafters' relocations, the transition from production in households to "industrial" locations may have brought with it other important changes in the division of labor within the household and community. The segregation of production areas from households and the presence of highly specialized technologies may signal a more specialized economy in which some items were produced by specialist producers in the population.

Such valued goods produced often serve as major carriers of culture, represent items of exchange in the marketplace, establish alliances, build social relations, signal affiliations and are indispensable parts of ritualistic performances. Even though such generalizations are imperfect, given the lack of written records with which to document the systems of value adopted, the specialized nature of the production techniques and the manufactures from precious, nonlocal materials serve as proxy measures of ideas of value underlying the material culture.[8] Implied by their presence is an inequality of access giving rise to ideologies of difference.

A related factor is the broadly distributed settlement of regions with distinctive material culture accompanied by evidence for long-distance exchange in the form of raw materials and similarities in ceramics and other finished objects. A chain of regional polities devoted to agropastoral economies lay between unsettled areas, though conceivably inhabited by mobile populations if we can assume the Cholistan data are representative. The mechanisms of exchanges facilitating these distributions reflect a larger system of relationships that surely blurred homogeneity in other aspects of the individual regional polities discussed.

The creation of written symbols, seals, and a measurement system suggests the presence of coordinating settlement units. The evidence at hand provides only a glimpse of social differentiation and virtually no basis on which to infer what forms of political control were in place to direct building projects, specialized manufactures, and exchange networks. However, it seems clear that embedded within the adoption of a rudimentary script or a measurement system, decipherable by relatively few, and the formalized identity represented by seals and sealings is an emerging, if not full blown, asymmetry of relations, albeit among small numbers of people.

In conclusion, important changes took place during the Pre-urban period when new regions on the alluvial plain were settled and a number of ideas crystallized. The scale of these developments, though significant, was not sufficient to suggest that full-scale urbanism had taken hold. What the currently available evidence does show are trends toward a greater complexity of social, political, and economic organization than in previous periods based upon elaborations of material culture in the production of objects and settlements. The coming together of specialized producers, alongside farmers, pastoralists, fishers, and craft specialists the expansion of settlement at Harappa, and increases in regional settlements during the final Pre-urban period are a basic framework for the later Urban period.

Even though these new changes provide us with indications of an incipient urbanism, we cannot identify the specific infrastructures underpinning these developments. In other words, what were the active forces behind the eventual urbanization of the Indus? I will address this question in Chapters 6 and 7 on agropastoral and craft-producing economies. In Chapter 5, I turn to the Urban period itself and outline the pattern of settlement and positions of cities as they were established in the Indus civilization. These cities represent the first urban climax in South Asian history.

5   Urbanism and States: Cities, Regions, and Edge Zones

In the preceding chapter, I discussed the development of increasingly large settlements and an expansion of population throughout the Indus and Ghaggar-Hakra Plains and their surrounding regions. Keeping pace with these changes were modifications in the physical layouts of settlements, intensified cultivation of agricultural crops, and diversification in animal husbandry. Similarly, stylistic and technological changes in the crafting of material culture took place. In relating these changes, I emphasized local differences, but at the same time, I recognized a hint of the emergence of common ideas with respect to community organization and stylistic preferences. The establishment of settlement linkages through trade and exchange is visible in the flow of resources and movement of goods. This likely enhanced and fostered the spread of ideas, as did new forms of transport and the pursuits of nomadic pastoralists.

As impressive as these developments are, they were relatively small in scale when compared to the Urban period that began in 2600 B.C. addressed in this chapter and those that follow. At the very least, we are now dealing with the development of five large cities and an increase in the number of sites from a total of 463 in the Pre-urban period to 976 in the Urban period (Possehl 1990:270).

My principal focus in this chapter is on urbanism and increased modifications to the landscape that included new conceptions of community planning, the development of regional exchange networks, and the creation of trading outposts, all key elements of the civilization. Corresponding increases in scale of economic specializations in agriculture, pastoralism, and craft production, as well as trade and exchange are addressed in Chapters 6, 7, and 8. The relationship of changes in landscape and material culture to economic and social differentiation is discussed in Chapter 9.

106

Indus Cities and States – The First Urban Climax

As noted in Chapter 4, there are two different but complementary approaches to the study of cities. One focuses exclusively on the city itself. These investigations include, among other considerations, establishing the periods during which the city was occupied, determining its overall layout, and reconstructing the activities conducted there. A second approach is based on studies of cities placed in regional contexts that include settlements in the city's countryside and outlying regions. Since urbanism involves the development of supporting networks between a city and the towns and villages in its surrounding area and wider world, the development of cities is often, though not always (Wright 2002a) part of a larger overarching state system.

As discussed in Chapter 1, the development of cities ushered in a new era and the coming together of many key features with which archaeologists identify the Indus civilization. Although early claims of "homogeneity" in the civilization are no longer supported by the evidence, many aspects of material culture and landscape elements are common throughout the region it encompassed. Among its defining characteristics are its system of standardized weights, distinctive seals and sealings, written script, pottery styles (see Box 5.1 and Figure 5.1), and terracotta human and animal figurines. New architectural features are planned cities and extensive public works. In addition, there was an expansion of settlement throughout the Indus and Ghaggar-Hakra Plains and neighboring regions.

Five major Indus cities are discussed in this chapter. During the Urban period, the early town of Harappa expanded in size and population and became a major center in the Upper Indus (see Figure 1.2 for cities referred to in the text). Other cities emerging during the Urban period include Mohenjo-daro in the Lower Indus, Dholavira to the south on the western edge of peninsular India in Kutch, Ganweriwala in Cholistan, and a fifth city, Rakhigarhi, on the Ghaggar-Hakra. Rakhigarhi will be discussed briefly in view of the limited published material.

The largest city was Mohenjo-daro estimated at between 125 and 200 hectares. Harappa was 150 hectares, while Ganweriwala extended over 81 hectares, and Dholavira, between 47 and 100 hectares. Population numbers for early cities generally are calculated by estimating 150 to 200 people per hectare based on analogies with present-day settlements.

Box 5.1 Determining Contemporaneity of Pottery Styles

One of the major characteristics of the Urban period is the uniformity of some pottery styles. Gonzague Quivron, a French archaeologist working at the site of Nausharo, used this "uniformity" to establish the contemporaneity of pottery styles among widely dispersed settlements. Quivron examined hundreds of whole pots and thousands of sherds (2000:152) from stratified deposits at Nausharo and conducted a stylistic analysis. The Nausharo pottery has a characteristic red surface color and is formed in a variety of shapes and sizes, some painted. Using these characteristics, along with decorative motifs and surface treatments, Quivron was able to break down the pottery at Nausharo into different types. In order to establish changes in pottery styles through time, he then correlated his types with the stratigraphy at Nausharo. His study was extensive involving correlations of shapes, forming methods, and decoration. Here, I focus on just one aspect of his very detailed examination of the painted pottery, preparation of a catalog of decorative motifs, and correlation of stylistic elements with specific occupational periods. This method made it possible for him to trace shifts through time as is shown here. As a final and major step in his analysis, Quivron compared pottery styles and motifs throughout the greater Indus Valley during urban occupational levels at Amri, Kalibangan, Harappa, Banawali, Cholistan, Mohenjo-daro, and numerous other sites. To demonstrate this aspect of his analysis, Figure 5.1 compares pottery from Mohenjo-daro to a site from the Cholistan survey. In the segments marked A, B, and C, design elements corresponding to the first stage (earliest period in which the type was found) at Nausharo are shown for Mohenjo-daro; in F, motifs from a site in Cholistan (known only from surface surveys) are compared. Quivron notes that the leaflike motif (water weeds or seeds) is a common decorative element in the early stages of the Urban period; motifs are drawn in registers and separated by double bands and/or dots arranged in loops. In a second stage, depicted in D and E for Mohenjo-daro and G for the Cholistan site, some design elements continue to be employed, but there are modifications documented by the introduction of a new checkerboard pattern and the hatching of stylistically rendered leafs. Quivron's study demonstrated the widespread uniformity of pottery styles and designs distinctive of an early phase of the Urban period throughout the greater Indus Valley (2000:186), while at the same time contributing toward refining our chronologies both from on-site excavations and surveys (Quivron 2000:152, Figure 10).

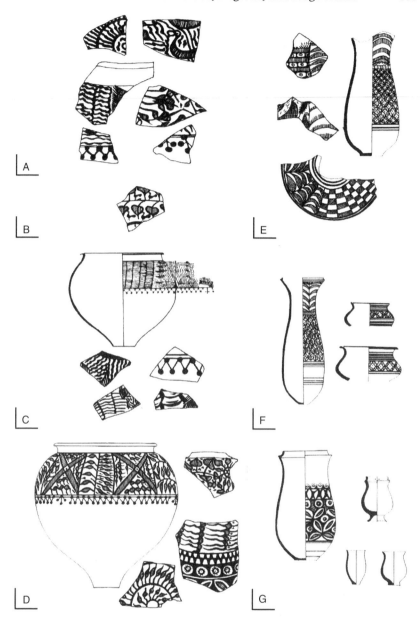

Figure 5.1. Comparison of decorative motifs and surface treatments of ceramics from Nausharo and other Indus sites. © Gonzague Quivron, French Archaeological Mission to Pakistan.

Using the lowest and highest estimates to calculate numbers of people, Mohenjo-daro's population would be between 20,000 and 40,000 and Harappa at 25,000 to 30,000.

I begin this chapter by discussing some general characteristics of Indus cities, focusing on Mohenjo-daro as a primary basis for comparisons with Harappa and Dholavira. My discussion includes both their similarities and unique qualities. I follow by comparing regional settlement patterns in the Ghaggar-Hakra region (Ganweriwala and Rakhigarhi) with the Upper and Lower Indus (Harappa and Mohenjo-daro, respectively). Finally, I discuss some villages and towns located on the margins of the alluvial plains.

Indus Cities

The development of cities signals a major change in the social environment in which people live. Even today people who move from rural areas experience a kind of "culture shock" when confronted with city life. Different experiences and the need to accommodate oneself to strangers requires adapting to new situations. Given that the Indus cities are the first in South Asian history, we can only imagine the kinds of adjustments people would have made.

Today, cities constitute an essential component of modern society as major centers of population. Cities in antiquity served the same function, but our population numbers now are much greater than in the past. In the case of Indus cities, populations of 20,000 and 50,000, though small in modern terms, were at least five times larger than villages and towns that coexisted with them. Whatever the absolute numbers of people living in them, cities were meeting grounds for a variety of social groups drawn to them as major centers of social, political, economic, and ceremonial life. In addition, they were places in which people engaged in a variety of occupations, including farming, pastoralism, craft production, and civic leadership.

The crowded buildings and streets visible on the plan of Mohenjo-daro (Figure 5.2) and a section of the city (Figure 5.3a and b) provide a glimpse into the kinds of adjustments people had to make to city life. Figure 5.2 is an overall plan of the occupied area of the city. The dark shaded areas have been excavated and the letter designations represent the initials of different excavators. The SD area is elevated and contains several large structures (to be discussed later). The HR-area (labeled A and B) lies to its south and east. A portion of this area is represented on the reconstructed grid shown on Figure 5.3a and b. This

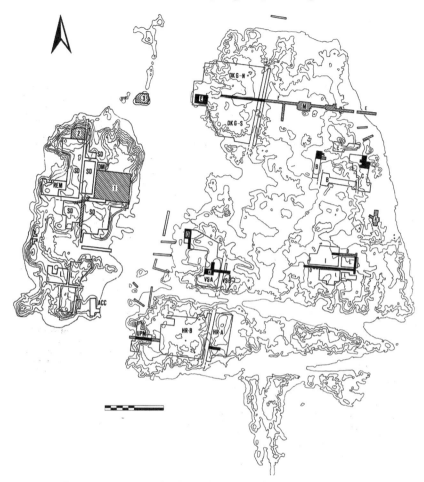

Figure 5.2. Mohenjo-daro site plan. Courtesy M. Jansen, Aachen Research Project Mohenjo-daro.

plan shows the dense nature of occupation at Mohenjo-daro. Areas designated with Roman numerals represent individual buildings, and the small Arabic numbers are rooms within each unit. Buildings were constructed of baked brick and lined up along streets oriented to the cardinal points with major streets in a north-south direction and smaller lanes, east and west. Other features represented on the map include a system of public works, which are discussed briefly here and more extensively in Chapter 9.

HR-B

Figure 5.3a. Redrawn site plan of HR A-B at Mohenjo-daro. In HR-B, Houses XXIII–XLVII (top center) are among two rows of small buildings. Courtesy of M. Jansen, Aachen Research Project Mohenjo-daro.

HR-A

Figure 5.3b. Redrawn site plan of HR A-B at Mohenjo-daro. In HR-A, House VIII is at the top right of the main street. Courtesy of M. Jansen, Aachen Research Project Mohenjo-daro.

This well-conceived city plan and its urban amenities rivaled any of its contemporaries in the ancient world. Even today, sections of Mohenjo-daro are well preserved, enabling visitors to walk through its streets, enter the ruins of its houses and observe its magnificent engineering accomplishments. (see Figure 1.6 for a street and houses at Mohenjo-daro.) However, due to erosional problems that occurred after excavation of some sectors of the city, many areas have been restored (Box 5.2).

In the following, I briefly describe the city plans, physical layouts, and residential and nonresidential structures at Mohenjo-daro, Harappa, and Dholavira. In so doing, I point out their common characteristics – such as wall constructions, sectors separated by walls or open spaces, and water-control systems. I also discuss differences among them that reflect local needs and interests.

Box 5.2 Recent Explorations at Mohenjo-daro

The city of Mohenjo-daro has been designated a World Heritage site by UNESCO and is perhaps the most famous of Indus cities. The site has experienced significant erosional problems due to a high saline water table and harmful atmospheric conditions. Because of these preservation problems, the government of Pakistan has banned further excavation there. This prohibition provided a unique challenge to a team of German and Italian architects, archaeologists, and geologists interested in conducting research at Mohenjo-daro. The various methods they employed demonstrate the kind of detective work that archaeologists routinely engage in. The team used a system of *unmanned hot air balloons* to which cameras were attached to obtain aerial photographs. These photographs were compared to older ones taken during earlier excavations. Plans were drawn from the photos and then compared to *on-the-ground surveys* of individual buildings. They also used specially designed *"vacuum cleaners"* to remove loose surface layers of debris to determine how deeply artifacts had penetrated into the subsurface. Other subsurface techniques included the selective *drilling of cores* sunk deep into the earth (50–60 feet). When the cores were removed intact, they were examined for cultural materials, to establish times of occupation and types of activities conducted, as well as to acquire environmental data. The color and texture of the core sediments gave clues to the types of activity that took place in a given area. For example, household waste dumps were grayish brown in color, suggestive of fire burning. Light brown and gray areas, especially

Box 5.2 (*Cont.*)

when mixed with fragmentary bones and tiny pieces of broken pottery, were suggestive of normal household dumping. In contrast, the identification of structures was based on the presence of fired brick. The use of "nodules" for foundations was also discovered in the core drillings. Other high-tech instrumentation was employed to identify subsurface features without drilling. These included *magnetometers* and tools that measured *electric conductivity*. *Magnetometers* detect subsurface materials that have been magnetized and altered by the earth's magnetic field. By walking over the surface with the magnetometer, a sensor records anomalies that signify contrasts between the surrounding soil and a magnetic material. For example, heated materials like baked clay become magnetized during cooling and capture the earth's magnetic field. In addition, iron oxide, an element found in clay, can be transformed to magnetite when fired under certain atmospheric conditions. Features like pottery kilns or baked brick, therefore, can be detected with this method, as can brick, a major building material. *Electric conductivity* measures the variation in resistance of the ground to electric current. Since different soil types vary in their degrees of resistance, some subsurface features can be detected. Using these methods, M. Cucarzi (1987) was able to identify a mudbrick platform 700 meters long, six meters wide, and six meters deep in the lower town and another in the upper town at Mohenjo-daro. In this case, the low levels of conductivity identified the platform. The geophysical prospecting also identified an empty corridor (or street) that divided the lower town and the upper town.

City Plans and Physical Layouts

Inside their walled enclosures, each of the cities was constructed according to well-defined city plans. At Mohenjo-daro, the city's north–south, east–west axis was oriented, with slight divergences, to astronomical data (Wanzke 1984; see Chapter 9 for details). Its well-planned grid cut across the entire city, thereby linking all of its parts in a coordinated plan. Harappa's city plan was similar, but there was a slight variation. Although it had a grid-like plan, some streets ran parallel to the interiors of enclosure walls that circled parts of the city.

The cities were divided into separate sectors. At Mohenjo-daro and Dholavira, but not at Harappa, sectors were separated visually into high and lower towns. As discussed in Chapter 4, the "high place/lower town

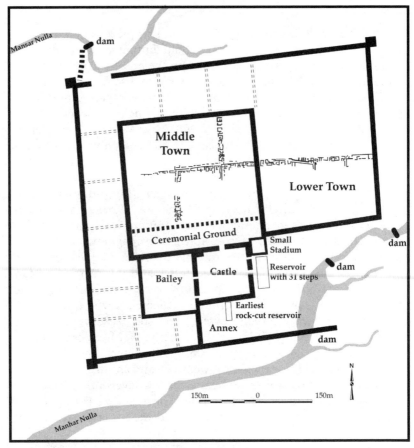

Figure 5.4. Plan of the site of Dholavira.

settlement layout" was common to the Amrian and Kot Dijian sites (Flam 1981:148) and may represent a tradition carried forward into the Urban period of the Lower Indus. At Mohenjo-daro the high parts of town sat prominently to the northwest (designated L, SD, REM, and ACC in Figure 5.2), and sectors were separated by uninhabited "empty" zones. At Dholavira the high ground also was to the northwest, where the Castle and Bailey (the names the excavator gave to these areas) were located (Figure 5.4). Walls further divided the high part of town at Dholavira and its lower town. At Harappa there were at least four sectors divided by walls (designated AB, E, ET, and F in Figure 4.2) (see following discussion of the wall shown around Mound E on the plan).

At Mohenjo-daro and Harappa, the majority of the city was made up of residential areas. The baked brick residential structures at Mohenjo-daro were connected to their neighbors by shared walls, much like town-houses in major cities today. With rare exceptions houses contained a courtyard and one or two sleeping rooms. Some, however, were more elaborate and had additional rooms. There was significant variation in the size of houses, however, such as the large house (House VIII) in HR-A compared to the smaller units (for example, XLIII–XLVII) in HR-B (Figure 5.3a,b). Inside of its walled sectors at Harappa, houses contained many of the same elements (large courtyards and bathing platforms) present in the houses at Mohenjo-daro, but the basic structure was constructed of mudbrick.

Nonresidential Structures

Perhaps the most dramatic differences between earlier villages and towns and the great Indus cities are the presence of large, nonresidential structures. At Mohenjo-daro and Dholavira, these were located in the elevated sections of town. The upper town at Mohenjo-daro was approximately eight hectares in size and currently rises eighteen meters above the plain (Jansen 1993b:31). Buildings on this mound have been labeled by previous excavators according to what they assumed their function to have been. It now seems doubtful that the buildings were used as originally thought; nevertheless, the names have stuck. One building, a large structure containing a colonnade surrounding a sunken pool, is referred to as "The Great Bath"; another has been dubbed "The Granary" based upon the presence of a possible wooden staircase or ramp for moving grain. Yet another, a building with small cell-like rooms, is known as "The College" (Wheeler 1968). Finally, the most visible building at Mohenjo-daro is the so-called "stupa." This structure looms over the northwest section of the site, where another building there was named a "monastery," by Marshall (1931:113) and R. D. Banerji (unpublished report 1921–2; see Box 5.3) and was thought to date to a later occupation of the site during Buddhist times. All that can be said about them is that they represent a cluster of large buildings of a type not found elsewhere in the city. I will return to the function of some of these buildings in Chapter 9.

Box 5.3 Mohenjo-daro – The Stupa and the Monastery

The reanalysis of excavation reports, some of which have been published only recently by G. Verardi has significantly altered our understanding of two major structures that make up the city's urban plan. They had been attributed to the Buddhist period by R. D. Banerji. He assigned the buildings to the Buddhist period based on what was then known from excavations and plans at several Buddhist sites excavated by Cunningham, Hargreaves, Marshall, and others. He believed the buildings were part of a "cluster of five shrines" (Verardi 1987:45). Banerji excavated these structures in 1921–2, but his full report was not published until 1984, and then without its photographic material. Since many of the artifacts he excavated have now been lost, it has been difficult to assess Banerji's statements about these structures.

Marshall later included the stupa area in his report, and although his conclusions appear to have been in disagreement with Banerji's, the excavation of the area had been completed by then, and he was left to rely on the unpublished report. It is unclear how many of the antiquities from the stupa area Marshall examined. He seems to have followed Banerji's interpretation of their Buddhist origin though he was clearly aware of the incongruity in the objects associated with the structures (Marshall 1931:120). Many are artifacts well-known in the Indus assemblages. They include Indus vessel shapes, especially a distinctive goblet with a pointed base found in great quantities in the final phase of the Urban period at Indus sites. In addition, there were various large jars, shell bangles, and terracotta animal figurines characteristic of the Indus Urban period. These items, according to Banerji's report, were not intrusive but *in situ*.

These doubts aside, Banerji did find some artifacts from the Buddhist period. They included large hoards of coins, one of which contained as many as 1,684. Verardi's reanalysis of the excavation report suggests the hoard was buried in a pit, and that it could have been put there at any time. In any event, he claims that "They [the coins] do not give reliable information about the monuments, and do not seem in any case to be referable to the most ancient historical layers" (Verardi 1987:50).

Perhaps the greatest discrepancies relate to the plan of the complex and the structures since they differ in a number of ways from Buddhist monuments of the period. Discrepancies include

Box 5.3 (*Cont.*)

various structural differences, unclear stratigraphy, and an absence of Buddhist iconographical material. One structural difference, for example, is in the form of the drum of the stupa. Marshall believed the "drum" of the stupa was hollow and too vast "to have been vaulted in unbaked bricks" (Verardi 1987:46). Furthermore, its internal facing did not show traces of plaster, and he doubted that the painted fragments described as coming from the interior of the drum were correctly interpreted.

These doubts about the interpretation of this important structure raise questions about the plan of Mohenjo-daro and the function of this building. The matter can only be resolved by putting together the objects found by Banerji, reexcavating what remains and collecting organic materials for dating purposes.

While the upper town at Dholavira contained large buildings in its high town, they were unlike those at Mohenjo-daro (Figure 5.4). The terms "castle" and "bailey" have been used to describe them because their plan resembled European castles "having two well-fortified areas, called inner and outer baileys" (Bisht 2005:74). There also were large open spaces in this sector at Dholavira that its excavator believes was a stadium or ceremonial area for special, community occasions.

When the three cities are compared, there are similarities and differences in the plan of nonresidential buildings. At Harappa, there were non-residential structures on the west and northwest of the city (labeled AB and F on Figure 4.2),[1] but as noted earlier, they were not elevated above any of the other sectors of the city. Mound AB was surrounded by an impressive wall. Abutting the wall was a platform made of baked brick on top of which were a series of buildings that were rebuilt on several occasions. Like the buildings at Mohenjo-daro, their function is uncertain.

The second sector (Mound F) was accessible to AB's north gate. Within the walled area, there was a set of buildings described as barracks by its early excavator, principally because each had a similar architectural layout and were lined up in rows. To their north, rows of bricks set in circles were originally thought to have been workmen's platforms used for grinding grain (Vats 1940) (Figure 5.5). However, recent research at Harappa casts doubt on this interpretation, since renewed excavations have shown that pits associated with the circular platforms neither contained straw nor husks or seeds indicative of grain processing. They also did not contain the wooden mortars for husking grain

Figure 5.5. Circular platforms at Harappa. Photograph by the Harappa
Archaeological Research Project © HARP.

that Wheeler (1947) had suggested lay at the center of the platform.
Instead, the central depressions of the platforms were found to consist
of compact layers of silty clay and a greenish brown stain consistent with
a waterborne deposit. The platforms themselves were found not to have
been out in the open but enclosed in rooms approximately 5.5 meters on
a side. Room walls were made of baked brick (Kenoyer et al. 1999:15ff.).
Although Wheeler's interpretation of the function of the platforms
was clearly incorrect, there is no current consensus on how they were
actually used.[2]

A large structure to the north of the platforms (Mound F) was first
excavated in 1921 by the archaeologist, D. R. Sahni. Although Sahni was
unable to identify the function of the building, when M. S. Vats (1940)
conducted his excavations, on the advice of Sir John Marshall, the director of archaeology at the time, he interpreted the large structure in this
sector of Mound F as a granary (Figure 5.6). Because of the proximity of
the houses, the circular platforms, and the granary, Vats (1940) believed
that the whole area was a "workmen's quarters." Later Wheeler compared it to villages found in pharonic Egypt or possibly Mesopotamia and
he imagined a type of labor organization in which workers engaged in
employment for the state in a "semi-servile" position (Wheeler 1968:34).

Figure 5.6. Granary at the site of Harappa. Photograph by the Harappa Archaeological Research Project © HARP.

There was, in fact, and remains very little evidence for the type of organization Wheeler imagined or even that the large structure was a granary, although it must have been a spectacular building. It consisted of a series of twelve symmetrically arranged rectangular structures raised four feet above the plain. The structures were built in rows of six and separated by a central lane. While all that remains is the baked brick from the walls, the buildings may have been roofed, as has been proposed for the granary at Mohenjo-daro, since there were remnant stains of wooden posts or piers possibly used as roof supports still visible in one of the structures. The building was compared to the granary at Mohenjo-daro, but these interpretations were ultimately based on comparisons with Roman structures that were better known by the archaeologists, many of whom had been trained in classical archaeology.

Despite renewed excavations of this large structure in 1998 and subsequent field seasons at Harappa, archaeologists have not resolved how the building functioned. However, it has been determined that aspects of the building as described by Vats are not representative of the complexity of the architecture. For example, one basis for interpreting the structure as a granary was the hollow "air holes ... for the circulation of air" (Vats 1940:21) presumably for better grain preservation. New excavations have established that the holes were not hollow but filled with mudbricks (Kenoyer et al. 1999). At this time, we can only state that these larger structures were not residential. They did not have the essential components of other residences in any of the cities – courtyards, ovens, and domestic quarters, and, as Vats had noted, they were absent of the types of objects usually found in residential buildings (Vats 1940:22). On the other hand, massive efforts were made to construct them, and they were set in expansive open spaces evocative of gathering places for large numbers of people. Furthermore, their separation from other sectors of the city, either visually or by impressive walls and restricted access suggests that some recognized civic authority in which the community was invested was responsible for their construction.

Public Works

One of the more innovative aspects of Indus cities not known from previous periods was its system of public works (Jansen 1989, 1993b). In fact, if there had been a *Guinness Book of World Records* 4,500 years ago, the Harappans would definitely have won recognition for their engineering feats. Harappan engineers specialized in many innovations designed to control waste disposal and to prevent encroachment of floodwaters on city buildings and their destruction from a rising and saline water table. Probably not until later Roman times did people devise so many clever construction techniques to deal with comforts and discomforts related to water. Although less elaborate waste disposal systems had been designed at settlements in Syria and Iran about a thousand years earlier, it seems unlikely that the Harappans knew about them. Even if they did, the Harappans did it better! One new device invented by the Harappans was the *toilet*. Toilets were built of baked bricks and possibly wood. Some were fitted with seats, while others consisted of a hole in the floor. They were not equipped with a water tank to flush out waste, which flowed along built-in chutes that spilled into street drains or cess (sump) pits. More numerous than toilets, since only a few toilets have been found thus far, were *bathing platforms*. They were built either as separate rooms or in the corners of multipurpose rooms. Most were built on platforms raised slightly above the floor level and sloped toward a drain. Some had stairs and platforms above them, possibly used to shower water on the bathers. Waste from these activities flowed into elaborate *sewage* systems (see Figures 9.1 and 9.7). Sewage drains included outlets for each house that spilled out into drains that ran along the edge of streets or into sump pits. In areas where street drains extended over long distances or where two or more drains met, cesspits were built to avoid clogging. Solids would sink to the bottom and liquids would flow into a larger system

Figure 5.7. A typical Harappan well from Mound AB at Harappa. Photograph by the Harappa Archaeological Research Project © HARP.

of drains. Since the sump pits were outfitted with stairs, waste could be scooped out of them. Large ceramic vessels also were set on the exterior of household courtyards as a reasonably inexpensive means of catching waste from various household activities. Like the sump pits, solid materials sunk to the bottom. Since ceramics are porous, liquids would leach out. When the ceramic sump pots were full, they could be replaced by simply setting a new pot on top of the old one (possibly scooping out debris beforehand).

Harappans also invented a new way to bring bathing and drinking water into their houses. This was accomplished through a system of vertical shaft *wells* (Figure 5.7). These were discovered by archaeologists in Harappan cities and in small villages. Wells were constructed with specially designed wedge-shaped bricks. The Harappans placed the bricks with their smaller end facing toward the center of the well. Built in this way, wells were able to withstand lateral pressure when they were sunk into the ground.

Another innovation at many Harappan cities was the construction of massive *platforms* designed to raise the level of buildings. Some rise as much as 7.3 meters above the plain. They are made of baked brick and fills of earth and debris. These platforms most likely were constructed to prevent destruction from the encroachment of floodwaters that may have occurred from time to time. Finally, Harappan buildings may have been subject to destruction by a rising saline water table. Salinized water promotes the decay of mud and baked brick and to prevent this the Harappans fired clay that was formed in the shape of modern Idaho potato-sized nodules. These "nodules" were used as foundation stones to insulate buildings from the saline groundwater and to provide an efficient drainage system. Stones would have been an alternative but they are few and far between on the Indus Plain.

This public works system is best known from Mohenjo-daro. As discussed, many of these public amenities lined its streets and lanes and included the sewers, sump pits, and drains designed to move water and waste away from structures and other public areas. The vertical shaft wells were located along city blocks either within houses or at locations where they would be accessible to several houses. Wells and sewage disposal seem not to have been restricted to a particular segment of society. At Mohenjo-daro wells were shared with one to three other dwellings.

The same amenities have been discovered at Harappa. Many of the interiors of houses were equipped with bathing platforms and water or waste management systems and in others individual householders improvised by using ceramic sump pots for collecting human and other waste, by positioning them on the exterior walls of courtyards.

A feature common to Mohenjo-daro and Harappa was a large drain with a corbelled arch. The drain at Harappa is almost identical to one associated with the Great Bath at Mohenjo-daro. At Harappa, however, the drain was built under a gateway linking mounds E and ET to a major entrance to the city leading archaeologists to conclude it was a principal drainage point for that sector of the city.

At Dholavira, there was an elaborate water management system that appears as an innovative adaptation to the dry, environmental conditions in Kutch. It included a dam constructed of blocks of stone used to retain water. The water was then channeled into terraced reservoirs that bank an outer fortification wall of the city. Water-retaining devices of this and other types make up 17% of the walled area at Dholavira.

Walls and Separated Sectors (Neighborhoods)

In the preceding discussion, I referred to the construction of walled enclosures and empty zones separating sectors of Indus cities. As a general rule, walls were large in size. As discussed previously, at Dholavira a wall in the high section of town enclosed an area that measured 47 hectares. It was constructed of stone rubble and mudbrick and enclosed the entire

Figure 5.8. Mudbrick wall on the south side of Mound E at Harappa.
Photograph by the Harappa Archaeological Research Project © HARP.

complex, where additional walls divided portions of the interior spaces. At
Harappa, there were several walls, each of which enclosed widely dispersed
sectors of the city. Most walls at Harappa were constructed of mudbrick
though some had baked brick exteriors. One wall, for example, consisted
of a 13.7 meter wide base made of mudbrick and an exterior baked brick
facing of 1.2 meters (Figure 5.8). Walls may have existed at Mohenjo-daro,
but the empty zones served as a similar separation of sectors.

The walls at Dholavira and Harappa could not be entered except at
special gateway areas. One wall at Dholavira, for example, was accessible
through gates on three sides. Another featured mudbrick-filled ramparts
faced with stone and several gates, some of which contained stairways.
It also had sunken passageways and screenwall(s). Screenwalls created
alleys or corridors between the two walls. At Harappa, gateways were
flanked by guardrooms and ramps. Wheeler described a portion of one
such wall that he excavated as follows:

On the western side a curved re-entrant in the defenses, controlled by a bas-
tion, led to a system of extra-mural ramps and terraces approached by gates and
supervised from guardrooms. At the southern end of this system there seems to
have been a ramp or stair leading up on to the citadel. It is likely enough that the
normal ascent from the flood plain was by steps. (Wheeler 1968:30)

The most spectacular wall at Harappa was between Mounds E and ET. Consisting of an elaborate gateway with pylons and side rooms built of baked brick, it was a major entryway into the city, providing access to a street that ran the full length of the two separate mounds. Thanks to the careful excavations being conducted at Harappa, we have been able to document episodes of destruction and rebuilding of some of the wall.

City Plans and Physical Layouts Summarized – Nonresidential Structures, Public Works, Walls, and Neighborhoods

This discussion of three Indus cities provides an introduction to both their shared and unique physical qualities. The plans of all of the cities included walled sectors linked by a uniform set of streets and lanes oriented to cardinal points. Some walls contained bastions and guardhouses that restricted entry to the separate districts, while others did not. There is no evidence to suggest that the walls were built for defensive purposes, and the most that can be said about them is that they imply civic control, whether imposed within individual neighborhoods or by rulers within the city. Although there is some variability, a major amenity of Indus cities was their public works. The presence of bathing platforms and toilets is fairly unique in the ancient world, and the elaborate drainage systems are truly extraordinary.

At the same time, there are a number of features that differ when the three cities are compared, especially in the variability of public structures. For instance, the elaborate colonnade, pillared corridor, and sunken pool in the "The Great Bath" at Mohenjo-daro has no counterpart in the other cities. The "workmen's platforms" at Harappa, whatever their function, are unique. Although Wheeler had thought that both Harappa and Mohenjo-daro had granaries, this interpretation is now in doubt given the absence of grain or food-processing equipment at either location. Moreover, the two structures bear no similarities in their construction, making them unique in each city. The "castle and bailey" at Dholavira, the large open courtyard associated with them, and terraced reservoirs have no counterparts at Mohenjo-daro or Harappa.

These differences suggest the presence of localized authorities capable of investing substantial human labor in building projects unique to their own cities. Though functional designations for these buildings as workmen platforms, granaries, great baths, castle, and bailey may be misleading, they do evoke the concept of civic authority. This lack of uniformity in the construction of public structures differs markedly, for example, from the restricted layout of public buildings found in other civilizations, such as in Mesopotamian temples, where a standard plan was employed in its various cities (see Pollock 1999). The lack of uniformity in the Indus argues against a strictly shared conception of religious or administrative buildings or an overarching authority common to all cities.

Finally, house layouts and public amenities were not uniform. From these variations, we can gain insights into the ways in which people and groups experienced life in the city. This aspect of the city landscape is discussed in Chapter 9.

City and Countryside

As discussed earlier, a view of urbanism that concentrates on cities alone is only half the story, since large segments of the people who populate urban societies live outside of them. A more common pattern in early cities was a mutual dependency between rural and urban dwellers. Although many city inhabitants most likely had agricultural fields and kept animals, the products of farmers and herders living in rural areas were necessary to sustain specialists living in cities who were not food producers. Cities also were centers of commerce and served as meeting places for the exchange of goods among urban and rural people. The sustaining networks of small settlements provided strategic links for the movement of goods and the development of trade networks and craft products not produced in cities.

To understand the degree to which Indus cities were integrated with their countrysides, we need to return to the regional settlements introduced in Chapter 4. Three areas in the Upper Indus are discussed in this section and shown in Figure 5.9. From left to right, they are the upper Indus near Harappa, the Ghaggar-Hakra plain in Cholistan in the regions of Derawar Fort and Fort Abbas, and to its east, settlements in northwest India.

The Upper Indus and Beas Regional Surveys
near Harappa

The results of surveys near Harappa do not represent the original settlement pattern. Sites near Harappa were subject to a great deal of overburden due to modern disturbances and may be deeply buried. Sites below ten hectares, for example, are easily disturbed by modern cultivation practices. Our observations, therefore, may be skewed because of differential site preservation resulting from modern cultivation and irrigation installations.

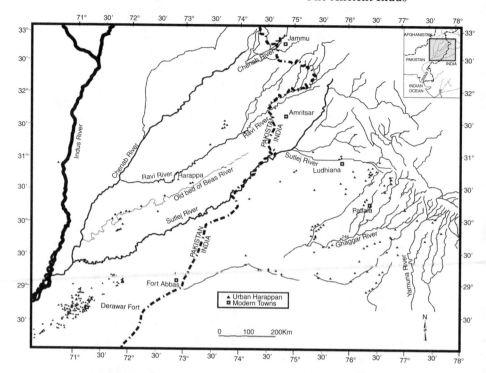

Figure 5.9. Upper Indus and Ghaggar-Hakra settlement patterns in the Urban period. Left to right: Chenab, Ravi, and Beas sites; Cholistan and northwest India. © R. P. Wright.

Our knowledge of settlements to the west of Harappa that are located either on or near the Indus, the Chenab, and the Ravi Rivers is based on the reconnaissance surveys conducted by the Punjab Archaeological Survey, as discussed in Chapter 4. The locations of settlements during the Urban period are shown in Figure 5.9. As can be seen by comparing Figure 4.5 and 5.9, all seven Pre-urban settlements along the Chenab and four of nine on the Ravi discussed in Chapter 4 were abandoned in the urban period. On the Indus, a single site, less than 2 hectares was occupied during the Urban period. With the exception of Harappa, two of the settlements on the Ravi were small towns (between 10 and 20 hectares) that had been occupied in the Pre-urban. The total abandonment of the Chenab settlements and limited occupations on the Indus cannot be determined without more intensive study of these settlements.

As discussed in Chapter 4, the settlements along the Beas River are better documented than others from the Punjab survey. We were able to

Table 5.1. Beas River Settlements and Harappa

	Small Village	Large Village	Small Town	Large Town	City
Hectares[a]	0.1 5	5.1–10	10.1–20	30+	80+
Urban	9	7	1		1

[a] A hectare is equal to 2.47 acres.

conduct more intensive research involving extensive mapping, systematic sampling of surface collections, and environmental reconstructions (Schuldenrein et al. 2004; Wright et al. 2005a,b; Wright et al. 2008).

Table 5.1 tabulates the number of settlements and site size categories along the Beas, including Harappa, in the Urban period (Wright et al. 2005a,b).

The majority of villages and towns along the Beas during the Urban period are in the 1- to 5-hectare size range. Larger sites are more limited. They include seven 5- to 10-hectare large villages and one 14-hectare small town. The onset of settlement along the Beas was fairly rapid and correlates with the known period of climatic optimization across this region, suggesting it was partially motivated by changing environmental conditions (Schuldenrein et al. 2004; Wright et al. 2005a), at about 6,000 years ago. The founding of settlements along the Beas extended the ecological niche for the Harappa region and represented a dispersal of settlements into a new resource zone enabling the intensification of agriculture and potential increase in the availability of plant resources for cultivation and animal grazing. The continued expansion of settlement throughout the Beas occupations is indicative of a successful adaptation to the new environmental conditions on the plain.

While more study is needed before we can determine exactly how the Beas settlements functioned, their alignment and site size categories indicate that Harappa was the major urban regional center.

The site of Vainiwal, part of the Beas survey, is one of the few settlements whose internal settlement plan is fairly well understood. It consists of three mounds measuring a total of four hectares, though the settlement originally was much larger, measuring at least seven hectares in size and rising to between seven and twelve meters above the Beas Plain. As noted in Chapter 4, Vainiwal was first settled in the Ravi and Early Harappan/Kot Diji periods and abandoned in the Post-urban/Late Harappan.

The plan at Vainiwal is based on the results of surface maps, the weighing and counting of artifacts from randomly selected units, and the

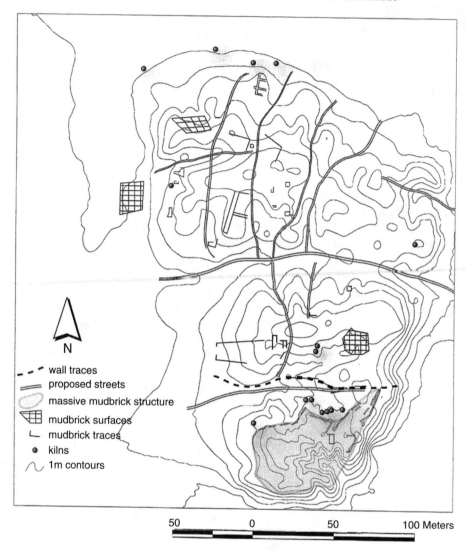

Figure 5.10. Site plan of Vainiwal from Beas landscape and settlement survey. © R. P. Wright.

excavation of a small test trench. Substantial evidence for past activities is still visible on the site's surface (Figure 5.10), including foundation walls, streets, a mudbrick platform, and craft activities. Within the seventy-one units sampled, the 12,451 diagnostic ceramic sherds and 3,506 small

Figure 5.11. Seal impression on pointed base goblet ceramic from Lahoma Lal Tibba, Beas Landscape and Settlement Survey. Photograph by the Harappa Archaeological Research Project © HARP.

finds including terracotta animal figurines; carts and wheels; terracotta and shell bangles; chert blades and cores; faience, steatite, and terracotta beads; grinding stones and pestle fragments; and copper and unworked stone, including lapis lazuli were recorded (Wright et al. 2005b).

Artifact styles and production technologies at Vainiwal and many other Beas settlements are similar to those at Harappa. The ceramic kilns visible on the survey are identical to the two-chambered kiln (see Figure 6.6 and accompanying discussion) at Harappa. The use of Indus script etched on pottery fragments at Vainiwal and seal impressions on pottery at the Beas settlement of Lahoma Lal Tibba (Figure 5.11) indicate that close ties and frequent interaction existed between the city and its outlying communities. At the same time, there are many artifacts and raw materials from outside of the sphere of Harappa, indicating that rural people at the Beas settlements engaged in interregional contacts conceivably independent of their connections with Harappa. The strategic locations of Beas settlements provided a natural corridor between Harappa and Mohenjo-daro. They also were situated at an east–west intersection between Cholistan and upland regions to the north and west.

The Ghaggar-Hakra Plain – Cholistan Regional Surveys

Table 5.2 lists the number of settlements in the Pre-urban (Hakra and Early Harappan/Kot Diji phases) with which to compare the expansion of settlement in the Urban period.

Table 5.2. Comparisons of Hakra, Early Harappan/Kot Diji, Urban Phases in Cholistan

	Small Village	Large Village	Small Town	Large Town	City	Totals
Hectares[a]	0.1–5	5.1–10	10.1–20	20.1–30	31+	0
Hakra	21	5	7	4		37
Kot Diji	19	8	3	2		32
Urban	44	20	8	0	1	73

[a] A hectare is equal to 2.47 acres.

Figure 5.9 shows the locations of settlements during the Urban period and should be compared to Figure 4.5. Although the number of settlements is fairly stable in the Pre-urban, there are differences when specific areas are compared. Pre-urban sites decrease sharply in the northernmost area near Fort Abbas, whereas in the Urban period, a larger number of settlements emerge at the southern end of distribution. Midway between this southern cluster where Ganweriwala is located and Fort Abbas, site density is lower than in the Pre-urban. During the Urban period, the major center at Ganweriwala, now was situated equidistant from Harappa and Mohenjo-daro – 314 kilometers northeast of Mohenjo-daro and 290 kilometers southeast of Harappa – as well as being conveniently located with respect to regions to its east, where important natural resources were located. It, therefore, was positioned strategically for agriculture, pastoralism, and trade.

The city of Ganweriwala has not been excavated.[3] The two mounds visible on its surface suggest that, like other Indus cities, it contained at least two sectors divided by walls or an empty zone. All surface materials indicate that its occupation was confined to the Urban period. The two large towns from the Pre-urban period were abandoned. The city was the only major center (listed as a 31+ size in Table 5.2) in the Cholistan region during the Urban period. Refer to Table 5.2 to compare the expansion of settlement between the Urban and Pre-urban periods.

There also were many small, single-function sites (some not included in these numbers because they were too small to measure). They are tabulated on Table 5.3. These are primarily industrial sites for stone working, metallurgy, and pottery production. "Camp" sites, likely occupied by pastoral groups moving through the area with grazing animals, also were found.

There are two observable changes at the single-function sites between the Pre-urban and Urban periods in Cholistan shown on Table 5.3.

Table 5.3. Comparison of Single-Function Sites in Cholistan

	Hakra Pre-urban	Kot Diji Pre-urban	Urban
*Sites with kilns	2	14	33
Camp sites	52	3	10
All industrial	0	0	79

* A hectare is equal to 2.47 acres.

First, in the Kot Diji Pre-urban, the number of camp sites is small compared to the Hakra phase, suggesting that in the Kot Diji/Early Harappan phases pastoral groups were becoming increasingly sedentary; the increase in camp sites in the Urban period may suggest a reverse trend in which pastoral groups were attracted to permanently settled areas but remained on their margins. Although the number of industrial sites increases (places where "craft related activities and kilns for firing pottery and other materials are concentrated"; Mughal 1997:56), they are a smaller percentage of the total number of settlements, when compared to earlier time periods. This pattern may indicate that some production moved from inside of settlements to their outskirts. Alternatively, there may have been an influx of artisans into the region drawn by the large center at Ganweriwala, even though they remained outside of villages, towns, and cities. In any event, it suggests that there were many coexisting groups engaged in diverse activities (Mughal 1997:50).

Ghaggar-Hakra Plain – Northwest India

There are a large number of settlements to the east on the continuation of the Ghaggar Plain in northwest India (Figure 5.9). According to Possehl (2002:241), these settlements number 218, demonstrating a large population density in excess of Cholistan. Kalibangan, Rakhigharhi, and Banawali are located here. Rakhigharhi was over 100 hectares in size. Kalibangan was laid out in the classic model with a raised area in its western sector and a wall and towers restricting entrance. Its lower town, oriented to a north–south axis, was residential. Banawali was now enclosed by mudbrick walls and an interior divided into two areas by a wall (Bisht 1982). The smallest sector, located in the south central portion of the village, was elevated above the rest of the village and surrounded by a thick wall. A gate with massive bastions on either side served as an entryway to its lower town. Many of the traditional architectural features were present in its mudbrick houses, such as bathing areas, courtyards, and pottery jars for waste disposal. Also present were wells constructed with wedge-shaped baked bricks like those built at Mohenjo-daro and else-where. Among several unusual features were a moat and berm along at least one side of the "citadel" wall, with a flight of stairs leading to them. Finally, unlike most other Indus settlements, streets were laid out radially or semiradially and converged on the east gate of the citadel wall.

The Lower Indus Regional Surveys

As discussed in Chapter 4, two major survey projects have been con-ducted in the Lower Indus near Mohenjo-daro. They include the Sindh Archaeological Project (Flam 1981, 1993a,b) and Shah Abdul Latif University, Khairpur surveys (Shaikh, personal communication). The Sindh survey included sites on the Lower Basin (alluvial plain) as well as others on its western margins in the piedmont and parts of the Kirthar range as discussed in Chapter 4. A second project, under the direction of Nilofer Shaikh of Khairpur University, includes exploration in several loca-tions to the east and north of the Sindh project and is largely unpublished.

Figure 5.12 combines the most recent results of the Khairpur project, sites discovered by the Sindh project on the alluvial plain, and previ-ously known settlements, such as Mohenjo-daro and Chanhu-daro (see Figure 1.2).[4] In the following, I discuss the two projects separately, since available documentation differs.

In contrast to the Pre-urban (discussed in Chapter 4), the Urban period sees an explosion of sites and an apparent shift from a more dense settlement pattern in areas west of the plain (in the Piedmont and Kirthar areas) on to the plain itself. This movement suggests a greater dependence on floodwater farming and husbandry, a weakening of ties with settle-ments to the west, and a greater focus on the major center at Mohenjo-daro. This is a pattern similar to that of Ganweriwala and indicates an increased importance of trade networks along the rivers and coastal set-tlements and a close network of interaction (Flam 1981:173–8).

The new evidence from the Khairpur University survey represents a major advance in our understanding of urban settlements on the Lower Indus alluvial plain. The Khairpur team has identified sixty-five settle-ments in the urban period, an increase in numbers from the sites identi-fied in the Pre-urban (Hakra and Kot Diji) periods (Figure 4.7). As noted in Chapter 4, four areas were surveyed (see Figure 5.12 for locations). In several areas the settlements are described as densely packed workshop complexes. They include Dubi (12), Rohri (18), Veesar Valley (3), and Kandharki (2) workshops that are relatively small in size. In the Thar area, there are thirty-two urban settlements, some of which are noted on Figure 5.12 and are generally located in the cluster of settlements south

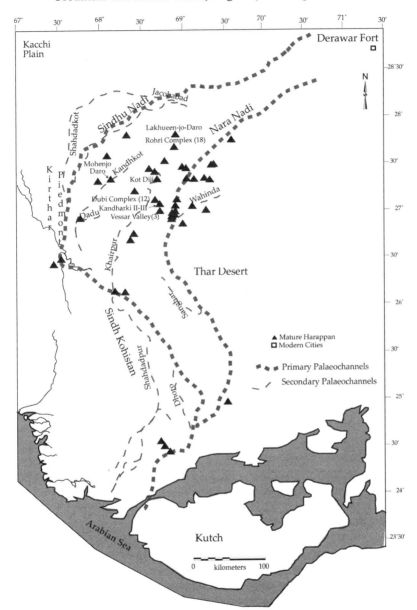

Figure 5.12. Lower Indus settlement pattern in the Urban period.
© R. P. Wright.

of the Rohri complex and east of the Veesar Valley. The sizes of these settlements are not yet published.

The Dubi workshop sites are found in clusters and are identified based on diagnostic pottery and stone tools. The sites are situated on sand dunes and lie in an inhospitable zone between the alluvial plain and the Rohri Hills. Occupation in the Dubi area at present is principally by nomadic pastoralists who gather in this area during periods of monsoon rains. Although the environmental conditions of the area have not been studied extensively, there is some indication that conditions differed in the past, since all the sites are located near small backwater lakes, "corresponding to an old river bed" (Shar et al. 1996:39).

Many other small settlements in the area of study are associated with sand dunes. Gharo Bhiro, for example, a less than 1.5-hectare site, is located on the slope of a sand dune. There are also large quantities of chert blades, ceramics, and clay bangles and animal figurines typical of the nearby site of Mohenjo-daro. More diverse finds included a variety of triangular-shaped cakes known throughout Indus sites as well as chert blades and shell objects typical of residential areas. A kiln was described as being "similar" to the ones identified at other Harappan sites such as the kiln excavated at Harappa and discussed in Chapter 7 and the one at Cholistan and Chanhu-daro (see Chapter 7 for description and photograph; Laghari 1996).

The principal difference between the pattern of settlement in the Lower Indus from that revealed in the Cholistan and the Beas surveys is in the site size distributions. Of the twenty-two sites identified by Flam, all are less than 5 hectares, with the exception of Mohenjo-daro. In addition, the site of Lakhueen-jo daro discovered by the Khairpur team is fifty hectares. One other site located on the top of a sand hill was spread over thirty-four hectares. Though large, occupation was brief, given the shallow depth of the deposit. Seven other sites located in the northeastern part of the region, near the Nara Nadi are situated on the top of sand hills and also have shallow deposits. Flam suggests that, like the 34-hectare site, they may have been occupied by people seeking refuge from abnormal flooding (1981:96). Alternatively, they may have occupied a restricted ecological niche.

Interpreting the Evidence for Indus Cities, City-States, and Regional Surveys

This outline of the spatial distribution of settlements and the size of area occupied (where available) provides a basic framework for understanding Indus cities and their rural areas. In later chapters, I will discuss some specific activities that took place in cities and at smaller settlements, but here I focus on models developed by geographers and city planners to understand the infrastructure behind major centers, villages, and towns in their countrysides within the Greater Indus and Ghaggar-Hakra as a whole.

Modern geographers who interpret spatial distributions of settlements view them as economic and administrative indicators. One geographical model that fits the Indus evidence and is useful in understanding their political and economic function is Central Place Theory (Christaller [1933] 1966). Christaller proposes that whereas settlements may be aligned with natural or modified features such as Indus waterways, an optimal pattern of settlement for the flow of goods is one in which a "central place" or city coexists with peripheral and secondary centers. Site-size distributions would consist of a single, large primary center, midsize secondary centers; and smaller peripheral settlements. Secondary centers in the central place model function as production and distribution points for particular goods and provide a social and economic infrastructure for populations performing production related tasks.

The *central place model* fits the available evidence. Ganweriwala and Harappa were the focal points of outlying production areas – serving as central places for the Cholistan and Beas settlements. In addition, the settlement-size distributions for the Mohenjo-daro, Harappa, and Ganweriwala central places all have at least one potential secondary center larger than ten hectares and numerous smaller settlements. This pattern is in contrast to one in which a single center exists in isolation and lacks interlocking support systems.

A model that complements the central place is the concept of a *city-state*. Although this concept was originally defined with the Greek polis in mind with specific reference to "active citizenship and participatory democracy" (Stone 1997:15), definitions have broadened to include other cities in the ancient world. Cities in ancient Mesopotamia and the Maya come to mind, and examples exist from seventh to fourth century B.C. polities in India (Kenoyer 1997a:65).

The environmental settings of Indus cities were optimal for the development of city-states. Able to control the vast sustaining network of their region in terms of subsistence needs, cities developed an interlocking network of smaller towns and villages and linkages to outside regions for the procurement of essential raw materials and the processing of goods as documented in all the surveys discussed. City-states that adopt this strategy typically are evenly spaced geographically, as is the case of the Indus settlements. Transport systems to be discussed in later chapters facilitated the development of these exchange networks and integration of the civilization.

These broad definitions of city-states emphasize the political and economic nature of city-states and link them to a particular settlement pattern. In them, the city is territorially based and includes "an economically and socially integrated adjacent hinterland" (Nichols and Charlton 1997:1). City-states are politically independent of, although culturally unified, other city-states within an overarching civilization. This pattern is in distinction to other state systems in which centralized political and economic power are focused on a single city or capital that dominates an entire nation and serves as its primary center.[5]

Another way to view cities is through *spatial models* as city planners have done in order to understand their political and economic functions. They adopt a broad, cross-cultural approach that examines the internal settlement plan of the city itself. Kevin Lynch, a city planner, identified a city type that he named "practical." According to Lynch, practical cities work toward some end. They typically have a regularity of plan that subscribes to a few simple rules (Lynch 1981:83,88). These rules are tied to the city's function and are organized to facilitate flows of people, services, or products toward a particular purpose. The city of New York with its well-planned streets and avenues in a gridlike plan is a typical practical city. In contrast, the city of Boston, with its twisted streets and apparent lack of a city plan, is an "organic" city. Boston streets, in fact, emanate from a symbolic center that binds the city to its early history.

The city-state and central place models both emphasize the political and commercial nature of the city. Like Indus cities, they have a regularity of plan and their layout subscribes to a few simple rules. Practical cities, though integrated through a coordinated city plan, typically consist of small, autonomous, undifferentiated parts that preserve the autonomy of each. The divided sectors of Indus cities clearly followed this type of plan.

Adopting the above analyses for Indus cities suggests the following. Indus cities were organized into several city states loosely integrated by a common material culture. Individual cities were centers of political and economic activities for rural networks of outlying settlements with which they interacted. Though rich in their agricultural potential, a condition that fostered self-sufficiency regarding subsistence and the production of some material goods, people in cities and rural dwellers were mutually dependent upon regional networks for craft and food products.

Urbanism at Its Margins, Gateway Towns and Edge Zones

In reconstructing the development of cities, I have emphasized their coordinating efforts in the production and distribution of resources, but I have not touched upon the infrastructure that lay behind their ability to acquire materials and resources beyond regional networks. Although cities and their surrounding countrysides were central features of the civilization, there were many other settlements – villages and towns – on the frontiers of the Indus away from the major river systems of the Indus and Ghaggar-Hakra Plains that were integral to the establishment of *loci* or were themselves loci for distribution and exchange among different regions.

In this section, I draw on another model from cultural geography and the concept of "gateway" communities or contact zones for lines of exchange. Typically, gateway settlements are located in places that facilitate transportation (Possehl 1980:76) – along coastlines, at the foot of passes, or the juncture between distinct cultural groups. In the remainder of the chapter, I describe a number of settlements that fit these criteria.

During the Urban period, the Indus civilization spread over a large area (Figure 1.2). The presence of artifacts and raw materials outside of the sphere of the major cities is indicative of contact throughout a vast region beyond the alluvial plains. Many settlements lie outside the direct Indus sphere.

Settlement distributions of the peripheral sites were radically different from the pattern observed for cities and their hinterlands. Although there were many others, six key settlements (Shortugai, Rehman Dheri, Nausharo, Balakot, Sutkagen-dor, Sotka-koh, etc.) on the frontiers or margins of the heartland of the Indus are discussed here.

The most distant settlement, Shortugai, was in northern Afghanistan near the Oxus River, some 500 kilometers from any other Indus villages and towns. Shortugai measures 2.5 hectares and lies north of the Hindu Kush along a route that centuries later became the Silk Road between China and the west. As noted in a preceding chapter, this settlement is strategically located near the world's largest lapis lazuli mine in northeastern Afghanistan. Most of the inhabitants at Shortugai lived in domestic structures and engaged in farming, pastoralism, and craft production, while others did not farm but were full-time craft producers. A monumental building was located in one area of the site. It contained large quantities of shell bracelets and beads, but its function is unknown (Francfort et al. 1989). Some of the material culture at Shortugai, such as ceramic styles and ornamentation, were produced in the Indus style. In view of the similarities of material culture and its proximity to important natural resources (lapis, gold, silver, copper, and tin), there is a strong possibility that Shortugai was founded by people from the Indus, as an outpost for trade. During the final period at Shortugai, its connections with the Indus diminish. More details about Shortugai, its site layout, production of lapis ornaments trade, and its final days of occupation will be discussed in Chapters 7 and 11, respectively.

Its nearest neighbor, Rehman Dheri (Figure 1.2), some 500 kilometers distant, was to its south and east, near the confluence of the Indus and Zhob Rivers. Rehman Dheri is approximately twenty-two hectares. The town was surrounded by an enclosure wall (Durrani 1988), and, like Indus cities, a main street served as a central axis (northwest/ southeast). Perpendicular to the main street are side streets and lanes, a plan present from the earliest levels of occupation. What is remarkable about Rehman Dheri is that Kot Diji style ceramics, known only in the Pre-urban period on the alluvial plain, continued to be produced in the Urban period until at least 2300 B.C. The new ceramic types associated with the Indus are absent, suggesting this region was not eclipsed by the Indus and maintained its indigenous culture during the Urban period. Other artifacts include beads made of lapis lazuli and turquoise and human figurines that are typical of settlements in Central Asia to its north. Like Shortugai, then, Rehman Dheri appears to have been a trading outpost, but unlike Shortugai, its local culture flourished during the Urban period, in spite of its interaction with the Indus civilization.

The village of Naesharo (Figure 1.2) lies south of Rehman Dheri, a 5-hectare site on the Kachi Plain at the western margin of the Indus Plain. As discussed in Chapter 3, Nausharo is 11 kilometers from Mehrgarh. Like Shortugai, it possesses a standard corpus of Indus material culture. The Pre-urban period at Nausharo was contemporary with the latest occupations at Mehrgarh (discussed in Chapter 3). While Mehrgarh was abandoned just before full-scale urbanization on the Indus plain, Nausharo continued to be inhabited.[6]

Architectural elements at Nausharo are typical of the Indus style and though every aspect of the settlement suggests continuity with Pre-urban levels, there is an influx of new ideas and material culture from the Indus superimposed upon it. Large walls and platforms of mudbrick, baked brick drains, streets, and lanes oriented to an east–west and north–south grid show evidence of town planning. There also was uniformity in construction and plans of housing units. The excavator of one of the blocks at Nausharo, Catherine Jarrige, has described the houses as follows:

They all show a large central space [a courtyard], most probably open, sometimes partly covered by a shelter on one side, as indicated by pillars or postholes, and two or three small compartments probably covered by a roof… [There is] … a direct correlation between the size of the house and that of the courtyard. (1995:2)

The outside walls of houses, at least on one side of the house, bordered streets or lanes. There were drains in houses that spilled out into streets with well-constructed baked brick drains. Some houses also had bathing rooms with paved floors, either of fired bricks, reused stone or pottery shards. In some instances, large jar types typical of Indus settlements served as soak pits for refuse.

Other sites on or near the Kachi Plain lie at the frontier of the Lower Indus alluvial plain to the east in the Kirthar and Piedmont areas surveyed by Flam (1993b). Numerous sites dating to the Urban period have been discovered including Ghazi Shah (see Figure 1.2) (Flam 1993b). These sites are located in a presently arid and semi-arid zone, where precipitation levels are low. As discussed in Chapter 4, Flam identified in this region important water retention devices called gabarbands which suggest that climatic conditions there may have differed in the past. During the Urban period, as was the case in the preceding Pre-urban, most sites were located near intermittent stream channels or spring water providing "a perennial supply of water" (Flam 1999:321). The use of gabarbands continued during the Urban period. Though produced from stone and mud, the diversion of water through the construction of walls in this manner is a form of artificial irrigation (Flam 1998:322). Devices of this type have not been found on the alluvial plain.

In the Urban period at Ghazi Shah, assemblages include materials common to other Indus sites. They include typical Indus ceramic types, terracotta beads, disks, bangle fragments, and a bull figurine, as well as imported materials of lapis lazuli, agate, carnelian, marine, shell, and steatite. Also present are potter's marks or inscribed signs on several vessels.

In southern Baluchistan, three sites are of interest. Balakot in Las Bela, occupied during the Pre-urban period and discussed in Chapter 4, was briefly abandoned and then reoccupied. In its new levels, it contains typical Indus pottery. Two villages also have typical Indus materials. Sutkagen-dor and Sotka-koh were ports of trade and accessible from the Indus plain through Las Bela or by traveling through mountain valleys directly south of villages like Nausharo. Sutkagen-dor and Sotka-koh have a lower town and a "citadel," surrounded by walls and towers flanking entrance gates. Locally available stone was the major building material.

Wedged between Balakot and Sutkagen-dor and Sotka-koh are settlements referred to as the Kulli culture (Franke-Vogt 2005:75). The material culture at Kulli sites is sufficiently different from the Indus assemblages that they may represent an entirely separate culture. These small and large settlements are distributed over a broad area in the region of Las Bela and positioned in strategic locations, on mountain, tops, overlooking valleys, and controlling plains and passes (Franke-Vogt 2000). They will be discussed in more detail in Chapter 8.

Other settlements that may have held strategic positions in distribution networks lie to the east beyond Dholavira. Of special interest is the small village of Lothal (less than five hectares) near the head of the Gulf of Cambay. A massive brick wall surrounds the site, which was built in identifiable districts. These districts included an upper town constructed on a large platform raised above the settlement and a lower town (Possehl 1980). Mud and baked brick structures were found along the streets of its upper town. One building had a large mudbrick foundation that was similar to the "granary" at Mohenjo-daro. Like Mohenjo-daro, very little was left behind with which to substantiate its function as a granary.

Streets in Lothal's lower town were oriented to the cardinal directions and contained residential structures. The houses were constructed around courtyards and had bathing areas paved with baked brick that were hooked up to a system of drains. Lined up on streets and lanes, workshops were interspersed in neighborhoods. A third feature, and the most controversial sector of the town, is a "dockyard" (S. Rao 1979), consisting of a depressed rectangular space enclosed by a baked brick wall. Based on the presence of post holes, anchor stones possibly for tying ships, Rao believes the area was connected to tidal flows from the sea and the depressed space was used for docking. Although Rao's interpretation has been criticized, scholars have not offered feasible alternative explanations, though one possibility is that it was a tank for collecting water as Bisht has suggested at Dholavira.

The settlements just described are relatively small, certainly not urban in scale and to some degree spatially isolated from each other and the heartland of the civilization. The extraordinary uniformity in their spatial layouts is, therefore, all the more remarkable as they demonstrate a degree of conformity to Indus "rules." Some general principles of city planning noted for Indus cities appear to have been shared, although there were local variations in planning and material culture. These similarities and variations suggest a high degree of interaction among the major settlements and its frontier zones as well as local autonomy.

Uniformity and Diversity – Cities, Regions and Edge Zones

In this chapter, our focus has been on using evidence from excavations and surveys of settlement patterns drawn from major cities, their regional networks, and others on the margins of the civilization to structure local and far-reaching settlement systems. Using models from geography, city planning, and history, we can construct a picture of early *Indus cities* as central places involved in the movement of goods and reciprocal exchanges with towns and villages in their countrysides and beyond the alluvial plain with gateway settlements. Their practical layouts and equidistant spatial positioning from each other were supported by an ever-expanding network of reciprocal settlements, a successful strategy that integrated local production and distribution, creating the context for an effective urban infrastructure of city-states. Viewed from the perspective of these spatial configurations, we observed significant uniformities of community planning – their two-part divisions, mudbrick platforms, segregated neighborhoods, massive walls, and public amenities (drains, disposal points, and wells) – sufficient to indicate an overarching set of ideas. On the other hand, local variations in spatial planning at many of the settlements, as discussed at Harappa, Mohenjo-daro, and Dholavira, argue for a strong local impulse that defined and reinforced community identities.

Regional settlement plans demonstrate an overall increase in rural settlements, presence of new settlement types and increased level of site size hierarchies. These urban concentrations signify an influx of populations possibly from peripheral regions to riverine locations. Significant factors were the availability of water for agriculture, pastoralism, and transport networks.

There is evidence for functional differentiation of settlements. On the one hand, there is an integration of city and countryside evident in the strong similarities in material culture and aspects of village plan, indicating sustained interaction and movements of resources with a strong base of agriculture, pastoralism, and craft production. From Cholistan, the evidence for pastoral camps suggests reciprocal arrangements between nomadic pastoralists and urban dwellers, and it seems most likely that similar exchanges occurred between village, town, and city there and elsewhere. At some Beas settlements, for example, Vainiwal discussed earlier, there are substantial quantities of finished products that may actually be objects produced by specialists at Harappa. The rich agricultural and pastoral potential of the Beas settlements provided Harappa with an essential ecological niche from which to provision the city. Other aspects of the evidence argue for a degree of autonomy within rural regions in the presence of a mix of local materials with others from distant settlements in Baluchistan and elsewhere. Thus in understanding the dynamics behind the expansion of settlements into new territories, it is important to emphasize that the civilization was not a monolithic entity and that the linkages to the centers on the Indus plain were variable.

Viewed in more broad geographical terms, there is the same variability in the vast geographical area encompassed by the civilization and by those settlements on its extreme margins at *gateway towns*, expanding as they did with the founding of new towns and the influx of ideas and materials present in regions occupied in the previous periods. Relations with these outlying regions were by no means homogeneous with respect to the degree to which Indus centers held sway over outlying settlements. At its greatest geographical extreme are several known villages, where full-blown settlements were established as trading stations at Shortugai, Sutkagen-dor, and Sotka-koh, possibly Lothal. Speaking specifically of Lothal but very likely applicable elsewhere, Possehl notes a symbiosis between its residents and local hunter-gatherers. Evidence for this interaction is in the form of typologically similar patterns in tool types at the small site of Langhnaj (Possehl 2002:71) and physical characteristics derived from the examination of human skeletal remains that link local hunter-gatherers to the Lothal population (Kennedy et al. 1984; Possehl 2002:72). Possehl makes a convincing argument that hunter-gatherer populations likely provided Lothal with important raw materials, "agate, carnelian, rock crystal, steatite, shell, ivory, as well as wood, such as teak" (Possehl 2002: 73), a method of procurement that may have been common in other parts of the Indus.

There is a strong Indus presence at Naushahro, but settlement on the Kachi Plain had a long history (see Chapter 3), well before the expansion of the Indus civilization. It most likely possessed a degree of autonomy based upon preexisting leadership. Another variation on a similar theme is the town of Rehman Dheri, already in existence in the Pre-urban period. Even though contact with the Indus is present, this settlement remained relatively independent of the larger civilization. By far, the most dramatic and somewhat unprecedented evidence is for the Kulli in the region of Las Bela. Although the Kulli might simply reflect a manifestation of the Indus culture overlain with other local elements (Possehl 2003) rather than a separate culture as I have suggested, it clearly represented a pocket of resistance to the Indus civilization.

These complexities in defining the margins of the civilization and its dialogs with neighboring groups suggest that, even though it was an expansive state, some boundary cultures were not incorporated into the civilization and remained wedged between its heartland and extended territory. This is consistent with an image of the Indus as a state that engaged in negotiations and established affiliations as a practical model of exchange.

Taken together, the preceding discussion suggests that embedded within the visible remnants of Indus urbanism, there were infrastructural elements within its centers and others that stretched beyond its famous cities. In its cities, a growing population was brought together into an urban way of life, in which a key element was the organization of flows of resources between city and countryside and the ever-widening territory encompassed by the civilization.

In the chapters that follow, I investigate these infrastructural elements in more detail, first by focusing on the agropastoral and craft-producing economy and the interregional distribution of resources in Chapters 6 and 7 and on foreign trade in Chapter 8.

6   Agropastoral and Craft-Producing Economies I – Intensification and Specialization

In the preceding chapters, I discussed the development of urbanism on the Indus and Ghaggar-Hakra Plains and in neighboring regions. These developments ushered in new ways of life, transforming the Harappan political economy. As cities grew at Mohenjo-daro, Dholavira, Harappa, Ganweriwala, and Rakhigarhi, regional networks were established and rural villages and towns developed over a broad geographical area.

Parallel to this expansion, there were significant changes in agriculture, pastoralism, and craft technologies. Like most other early states throughout the ancient world, people's livelihoods were based upon an agropastoral and craft-producing economy, in which farming (selection, nurturing, and maintenance of plants), pastoralism (breeding, raising and managing domesticated animals), foraging (hunting and foraging of wild plants and animals), and crafting technologies were transformed into highly productive activities. As a result, food yields were increased and a widened variety of agricultural and animal products provided a sufficient surplus to provision individuals engaged in nonagrarian, craft-producing activities.

These changes were the result of a complex interplay of environmental factors and human choices. To understand these complexities and their impact on politics, society, and the economy, this chapter focuses on *intensification, diversification,* and *specialization* of the Indus's agropastoral and craft-producing economy. *Intensification* in the context of farming and pastoralism refers to the development of ways and means to increase yields or output from a unit of land; it also applies to craft production and technological activities involving the production of new products and increased numbers of producers. *Diversification* refers to the development of increased numbers and diversity of food and craft products. The closely aligned concept of specialization relates to movement toward allocation of resources to specific but diverse activities and the acquisition of specialized skills necessary to undertake the tasks involved. *Specialization* in agropastoral and craft-producing economies involves increases in divisions of labor and the exchange

145

of products because no single producer is likely to maintain self-sufficiency (Morrison 1994:144). (See Box 6.1.) In this chapter, I concentrate on intensification and specialization. In Chapters 7 and 8, my focus is on diversification and the organization of production, distribution, and exchange of products. These aspects of the Urban period – intensification, specialization, diversification, and the organization of production, distribution, and exchange – comprise the infrastructure that fueled the Indus social and political economy.

The Harappan economy was dependent upon a variety of technologies. Although the use of plows drawn by cattle was a significant innovation, many tasks were performed manually. Sickles for harvesting were made of small stone blades bonded to a handle, although some may have been made of metal. Tasks such as planting and milking were done by hand without the aid of specialized tools. Craft producers continued to rely on a limited range of raw materials in the production of utilitarian and nonutilitarian objects.

As we have seen in Chapter 5, farmers and pastoralists at rural settlements provisioned cities at least in part. Additionally, based on the presence of animal bones and plant remains, we can assume there were substantial numbers of individuals engaged in farming and pastoralism living in the urban centers. The physical separations we see in many places today in which farmers live in remote farmsteads while craft producers are engaged in "industrial" settings were rare on the Harappan landscape. Although it may seem strange to think of farmers, animals, and craft producers living all together, especially in fairly large cities, these activities most likely coexisted comfortably in villages, towns, and cities. If we were able to turn back time and walk through an Indus settlement, we likely would find people engaged in a variety of agriculture, pastoral or craft-related tasks, encounter an occasional sheep or goat, or pass a zebu tethered to a stake or hitched to a cart in an alleyway, all in the company of a metal worker producing tools. If we entered the courtyard of one of the homes, we might find someone milking a water buffalo. Nearby, another individual might be weaving or making a clay pot.

If all these changes were indeed the case, in what ways *was* the agropastoral and craft-producing economy of the Indus civilization intensified and specialized? How was production organized? And what does this information tell us about its political economy? In this chapter, I address each of these questions, beginning with a discussion of the intensification and specialization of craft production, followed by its farming practices and pastoralism.

Box 6.1 Agropastoral and Craft-Producing Economies – Intensification, Specialization, Diversification, and the Organization, of Production, Distribution, and Exchange

One way in which to understand the economic and social impact of agropastoral and craft-producing economies is to consider four interrelated factors: intensification and specialization (Kaiser and Voytek 1983, Morrison 1994), diversification and the organization of production, distribution, and exchange. *Intensification* refers to increases in output, for example in outlays of resources, per unit of labor in the case of craft production or land when considering agriculture and animal husbandry. It may, for example, result in increased agricultural yields per unit of land; the exploitation of new species or multiple products from a previously known species; and increases in the numbers of craft producers and the production of new products. *Diversification*, with respect to crafts, refers to the movement towards and making choices about crafts and styles in which there is an increase in the number of different craft products being produced and consumed. Similarly, in agriculture and animal husbandry, it relates to an increase in the number of different foods produced or the different uses to which resources are assigned (Dorsey 1999). Each of these factors may result in the proliferation of specialists engaged in the production of plant, animal, and craft products. *Specialization* refers to the process of allocating resources and labor to these specialized tasks. In the case of agriculture, it includes specialized farming strategies, such as irrigation agriculture in addition to dry farming; for animal husbandry, it can include the diversification of breeding and herding practices in order to develop specialized characteristics such as enhanced wool-bearing sheep. The specific knowledge and skill involved in developing agrarian economies may result in or be the result of divisions of labor among producers. Similarly, artisans involved in craft production may possess high levels of skill and technical knowledge not accessible to other members of the community. Specialists often produce products that are standardized, the result of repetitive ways of handling materials that maximize output and minimize production and labor costs (Sinopoli 2003). Farmers, pastoralists, and craft specialists can be part-time or full-time and be independent (produce for themselves) or attached (produce for a client). There is no one-to-one correlation as to whether any of the

Box 6.1 (*Cont.*)

preceding will take place within household or nonhousehold contexts. *The organization of production, distribution, and exchange* refers to the economic and social relationships surrounding agriculture, animal husbandry, and craft production; for example, whether producers are producing for themselves in the context of a household engaging in community or centralized production and exchange or pursuing some other more complex arrangements.

Craft Production

The production of crafts made a major contribution to the agropastoral and craft-producing economy and contributed to the overall expansion of production diversity. Some skilled artisans developed specialized technical knowledge, producing high-quality and diverse goods for exchange while others produced and consumed their own products. In the following, I begin with a general discussion of the intensification and specialization of Harappan craft production. Subsequently, I discuss three crafts – ceramics, stoneware bangles, and seals – in greater detail as illustrations of intensification and specialization.

Craft Production and Intensification

Documentation of crafts has been a topic of long-standing interest in Harappan studies. Researchers have painstakingly reconstructed each of the steps artisans have taken in producing an object. These studies indicate that the Harappans approached crafts with very strong perceptions about production technologies, many of which were holdovers from techniques developed by artisans at Mehrgarh and discussed in Chapter 3. The intensification of craft production is demonstrated in the elaboration of technique and style of those previously known technologies, such as ceramic production, and in the creation of entirely new products, such as the seals and stoneware bangles discussed later. These innovations involved skilled personnel who employed a technical virtuosity that rivaled many other craft producers in the ancient world.

Archaeological reconstructions of crafts can be thought of as "mini-excavations" in which archaeologists reconstruct each step taken by an artisan in producing an object. Such studies typically are done by examining the object macroscopically and microscopically, a method I have used in my pottery studies at Harappa. Macroscopic characteristics include features such as form and shape. Microscopic characteristics consist of minerals present in clays and temperatures at which pottery is fired. These features provide evidence with which to evaluate the durability, porosity, and overall strength of the end product. Other invisible aspects of production can be learned through sourcing techniques, such as neutron activation analysis, a technique that provides a chemical fingerprint of the clays, which can be compared to "fingerprints" from known clay sources in order to determine where potters procured their clays.

The reconstruction process effectively turns the pots "inside out," as we learn each of the steps from clay procurement, preparation of clays, forming vessels, recipes for paints applied, and firing procedures. While these factors can be used to assess the durability of the final product and how it might have functioned, the reproduced production steps reveal the creative process engaged in by the potter, such as scheduling, planning, control, and vision involved in producing the object.

Most crafts involved working with stone, metal, shell, fiber, and clay. With the exception of textiles, artisans approached them using either reductive or pyrotechnological techniques. Reductive technologies involved the chipping and reshaping of an object. Stone and shell are some examples of materials on which this technique was employed. Pyrotechnological techniques involved subjecting a raw material to heat. Clay and ores are typically worked in this manner. The Harappans also applied pyrotechnological meathods to stone – crushing, grinding, and firing the prepared "pastes" in kilns. H.M.L. Miller refers to the creation of new materials "through pyrotechnology or chemical processes" as "transformative crafts" (2007:44).

This "technological style" was consistently employed by Indus artisans. Studies of pottery production reveal an emphasis on the restructuring of materials and juxtaposing shapes, textures, and colors (Wright 1993). Many forms were built in segments that required fitting components together, a technique that imposed new structure on the natural clays and pushed them beyond their natural workability range. Other forms required a substantial vision and experimentation with known techniques. The same form was produced with unmodified surfaces, yet others had surfaces into which deep permanent marks were carved to which contrasting slips were applied (see details below). These techniques drew attention to the transformations achieved by the potter, through use of new color effects by controlling atmosphere and temperatures in kilns.

Although it could be argued that the transformations described are always the case when working with clay, a brief look at other Indus crafts reveals the same impulse to break down, re-create, and transform certain other materials. A good example of this manner of working is in the

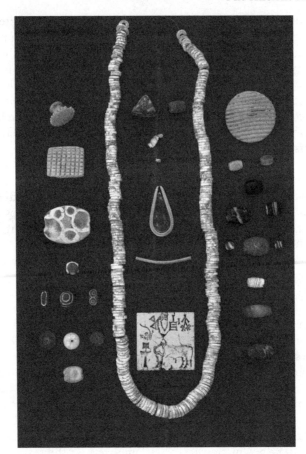

Figure 6.1. Harappan ornaments produced from different materials and production technologies. Photograph by the Harappa Archaeological Research Project © HARP.

modification of steatite (talc) to produce disk-shaped beads. Disk beads are small, round, paper-thin ornaments. They are produced from steatite or talc and are first known from Mehrgarh in 5000 B.C. These early beads were produced using a reductive technique that involved cutting them from rod-like blanks; however, sometime around 4500–3800 B.C., the artisans at Mehrgarh began to glaze the disk beads with a coating of finely ground sand, lime, and clay to which ash or a substance with a mineral colorant was added, and firing them to about 1,000 degrees centigrade (Bouquillon and Barthelemy de Saizieu 1995). In a later stage during the manufacturing history of disk bead production in the Urban period, extraordinarily thin (0.8–1.0 millimeter with 0.4 millimeter. inner holes) microdisk beads were perhaps produced from a "paste"

RAW MATERIAL ACQUISITION

MINE

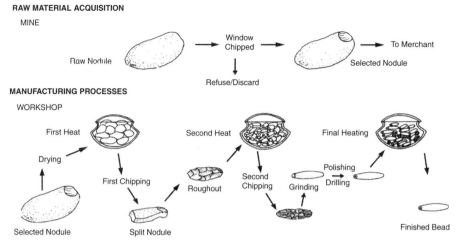

MANUFACTURING PROCESSES

WORKSHOP

Figure 6.2. Reconstruction of Carnelian bead production. Redrawn from Kenoyer (1998).

(Vidale 2000:64). It took three hundred very fine tiny beads such as the necklace at the center of Figure 6.1, produced in this way to create one necklace (H.M.L. Miller 1997; Vidale 2000).

During the Urban period, the Harappans combined reductive and pyro-technological techniques in other inventive ways. The production sequence for carnelian beads has been reconstructed from microscopic examination of archaeological examples and observation of modern artisans in India who produce similar beads. The sequence of production has been recon-structed in Figure 6.2 (Kenoyer 1991, 1998). The production techniques demonstrate the extensive technical knowledge and skill required to pro-duce the beads. Production begins with chipping the stone to form the desired shape along with intermittent heating to make the raw material easier to modify. The final steps involve polishing, drilling, and reheating the completed beads in a reducing atmosphere, a procedure that draws iron oxide from the stone thereby deepening the red of its original color.

Harappans fashioned many objects using the various techniques described either alone or in combination. They also created different ver-sions of a single object. Figure 6.3 shows a collection of beads made from a number of different raw materials and various manufacturing techniques. This wide array of products suggests that objects were produced for a range of consumers (Vidale 2000; Vidale and Miller 2000; Kenoyer 1992).

This style of production was not, of course, employed with all crafts. The study of weaving techniques is underdeveloped because of poor preservation and the small number of surviving cloth remains. Weavers worked with animal fibers and plants including cotton, linen, and jute

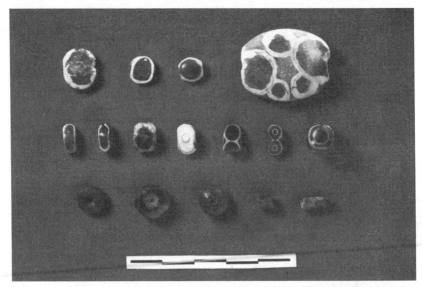

Figure 6.3. Carnelian and faience beads from Harappa. Photograph
by the Harappa Archaeological Research Project © HARP.

producing basketry, cloth, and other woven items. In distinction to the
"hard" remains of pottery and stone objects, textiles are "soft" and do
not preserve under the hot and humid environmental conditions of
the Indus. Figure 6.4 is an example of the impression on a clay pot of a
cloth woven of jute in a simple weave, in which the structure of the cloth
survived the kiln firing (Wright et al. in prep). It is unusual for the structure of a fiber and weave to be preserved in this manner. One possibility,
based on replicative experiments (H. Beaubien personal communication) is that cloth wetted in clay wash was placed on the ceramic to hold
its shape. Before the pot was fired, clay crept into the spaces between the
fibers, leaving an impression of the weave and fiber.

Craft Production and Specialization – Resource Availability and Selection, Technical Skills, and Specialized Production

Among the factors to consider in discussions of specialization are the
natural resources used in manufacture and the level of skill and technical
knowledge required to produce objects from a given raw material.

In the following section, I discuss three technologies to illustrate the
relationship among resource availability, technical skill, and specialization. They include ceramics, stoneware bangles, and seal production. In

Figure 6.4. Pseudomorph of jute cloth from Harappa. © R. P. Wright.

each example, I outline the very specific technical knowledge and artisan skills required to produce the objects discussed, including the complexity of each craft, with respect to processing and selection of materials.

Ceramic Production

Producing ceramics was one of the most basic and important utilitarian crafts. Ceramics served a variety of functions that included containers for liquid and dry food and storage and transport of products over long distances. Among the over 100 different varieties of pots known from Harappan contexts, the majority were used for ordinary pursuits, for cooking, serving, eating, and bathing. Others were used for more specialized tasks, such as transport (Figure 6.5). Jars of this type have been discovered as distant as the Arabian Peninsula in Oman and the United Arab Emirates. (See Figure 8.1 for locations.) Chemical analyses have shown that transport jars like these were produced in the Indus, probably at both Mohenjo-daro and Harappa (Mery 2000).

Natural clays were readily available in most regions of the civilization. As I noted earlier, potters demonstrated significant skill by pushing the natural clays beyond their normal workability range. They also devised a variety of techniques to decorate their pottery in colorful and exotic

Figure 6.5. Black slipped storage jar from Harappa with Indus inscription near rim. Photograph by the Harappa Archaeological Research Project © HARP.

ways by employing a limited range of pigments, some of which may have been procured from some distance, while others were locally available in waterborne sediments.

Kilns were needed to fire the ceramics and several different kiln types have been discovered. They include (Figure 6.6) open air, pit, single-chamber (not shown), and double-chambered up-draft kilns. Open air kilns can be dug into a sloping surface such as one discovered at Nausharo dated between 2500 and 2400 B.C. to encourage a strong draft and more even firing. Pit kilns, examples of which were found at Harappa, involved digging a shallow pit into a flat surface with openings at one

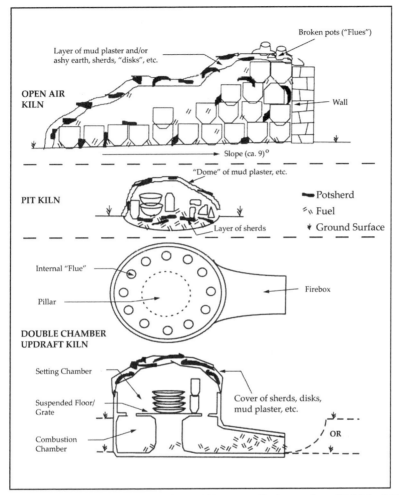

Figure 6.6. Three different kiln types. Redrawn from H.M.L. Miller (2007).

end either to feed in fuel or to facilitate the escape of air. Generally, this type is smaller and has lower vessel capacity than the open kilns. The pit kiln at Harappa contained "cakes, lumps, and stones ... [that would absorb] ... heat early in the firing sequence, then radiate heat as the fuel was consumed" (H.M.L. Miller 1997:52).

It was most likely used for firing small vessels or figurines (Dales and Kenoyer 1992:60). Double-chambered kilns have been discovered throughout the Indus civilization.[1] At Harappa, a kiln located on the northwest corner of Mound E (Figure 6.7) is a typical two-chambered

Figure 6.7. Double-chambered kiln from Mound E at Harappa.
Photograph by the Harappa Archaeological Research Project © HARP.

kiln. Double-chambered kilns contain a lower chamber for fuel and an
upper chamber on which to place the pots. They are built with central
pillars that support the floor of the setting chamber, thereby separating
it from the fuel chamber. With double-chambered kilns, potters are able
to control temperatures and atmospheric conditions to a greater degree
than with any of the other types described since the separation of the fuel
chamber from the setting area makes it possible to regulate heat and air
intake. In a double-chambered kiln I excavated near Mehrgarh at Lal
Shah, a regulating hole connected the chamber with the exterior of the
kiln, making it possible for the potter to view conditions in the interior of
the chamber to control the circulation of heat.

The pottery types associated with the kiln on Mound E at Harappa
demonstrate a high level of skill. The pots produced in the kiln were
restricted to 20 of the 100 or more types discovered in the Urban period.
All demonstrate the transformative technological style discussed above.
Some were simple wheel-made vessels. Cylindrical forms (shown on
Figure 9.12) were raised from a single lump of clay (referred to as the
"hump"). By establishing a rhythm through a repetition of movements,
potters produced a standardized cylindrical shape in different sizes.
Their surfaces are plain and unmodified, although traces of the pot-
ter's hand are visible in the presence of thumb and other finger marks.
Other pots were produced in several stages. The examples in Figure 6.8

Figure 6.8. Harappan pottery showing different textures and designs applied to a single form. © R. P. Wright.

show a single form on which potters created innovative methods of taking the single shape to which different surface textures were applied. Traces of the potter's hand are visible in the scraped surface of diagonal lines that are etched after covering with a cream slip or wash. This transformation of the clay surface affects a clay body that is raised in areas and slipped in around the depressions. The result is a surface that is enhanced by color and textural contrasts on which the upper surfaces of the pot are a velvety rose paste and at their midsections, a manipulated surface that highlights the deep permanent marks made in the clay. Other pots like the large black jar (Figure 6.5) used for transport required great skill and were produced in sections. A mold was used to form the base for the lower part of the jar. After drying in air, this base was placed on a potter's wheel, and a middle section was added. Finally an upper section, also produced on the wheel, was added. The joining of the two sections occurred at just the right moment when the drying clays were still wet and pliable but sufficiently dry to be stable (Wright 1991). The ability to produce the pot in sections shows a high level of skill and knowledge of the workability of the clays used. All the joins needed to be smoothed over, a process that was very carefully attended to on the exterior, less so on the interior, leaving the telltale marks of the joins. After drying, the pots were coated both on their interiors and exteriors with a thick application of fine clay mixed with iron oxide pigment to produce the black exterior and red interior color of the pots based on the manipulation of atmospheric conditions in the kiln.

In addition to possessing a high level of skill, potters demonstrated their expertise in other ways. Among the debris associated with the kiln, there were devices for drying pots and tools for finishing them, including tools made of bone and stone for trimming pots, molds for forming bases, and irregular terracotta slabs used as kiln furniture to separate the pots in the kiln or as supports while pots were drying before firing. Therefore, we can assume that the entire production sequence was carried out and known to the potters on Mound E at Harappa. The output and scale of workshop production can only be estimated, since the excavations around the kiln are not complete. In any event, its capacity was well beyond what is required by a single family.

Stoneware Bangle Production

In addition to using clays for vessels, the Harappans produced many body ornaments from clays but arm bangles were the most ubiquitous. Beads, some of which are illustrated in Figure 6.1, and bangles were made from a variety of materials that required different levels of technical expertise. Simple, relatively low-fired terracotta bangles were produced by forming narrow strips of clay and firing them. Others made from metal and shell were the result of more complex processes. Stoneware bangles were the most technically sophisticated and limited in number.[2] These stoneware bangles were restricted in access to the major cities of Mohenjodaro and Harappa, although three have been found at the site of Balakot (Franke-Vogt 1989; Vidale 2000).

Stoneware bangle production was truly innovative because it took advantage of previously known techniques such as selecting and processing specially refined clays and reduction firing (Wright 1985). With minimal changes, potters altered conditions in kilns and created an entirely new product. The secrets of its production were lost until archaeologists reconstructed it. Perhaps because of the specialized technology involved in their manufacture, which most likely was scrupulously guarded, we assume the stoneware bangles were among the Harappans most highly valued possessions. Unlike most other bangles produced from different raw materials, many of these bore personal inscriptions, etched onto their exteriors before and/or after firing (Vidale 2000:90).

Stoneware bangles were produced from highly refined clays under strictly controlled temperatures and atmospheric conditions (Vidale 1990:

2000). The same impulse to break down, recreate, and transform materials was achieved through a complex process in which the clay was highly refined through levigation (Blackman and Vidale 1992). The refined clays were shaped into bangles by throwing hollow clay cylinders on a potter's wheel and subsequently grooving or cutting them from the cylinder. The bangles were hardened in air, returned to the wheel where they were refined with tools and then fired in cylindrical pottery containers called saggars, which were stacked and encased in a large jar (Figure 6.9). Firing in airtight sealed saggars provided optimal control of atmospheric conditions and attainment of higher temperatures. The final product reveals a hard, uniformly textured surface that when broken has a glasslike fracture.

The bangles were produced in two colors. The black-gray bangles were fired in a reducing atmosphere in the sealed containers (saggars). These strong reducing conditions lowered the melting temperature, sintering

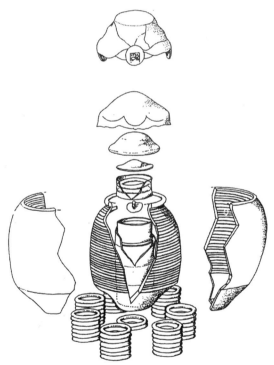

Figure 6.9. Reconstruction of firing system of stoneware bangles, including upper cap and sealing, coatings of inner vessel and outer vessel. Redrawn from M.A. Halim and M. Vidale (1984).

the clay and giving the bangles a shiny metallic luster (Vidale 2000:90). In order to create red products, the potters used different clay compositions, fired the red bangles at lower temperatures, or altered atmospheric conditions by opening the saggars.

A stoneware workshop at Mohenjo-daro was discovered in an abandoned residential area of the city that had been reoccupied by stoneware artisans. There are post holes (wood stains in the soil), indicating that the artisans erected wooden structures within the walled areas of an abandoned residential compound, thereby enclosing the workshop space (Vidale 1990). Within the workshop's walls were found storerooms, collapsed brick walls of kilns and dump heaps. The dump heaps included pieces of kiln linings, vitrified ash, overfired bricks, and the saggars in which the bangles were fired. The kilns were large and rectangular in shape and contained a suspended "grid" with holes (Vidale 2000:92). The artisans reused bricks and preexisting walls to make their kiln. Since the kilns were not excavated, it is unclear whether the stoneware bangle kiln fits with any of the kiln types illustrated in Figure 6.6.

Seal Production

Seals are well-known objects throughout the Indus and contemporary cultures in the Near East in southern Mesopotamia and at Iranian sites. They are "hallmark artifacts" of these ancient civilizations (Pittman 2001b:231).

Indus seals are broadly distributed at both large and small Harappan settlements (Box 6.2). Although they may have been used as amulets or talisman, in the Harappan context, they clearly functioned as a kind of "signature" or marker of identification. When impressed on a pliable surface such as clay, an image was preserved. This image is referred to as a sealing (for an example of a sealing and seal types, Figure 6.10).

Seal production was widespread throughout the Indus Valley, since there are unfinished seals and blanks are recovered at large and small sites. In this discussion, I focus on the square, engraved seals and highlight aspects of their production and style that demonstrate the specialized skills and technical knowledge required to produce them.

The manufacturing techniques of Indus seals are fairly uniform and involved a combination of reductive and pyrotechnological techniques. The seals were cut using copper or special stone tools and carved with "thin-pointed copper-bronze chisels" (Vidale 2000:62). The whitish outer surface (referred to as "glazed") is thought to be the result of soaking the prepared seals in a chemical solution and subjecting them to heat, possibly in kilns and perhaps as high as 1,000 degrees centigrade. This

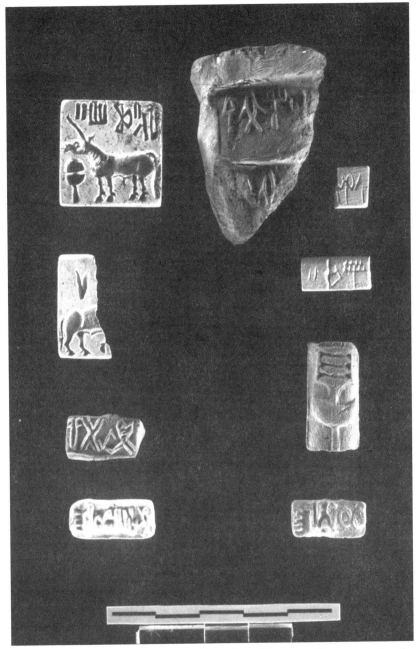

Figure 6.10. Seals and sealings from Harappa. Photograph by the Harappa Archaeological Research Project © HARP.

Box 6.2 Seals and Sealing Devices

There are several different inscribed objects that fall into the category of seals and sealing devices. Rissman's research on seal motifs is based exclusively on studies of the square seals, the predominant seal type. At Mohenjo-daro, 75% of the 1,501 seals discovered there until 1938 were square and depicted a single animal or hybrid creature. Of the animals depicted at Mohenjo-daro, the unicorn is the most frequent, followed by short-horn bulls, zebu, and elephant. The same frequencies are found when all known Indus stamp seals are considered (Franke-Vogt 1992:103). There is no consensus as to whether the single horn depicted on the unicorn was a stylistic convention based on the animal's profile stance or a mythical animal. The discovery of a terracotta figurine with a single horn (Kenoyer 1998) lends support to the latter, though such figurines are rare. Square seals at Mohenjo-daro were found in both the upper and lower parts of the city, though more have been discovered in the lower than the upper town. At the deepest levels at Mohenjo-daro, the iconography, writing and style were uniform, but there were changes over time that included a decrease in variability that became "more standardized in the upper levels" (Franke-Vogt 1992:108).

In distinction to the engraved square seals, faience and terracotta tablets are produced in high relief and have from two to four sides. Indus faience is produced from a heat-treated steatite or talc-based material that was ground and mixed with a substance (a flux) that lowered the material's melting point and caused fusion upon heating. By exerting pressure, the "paste" could be shaped into a form by hand or pressed into a mold (Miller 1999a:3) and hardened. Imagery on the faience consists of pictorial representations and/or script. Terracotta tablets were produced by impressing a pliable clay into molds and firing them to a hardened state. Figure 10.5 discovered at Harappa is an example of a pictorial image in which a narrative theme is depicted. Seals identical to this image were found in other locations at Harappa, indicating that the same master mold was used several times. Finally, a different type of tablet was produced from steatite and incised with a sequence of signs on "blocks of steatite which were subsequently fired" (Meadow and Kenoyer 2000:333).

A major question with respect to the seals and tablets is how they functioned. Many of the tablets from Harappa were found associated

Box 6.2 (*Cont.*)

with perimeter walls along with other debris. Why the tablets were discarded in this manner is a puzzle. Possibly their discard indicates a kind of "'death'" of the seal (Meadow and Kenoyer 2000:336), the end of their utility, or a reflection on the owner of the tablet, their "change of status, or death, or the passing of an amount of time during which the seal was considered current" (Meadow and Kenoyer 2000:336). The lives of seals or their owners, however, most likely differed depending upon the type of seal.

The engraved square seals have a broad distribution at Indus sites and are present in the greatest number (Frenez and Tosi 2005) and from the earliest phases of urban development (ca. 2500 B.C.) to its latest. Although seals that traveled great distances are limited, the presence of Indus seals or motifs associated with them extends as far afield as Mesopotamia where sealings, lumps, or "tags" from applying a seal to a pliable material also have been found. At the site of Umma, for example, a clay lump with an impression from an intaglio seal depicting a unicorn and Indus script, is one such instance (Parpola 1994:13, figure 7.16). Other seal impressions or seals with Indus motifs are found at sites near the Mesopotamian coast (at Ur, Lagash) and inland (at Tell Asmar), accessible on coastal and overland routes. Indus-type seals (some with unconvincing Indus script) have also been found in western Iran at proto-Elamite sites, in Central Asia, and in the coastal Arabian Peninsula. The largest number of sealings impressed with a stamp seal or tablet at an Indus site was discovered at the site of Lothal. Of the total approximately 130 to 140 sealings known in the Indus, 93 have been found at Lothal (Frenez and Tosi 2005), a possible trading port located in Gujarat (see Figure 1.2 for location). Based on their shapes, they were used for various locking or securing devices, either for doors or storage spaces, while some appear to have been affixed to movable structures like crates or architectural elements (Frenez and Tosi 2005). As Dennys Frenez and Maurizio Tosi have noted, the use of seals and sealings at Lothal is conceptually related to a "Transcultural Administrative Sealing System," used in storage and safe-keeping of objects and known since the sixth to fifth millennia B.C. throughout the Middle East and widespread among cultures contemporary with the Indus civilization. I discuss the imagery on the square intaglio seals and the faience and terracotta tablets in greater detail in Chapter 10 and their relationship to the widespread sealing system in the third millennium B.C.

technique hardened the stone, making the seal more durable (Kenoyer 1998:73).

As discussed in Chapter 1, engravings on the square seals were of a fairly standard composition in which an animal is represented at the midpoint of the seal. The most common animal depicted is referred to as a "unicorn," shown at the top left in Figure 6.10. The animal is shown with one horn and may either represent a mythical creature or an artistic convention in which two-horned animals are shown in profile (Franke-Vogt 1991b:182). Inscriptions were engraved in the top register of the seal, suggesting that seal carvers either were literate or worked in association with other individuals who were. A third image, referred to as a "standard" on many seals, was placed in the bottom corner of the seal. Looking again at Figure 6.10, the standard is a somewhat mysterious object consisting of two parts, an upper element that looks like a cage and a lower one, resembling a bowl. Some scholars believe this object has ritual significance.

Paul Rissman (1989) examined 601 seals from Harappa, Mohenjo-daro, Chanhu-daro, and Kalibangan as a pilot project for determining stylistic conventions and whether "schools" of producers could be identified. Rissman focused on the composition and iconography of the seals with depictions of unicorns, including such attributes as "the animal's face and horn, the rendering of the 'standard' that the animal faces, the detail of the ear, the deep relief at the hindquarters, the depiction of the junction of chest and front legs, and the modeling of the rump" (1989:159).

Rissman recorded various stylistic elements in detail. Here, I refer to just two of these – the treatment of the head and neck and the upper section of the standard. He found that with few exceptions the head and neck treatments of the unicorns fell into the three types illustrated in Figure 6.11. These included the "collared neck," a double line at the animal's neck that was sometimes hatched; a "hatched face," vertical hatching on the face and neck; and a "hatched neck," vertical hatching that extended the length of the neck. In a study of seals at Mohenjo-daro, Franke-Vogt (1992:107) also identified the collared neck and hatched neck among major clusters. When Rissman examined the upper section of the standard, he found similar restrictions in stylistic elements. One style, a "straight cage" was a vertical rectangle with straight or concave sides. A second style, "zig-zag cage" had a similar rectangular shape but was filled in with a zig-zag motif. A third type, the "rounded cage," was a rounded rectangle with a vertical/horizontal motif. Rissman used these results to conduct additional studies comparing seals from various sites and time periods. He was able to verify his observations based upon style frequencies utilizing statistical analyses (simple chi square tests).

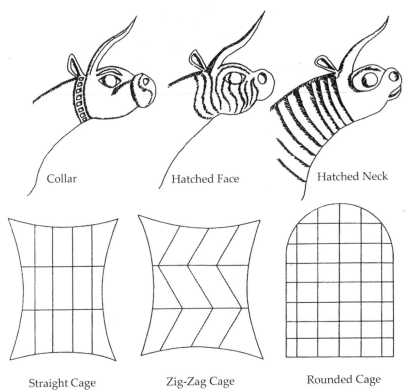

Figure 6.11. Head and cage patterns on Harappan seals. Redrawn from Rissman 1989.

The comparisons demonstrated that certain styles, the hatched face and zig-zag cage, occurred most frequently at Harappa, while the collared neck and straight cage were found at Mohenjo-daro or the nearby site of Chanhu-daro, but were absent at Kalibangan.

These variations and clusters of stylistic elements were sufficiently convincing that Rissman referred to them as "schools" of producers recognizable on a regional level. Based on these criteria, he concluded that several of the seals examined were nearly identical and may have been "either made by the same person, or by two people, one apparently copying the work of the other" (1989:159). In distinction, when he examined another small group, the engravers used different stylistic conventions suggestive of different producers. On the other hand, the fact that Rissman could identify a limited number of stylistic elements across a significant geographical area meant that styles of representation were "extra-local" in scope, either the result of "rigid bureaucratic guidelines" or more informal mechanisms such as visits among relatives or friends who labored in separate workshops" (Rissman 1989:168).

Intensification and Specialization of Craft Production

There was a broad versatility of technology and specialized knowledge employed in producing objects from different materials. Pyrotechnical techniques were widespread especially in view of the availability of raw clays and specialized skills developed by craft producers, ranging from the manufacture of simple pots to the stoneware bangles. As the crafts known in early periods were absorbed into the urban economy, Indus artisans, with great ingenuity, honed their technologies and created a remarkable assemblage of artifacts with which we now identify the civilization.

Agropastoral Production

Significant modifications in farming and animal husbandry kept pace with changes in craft production. Agropastoral production subsumes plant- and animal-using livelihoods. Agricultural and pastoral production can take many forms, ranging from a single individual or group engaged in both farming and animal keeping or a concentration of people and resources devoted to one of these activities. Pastoralism, especially, is practiced in many different ways to be discussed later. Both of these forms of production were important aspects of the Harappan economy. Some crafts, for example, were dependent on agricultural products, such as cotton, wool, and jute for raw materials in textile production. In fact, craft production was made possible in part by the surplus generated from agrarian pursuits.

Agriculture and Intensification

One measure of agricultural intensification is the increase in crop yields per unit of land. Included in this measure is the expansion of settlement to riverine environments. Although many Indus settlements, particularly villages and towns, continued to depend upon the dry farming methods employed at places like Merhgarh, as discussed in Chapter 3, the civilization's heartland was in the riverine environments of the Indus and the Ghaggar-Hakra Plains. The natural seasonal flooding cycles of these rivers provided fairly reliable water sources and conditions conducive to the intensification of agriculture.

Throughout the ancient world, riverine environments offered early agriculturalists an effective means of increasing agricultural yields in regions where dry farming is marginal because of inadequate rainfall, or even in places such as at Harappa, where good rainfall and fertile soils were favorable for a good harvest (Weber 2003). Even though the characteristics of river regimes differed in the Upper and Lower Indus and along the Ghaggar-Hakra, as discussed in Chapter 2, they all provided the necessary conditions for establishing extensive tracts of land for farming.

The most desirable areas for cultivation were within the reaches of the expansive floodplain. Although farmers may have used simple technologies to store water, regulate flows, or create embankments to hold water, thus far there is no evidence in the Upper Indus or the Ghaggar-Hakra for water-restraining devices. This absence of evidence may be due to severe modifications to the landscape from modern cultivation and natural forces, such as erosion, that have obliterated all signs of channeling. Although possible canal irrigation on the northern extension of the Ghaggar River had been proposed (Francfort 1986), subsequent studies of soil sediments (Courty 1995) were unable to confirm the presence of canals associated with occupations contemporaneous with the Indus civilization. Studies (Flam 1981, 1993a; Jorgenson et al. 1993) in the lower Indus have shown that agriculturalists living at settlements south of Mohenjo-daro depended on sheet flooding to water their crops and that their settlement locations were very much conditioned by the distances inundated by water. As a primary example, although Mohenjo-daro was 25 kilometers from the Sindhu Nadi (see Figure 2.2 and 2.3), the flow of water would have come dangerously close to the city during flood stages. What saved the town from being flooded was its location on the naturally raised landform that protected it.

Elsewhere, beyond the floodplains, there is some evidence for the construction of water-retaining devices of several types. As discussed in Chapter 2, damlike structures known as gabarbands, were built across valley floors to store water, trap runoff, and slow water speed. Although poorly dated, these structures have been observed in the hills of Baluchistan (Stein 1937; Dales 1962; Fairservis 1967; Flam 1998). A second type at the site of Dholavira (possibly Lothal) involved storage systems in an area of low rainfall, where several different types of water systems for the collection of runoff and rain were discovered. They include a complex of small dams or bunds constructed along a seasonal stream that runs near the site and an elaborate and technically sophisticated system of reservoirs. One reservoir, for example, was twenty-four meters wide and over five meters deep with a series of thirty-one steps leading from top to bottom (Bisht 1991). Conceivably, such systems existed elsewhere in the region.

The adoption of plant species included crops cultivated in both winter and summer. Most winter crops are known from the seventh millennium B.C.; summer crops, from the beginning of the third millennium B.C. Winter crops included cereal grasses (wheat, barley, oats), pulses (peas, chickpeas), and plants for fiber and oil (flax/linen). Summer cropping involved millets, mustard, grapes, dates, sesame, cotton, hemp, and jute. Winter crops (today locally referred to as *rabi*) thrive best during cooler months; their growing season would have been between November/December and April/May to avoid fields being flooded before harvest. Planting of the drought-resistant summer crops (*kharif*) would have taken place in May for an October harvest (Weber 2003). Many of the summer crops listed in Box 6.3 are perennials; in those cases, special plots of land would have been dedicated to their cultivation.

An obvious benefit to the Harappans was an increase in the variety of available food and fiber (Box 6.3). In some locations where both summer and winter crops could be grown, there was an overall increase in agricultural yields per unit of land, since land could be cultivated year-round.

Box 6.3 Some Archaeological Indicators of Agriculture

Plant and Fiber Remains	Potential Use/Benefit
Wheat and barley (W)	Bread, porridge, beer
Lentils, peas, chickpeas (W)	Raw, cooked, dried food
Linseed/flax (W)	Oils, fiber, cloth
Cotton (S)	Oils, fiber, cloth
Mustard (S)	Oils, cooked foods
Sesame (S)	Oils, cooked foods
Jujube fruit (W)	Raw food
Dates (S)	Raw and cooked food, wine
Grapes (S)	Raw and cooked food, wine
Millets (S)	Bread, porridge, fodder
Jute (S)	Fiber, cloth
Hemp (S)	Fiber, cloth
Rice (S)	Cooked food

Artifactual Evidence	Intensification and Specialization
Models of terracotta ploughs	Soil preparation
Models of terracotta carts	Traction, transport
Sickle blades	Harvesting
Figurines of women bearing carriers	Transport of produce and other products?
Terracotta figurines of woman grinding	Grain processing, food preparation
Mortar and pestle	Grain processing, food preparation
Ovens, hearths, cooking pots, charred plant remains	Cooking
Cotton (corrosion products on copper and silver)	Cloth
Jute (remnant products on terracotta)	Cloth

Note: W = winter/spring harvested; S = summer/fall harvested.

For example, the introduction of millet would have made it possible to utilize individual plots throughout the year. Finally, people took advantage of the rich ecological diversity of the region by developing settlements in previously unsettled regions (Madella and Fuller 2006).

Specialization of Cropping Patterns and Regional Diversity

The spread of a variety of domesticated plants throughout the Greater Indus region and the preferential selection of particular plant foods for cultivation provided important additions to available food sources and involved the specialization of cropping patterns.

The best documented example of the intensification and specialization of farming is from the sites of Harappa in the Punjab and Rojdi in Gujarat (Figure 1.2), where seed remains from excavated contexts have been studied (Weber 2003). At Harappa the predominant cropping pattern involved the cultivation of winter plants and to a lesser extent millets, both of which were present in the Pre-urban period. Cultivation of millets and other summer crops intensified during the Urban period, though even then wheat and barley continued to be dominant. The exploitation of drought resistant summer crops continued even as the civilization began to decline at Harappa (S. Weber personal communication), and the variety of taxa cultivated increased (for example, rice is present for the first time). There was regional variability, however, since wheat and barley continued to be major crops at Harappa. At Rojdi, the drought-resistant crops were dominant and supplemented by small quantities of barley. Other summer crops cultivated in the Urban period included mung beans, melons, dates, grapes, and cotton. These foods added diversity to the diet, and crops like dates and grapes could be used for beverages.

In other parts of the civilization and beyond, our evidence for agriculture is uneven and dependent upon limited excavation. The dominant pattern in Baluchistan was winter cropping. East of the Indus at Banawali (Figure 1.2), wheat and barley were present from the later third millennium (Madella and Fuller 2006:1297).[3] Increased precipitation in the region may have facilitated the spread of winter crops (Fuller 2003:377), while to the south at Rojdi (Weber 1991), small millets of South Asian origin were the main crop supplemented by small quantities of barley. Near the end of the Urban period and beginning of the Post-urban/Late Harappan, African millets appear at Rojdi. In western and central India, rice and summer pulses also were grown.

In regions south of Banawali and Rojdi in South India, farmers were dependent upon monsoon rains for farming but grew both summer and winter crops. In the South Indian Neolithic, a culture that was outside of the Indus tradition (Fuller 2003; Wright in press), small millets and pulses were indigenously domesticated. They were grown between May/June and October/November. With the introduction of wheat and barley to this region at the end of the third or the beginning of the second millennium (Fuller 2003:356), irrigation would have been necessary, although there is no on-the-ground evidence for that at this time. Other millets that played a minor role there may be of African origin.

The widespread distribution of diverse plants raises questions about the routes taken in their diffusion. With respect to wheat and barley, their presence at Balathal in the pre-urban (Early Harappan) suggests they spread from the Indus Plain, but whether the diffusion of wheat and barley to peninsular India was via Balathal or directly from the Indus settlements is unclear. The spread of millets is equally complex. Whether their origins were indigenous, African, or Chinese is not yet determined. In any event, this movement of crops indicates that people engaged in contact over fairly long distances and there was a sharing of technological innovations.

Pastoralism and Intensification

As discussed in Chapter 3, animals appeared in both wild and domesticated forms at Mehrgarh several thousand years before people settled on the alluvial plains. The intensification of pastoralism included the continued raising of sheep, goats, and zebu for meat and nonmeat products, such as dairy foods, traction, and wool. These secondary products are important examples of the specialization of animal husbandry (Box 6.4).

Box 6.4 Some Archaeological Indicators of Animal Exploitation in the Indus

Animal Bones	Potential Use
Sheep	Meat, dairy products, wool, skins, hair
Goats	Meat, dairy products, skins, hair
Zebu and other cattle	Meat, dairy products, skins, traction
Water buffalo	Meat, dairy products, skins, traction
Various wild species (boar, deer, etc.)	Meat, wool
Marine and riverine fish	Meat, oils
Camel ?[a]	Meat, traction, transport, skins
Horse ?[a]	Meat, traction, transport, skins
Donkey ?[a]	Meat, transport, skins
Various fish	River and marine catfish?

Artifactual evidence	Intensification and Specialization
Cut marks on bone	Butchering for meat, skins
Scarring on bone	Dairying and traction
Fish hooks, net weights, imagery	Fishing
Terracotta cart models	Animal transport, traction
Terracota yokes	Animal transport, traction
Terracotta plows	Animal traction
Plowed field and cart tracks	Animal traction
Imagery of tethered animals	Animal keeping
Hearths and ovens	Food preparation
Ceramic jars	Dairy processing and containers
Figurines, sculptures, masks, seals	Representations of domestic animals

[a] Late in sequence – ca. 1800 B.C.

Evidence exists for the use of selective breeding (a form of intensification) in the Indus. A good example of selective breeding for nonmeat uses is a study conducted by Richard Meadow in which he compared the skeletal remains at Nausharo and Harappa from urban deposits. As discussed in Chapter 3, a common pattern when sheep are domesticated is that they decrease in size, which is exactly what had occurred at Mehrgarh. Later in the Urban period, Meadow (1989a) noted other differences when he compared the sheep at Nausharo and Harappa. The sheep at Nausharo remained relatively small, while sheep bones found in deposits at Harappa were larger. He also noted that kill-off patterns for sheep indicated that more than half of the animals were older than 5 years. Though unconfirmed, the differences in kill-off patterns suggest that sheep may have been bred principally for wool. Along with cotton, a summer crop, these two fibers diversified the Harappan textile base.

Of additional interest is the use of cattle for dairying and traction. Bone assemblages show a wide range of ages at death and the presence of many young animals (Meadow 1998:15), a pattern suggestive of the use of cattle for secondary products exploitation. Other indications, discovered by Laura Miller (2003), are pathologies on cattle bones indicative of physical stresses associated with traction for transport and plowing fields. Finally, the use of animals for traction is suggested by a miniature clay yoke discovered at Nausharo (Meadow 1996:405). Models of bullock carts discussed in Chapter 4 and remnants of a plowed field found at Kalibangan in Pre-urban levels complement these studies of skeletal remains. As Raymond and Bridget Allchin (1997) have pointed out, the use of plow cultivation represented a major advance in agricultural practices and the potential for "great increases in crop production" (Allchin and Allchin 1997:169).

Water buffalo also were domesticated at least by the Urban period. Based on the study of faunal remains at the site of Dholavira, Meadow and Patel (2003) have identified both wild and domesticated forms. Meadow (1996:403) also cites a "small and also tightly curled horncore" at Balakot, in contrast to the long and sweeping horn cores of wild buffalo, as possible evidence for domesticated buffalo at that site. However, since it came from a young individual, it is unclear whether the animal was wild or domesticated (Patel and Meadow 2003).

Three other animals – the camel, horse, and donkey – are present possibly by approximately 2000 B.C., but they were not widespread until the second millennium B.C. (Meadow and Patel 2003:83). These animals likely were introduced into the region from Central Asia to the northwest. Their presence constituted a major transportational innovation, since camels, donkeys, and horses were able to travel long distances, bear heavy weights, and tolerate a variety of environmental conditions. Additionally, the horse and camel could be trained for riding, although there is no evidence that this had occurred. Throughout history, the coming of the horse brought about a major advantage in warfare because of the combination of speed and power not possessed by other animals.

Pastoralism – Specialization and Regional Diversity

The preceding examples of the adoption of new animals and the development of secondary products provide a basis with which to make inferences about specialization. While cattle were the most dominant species throughout the Indus civilization, there is regional variability with respect to the distribution and use of other animals. Goats, for example, were more at home in arid and semi-arid environments, such as existed at Nausharo and regions near Dholavira. In better-watered areas, such as the Punjab, sheep outnumbered goats. The situation for water buffalo is another case of regional difference. Water buffalo imagery is found on seals throughout the Indus, but whether domesticated forms spread to all regions remains unclear. As noted previously, the only evidence for them in the Urban period is from Dholavira (Meadow and Patel 2003:78). Today, most visitors to the Indus Plain are familiar with the sight of water buffalo wallowing in canals or other watered areas. Far from a slothful activity, wallowing is essential for water buffalo survival because they must be watered-down daily. The series of reservoirs at Dholavira, discussed in Chapter 5, likely were used for this, as well as other purposes (Bisht 2000a, 2005; Patel 1997).

Many different forms of pastoralism could accommodate the keeping of domesticated animals in the Harappan context. The term "pastoralism" refers to the breeding and raising of animals. It involves what Richard Meadow has referred to as a "continuum of lifestyles" (Meadow 1996:401; Khasanov 1984) marked by degrees of mobility. *Nomadic pastoralists* live a "portable" life suited to the constant movement of animals but within a fixed range (Barfield 1989). They move about on a seasonal basis seeking pastureland for their animals. Along the way they may trade items they produce (milk products, meat, textiles, for example) with settled farmers in exchange for agricultural products. *Semisedentary pastoralists* have a home settlement, which may be in an agricultural community, where they remain part of the year; some members or the entire family leave for short periods. Movement typically occurs during dry periods or when available land is being used for agricultural purposes. Some members of a family will move their animals to areas of preferential grazing (Abdi 2003). *Sedentary pastoralists* remain in one location throughout the year and may engage both in farming and pastoralism. The modern small farm is a pattern common in many parts of the world today (Poyck 1962).

The full range of specialization types was present in the Harappan world. At cities like Harappa and Dholavira, a form of sedentary pastoralism is reflected by the large numbers of animal bones and cart tracks found in street deposits at Harappa, and the water storage tanks at Dholavira. Judging by the current evidence, it appears that animals were kept by urban dwellers to supply dairy foods, such as milk and yogurt. Settled pastoralists on the alluvial plains most likely took advantage of its varied landscape, seeking out well-watered areas for water buffalo. Sheep and goats could graze on marginal lands on the outskirts of agricultural lands and on stubble from harvested fields.

The pattern of semisedentary pastoralism, also referred to as transhumance, described at Mehrgarh in Chapter 3, continued in the Urban period. At Nausharo, for example, pastoralists moved seasonally between upland and lowland settlements to avoid harsh winters and hot summers when grazing areas were reduced.

On the Ghaggar-Hakra Plain, the distribution of small camp sites discovered by Mughal (1997), as discussed in Chapter 5, suggest a pattern of nomadic pastoralism. Nomadic pastoralists move beyond the limits of agricultural zones and typically return to the same location on a seasonal basis.

Elsewhere, hunting and gathering populations living in the interstices of the marginal areas of city-states and beyond, at places like Langhnaj in Gujarat (discussed in Chapter 5) engaged in symbiotic relationships with village and town dwellers (Possehl 2002; Morrison 2006).

Continued Use of Wild Plants and Animals – Foraging and Fishing

There are many different species of wild plants, animals, and forest products in the archaeological assemblages of the Indus world. These resources either were items traded with hunters and gatherers, nomadic populations, or permanently settled people. They include fish, fish oils, wool for cloth, feathers, ivory, skins, bone tools, and wood products. As Meadow and Patel (2003:75) have pointed out, crop growing would have been carried out in well-watered areas, leaving areas "open to other kinds of exploitation, including hunting, fishing, fowling, plant gathering, wood cutting and pastoralism."

The principal evidence for the continued use of wild plants is from wood used for furniture and fuel. Woods identified from archaeological

Figure 6.12. Forested area at Harappa (1994). Photograph by the Harappa Archaeological Research Project © HARP.

remains include tamarisk, acacia, and prosopis, species that grew locally in wooded or shrub areas (Figure 6.12). The tamarisk and acacia would have been present in gallery forests along watercourses, whereas the prosopis could grow in dry, open woodland some distance from watercourses (Tengberg and Thiebault 2003). In addition, wood was brought from great distances as is attested by a wooden coffin at Harappa that was made from elm and cedars brought from the Himalayan forest to the north and Indian rosewood from inner India (Tengberg and Thiebault 2003).

The presence of bones of wild species of animals and fish attests to the continued utilization of wild animal resources. Many of these animals may have been unwanted or dangerous intruders, like the tigers on Indus imagery (Figures 10.4 and 10.5), who roamed the agricultural fields, lands set aside for the grazing of domestic animals, and forested areas not under cultivation. Among the wild species depicted on Indus imagery are birds, rabbits, rhinoceros and elephants, peacocks and ducks, and many others.

The clearest evidence for continued dependence on wild resources is William Belcher's (2003) study of fish bones from Harappa and three village settlements at Nausharo, Balakot, and Allahadino. As discussed in previous chapters, Nausharo is near the site of Mehrgarh; Balakot is in Las Bela; and Allahadino, east of the Indus River delta (Belcher 2003). Fishing likely was a seasonal activity. Winter backwater areas would have provided optimal locations in which to procure catfish, the principal fish exploited at all sites and used for food and fish oils. In addition to fresh-water catfish, there is evidence at Harappa for a few specimens of marine catfish that was imported from coastal settlements. The distribution of catfish over such an extensive area is discussed in Chapter 7.

Specialization and Intensification of the Agropastoral and Craft-Producing Economy

Earlier in this chapter, I concentrated on bringing forward the changes in technologies that ushered in new ways of life during the Urban period. With respect to agriculture and pastoralism, the most visible changes were the dependence upon seasonal flows of water and specialization and diversification of animal and crop selection, including selective breeding of animals and a broad spectrum of crops. Viewed in broad terms, farm-ing, pastoralism, foraging, and fishing economies contributed to a level of productivity beyond subsistence needs of individual producers. As previously discussed, there was much diversity in these pursuits within settlements and on a regional basis. For craft production, techniques known in previous periods were put to use with specific new products involving significant technical knowledge and skill in their implementa-tion. In addition, the number and types of objects available increased.

With respect to food production, I have emphasized the dramatic changes that occurred sometime between 3200 and 2000 B.C. on the allu-vial plains. When we consider the Indus civilization as a whole, includ-ing urban settlements in riverine, coastal, and inland sites, and the range of cities, small villages, and towns, the intensification and specialization of production appear as an integrated process. A large measure of its suc-cess is based upon the exploitation of a diversity of ecological zones and resources. Based on the evidence we have, two complementary types of agriculture were practiced during a one-thousand-year period in the Harappan region, one in which crops were grown in winter and summer, although winter cropping predominated. With respect to animals, for the most part, those that were exploited in earlier periods continued to be the dominant species; the principal changes that occurred involved greater dependence upon domesticated species, innovations in selective breeding, and the exploitation of animals for their secondary products, such as dairy, traction, and wool.

Although significant fluctuations in climate no doubt influenced changes in agropastoral practices, in this chapter and Chapter 2, I have emphasized the importance of elements of human choice in implement-ing the changes adopted. At Harappa, for example, the adoption of new animal and plant species did not appear to be related to food stress but conscious choices motivated by a desire to broaden the agricultural base since none of the earlier species disappears. The continued effort at Harappa to diversify crops is interconnected to the changing needs within Harappan society and "an indicator of culture change ... [related] ... to issues dealing with storage, trade, and the centralization and control of the food supply" (Weber 2003:198). As Dorian Fuller has suggested in a different context, certain foods may have taken on "prestige associations." Since cuisine often functions as a "prestige technology," it may effectively increase social hierarchy and provide motivations for the adoption of new foodstuffs, including novel forms of preparation and new cultivars (Fuller 2003:377ff).

The diversification of crops and animals exploited also suggest that a large range of habitats were exploited. The founding of settlements along the Beas, discussed in Chapters 4 and 5, is a primary example of this type of intentional diversification and exploitation of habitats. They provide one instance of the changing nature of productive systems and potential social relations among producers and consumers.

By intensifying and specializing production, people increased the long-term survival of their communities. Resource specialization in agriculture and pastoralism increased availability and variability of food supplies, providing a hedge against risk of failure in an economy increasingly capable of withstanding fluctuations in productivity in any one resource. The interaction with hunting and gathering groups also added to the resource base. Additionally, specialist producers necessarily engage in social and economic networks with consumers and other producers, creating exchange systems that are inseparable from the social relationships that underlie them. In other ancient settings, the control of products and provisioning of food and objects were major factors in the development of a varied political economy, offering the potential to confer prestige, political influence, and symbolic material wealth (Helms 1993).

Craft technologies grew in pace with these changes. The wide variety of utilitarian and prestige products consumed and exchanged suggests that a significant segment of the population was likely engaged in craft activities. In either event, they indicate that broader social roles and positions existed along with a range of associations among individuals and communities. These changes have wide-ranging social and political implications with respect to internal social relations within Indus cities, towns, and villages and on a regional level. Taken together, the Harappan economy included both large-scale and smaller-scale production systems, a diversity of products, and a vibrant mix of professions.

The examples discussed in this chapter raise important questions about the ways in which the agropastoral and craft-producing economy was organized and the distribution and internal exchange systems of plant, animal, and craft products. What social changes underlie the processes of intensification and specialization and these important advances in the economy? Were Harappan specialists independent producers who controlled and distributed their own products or were these controlled by others? And is it possible to discern the exchange systems that had developed around the raw materials and finished products they produced? These are topics taken up in the two chapters that follow.

7 Agropastoral and Craft-Producing Economies II – Diversification, Organization of Production, and Distribution

The domestication of plants and animals, the development of secondary products, and important innovations in craft production discussed in Chapter 6 were central features in the process of Indus urbanization. The focus of this chapter is on the diversification and the organization of production, distribution, and exchange of the material objects that characterized this expanding economy.

In studies of early states, archaeologists work under the premise that the appearance of innovative manners of resource procurement, new technologies, technically more sophisticated crafts, and the expansion of interregional and long-distance trade and exchange signal important increases in social and economic complexity and bring about divisions of labor within a society. As sectors of specialization and social differentiation intensify, structural changes occur in which the organization of production, distribution, and exchange become increasingly complex as a result of the implementation of various mechanisms by individuals and groups as they attempt to control aspects of the agropastoral and craft-producing economy. In many discussions of early societies, it is assumed that *one of the ways* in which states and individuals gain their power is through the control of producers' labor by appropriating and controlling the distribution and exchange of their products. Indeed, studying production and exchange systems is very interesting because it can potentially bring to light arenas or opportunities for control.

Archaeologists continue to debate these issues and their significance in the development of the Indus civilization. They call on various types of evidence to fuel their discussions. In this chapter, I focus on the archaeological evidence for diversification and the organization of production, the internal distribution of raw materials and finished products, and the exchange networks that were critical to provisioning local markets. Equally significant is long-distance trade, discussed in Chapter 8.

As will be shown in the following discussion, there was a diversity of production organization within individual settlements and in networks of exchange that extended beyond local regions. Organization of the

179

agropastoral and craft-producing economy varied and included independent household, communal or kin group, and centralized production and exchange. A key factor in this process was the accessibility of raw materials and the degree of technological complexity and technical knowledge required to produce objects. With respect to farming and animal husbandry, the diversity of occupations increased along with the availability of new foods and labor-enhancing devices such as plows and traction animals.

Throughout the periods discussed in the preceding chapters that led up to urbanization and movement to the Indus and Ghaggar-Hakra Plains, people engaged in extensive networks of exchange, maintaining contacts over large areas. Whatever deficiencies may have existed within a given location, they took advantage of this ecological diversity and established strong interregional ties. This same pattern is evident during the Urban period but involved more extensive networks of exchange and a variety of production organization.

Diversification and the Organization of Production, Distribution, and Exchange

Archaeologists who investigate agropastoral and craft-producing economies are interested in how societies organize their diverse and expanding economies. Their research indicates that one way to understand this is to investigate whether people are producing for their own consumption or for others outside of their own agropastoral or craft-producing units. Additionally, are producers engaged in crafts and agrarian pursuits on a part-time or full-time basis? If part-time, are they engaged in both agriculture and craft production?

Of additional importance is the question of control. Studies of early urban societies and states have shown that accelerated changes in economies are the result of initiatives undertaken by social and political groups within the society. Under such conditions political leaders and other segments of the society seek to control labor and production in order to garner prestige and political influence.

There are many examples of early states in which leaders and other segments of the society controlled economic activities. In Mesopotamia, for example, where meticulous written records were kept by the state, large tracts of land and animal herds were owned by political leaders, religious institutions, and private individuals. On state lands, cultivation and animal care were maintained by workers either employed seasonally or permanently attached to state-run work groups (Adams 2006; Steinkeller 1987; Wright 1996). In both instances, workers were compensated from the state's agricultural and herding "industries."[1] Still, there also were independent farmers and pastoralists who maintained their own herds and land. As for craft producers, the same pattern of seasonal or permanent employment in state workshops occurred. Weavers, principally women, were employed full-time by the state; in contrast, potters were employed for short periods during the year, when their outputs were state controlled. At other times, these same potters worked independently and controlled the distribution of their products (Wright 1991).

Still, the archaeological evidence presents an altered picture of the degree to which craft producers were subject to state control in Mesopotamia and elsewhere. Stone and Zimansky (1992, 1994) and Postgate (1990) found that in Mesopotamia manufacturing was embedded in residential neighborhoods. The evidence reveals a pattern of state control and independent production and distribution of craft products. Similar conditions are known in other early states and ethnographic studies where state control was limited or totally lacking and social groups operated independently (Trigger 2003). In such instances, craft specialists played an important role in the economy in varied ways. For example, in the Vijayanagara Empire (A.D. 1350–1650) in south India, artisans were based in villages and cities and engaged in their craft in independent, household contexts as well as under more restricted control in temples. There is no evidence for "a high degree of centralized administrative involvement in or control of craft production" (Sinopoli 2003:302). There also is little evidence for high demand production based in large-scale workshops. Many Vijayanagara artisans controlled their conditions of employment and compensation and maintained high social standing. In South Asia today, the knowledge of craft technologies like the carnelian bead manufacture described in Chapter 6 is tightly guarded and handed down from generation to generation. Under such circumstances, artisans resist attempts to tamper with the intergenerational pattern of organization.

These examples raise important questions about the ways in which this diversified economy was organized in the Indus civilization and whether the great variability of products and task-related activities was matched by a complexity of production organization. Additionally, the forms these infrastructural aspects of the agropastoral and craft-producing activities took also come into question.

In the absence of decipherable written records, determining how production and distribution of products was organized in the Indus is necessarily dependent upon archaeological evidence. In Chapter 6, I discussed the technical knowledge and skills possessed by artisans and agropastoral producers. In this chapter, I examine the spatial contexts in which the evidence for production and distribution were discovered. This evidence is clearest for craft production. Consideration of the agropastoral economy will follow the discussion of crafts.

Diversified Crafts and the Organization of Craft Production

Box 7.1 outlines some factors archaeologists consider when determining the organization of Indus craft production. As the outline shows, these criteria include architectural features, scales of production, and the presence or absence of record-keeping devices – such as seals or seal impressions (Figure 6.10), Indus "tablets" (see Figure 7.1), and weights and measures – all possible indicators of the control of manufacturing. For example, based upon the absence of record-keeping devices, a recent study of spatial distributions of crafts at Harappa and selected evidence from other settlements concluded that there was "noevidence that these patterns are based on control of organization by non producer elites" (H. M. L. Miller 1999:527). On the other hand, the fact that some crafts were spatially segregated and that extractive/reductive and pyrotechnological crafts were separated suggested that there may have been basic differences in the organization of different crafts (Miller 2007:41–3).

Box 7.1 Archaeological Indicators of the Organization of Production

Spatial Contexts

Evidence for production
Raw materials, manufacturing tools
   Fixed installations (kilns, storerooms)
   Debris (discard/recycle)
   Finished/unfinished products
Scale – Production of a single product
   Production of multiple products
   Quantity of goods produced
Production occurs in residential workshop
Production occurs in segregated, separate workshop
Production occurs in association with special function building

Record-keeping Devices

Seals
Tablets
Standardized graffiti
Sealings
Weights and measures

Figure 7.1. Seals and tablets from Harappa with the same script sequence. Photograph by the Harappa Archaeological Reasearch Project © HARP.

Production of the three crafts – seals, ceramics, and stoneware bangles – discussed in Chapter 6 provide examples of several types of production organization, as would be expected from our knowledge of the other early states. I discuss each in terms of diversification and organization of production.

Seal Production

During the Urban period, there was an increased diversification of inscribed devices and in seal production. It included the engraved square stamp seals that most typically contained images of animals, Indus script, and the so-called Standard. In addition, small molded tablets in a variety of shapes included Indus script and/or narrative images. Other objects with script were etched or molded (Box 6.2). In this section, my discussion is focused on the square stamp seals.

As discussed in Chapter 6, Rissman (1989) found strong coherence in the stylistic conventions indicative of controlled stamp seal production. Rissman suggested that the employment of uniform stylistic criteria for seal production and their distribution were controlled under "rigid bureaucratic guidelines," but he also left open the possibility that arrangements may have been more informal, involving visits among relatives or friends who labored in separate workshops (Rissman 1989:168) and maintained close contact.

Complementing Rissman's research is a study by Vidale of a subset of seals in which a "short-horned bull" is represented. The bull may be a wild, South Asian bovid (*Bos gauru*). Vidale considers the animal icons as social markers and singles out the short-horned bull seals because the image is widely distributed, though rarely represented on seals at Indus centers. It is an easily identifiable symbol that may have been adopted by trading families who left the Indus in the last half of the third millennium B.C. for centers in southern Mesopotamia and the Iranian plateau (Vidale 2005:153).

Using the criteria outlined in Box 7.1, the spatial contexts for stamp seals at the site of Chanhu-daro complement Rissman's data. Chanhu-daro is much smaller than Mohenjo-daro, but its layout reflects the same attention to planning and amenities. What makes the site unique is the evidence for production of many diverse, specialized crafts. The quantity of production debris and variety of crafts was significantly vast that Ernest Mackay, the original excavator of the site, suggested that it was "populated chiefly by artisans" (Mackay 1943:38).

Production at Chanhu-daro was spatially segregated by craft. Seal production was restricted to the northern quarter of the town, while other crafts (beads, weights, metal) were produced in the southern portion. Mackay provided lists of small finds based on the excavation units in which the unfinished seals were discovered. They are unremarkable when compared to artifacts in the southern portion, consisting of pottery vessels, figurines, shell ornaments and cones, net weights, whetstone, faience bangle, carnelian beads, flint saws, copper knives, and chisels. Only one locus (#459) is in a recognizable structure. It was sizable (17'8″ × 14'8″), had substantial walls, and a bathing platform (Mackay 1943:39); otherwise, nothing more is known.

If Mackay's interpretation of the site layout is correct, production took place in residential structures or possibly in a workshop. The presence of net weights and seals, using the criteria outlined in Box 7.1, follows Rissman's suggestions that seal production may have been organized on a guild structure or within the context of a family group. The separation of seal production from all other crafts and the fact that they are themselves record-keeping devices and measures of social status indicates a level of control. Coupled with Rissman's stylistic analyses, we can neither state with certainty nor rule out the possibility that the workshops were state-administered. Kenoyer (1997a) and Vidale (2000), based on the bead production areas, the high quality of the beads, and the possibility that they were traded to southern Mesopotamia (beads using similar technologies were discovered at the Royal Cemetery at Ur – see Pollock 1999), have "hypothesized" that the organization of bead production at Chanhu-daro was "centralized production controlled by state institutions or important merchants connected with political *elites*" (Vidale 2000:58). (See Box 7.2.)

Box 7.2 The Indus Script

As discussed in Chapter 1, it was the presence of seals with an unknown script that alerted Marshall and his colleagues and fellow researchers in the Near East to the presence of an unknown civilization. Literacy in ancient societies is often presumed to be associated with leadership since the use of writing is considered to have been a means of controlling transactions and management. Though undeciphered, the script can be used as a proxy indicator for control of specific activities, as indicated in Box 7.1.

When Gadd and Smith noted similarities in individual signs between Mesopotamia and the Indus, they launched the first attempt to actually read what was written. Though the signs they identified were similar looking and indicative of contemporaneity, they represented different pictographic values; in other words, the Indus script was not derivative of the Mesopotamian languages. Since that time, linguists have not been successful at deciphering the script, although many attempts have been made. The decipherment of other unknown scripts, for example Egyptian hieroglyphs and cuneiform in Mesopotamia, only took place after the discovery of trilingual texts in which known languages were compared to an unknown ancient language. From the identification of a few signs (in Egypt based on the Rosetta stone and in Mesopotamia, an inscription carved by the Persian King Darius), scholars were able to establish baseline knowledge with which to build vocabularies and establish whether the language was logosyllabic (Do the signs represent words or are they phoneticized?), syllabic (Do they have a phonetic, syllabic value?), or alphabetic. Asko Parpola, a leading scholar in decipherment, believes the script is logosyllabic, that is, it is not syllabic or alphabetic (2000:4). Another difference between Egypt and Mesopotamia and the Indus is that the Egyptian and Mesopotamian civilizations were long-lived so that their ancient writing systems were preserved and could be compared to a more recent language (in the case of Mesopotamia, the comparison of cuneiform to the Old Persian inscribed on a rock by Darius). The Indus civilization lasted less than eight hundred years.

Box 7.2 (*Cont.*)

The earliest known use of Indus signs are etched on Ravi and Kot Dijian pottery sherds discovered at the site of Harappa. The use of script on pot sherds to convey messages continued throughout the Indus periods, but on these early sherds only one sign was etched onto a vessel, whereas later there were as many as five. The presence of this early use of script signs is a clear indication that writing originated in the Indus among a population at least some of whom continued to be a part of the later civilization, suggesting that from an early set of signs the written language became increasingly complex.

In its fully developed form, the Indus script appears on a variety of media, principally on several types of seals and tablets. The predominant type is the square stamp seal, comprised of script at the top, an animal motif at the center, and the standard in a bottom corner. Not all stamp seals include script, suggesting that certain messages could be conveyed without the written symbols. Other inscribed devices include narrative scenes in which script may or may not be included, again presumably because the motifs conveyed sufficient information. Another type of inscribed device has several sides that consist solely of script. They are referred to as tablets. Script also appears on copper tablets, stoneware bangles, bronze tools, and pottery sherds. A single signboard at Dholavira consisted of ten signs. Taken together, the signs on these various media include no more than four hundred signs all tolled, a number thought to be too high to be syllabic, where about 100 signs is common in syllabic scripts and fifty signs in alphabetic scripts (Parpola 2000:4).

In spite of these difficulties, since 1875, "over 50 'solutions' have been published" possibly more (Parpola 2000:1), but without consensus. A major difficulty is determining the language family from which the script was derived. Dravidian is represented among present-day languages in several areas of South Asia and has been a frequent starting point. Parpola's decipherment, for example, begins with the premise that the Indus script is a logo-syllabic type and that it belonged to the Dravidian family. Using these two premises as "working hypotheses," he interpreted various Indus pictograms by establishing individual sign meaning through a comparison of ancient Indian languages and mythology and symbolism in Mesopotamia, though again there is no consensus.

Indus scholars are always hopeful about script decipherment; meanwhile, archaeology will reign in "solitary splendor" (Trautmann and Sinopoli 2002:494). There are, of course, always surprises. The

Sumerians in Mesopotamia were without a doubt curious about other languages. They were bilingual, some apparently were comfortable both with Sumerian, a more ancient language, and the more modern Akkadian. During the Akkadian period (ca. 2350 B.C.), texts speak of translators, referred to as "language-turner" or later "word-turner." Accounts refer to specialists who engaged in "turning the languages" of Meluhha during the Akkadian. In later periods, there were "traveling interpreters" (Hallo 1996:350). A related phrase was "tongue interchanger." We await the news that they were successful.

Ceramic Production

Ceramic types became increasingly diversified during the Urban period. In contrast to the Pre-urban period when there was a limited range of shapes and decoration with variations in localized regions, Indus ceramics were more standardized and uniform throughout the Urban period. Over one hundred different types have been identified (Dales and Kenoyer 1986) and within each type the variations in decorative elements.

As discussed in Chapter 6, our best evidence with which to discuss the organization of production is a ceramic production area that was discovered on the northwest corner of Mound E at Harappa. It included a two-chambered kiln and various production tools as well as pit kilns, some of which had been in use before the Urban period. A mudbrick wall is associated with the workshop. Although excavations are incomplete, the wall most likely was part of a residential building similar to those excavated in other locations in the city. No record-keeping devices such as seals or weights and measures were present. In addition to the two-chambered kiln, there were two other small pit kilns associated with the workshop. One of the kilns was contemporary with the two-chambered kiln, but the other was constructed several hundred years earlier, suggesting that a group of specialists had produced clay objects in this location over a period of several hundred years (Wright 1991). They began with small-scale production in the Pre-urban settlement and later intensified during the Urban period. The continuous use of the area for ceramic objects implies that the site was handed down over successive generations of potters. Along with the lack of record-keeping devices, such as seals associated with "administered" production, the evidence is consistent with an independently operated workshop handed down from generation to generation as a *family-operated craft*.

Ethnographically, no single pattern accounts for how family-operated workshops are organized, but in general, all members of a family participate in production in one way or another. For example, adult males may procure clay and produce the pots using a potter's wheel or hand-building methods, while adult females process the clay and paint the pots. Everyone in the family, including children, assists with loading the kiln, firing the pots, and storing and marketing them (Wright 1991). Although not necessarily the case for the Harappan workshop, in many family-owned potteries, farming and pastoralism are also part of the family's seasonal occupations, and the production of pottery (or some other work) is timed to coincide with periods when agricultural work is slow (Arnold 1985). These arrangements would have the advantage of spreading risks within the family, providing them with products for internal consumption and for exchange.

Stoneware Bangle Production

During the Urban period, there was a proliferation of diverse types of bangles. They included bangles that were simply constructed of low-fired terracotta, shell, faience, metal, and stoneware. My discussion of stoneware bangles in this chapter follows from Chapter 6 and the production area known from Mohenjo-daro.

Using the archaeological indicators shown in Box 7.1, the archaeologists who examined stoneware production at Mohenjo-daro believe the workshop there was an "industrial" area under administrative control. They base this assessment upon four factors. First, the production area was intentionally bounded by a walled enclosure, an attempt at spatial control. Second, the outer jar containing the saggars in which the bangles were fired bears the impression of a unicorn seal on its exterior just at that point where the jar would have been sealed closed before firing. (See Figure 6.9.) Third, many stoneware bangles were etched with signs of the Indus script, an additional indication of some type of undefined, *administrative control* (Vidale 1989:178). Finally, the distribution of stoneware bangles was limited to Harappa and Mohenjo-daro. A neutron activation analysis indicated that they were produced at both Harappa and Mohenjo-daro (Blackman and Vidale 1992).

The Diversification and Organization of Production – Seals, Ceramics, and Stoneware Bangles

The several examples discussed previously show varied organization of production. Ceramic and stoneware bangle production are examples of two different ways in which ceramic crafts were organized, one possibly controlled by a family-based operation and the other, an administered craft. At Harappa, some pottery-producing groups had been employed in ceramic production for several generations in household workshops. The stoneware bangle producers set up their workshop away from their households in an abandoned area of Mohenjo-daro. Seal working, on the other hand, was a formalized craft in which producers followed well-defined conventions of composition and style. They also were highly skilled artisans, linked either through family ties, guildlike communities of seal producers, or an as yet undefined bureaucratic structure, possibly state-administered.

Even though these examples are from several different sites, they represent the variability that existed within the Indus civilization. The pottery, stoneware bangles, and seals are three examples, but many other crafts attest to significant variability of organization.

Diversification of Raw Materials and Finished Products – The Organization of Interregional Exchange

The raw materials exploited by the Harappans included stone (lapis lazuli, turquoise, chert, agate, quartz, basalt, ochre, and many other materials) and metal (gold, tin, and copper). Marine shell also was important. Figure 7.2 shows the locations of some of the potential sources.

Harappan settlements are distributed over a broad geographical area conspicuously rich in raw materials and diverse ecological zones, including mountain, plain, and coast. Nested within these regions were sources of semiprecious stones, highly valued metals, and animal and plant products. The differential distribution of raw materials provided opportunities for local exploitation and control of production. The following are examples of production involving exploitation of raw material source areas located outside of the alluvial plain and where there is evidence for different organizational and distributional forms. They include chert quarrying sites and the production and distribution of lapis lazuli, shell, carnelian, steatite, and precious metals.

Chert

Chert is the principal source for a variety of stone tools and the system of weights that were a standard of measurement utilized throughout the Indus (Figure 7.3 for Indus weights). There is variability in the source areas exploited both spatially and temporally which may have been critical to weight production. In the Pre-urban period at Harappa, chert sources from the eastern Salt Range to the north of Harappa were most often used in addition to chert from the Rohri Hills. In the Urban period,

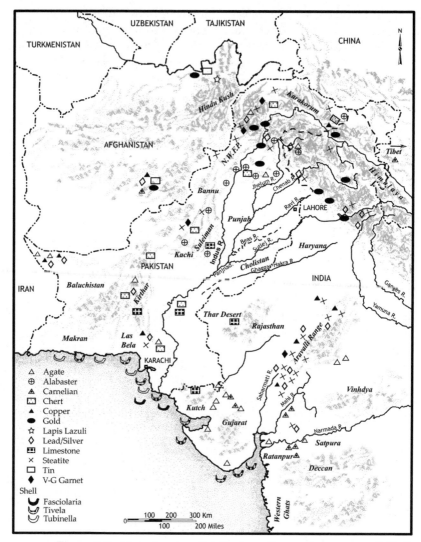

Figure 7.2. Map showing distribution of natural resources. © R. P. Wright.

the Rohri chert was the principal source (Law 2008). In general, analysis of chert artifacts from other settlements indicates that sources nearest to sites were the ones exploited (Law 2008).

Rohri chert can be identified by its distinctive "buff or grey with a patina either of cream or mottled black and rust colour" (B. Allchin 1976:477)

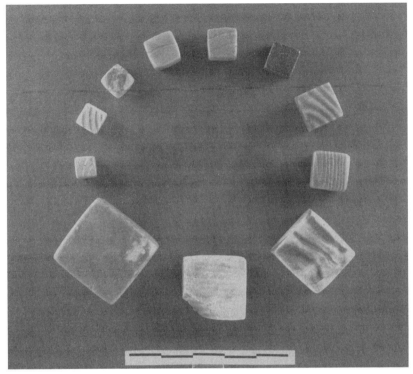

Figure 7.3. Chert weights from Harappa. Photograph by the Harappa Archaeological Research Project © HARP.

or "banded" appearance (Kenoyer 1984:118).[2] Chert artifacts with these characteristics have been found throughout the Indus and on the Arabian Peninsula.

The information on quarrying and production comes from a large chert deposit in the Rohri hills (Figures 1.2 and 5.12), where Italian and Pakistani researchers have discovered thousands of mining and production sites (Biagi et al. 1991, 1995). The principal activities conducted at Rohri involved mining, reducing chert nodules, preparing cores, and pressure-detaching blades and bladelets (Vidale 2000:36). Each of these activities took place in separate locations. This spatial segregation of production tasks suggests that relatively small groups of miner/craft producers were involved in the operation and that the nodules, cores, or blades and bladelets were their end products. These prepared materials were unmodified and then exported to production areas. Only a very few were "retouched" (Negrino et al. 1996), that is, subjected to additional modification of blades or with specialized tools, such as drills for bead production or chert weights. Nonetheless, the workshop areas at Rohri provide conclusive evidence for mass production of blades and bladelets and a pattern that clearly reflects an extensive "trade and exchange ... of the Harappan civilization ... over a wide geographical area" (Negrino et al. 1996:102).

When Rohri chert is found at archaeological sites, the evidence complements what researchers have found at the quarry. At Harappa, for example, the production of chert weights began with the prepared nodule (Dales and Kenoyer 1989). Similarly, at some small settlements along the Beas, chert cores (Wright et al. 2005 a,b) also have been found, but none of the debris associated with their preparation has been uncovered. On the other hand, at Allahadino and Balakot, cores are underrepresented (Dales 1982:156); prepared chert blades appear to have been imported and subsequently modified by chipping and fashioning into drill heads and scrapers.

The control of these mining operations and the people who conducted the work likely varied, depending upon the end product. Vidale provides a vivid picture of the people involved and the organizational structure of blade production:

We have to imagine that Harappan craftpersons and traders traveled to the mining areas and back on bullock carts loaded with people, tents, poles, containers. The under-representation of well-defined blades' size classes ... in some Rohri sites suggests that these were the products which were mainly traded to the cities and villages of the Indus plain ... The chert blades were detached on the spot and collected in bags or baskets and brought back to camps or settlements on the plains. (2000:103)

But whether these individuals were independent entrepreneurs and their families members of elite groups or state institutions is uncertain.

A distinct possibility is that the end products produced at the quarry were subject to different forms of control, a suggestion made by Kenoyer (1991). He observed that selected, special varieties of chert from Rohri were used to produce weights. The banded varieties of chert were preferred for the production of Indus weights, since they would have been more easily recognizable. They also have a constant density, thus providing good material for producing a standard weight. Procurement of the banded chert may have been more closely monitored and controlled by merchants since the weights were a standard with which to maintain control of production and distribution (Kenoyer 1991) of other products.

Lapis Lazuli

Lapis lazuli was highly prized throughout antiquity and continues to be a favorite stone for use in jewelry and other ornamental objects. Today, the most valued lapis is the deepest blue with tiny flecks of pyrite that give the appearance of shiny gold flakes and impart a startling contrast.

As noted in previous chapters, the world's largest lapis lazuli mine is in northeastern Afghanistan at the base of a beautiful and yet forbidding landscape. In 1975, I was one of four archaeologists to traverse its narrow roadways as our jeep skirted along the Kokcha River often passable by only one vehicle. Figure 7.4 shows a view of the Kokcha Valley in 1975, where today's farmers and pastoralists exploit its rich soils. Our goal was to identify third millennium B.C. settlements that may have been involved in the lapis lazuli trade with Mesopotamia (referred to in textual sources and discussed in Chapter 8). Although we were successful in identifying a number of promising sites (Kohl 1978), we were unable to return to Afghanistan due to political constraints.

Even though we lack evidence for on-site quarrying at the lapis mine during the third millennium B.C., the archaeological site of Shortugai lies within a short distance from the outcrops at the confluence of the Kokcha and Oxus Rivers. The site was discovered by a team of French archaeologists shortly after our survey (Francfort et al. 1989).

There are several reasons to suggest that Shortugai was founded specifically for the exploitation and trade of lapis by people from the Indus. First, the layout of the site, oriented to cardinal points and a

Figure 7.4. The Kokcha River in northeastern Afghanistan near the Lapis Lazuli mine in Badakshan. © R. P. Wright.

gridlike plan, shows an intimate understanding of Indus landscape planning. Second, the assemblage of artifacts, especially the ceramics, are stylistically and technically similar to those found at other Indus sites. Since they were produced from local clays and, therefore, not imported (Francfort et al. 1989:236), potters must have had an intimate knowledge of Indus technologies. Third, the same familiarity with Indus technology was exhibited by artisans in a lapis lazuli workshop (an atelier "de taille du lapis-lazuli" – Francfort et al. 1989:253) in which beads were found in various stages of manufacture, including flakes and some finished beads. The manufacturing technology involved a "grooving and splitting technique" typical of lapis working areas at Mehrgarh (Vidale 2000:108) and use of a specialized tool employed by Indus craftworkers. Fourth, the site is located near sources of gold, silver, copper, and tin and important overland routes for internal distribution and long-distance trade.

The settlers at Shortugai were in regular contact with several regions in the Greater Indus, providing insight into their exchange network. Nonlocal, imported raw materials discovered at Shortugai include carnelian, steatite, and chert. Possibly in return, lapis lazuli was exported to other regions, such as Nausharo (Figure 1.2, Chapter 3 for brief discussion) and Ghazi Shah (in Sindh near Mohenjo-daro), where reworked lumps of lapis have been found (Flam 1993b). Lapis production was also discovered at Nagwada in Gujarat (Sonawane 1992:165).

Shortugai's location represented a strategic move to control mineral resources. Still, the site appears as an outpost or frontier settlement and clearly was not part of any unified program of advance to colonize the region. Rather, its presence in northeastern Afghanistan appears more like the budding off of individuals from an Indus center to settle a new territory in order to exploit valuable resources rather than a major invasion.

Carnelian, Chalcedony, Agate, and Jasper

The source areas for carnelian, chalcedony, agate, and jasper are more varied than for chert and lapis lazuli. The most valued source today is in Gujarat, from which jewelry of the highest quality is produced; however, there are numerous other resource zones (Figure 7.2). Agate and jasper are erosion products from volcanic formations that appear in the form of pebbles in alluvial beds in the Upper Indus and elsewhere in larger outcrops. Carnelian is an agate variant that can be transformed from a red-brownish color to red by firing the stone in containers. In contrast to the prepared chert cores and blades shipped from the Rohri mine, the carnelian discovered at places like Chanhu-daro arrived unmodified "without any preliminary stage of reduction" (Vidale 2000:102).

Four main types of beads were produced from these stones (Vidale 2000). (1) The most common was a simple disk bead. (2) The most distinctive and difficult to produce was an elongated (long-barrel) bead, a type that was traded to Mesopotamia. Production of these beads required specialized knowledge that may have been known only to Indus artisans. In addition to the specialized drills and preparation required to produce the beads, they were fired in kilns to attain their intense red color. It has been estimated that one worker would have taken thirteen to fourteen days to produce a single carnelian long-barrel bead (Kenoyer 1998). (3) A third bead type involved selecting for white-to-red agate and exploiting the multilayered interior structure of the stone to produce beads with eye-like patterns. (4) The most complex bead technology involved bleaching or etching patterns by applying a chemical solution to their surfaces and refiring them in order to permanently affix the white on the surface (see Figure 6.4 for some examples). The long-barrel and bleached beads are examples of a technological style, or transformative approach, that merged reductive and pyrotechnological techniques.

Drills, debris, and unfinished carnelian/agate beads have been found at many Indus sites, such as the workshops at Chanhu-daro and Mohenjo-daro. However, several sites are located near to the sources in Gujarat (Nagwada and Kuntasi), in Kutch (Dholavira, Surkotada, and Lothal), and Rajasthan (Banawali). Moreover, the presence of carnelian at Chanhu-daro, Mohenjo-daro, Harappa, and Shortugai, all some distance from carnelian sources indicates there were wide-ranging exchange networks that involved long and arduous travel hundreds of kilometers distant from the quarry sites.

Limestone

As will be discussed in Chapter 9, limestone was used to produce rare statuary at Mohenjo-daro. In addition, Indus artisans produced ring-stones, variously described as "yoni" stones (Marshall 1931:158ff.), columns (Mackay 1938:597), drain covers, and architectural elements such as column bases (Bisht 1991) and calendar stones (Maula 1984). Like the statuary, they are found only in Indus cities.

Research on limestone is limited, but a recent study by Randall Law (2008) identified several source areas (Figure 7.2). At Dholavira, the nearby source was used for the construction of wells, houses, reservoirs, and city walls; most other Harappan sites used baked and mudbrick for these architectural features. Law conducted a small pilot study, in which he compared geologic samples to limestone artifacts from Harappa. All of the archaeological samples clustered with the geological stones from Gujarat (Law 2008). This evidence, coupled with the wide distribution of shell from Kutch to other areas in the Greater Indus suggests it was an important source area and likely was part of a complex of trade comprised of rare raw materials.

Precious Metals – Copper, Gold, Lead, Silver, and Tin

The production of copper-based objects far outweighs that of other metals such as gold, lead, silver, and tin. The principal objects produced were ornaments, tools, and vessels (copper and silver), the last often produced in shapes identical to ceramic forms. The production of metal vessels in common forms that were nearly identical to others produced in clay is another example of the creation of objects of higher value that reinforced social difference. In the Urban period, some stone tools were replaced with copper. New objects were produced in the Urban period, some of which may have been weapons (Figure 7.5 for some copper objects). Indus metal tools were unsuitable for serious militaristic purposes since they lacked the strengthening midribs of metal weaponry produced by their comtemporaries. More rare objects included copper mirrors, seals (silver and copper), gold ornaments, and minor objects made of lead. Tin was used as an alloy in copper production to produce bronze.

There are numerous copper sources, though few analytical studies have been conducted to determine the sources of metals employed by Indus craft producers. Known sources of copper are in northeastern Afghanistan near the lapis mines, in Baluchistan, and along the Aravalli range in Rajasthan. A third source exploited during this period is in today's Oman (Weisgerber 1984).

Indus objects were produced either from pure copper, copper and tin, or arsenical coppers, in that order of relative use. These differences provide important clues to the particular sources utilized. At Harappa and Mohenjo-daro, coppers rich in arsenic were predominant, secured most likely from arsenic-rich sources in Baluchistan and Afghanistan. In distinction, in Gujarat at Lothal, copper objects have low percentages of arsenic, suggesting the raw material from which they were produced came from nearby sources in the Aravalli range.

A third metal technology involved the alloying of copper with tin. Tin is of major significance in the study of the development of metallurgy. Known tin sources are in eastern and northeastern Afghanistan. The addition of tin imparts important qualities having to do with strength,

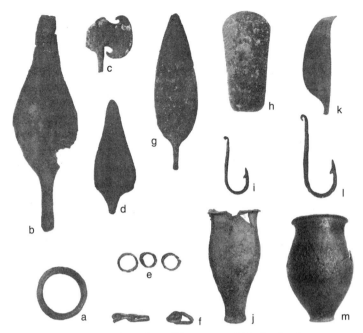

Figure 7.5. Metal objects from Harappa and Mohenjo-daro.

color, and working properties of the final product. For example, "The addition of anywhere between 3% and 15% tin yields a significantly harder product and achieves a more goldlike colour, while lesser quantities (down to ca. 0.05%) lower the melting point, act as a flux and facilitate casting" (T. Potts 1994:153). In the Indus, percentages of tin varied when objects from Mohenjo-daro and Harappa were compared with metal objects from Lothal and Rangpur. At Mohenjo-daro half of the objects studied had percentages of tin above 5% (9 of 18); of 29 sampled at Harappa, seven had percentages over 5%; at Lothal where sixty-three were sampled, only six had percentages over 5%; and at Rangpur, four of twelve had percentages between 5% and 11% (Kenoyer and Miller 1999). These variations and differences in percentages of arsenic (of the samples analyzed from Lothal and Rangpur, only four had traces of arsenic), suggest that different raw material sources and exchange networks were involved in resource procurement.

When it comes to other metals, there again is variation in sources and techniques employed. Major gold sources are known from Karnataka and southern India, but it is unclear whether these sources were utilized by the Harappans. Small gold nodules (gold dust?) are fairly widespread, available in some Indus rivers in the Upper Indus, Baluchistan, and Uddar Pradesh (Ratnagar 1981). Other reported gold sources are in the Kokcha Valley in northeastern Afghanistan (Figure 7.4). Sources in the north were more likely the major source areas for gold in the third millennium B.C. (Law personal communication).

Lead is found in Baluchistan, Afghanistan, Rajasthan, and the Himalayas (Kenoyer and Miller 1999). Silver mines are reported in Baluchistan and Afghanistan.

The production of metal objects requires a high level of skill and source material is rare. As a consequence, metallurgy frequently is associated with craft specialization. For these reasons, many archaeologists have regarded the coming of metals as an indication of increasing social complexity since the new technology and rare sources could be controlled by a small, elite segment of the population. The Indus may be a special case, however, since metal has multiple sources of access (for an extended discussion see Kenoyer and Miller 1999). The control of metal sources was mitigated by its relative abundance, and although technical skill was involved in metal production, specific skills varied depending upon the desired end product and even the different stages of production (Kenoyer and Miller 1999).

The sorts of detailed studies needed to make the proposed finer-grained assessments, involving questions related to "independent and derived invention, shared and restricted knowledge, and the adoption of technological innovations" (H. M. L. Miller 1999b:283), are yet to be conducted. At present what we do know indicates that metal production varied, both in what was being produced and the sources being exploited, suggesting that multiple organizational strategies and exchange networks were in place for its raw materials and finished products.

Shell

Objects produced from marine shell are widely distributed. They provide an important resource for archaeologists interested in distribution systems, since certain species of shell are confined to restricted areas. Of the principal shells utilized, conch (*Tubinella*) is found on the Makran coast, Kutch and Khambat, clam shells (*Tivela* or *Meretrix*) come exclusively on the Makran coast, and *Chicoreus* and *Fasciolaria*, are derived from along the Omani coast and in Kutch (Kenoyer 1997b:274). See Figure 7.2 for a map showing general locations. There also is significant variation in shell production, organization, and distribution. I discuss the evidence from three sites, Balakot, Nageswar, and Kuntasi, (see Figure 1.2) next.

Shell bangle production areas at Balakot were segregated depending upon the types of shell utilized, indicating different forms of organization of production and distribution. In one workshop, clam shell bangles were produced by chipping and grinding; a single bangle was produced from each shell. The workshop was located on a mudbrick platform onto which a temporary shelter had been erected. Associated with the shelter were large quantities of shell-working debris and unworked shells. The temporary nature of the workshop and the large quantities of bangles, likely beyond what would be consumed at this relatively small site, suggest the bangles were not for local consumption but for export. One of several possible scenarios are suggested by Vidale. One leads to the interpretation that shell manufacture was under the organization and control by elite merchants living there (Vidale 2000). In a second workshop, bangles were cut from conch shells with bronze saws that have strong cutting edges. Several bangles could be produced from a single shell (Kenoyer 1997b:275). The context of the conch workshop was in a badly damaged multiroomed building, leaving open the question of whether production was in a household or an unoccupied ruin. However, the small percentages of conch bangles produced in the conch bangle workshop have led to the interpretation that local artisans were producing for local consumption (Vidale 2000:105).

The separation of shell-working technologies in different workshops and the differences in forms of organization are in keeping with evidence from other Indus settlements. At Nageswar (Bhan 1986) and Kuntasi, a possible seaport (Dhavalikar 1992) (Figure 1.2 for locations), specialized areas were devoted to specific parts of the shell production sequences, indicative of different forms of specialization and organization of production and distribution. At Nageswar, shell-working debris is segregated from residential areas. The division of labor is reminiscent of assembly line production in which only one step in the production process is present at each station. In one workshop, for example, waste from conch shells included chipped and sawn shell, the last step in production, while in another only the apexes of the shells were present representing the first step in production (Vidale 2000:105-6). In other workshops segregation of production was based upon the end product and/or the type of shell being exploited. For example, in one conch workshop inlay pieces, beads, and other items were being produced, while in another, ladles were made from spiney murex shell. The variety of end products and the presence of extensive workshops has been interpreted as production intended for long-distance trade to inland settlements (Bhan and Kenoyer 1983).

At Kuntasi, shell-working debris was found throughout the site. This included habitation areas associated with buildings assumed to be residential. However, a more extensive production occurred in a separate area described as an "Industrial Complex" (Deshpandi-Mukherjee 1998:73), in which many different shell types were being exploited.

Shell working has been discovered at inland sites at great distances from the raw material sources, further demonstrating the importance of shell in trade. They include significant quantities of shell-manufacturing debris, such as a *Tivela* fragment at Harappa, providing an obvious connection between the urban center and the Makran (Kenoyer 1984, 1997b:275). Also there is evidence of shell working at Mohenjo-daro in the VS area. In a substantial and well-preserved building with twenty-eight rooms, forty-one cores of shells were discovered for the production of bangles (Mackay in Marshall 1931:219).

From these several examples, a clear picture emerges of production and distribution of shell species from nearby sources and the exchange of shell over long distances. It demonstrates that shell, in its raw and finished form, was a highly valued commodity and integral to internal and long-distance trade. The large-scale and specialized production at the workshops at Balakot, Nageswar, and Kuntasi are examples of a highly organized activity intended for non-local consumption while at the same time objects (especially bangles) were produced for local use.

Steatite

Law's (2005) analytical studies of resource and procurement zones indicate that four potential sources of steatite were in use, though there were shifts over time. At Harappa, in the Pre-urban period, steatite was procured at source areas to the north of Harappa in the Khyber and Hazara in the NWFP areas. Later in the Urban period, while steatite continued to be obtained from the north, two other sources were also used from northern Rajasthan (Law 2008: Chapter 13).

Extensive research has been conducted on the transformative qualities of steatite (talc) represented by the so-called, "talc-faience complex" briefly discussed in Chapter 3, where heat-treated steatite is first known at Mehrgarh. As discussed in Chapter 6, during the Urban period, this technological style of working with steatite became common. When heated above a certain temperature (ca. 1,000 degrees Centigrade), steatite becomes hard. Heat-treated steatite was a favorite substance for beads (found in the thousands at Indus sites) and small objects. Although steatite was widely available, some sources have special qualities that made their resources more preferable to others for seals and tablets, two items central to Indus political economy. At Mohenjo-daro and Harappa, artisans utilized the preferred white firing dolomitic steatite from the Hazara area and the northern Aravalli range (Law 2008:Chapter 13).

Diversification of Craft Production, Organization, and Distribution

In summary, in this chapter, I returned to the ceramic workshop at Harappa, the stoneware bangle production at Mohenjo-daro, and the seal engraving at Chanhu-daro. Along with discussing other crafts and/or raw materials procured outside of the major centers, I summarized our current understanding of the organization of their production. Interpretations of the evidence suggest there was significant variability in the ways in which crafts were organized, ranging from independent household production to administered production.

Complementing these assessments, the evidence for interregional craft production and exchange demonstrated a similar variability. The variability was site-specific, again ranging from small-scale production for local consumption to fabrication of objects on a larger scale for nonlocal consumption. At some locations, raw materials were unprocessed and traded out to distant locations, while in others a limited number of production steps were completed before shipment. Preparation was in some cases geared to a specific final product, such as the banded chert cores that were transformed into weights at their destinations. Finally, the Harappans exploited diverse ecological zones, reaching out to areas in which desired materials were present, as demonstrated by the founding of Shortugai for exploiting lapis lazuli and other exotic raw materials.

Artisans successfully implemented innovative technologies involving traditional reduction methods and pyrotechnical techniques less frequently applied to stone. Stone, clay, and other materials were ground and heated producing interesting color effects that produced "copies" of natural materials. In addition, the new techniques produced easily manipulated media with which to produce an array of forms. The enormous variety of stylistically similar objects produced from widely divergent technologies and resources raises questions about consumers, their choices, tastes, and access to these different products.

H. M. L. Miller (2008:215), based on earlier charts published by Kenoyer (1992) and Vidale (1992), approached this question by developing an *"Axes of Relative Value"* of objects based on the degree of complexity of production and access to natural resources. In Figure 7.6, I modified Miller's scale to account for a wider range of products than originally considered. On the

	Low	Medium	High
High	Stoneware bangles Statuary	Faiences Glazed Objects Seal production	Lapis lazuli Elaborate Metal objects Etched carnelian Beads Limestone
Medium	Woven cloth Complex terracotta Objects	Fired Steatite Beads	Marine shell Ornaments
Low	Simple terracotta Bone tools Basketry Simple woven cloth		Simple stone beads

Figure 7.6. Axes of relative value: Technological elaboration and raw material access. Modified and redrawn from H. M. L. Miller (2007)

vertical axes, technological elaboration is rated from low to high depending upon the degree of complexity of the craft. Plotted on the horizontal and rated from low to high, is the degree of raw material access and procurement. For example, objects produced from locally available materials are ranked lower than those produced from precious stones or rare metals or other materials, though less than marine shell procured from coastal settlements. As an example of its application, the stoneware bangles would rank high on this scale of value because their production involved a highly complex technology. On the other hand, lapis lazuli would rank high on the scale in view of the physical distance to its source.[3] Additionally, simple terracotta objects rank low on the index of value because materials were locally available and the technology was relatively simple.

If value can be assigned to objects when crafts are compared, their relative "value" should be reflected in consumption patterns. For example, since long beads are produced from both carnelian (high index) and simple terracotta (low index), there should be a relationship between demand and diversification depending upon one's social and economic status (H.M. L. Miller 2008). Stated differently, whether an Harappan wore carnelian long beads or ones of a similar style made of terracotta was a reflection of his or her status and wealth. In that sense the technological style adopted by the Harappan artisans was a catalyst for important social transformations (Lemonnier 1992:13) and social differentiation in the Indus.

In Chapter 9, I return to a discussion of resource materials and production technologies and examine consumption contexts at several locations in light of the relative value of goods implied by the axes described. In this chapter I have provided the "nuts and bolts" of selected technologies, their production techniques and organization, and in the context of settlements outside of the major centers, their exchange; my interest in Chapter 9 is the distribution and social differences among Harappans in its major cities. My purpose is to establish the consumption contexts of materials produced from rare materials and/or objects produced with the greatest skill, by examining the contents of individual loci at Mohenjo-daro, where a large number of residential areas have been excavated.

Diversification of Land, Labor, and the Organization of Agropastoral Production

As societies specialize and diversify their agropastoral economy as discussed in Chapter 6, they must adopt strategies to effectively allocate land and labor use. Matters related to land concern areas for planting and harvesting coordinated with wet and dry seasons, and the dedication of land to specific crops. This specificity pertains to alternating uses of land for summer and winter crops and perennial species for which land must be dedicated throughout the year. Diversification of land use has its correlates in allocations of labor similar to strategies employed by craft producers who also engage in farming or pastoralism. The complexity of agricultural production, cropping patterns, and animal management change the balance of labor and land use.

My discussion is limited to three aspects of these complexities and is dealt with elsewhere in greater detail (Wright, in press). They include organizational matters involving the uses of land and labor in the context of diversifying food and fiber crops by employing techniques such as multicropping, plow agriculture, crop processing, fiber crops, and aboriculture.

Diversification of Farming – Multicropping, Plow Agriculture, Crop Processing, Fiber Crops, and Aboriculture

A variety of plant foods were grown and processed by the Harappans. As discussed in Chapter 6, wheat, barley, millets, legumes (peas, lentils, chickpeas), and the fruits of dates, jujube, and grape probably were the most important plant components of the Harappan diet. Cereal grains processed into bread and porridge provided a source of valuable carbohydrates. Legumes could be easily dried and stored as a good source of protein. Fruits were eaten raw or possibly fermented into wines. Wheat and barley were fermented to make beer or wine. These are nutritious beverages. The vegetative parts of certain millets and other plants may have been used for animal fodder. Other plants cotton, jute, and hemp – were valuable sources for fiber and cloth production.

As noted previously, Harappan farmers of the Urban period practiced a strategy of multicropping in which plants were grown throughout the year in a two-season pattern. Wheat, barley, and to a lesser degree millet, were the staple crops, and we can assume large tracts of land were devoted to their production. This diverse range of crops (see Box 6.3) necessarily required allocating land resources and labor to specific activities. As discussed earlier, the organization of production in early states varied so that we cannot assume that wheat, barley, or millet farming was monopolized either by elite groups or state institutions or carried out independently by farmers and pastoralists.

The evidence with which to make these distinctions (small-scale as opposed to large-scale centralized farming and, of course, a variety of other possibilities) is limited by the evidence from Harappa. It includes the introduction of plow agriculture and data on crop processing and, in no way do they represent all aspects of Harappan farming either for the city or elsewhere in the civilization. Due to these limitations, my interpretations of these data are preliminary.

As discussed earlier, two labor-saving devices – ploughs and the use of cattle for traction – were introduced into farming practice during the late Pre-urban, but accelerated in the Urban period. The increase in the use of cattle for traction is documented by their increased size, a change that is suggestive of an emphasis on males and castrates (L. Miller 2004:619). Evidence for ploughs comes in the form of clay models of yokes discovered at Nausharo and Banawali. The implementation of plow agriculture would have greatly facilitated soil preparation because it promotes modifications of soil structure that may increase yields per unit of land. Second, it makes farming larger tracts of land possible. The ability to prepare larger tracts using these semimechanized processes may have made agricultural projects involving larger numbers of people more plausible. In any event, individuals who possessed plows and draft animals would have an advantage over others preparing their fields manually, although these advantages would diminish under conditions of small-scale farming.

Evidence for crop processing at Harappa complements my interpretation that the use of draft animals suggests larger tracts of land were being farmed. When archaeobotanists examined crop-deposits from hearths and other occupational surfaces (Weber 2003:177,181)[4] from the Urban period of the Harappan sequence, they noted that some samples did not include the hulls of millets and chaff or rachises of wheat and barley. This evidence indicates that the crop was processed *after* harvesting and before storage at a location that was not an individual household. Fuller and Madella (2000) and Weber (2003) interpret this data for harvest and postharvest labor as possibly indicative of communal or even centralized organization of production.

The reliance on cotton, grapes, and dates for dietary, beverage, and fiber sources also impacted land resources and required new forms of labor organization that differed from that employed at large-scale tracts for the growth of wheat, barley, and millets. Successful cultivation of each of these plants requires summer harvesting and areas of land set aside for their sole use. Based on imprints of cloth and pseudomorphs on faience and metal objects, the cotton plant has been identified as *Gossypium arboretum*, a perennial shrub or small tree that is native to South Asia (Fuller personal communication). Cotton is more easily spun than linen, another fiber that probably was used, and could be woven into a lighter cloth than linen. Wool, also woven into cloth, would have been too hot to wear during certain seasons in the Indus. In addition, dried cotton stalks could be used as cooking fuel during winter and spring. Finally, stubble of unpicked cotton can be used to graze animals, a strategy practiced today by farmers near Harappa.

Similarly, developing a cropping pattern that involved the tending and nurturing of dates (along with grapes and cotton) would have presented challenges to Harappan farmers, again with respect to allocation of labor and land. Orchard farming requires annual care and setting aside of parcels of land for their exclusive use. Date palms, for example, grow best along river banks where they can reach down into the underground flow of freshwater for added moisture. They can be cultivated either from stones, which (under modern conditions) take from six to seven years to produce a crop, or from offshoots, which bear fruit in three to four years. Date trees reach their full maturity in about fifteen years and may continue to yield for as many as eighty. But both pollination and harvesting require large labor investments. The trees demand expert care and nurturance at certain times of the year (Wright 1980) unlike the annual crops, such as wheat and barley, which are grown in winter and could be planted on different plots of land in each season, cotton and arboriculture (dates and grapes) would have necessitated careful planning. Parcels of land exclusively for the fruit trees would have to be set aside and managed.

Land also would have been set aside for growing other plants, such as hemp (Madella 2003:221) and jute (Wright et al., in press). Residues of hemp were found placed under a sump pot (a vessel used to collect liquid and solid refuse), possibly acting "as a cushion pad that would have prevented breakage during the operation of removing and replacing the container to dispose of the refuse" (Madella 2003:221). The remnants of a jute cloth used to support the rim of a dish-on-stand before firing was recovered from a ceramic vessel (Wright et al., in press). Jute would be harvested near the end of the monsoon season. Seed gathering for planting in subsequent years would take place at the end of the monsoon.

Other basic transformations in landscape use and food and fiber production also took place (as discussed in Chapter 6) regionally. For example, in the Harappa region, settlements on the lower reaches of the Beas were situated in a zone with significantly lower rainfall than at Harappa. Drought resistant millets and other summer crops may have been grown at these downstream sites and traded for products produced at the center.

These examples of plow agriculture and crop processing of cereal grains; summer cropping of perennial dates, grapes, and cotton; and jute harvesting and seed collecting for planting in subsequent years, along with the exploitation of regional ecological diversity, represent an increase in the number of components in the productive system. Each technique required the development of management strategies for scheduling times, planting and harvesting, and dedicating appropriate land areas to specific crops. As Morrison (1994:144) has pointed out, this type of diversification in agricultural practices reflects the strategies employed by various groups within the society, and much as with craft production, the complexities involved with agricultural production, scheduling, and land management changed the balance of labor. As discussed, the exploitation of fibers like jute and cotton necessitated dedicating plots of land to their production and to the intensification and scheduling of labor to gather and process fibers. In that sense, while fiber production provided an additional economic resource, it conceivably necessitated the realignment of work groups.

The evidence described in the preceding examples suggests that the organization of production varied. Some farming may have been centralized or communally organized, perhaps within neighborhoods of related kin. Ownership of plows and traction animals clearly provided the farmers who possessed them with an edge, especially if they were engaged in large-scale farming. As discussed, aboriculture requires sustained maintenance over periods of years as trees are nurtured to their peak growing years, suggestive of specialist producers, whether individuals or groups. Cotton production presents other puzzles with respect to organization that must be left unanswered. Was this crop grown and processed and the cloth produced by a single institution or group? Was it a small-scale industry and the basic fiber used for the production of clothing?

Diversification of Pastoralism – Specialized Breeds,
Food and Fiber, Animal Provisioning, Mobility,
and the Organization of Production

Innovations in the pastoral economy clearly kept pace with the increased diversification of animal products and in the breeding of animals for specialized uses. As discussed in Chapter 6, different varieties of meat were made available from both domesticated and wild animals including fish. Even though most wild foods constituted a smaller portion of the diet, Belcher's research on fishing (referred to in Chapter 6 and discussed in more detail later in this chapter) suggests that fish may have been a major part of the Harappan diet and fishing a full-time occupation. It is uncertain whether hunting was practiced on a part-time basis by settled peoples or by hunter-gatherers who existed on the margins of urban areas and traded hides and meat for agricultural and other products.

As with farming, the diversification of pastoralism and the development of specialized breeds for traction, dairy products, and wool required the implementation of strategies for labor allocation and maximization of land resources. L. Miller's evidence for the development of special cattle breeds for traction and their use in plow agriculture is one example (2003:304). Cattle, however, also may have been harnessed to carts, like the clay models and cart tracks at major cities show (discussed in Chapter 6) (L. Miller 2003:274 and see Figure 7.7 for a modern cart in Pakistan today). The evidence for dairying at Harappa is ambiguous, although faunal patterns are consistent with dairy exploitation (L. Miller 2004:625). If present, dairy producers may have supplied households with fresh milk, possibly supplemented with storable products such as clarified butter and cheese (L. Miller 2004:622). With respect to sheep Meadow's (1989a,b) analysis of sheep bones from Harappa (based on kill-off patterns and size) suggests that they were specially bred for wool. Finally, at one small village at the site of Balakot, there is evidence for secondary products from cattle. L. Miller suggests that "rural settlements may have become incorporated into urban economic systems in which rural production strategies were focused towards

Figure 7.7. Modern cart driven by Zebu cattle. Photograph by the
Harappa Archaeological Research Project © HARP.

meeting subsistence needs in cities" (2004:623). Future explorations
of village sites and archaeological remains are critical to a better understanding of rural and urban relations with respect to production and
consumption of these important secondary products.

This diversification of animal breeds and their new uses has implications for allocations of land and labor and production organization.
The archaeological evidence gives every indication that sedentary and
nomadic pastoralists were present. At the major centers, for example,
the presence of sedentary pastoralists is indicated by the animal bones,
cart tracks, and plow animals discovered at Harappa. In contrast, the
small camp sites in Cholistan have been interpreted as the settlement of
pastoral nomads.

In urban contexts, sedentary pastoralists who kept herds of sheep or
cattle would necessarily have required large tracts of land for grazing.
Depending upon whether they were kept by shepherds who moved herds
outside of farm lands or they grazed on existing farmlands when land lay
fallow, provisioning animals would necessitate making adjustments in
land use and allocations of labor. Strategies in different regions necessarily varied. For example, Dholavira, because of its poor drainage and lack
of perennial surface water, is located in an area less suitable for farming

than Harappa. On the other hand, the region offers good grazing land (Bisht 1996:267) that would not have been taken over by farming.

These adjustments in land use, whether provisioning occurred on marginal lands or on agricultural fields, would impact the organization of pastoral production. The movement of cattle or sheep into marginal lands or farmlands required an allocation of tasks and scheduling of movement of animals in order to avoid conflicts (Abdi 2003:438). Similarly, provisioning and daily watering needs of water buffalo required the coordination of herders at Dholavira, for example, where water buffalo likely were watered down in the terraced complex.

Tom Barfield's ethnographic studies of pastoral societies provide some clues as to how different forms of pastoralism may have been organized. As the evidence from the Indus makes clear, several forms of pastoralism existed in and around the urban centers. This pattern is consistent with Barfield's research, as it indicates that sedentary pastoralists are likely to be among other pastoral forms coexisting in the same society. At Harappa, for example, some pastoralists may have specialized in dairying, while others living in nearby villages may have engaged in farming and keeping small herds of sheep or goats. Yet others may have spent periods of time away from home moving their herds out to marginal lands, returning sporadically to an urban center or village. In contrast, nomadic pastoralists are mobile, traveling throughout the seasons, in response to the needs of their herds.

As studies of historical and contemporary pastoral economies have shown, these different forms of pastoral production (sedentary, semisedentary, and nomad) may have stimulated social and political changes. Nomadic pastoralists, for example, may be alien to sedentary populations. In such conditions, relationships are "subject to misunderstandings and misinterpretations" (Barfield 1989:20). On the other hand, a mix of environments and specialization of husbandry would have provided rich resource variability and products that could be drawn on either through alliances, exchange or less peaceful means. Also drawn from ethnographic studies, nomadic pastoralists may have been the perfect conveyers of trade goods and their own products "on the hoof." The entire system would have been facilitated by their mobility.

As a byproduct of the overall success of new forms of agriculture and husbandry, an additional consideration is that a balance of demands would have to be achieved to accommodate different cropping and animal-keeping regimes within the pastoral community. Sedentary agropastoralists would have been more established in the long-term use of land and protective of their plots from intrusion by more mobile pastoralists. Nomadic pastoralists, on the other hand, would have placed higher value on the ownership of animals, privileging mobility, and the needs of livestock (Barfield 1989:20). They would have been less mindful, or at least less attentive to, property boundaries. In one case, prestige accrues from land resources; in the other, the prize animal is most valued.

Drawing on the ethnographic record, these different forms of pastoralism were organized in different ways. Among nomadic groups, units would have ranged from small numbers of related individuals ("families, extended households, and local lineages") to larger means of incorporation (clans and tribes) (1989:27). These might include brothers or other family units either working together or in competition based on a hierarchy of leadership. Laura Miller's ethnoarchaeological study of sedentary pastoralists near Harappa (2003) suggests that a mixed form of farming and pastoralism can exist within the context of nuclear or extended family forms of organization. This type of organization has been documented in other historical contexts in southern Iraq (Poyck 1962). The extreme more centralized form of organization has been documented in southern Iraq during the third millennium B.C., when the Ur III state held large herds of sheep. Shepherds there were integrated into a centralized and institutionalized bureaucracy and appear to have worked directly for the state (Adams 2006). We lack the evidence with which to determine whether the sedentary pastoralists in the Indus fit into any of these models.

The Organization of Interregional Exchange of Plant and Animal Products

The most successful discussion of the organization of production and exchange patterns is William Belcher's analysis of fish remains from different spatial contexts at Harappa (Belcher 2003:101) and the study's implications for the organization of fishing.[5] Belcher's study is based on a combination of ethnoarchaeological research, the examination of fish refuse in domestic contexts in urban and nonurban environments, and butchery patterns of fishermen and fishmongers in present-day markets. He noted that in villages and towns today, when people receive fish directly from fishermen, they tend to consume a variety of seasonally available fish. In contrast, when they procure fish indirectly from markets, there is less product diversity in terms of species present (2003:102). Since procuring fish represents an exchange of goods, determining whether distributions are direct or indirect provides a basis on which to infer social relationships among producers and consumers.

When Belcher examined archaeological fish remains from Harappa, he found there were shifts in distributions between the Pre-urban and Urban periods. In the Pre-urban, procurement was both directly from fishermen and indirectly from an intermediary source; in contrast, in the Urban period, fish remains were procured through indirect distribution, although some households exhibited both direct and indirect modes (2003:161). Furthermore, when he compared street deposits, the sizes and species of fish were more diverse in the Pre-urban than in the Urban period. These contrastive patterns reflect differences in the political and economic infrastructure of fish supply within and to urban centers (Belcher 2003).

Belcher's study of fish remains yielded important data on interregional distribution networks. He notes that at Harappa fish came predominantly from various riverine habitats and that their procurement was dependent upon seasonal factors. However, his major discovery was that a small percentage of fish (1.1%) bones came from marine species. These species were procured from coastal environments significant distances from Harappa, a clear indication of the expansion of resources, the presence of an interregional distribution system, and the availability of more varied food choices. Balakot, a small village, located near maritime resources (discussed earlier in Chapter 4), may have been a fish-processing station, an inference based upon the concentration of processed fish in a section of the settlement. Resettlement of the site during the Urban period, after an abandonment of two hundred years, may have been specifically for the exploitation of fish and shellfish resources. Belcher believes Balakot was colonized by the Harappans just for this purpose. Based on analogy with fishing practices at coastal settlements in Pakistan today, fish most likely were salted to ensure preservation and facilitate trade to inland settlements (Belcher 2003).

There is additional archaeological evidence for the movement of both wild and domesticated plant and animal products across diverse ecological zones. These included ivory, live animals and birds, wood, and a variety of foods. Ivory came from the tusks of elephants, animals that likely were distributed in forested areas throughout the Greater Indus. Some species of wood were common in the alluvial setting in pockets of forest that contained various tree/shrubs (acacia, tamarind, prosopis, ziziphus, salvadora, ficus, and tamarix). These are species known from charcoal assemblages from the Greater Indus Valley (Madella and Fuller 2006). But other woods discovered in archaeological contexts were from Himalayan and sub-Himalayan valleys. As noted in Chapter 6, they include elm and deodar (a coffin from a cemetery at Harappa), teak (Lothal), walnut wood, and night jasmine at Rohira in the Punjab, India (Madella and Fuller 2006).

People took advantage of the civilization's varied ecology as has already been discussed for the regional level. However, as I have already demonstrated, food resources moved over a broad area. Various "agricultural packages" (Fuller 2003) were dispersed in different ecological zones. Winter crops (southwest Asian barley, wheat, etc.) were most at home on the alluvial plain where water was readily available. Summer crops (millets) were drought-resistant and most at home in Gujarat and south India, and yet they were grown at Harappa. And at Banawali southwest Asian crops diffused from the settlements along the Indus or the Ghaggar-Hakra, and local farmers devised appropriate agricultural practices to grow a successful crop. Elsewhere, people refashioned their landscapes by building extensive water storage tanks to accommodate desired or needed animals. The water tanks at Dholavira, built for watering down water buffalo is an example.

Based on this variability, we can envision other possible exchanges in which animal byproducts, such as processed milk, cheese, wool, and animal skins were transported from regions rich in these sources to places desiring nonlocal products. Not surprisingly, as Meadow and Patel (2003) have suggested, certain animals were better suited to specific regions. In arid and semi-arid areas of Baluchistan and Kutch, goats were more commonly kept; however, in the better watered areas of Punjab, sheep greatly outnumbered goats (Meadow and Patel 2003:84).

Agropastoral and Craft-Producing Economies – Intensification, Specialization, Diversification, and the Organization of Production and Distribution

In this and the preceding chapter, my focus has been on intensification, specialization, diversification of products, and organization of their production and distribution. I have sought to demonstrate the mutual benefits and tensions derived from the dual aspects of an agropastoral and craft-producing economy. Additionally, my interests have been in identifying the internal dynamics or social actions that lay beneath the surface of the materials we recover. To catch a glimpse of this infrastructure, I have focused on the particularities of social actions taken to intensify production and the degree to which specialist producers dominated the scene, concentrating in this chapter on the effects of diversification on examining the organization of production and distribution of products. Finally, I have steered away from overemphasizing the centralized nature of production systems in favor of advancing our understanding of everyday practices and considering alternate possibilities.

In previous studies of the Indus economy, agriculture, pastoralism and craft production had not been considered as *integrally related* dimensions of the political economy. In these chapters, I have elaborated on the possible tensions and competition with respect to resources such as land and water, access to local and nonlocal resources, and labor allocation as a basis for inferring potential social relations among farmers and pastoralists and craft producers.

Belcher's research on consumption patterns and exchange provided a model for understanding local relations useful in the study of other agrarian pursuits in the greater Indus. In his studies of fish remains, local consumption patterns varied with different settlement types, and although studies of regional patterns between urban and rural populations have not been undertaken, it seems likely that exchange systems existed among them as well. The exchange of marine catfish over long distances between coastal sites and inland Harappa provides important evidence for well-coordinated distribution systems within the civilization.

Similarly, in analyzing the Harappan agricultural and pastoral system, there is great variability in the types of networks within which goods and services circulated. Local and regional patterns suggest that whereas aspects of agricultural production, for example the communal harvesting and processing of grains, suggest possible control of resources by a limited segment of the population, this control need not have been centralized because it might also involve more limited groupings of people in neighborhood or kin group contexts. Moreover, small-scale processing within individual households most likely have also existed.

The increase in surplus production of plants, animals, and crafts provided opportunities for access to new and varied resources, control of production and distribution, and ultimately to the development of social and political hierarchies. Here, we are again faced with variability. As we have seen, whether on the local or more global level, there were potentials for hierarchies that must have existed among agriculturalists and pastoralists in urban and rural contexts and among settlers in rural areas. Good examples are the pastoral nomads and hunter-gatherer groups that moved about the region's ecologically diverse landscape, contributing trade items most likely in exchange for agricultural and pastoral products. The interactions among these producers and consumers, though variable, very likely translated into relations of power.

With respect to craft production, our indicators of production organization suggest that the process was not uniform. Instead, various crafts and production systems were absorbed in the urban economy in different ways. The crafts discussed demonstrate a range of organizational types, including independent (ceramic production on Mound E at Harappa), administered (stoneware production at Mohenjo-daro), and some type of corporate control, perhaps administered or organized in guildlike groups for seal production. We still lack an understanding of the relative status of craft producers but are closer to more realistic appraisals of the variability in the social and political relations and the degree to which their social identity was linked to the craft in which they were engaged (Costin and Wright 1998).

The adoption of new plants (e.g., millets at Harappa), animals in climatically unsuited areas (water buffalo in poorly watered areas such as at Dholavira), the exploitation of distant resources (fish remains from the coast brought to Harappa), and the production of new craft items should be viewed as social choices among producers and consumers that facilitated links within communities and throughout the greater Indus. These activities provide a window into infrastructural arrangements that underlay the systems described.

Taken as a whole, the overall impression is that the people of the Indus were keenly aware of the potential for optimizing their economic activities in a diverse ecology. They openly engaged in networks of exchange from which various raw and finished products, along with plant and animal resources, were drawn. By exploiting diverse ecological zones, they constructed a world that not only maintained but enriched their economy. There was, of course, nothing "natural" or preordained about the end result. These outcomes were instead based upon social choices and acceptance of new resources as they became known and desired.

These exchanges within the civilization are only part of the story on the distribution of Indus goods. In the next chapter, I focus on long-distance trade between the Harappans and neighboring cultures. Some of our knowledge about trade is from textual sources in far-off Mesopotamia. Although the texts must be used with caution, they complement what is known from the artifacts recovered by archaeologists. Along with complementary archaeological evidence, they are the focus of Chapter 8.

8   The Lure of Distant Lands

In the preceding chapters, I discussed the intensification of the agropastoral and craft-producing economy and the exchange systems among groups within the Indus sphere of influence. My detailed inquiry into distribution and exchange revealed a significant movement of raw and finished products in which diverse ecological zones were exploited.

Indus forays outside of its sphere of influence were extended over great distances. Like many of their contemporaries, the Harappans participated in what Philip Kohl refers to as an "interconnected" and interdependent world that extended west to the eastern Mediterranean including Mesopotamia and Iran to beyond the boundaries of modern-day India. Its northern and southern limits were central Asia and the Arabian Peninsula (Aruz 2003; Kohl 2007). While the apparent rationale for this expansion was the redistribution of natural resources and acquisition of craft products, it brought with it new ideas and social relations.

Our evidence for long-distance interaction comes from a broad range of sources. I begin this chapter with a discussion of what can be gleaned from the Mesopotamian texts and the nature of its contact with the Harappans. In Mesopotamia, where conspicuous display was a cultural value, trade, warfare, and diplomacy were a major means of acquiring needed goods on many geographical fronts including the Indus.

The Lure of Distant Lands – Dilmun, Magan, and Meluhha

Mesopotamian texts cover a long span of history and are of specific relevance to this chapter. Sources cover the mid third to early second millennia B.C. Historical-literary archives and economic texts contain references to "Meluhha" and to other groups who might be contemporary with the Indus and had contacts with Mesopotamia and other lands.

In a frequently cited text, King Sargon, the first king of the Akkadian dynasty (ca. 2334–2154 B.C.), boasted that he had ships in his port loaded with cargo from Dilmun, Magan, and Meluhha. Dilmun has been identified as Bahrain, Magan as Oman, and Meluhha as the Indus.[1]

In another text, Meluhha is described in the following words:

He crossed to the land (*kur*) of Meluhha.
Enki, the king of the sweet-water ocean, decrees its fate:
Black land (*kur*), your trees will be large trees,
they will be *mesu*-groves of the highland (*kur*),[2]
    their thrones will be set in royal palaces.
Your reeds will be large reeds,
they will be reeds of the highland (*kur*),
    heroes work them as weapons in the battlefields.
Your bulls will be large bulls,
they will be bulls of the highland (*kur*),
    their roar will be the roar of the highland (*kur*).
The great laws (*me*) of the gods will be perfected for you.
All *dar*-birds (i.e., fowls) of the highland (*kur*) [wear] carnelian beards;
    your birds will be *haia*-birds,
    their cries will fill the royal palaces.
Your silver will be gold, your copper will be bronze-tin.
Land (*kur*), everything you have will [increase],
your people will [multiply],
    your male will go after his fellow male like a bull.

In this context, the reference to *kur* is to the Iranian plateau and locations east of Mesopotamia (Parpola 1994:14).

Mapping the Third Millennium B.C.

The Harappans did not have maps, but we can produce fairly reliable ones based upon site locations known from archaeological excavations and surveys and polities named in Mesopotamian texts. Figure 8.1 includes some of the major sites that have been subject to archaeological exploration. The same figure includes the names of places mentioned in Mesopotamian texts. Since opinions differ among researchers as to the precise locations of the polities referred to in texts, I have used the major names associated with each area. Where two names appear or a name appears at more than one location, there are conflicting interpretations. As Timothy Potts notes, it is unclear whether textual references are to countries, cities, or towns or whether they are for "regions of varying size and definition, for trivial and other ethnically-based territories, as well as for national-states, empires and transnational entities" (T. Potts

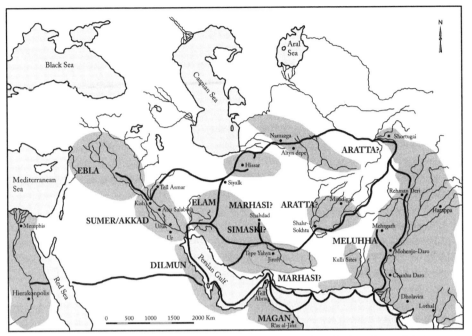

Figure 8.1. Map of ancient sites in the Near East, Indus, Central Asia, and Arabian Peninsula. © R. P. Wright.

1994:12). In any event, the major players, in addition to Dilmun, Magan, and Meluhha, were Elam, Mesopotamia's eastern neighbor with whom it seems to have been in perpetual conflict; Marhasi/Parahsum, a highland power possibly at the easternmost limits to which Akkadian kings ventured; Simaski, not well liked by the Mesopotamians and referred to in derogatory terms as persons who live in tents and know "not the places of the gods, Who mates just like an animal, and knows not how to make offerings" (Potts 1994:30ff.); and Aratta, a land with abundant resources of lapis, gold, silver, and tin.

The international world of the third millennium B.C. involved battles, acquisition of booty, diplomacy, and other ventures conducted over land and sea routes (Box 8.1). It was a period of great change and increasing social and cultural diversity in which materials and ideas were exchanged over a broad geographical area. The overall effect of these changes, with respect to trade and intercultural contact, was the development of numerous settlements that served as bridges between diverse ecological zones, landlocked cities, and multiple cultural groups.

Box 8.1 Routes of Conquest and
Trade – Whether by Land or Sea

It may be difficult for us to conceive of the long distances people traveled during the third millennium B.C. Although not denying that travel would have been difficult (It is staggering to think of the discomforts experienced), it should not be surprising to learn that far-flung contacts have been a necessary part of life ever since people settled down in one place. But getting about must have presented its own set of issues, such as finding water and natural passes through mountain ranges. The large expanses of desert in this region would have necessitated developing well-planned routes to bypass them. Granted, most average Harappans probably never ventured more than a few kilometers from their homes out to agricultural fields, to tend animals, or to procure supplies for crafts, but they likely saw others returning from travels to distant towns or, if living in rural areas, setting out for one of the major Indus centers or even journeying many hundreds of miles from home.

Whether travel was on foot, by cart, pack animal, or boat, there are many examples of efficient modes of travel in early societies. In the Indus, people would have seen or used carts pulled by cattle. This inference is based on the presence of clay cart models discovered in good archaeological context. Laura Miller's study of stress signatures on the skeletal remains of zebu cattle suggests cattle were used for pulling such carts. Other evidence for use of this type of conveyance includes cart tracks found in the city streets at Harappa, demonstrating that carts were used in cities to move goods from one place to another. Carts would have provided good transport on the flat alluvial plain and would have been suitable in other areas where there were rolling plateaus. Based on analogy with similar carts used in the region today, Kenoyer (2004) estimates that Indus carts could carry around 1870 kilograms of cargo. Their use was widespread judging by the clay models of carts found at Harappa, Mohenjo-daro, Chanhu-daro, Lothal, and other sites in Gujarat and Rajasthan.

People also may have seen river boats, as there are depictions of boats suitable for river transport on Indus seals (original in Mackay 1938:340–1, 657, pl. LXXXIX-A). Very likely the boats were made of wood and traveled up and down the rivers most of which were navigable once they entered the plains. We see this practice among the Mohanna, river nomads, in Pakistan today (Shar 1987).

In mountainous regions, different forms of transport would have been necessary. An obvious choice was humans, either through a dedicated "merchant" group or nomads who also kept animals. Either group could easily transport lighter loads, such as finished beads or unworked stone. For heavier loads, pack animals also could have been used. We do not have any direct evidence for the use of sheep and goats for this purpose, and evidence for the use of other animals, such as donkeys, is unclear. According to T. Potts (1994:45), in Mesopotamia, onager and ass may have been kept in a semi-wild state. He notes their depictions in Mesopotamian imagery and also cites the presence of their skeletal remains in Mesopotamian assemblages. Still, if zebu were used by the Harappans, they could carry 54 to 72 kilograms of goods, and sheep and goats, 5 to 18 kilograms. Today, all of these animals are used by farmers to transport grain and fiber from fields. With respect to the distribution of goods within the Indus, carts could have been used to reach places like Baluchistan and then traversed over various mountain passes. (Figure 8.1 shows some routes they may have taken.) Today, many of these routes are traversed by humans riding on the backs of animals; however, there is no evidence for riding animals during this period.

Maritime routes were the main corridors over which products from the Indus moved to Mesopotamia (Figures 8.1 and 1.2), stopping at a chain of settlements. Available routes would include ports in Gujarat from which boats would have moved, hugging the southern coast of present-day Pakistan, perhaps stopping on the coast near Sutkagendor and Sotka-koh and from there on to eastern Oman and Magan. As Maurizio Tosi notes, this area is "the major landmark for boats crossing from Pakistan towards the Gulf and Africa" (1991:123), and he estimates the distance from these sites to Oman at 450 nautical miles. Trading ships may have originated at the two latter sites, collection points for materials coming from inland Baluchistan and the alluvial plain. Passage to Mesopotamia was through the present-day Persian Gulf and likely included various ports-of-call along the coast of southern Iran (at the Straits of Hormuz and Bushire, for example) or on the southerly side of the gulf at ports along the Arabian Peninsula. While maritime routes were an efficient means of transport, shipping would have to be timed to coincide with prevailing winds (Ray 2003). The best times for travel probably would be confined to those months of the year when conditions were optimum. In any event, there likely was considerable risk and uncertainty with respect to delivery of cargo.

Box 8.1 (*Cont.*)

There are representations of boats adequate for sea travel. A boat, probably made of reeds, is depicted on a square seal from Mohenjo-daro (Mackay 1938:340–1, pl. LXXXIII.30). Thor Heyerdahl was able to sail a reed boat through the Persian Gulf, around the Arabian Peninusula, as far as the Red Sea. Reed boats would consist of tightly wrapped bundles of reeds coated with bitumen for waterproofing, such as has been found at the site of Ras al-Junyaz and other sites along the coast of the Arabian peninsula. Other depictions on a pottery sherd (Mackay 1938:183, pl. LXIX.4) and a clay model indicate that the Harappans possessed a knowledge of sailing vessels. Although no sail has ever been recovered, various fibers that could have been used for this purpose were available to the Harappans, including cotton, linen, or leaf matting.

For the great kings ruling Mesopotamia, the focus of interest on this wider world was based on economic, political, and military concerns. An important economic consideration was its political relations with cultural groups accessible over land and by sea. Political considerations turned on whether engagements involved antagonism (through military invasions), diplomacy, or trade relations. The world also was divided according to desired goods, including raw materials, finished products and people, some of whom became prisoners of war and were brought back to Mesopotamia as slaves (T. Potts 1994).

Important information about the Indus can be gleaned from Mesopotamian texts involving conquests and expeditions to lands to the east, in which Meluhha is named. In one instance, an expedition to the east in which a major battle occurred during the reign of Sargon's son, Rimush, is recorded. It involved a military engagement with people of Parahsum, Zahara (location unknown but apparently between Parahsum and Elam), in which the battle was sufficiently fierce that Rimush claimed to have killed 16,212 men and captured 4,216. Booty listed included copper, gold, and prisoners of war. Meluhha is also listed as being among the opponents in this battle (T. Potts 1994:101), though clearly Rimush had not reached the Indus. It is unlikely a Meluhhan "army" was present. Later, in a campaign conducted by Naram-Sin, the grandson of Sargon, reference is made to encounters with the "men" of Meluhha (T. Potts 1994:115).

There also is indirect reference to diplomacy involving Meluhha. They include a tribute involving a "speckled dog of Meluhha" (conceivably an exotic breed known only in the Indus) brought from Marhasi

(T. Potts 1994:140) to a Mesopotamian king at the end of the third millennium. References to trade suggest that water transport was a more efficient means of contact than overland trade, since larger and bulkier goods could be carried with superior speed. Certainly from the mid third millennium B.C., there was great emphasis on Persian Gulf trade as a major conduit for import of metals, stones, and timber, although contact along over land routes continued.

Indus and Mesopotamian Contact by Sea and Over Land – Texts and Archaeology

References to Meluhha in the gulf trade are frequent and archaeological evidence supports some of the Mesopotamian claims. Items referred to in texts received from Meluhha include the following (T. Potts 1994:148ff.): copper (from royal inscriptions, economic, and literary texts), tin used as an alloy (from a royal inscription from a late third millennium king), lapis lazuli (used for beads, inlay and cylinder seals in Mesopotamia listed as arriving in unworked "lumps"), various types of carnelian in raw and finished form, including stones speckled with white, black, mustard, yellow, and possible references to chalcedony, agate, jasper, and other stones used in Indus bead production. In fact, the Mesopotamian texts state clearly that Meluhha was the primary, "if not exclusive, origin" of carnelian (T. Potts 1994:197) and ebony (*mes.meluhha*). Other materials listed include pearls (fish eyes), and gold ("gold of Meluhha"; T. Potts 1994:160). Specific references such as a royal inscription from the late third millennium B.C. in which gold from Meluhha and silver (literary sources speak of silver from Meluhha) are recorded. Other items are various wood species, among them ebony, "thorn tree" (possibly mangrove), mulberry, sissoo, and date palm (Ratnagar 1981:100). Ivory also is mentioned, but with specific reference to "birds of Meluhha" (Ratnagar 1981:111).

These textual references to goods imported in Mesopotamia complement archaeological evidence there. They include many of the raw and finished products discussed in this chapter and in Chapters 6 and 7, such as pure and arsenical copper, etched carnelian and long-barrel beads, lapis lazuli, silver, and shell although none have been archaeometrically sourced. Among the objects found in Mesopotamia made of lapis were ornaments, statuary, ceremonial gifts, foundation tablets in temples, and cylinder seals (Ratnagar 1981:137) most likely produced by Mesopotamian artisans from imported lapis lazuli. Cubical dice found in a royal cemetery are stylistically the same as those known in the Indus (1981:146).

Important indicators of trade are seals and sealings. Seals were produced in different shapes and styles that make them readily identifiable with their place of origin. As discussed in Chapter 6, seals can be thought of as a device with which to identify the signatures of individual persons, kin groups, or large institutions. The most typical Indus seal was square, with its script along the top, an animal at the center, and an icon at the bottom. In Mesopotamia, in contrast, the typical seal was cylindrical (Figure 10.7). The latter often contained images of humans and gods engaged in various activities, some of which are derived from Mesopotamian myths.

The number of Indus-type seals discovered in southern Mesopotamia is small (approximately ten) and few are unequivocal examples of the square seals produced in the Indus itself. They include square seals with images of unicorns, zebu, short-horned bulls, tiger, and water buffalo and swastika and geometric designs. One square seal has an Indus motif and cuneiform writing, while a cylinder seal depicts animals associated with the Indus (an elephant, rhinoceros, and gharial) and two square seals (one with a swastika similar to ones known from the Indus and another with a geometric design) (Ratnagar 1981, Possehl 1996, 2002, Aruz 2003). Most of the seals are from Akkadian contexts, complementing the textual sources cited earlier, as well as the archaeological evidence for resources and objects from the Indus that have been discovered in Mesopotamia.

Sealings are the impressions made by seals when pressed against a pliable material (see Box 6.2). At the Indus site of Lothal, located near carnelian sources and the coast, there are ninety-three clay impressions, in which the typical square Indus seal has been impressed on packing materials. The reverse sides of the sealings bear impressions of woven cloth indicating that the cloth had been wrapped around a container before mud was applied and the package sealed. A seal impression from the Mesopotamian city of Umma also contains all of the elements typical of Indus seals (a unicorn with Indus script) and the cloth-backed impression on its reverse (Tosi 1991:369; Frenez and Tosi 2005). Four other sealing impressions with Indus imagery and/or script were discovered in Mesopotamia.

Many of the objects discovered in Mesopotamia are from centers near the mouth of the Persian Gulf and, therefore, are most likely to have arrived by sea. Others would have come on a northerly track over land through Iran (the old Khorasan Road, see Figure 8.1) possibly via Shortugai (see Chapter 5). Several artifacts at the site of Tell Asmar (Eshnunna) in the Diyala region (near modern Baghdad) are indicative of Indus contact, including two of the seals with Indus affinities, lapis lazuli, a crystal pendant representing a monkey, inlay and stamp seals, etched carnelian beads, and a distinctive ceramic referred to as "knobbed" ware. Finally, as Possehl has noted, one of the buildings at Tell Asmar has a "privy" comparable to those at Mohenjo-daro and a drainage system normally associated with the Indus (Possehl 1997:95).

The reciprocal nature of trade is attested by Mesopotamian recovered objects in the Indus. They include Mesopotamian barrel weights (Mohenjo-daro and Harappa), animal-headed metal pins (Mohenjo-daro), cylinder seals (three at Mohenjo-daro), a "toilet" set of copper implements (Harappa), and copper axe-adzes (Mohenjo-daro and Sibri) (Possehl 1996b:176ff).

The reciprocal nature of trade is attested by Mesopotamian recovered objects in the Indus. They include Mesopotamian barrel weights (Mohenjo-daro and Harappa), animal-headed metal pins (Mohenjo-daro), a "toilet" set of copper implements (Harappa), and copper axe-adzes (Mohenjo-daro and Sibri) (Possehl 1996b:176ff). There were, as well, other materials that very likely were traded to the Indus. These so-called "invisible" products because they do not preserve well in the Indus included woolen cloth, barely and oil (Crawford 1973, Ratnagar 1981).

Mackay discovered three cylinder seals at Mohenjo-daro (1938: 344ff.). However, all carried images that were known from Indus seals, for example, gharials, short-horned goats, a tree and a bird, possibly a scorpion, and two antelopes. He proposed that the Harappans had seen cylinder seals but did not find them useful for the type of packaging they developed and that the Mohenjo-daro cylinder seals were among a few seals produced in the Indus. This interpretation falls in line with the cylinder seal from Kalibangan (Figure 10.4). Several of the images on that seal are replicated on square seals, suggesting it was not imported.

Two types of evidence, one from a cylinder seal and the other from Mesopotamian texts, provide us with insights regarding the degree of contact between people living in southern Mesopotamia and the Indus. They suggest a remarkably close relationship, as they show that Indus people actually traveled to Mesopotamia and a few who may have emigrated to Mesopotamia.

One named individual is *Shu-ilishu*. But who was he? Our information comes from a seal bearing Mesopotamian script in which *Shu-ilishu*, is named as owner of the seal and is identified as a Meluhha interpreter. The image on the seal depicts a seated goddess (based upon her headdress and type of seat on which she is sitting). Two people, perhaps Shu-ilishu and his wife approach the goddess. The approaching woman carries a situla (or bucket) normally carried by a priest.

The two people approaching the goddess are wearing clothing known from Mesopotamian statuary and other seals; thus they are not represented as foreigners. Behind the goddess someone is brewing a drink. Because this seal has a well-established iconographical grouping, it has been suggested that it was "ready-cut" from a seal cutter's workshop to which the inscription was added (Boehmer 1965; Parpola 1994:132). A somewhat different interpretation of the image is that the two figures are paying tribute to a goddess, the man bringing a deer (at the top of the seal) and the woman, the situla. The bearded figure on the knees of the goddess "may evoke the birth of a young god personifying vegetation" (Aruz 2003:413), though others have suggested the seated individual is *Shu-ilishu*, represented "symbolically as a dwarf seated on the lap of a person of higher rank" (Tosi 1991:118). In any event, the fact that the seal was owned by a person from Meluhha is significant, as it reinforces the idea that "commercial or diplomatic relations with the region of Meluhha were regular enough to justify the existence of a professional interpreter" (Aruz 2003:413).

Mesopotamian texts refer to merchants from Meluhha living in Mesopotamia. Twelve texts dating from the Ur III period in Mesopotamia (2112–2004 B.C.)[3] refer to a village there called *me luhha* [written with a determinative *ki*]. The *ki* determinative suggests that the village originally was a trading settlement (a "village of traveling merchants") whose inhabitants had become acculturated (Parpola et al. 1977:145). They appear to have been permanent residents, since the texts date to a period of forty-five years. The village of Meluhha appears to have functioned "as a normal unit of local agricultural production" (T. Potts 1994:36). These arrangements and the acculturation of Indus traders living in a former trading settlement, now a proper Mesopotamian village, differ from the norm for Mesopotamians who lived abroad. Mesopotamian texts tell us that their merchants lived in garrisons and Mesopotamian-style households apart from local people.[4]

An additional text is dated to a slightly earlier period (the Akkadian). It concerns a "man of Meluhha" who was fined and required to pay the injured party a payment for a broken tooth, apparently due to a physical encounter! In this instance, unlike the men cited in the later texts, who are named as "citizens/inhabitants (*dumu* of this village)" and bear local Sumerian names, this individual's name was not Sumerian. It appears to have been translated from his native language into Sumerian as "just buffalo-cow," which "does not make sense in the Mesopotamian cultural sphere" (Parpola et al. 1977:161). This early text and the later ones suggest that the Meluhhans traveled to Mesopotamia over several generations and that acculturation took a period of several hundred years.

These texts provide a context for *Shu-ilishu*'s place in Mesopotamian society. We can imagine that, like the other Meluhhans, he had established some close ties within Mesopotamia. *Shu-ilishu* may have started out as a merchant and later, having become familiar with the language, forged a new profession as a translator. We assume he was bilingual and achieved some recognition, establishing a new life (he may even have been born there) a long way from his original home. Individuals with such worldly experiences clearly were limited to a very small number in the third millennium B.C., but it seems clear here, that it was not an experience reserved for royalty or the priestly class. Knowledge about merchants or "expatriate meluhhans" are important because they provide a glimpse into some of the experiences in which individual Meluhhans, whether they were traders, merchants, diplomats, or leaders, engaged when they traveled far from home.

Indus Contact beyond Mesopotamia – By Sea and Over Land

Indus trade did not begin and end with its interactions with Mesopotamia. It included a broad sphere of influence beyond Mesopotamia, involving contact along maritime and overland routes to places named in Mesopotamian texts and others extending into Central Asia.

Indus Contacts along Maritime Routes

There were a number of ports of trade located in the Indus region. They include the settlements at Kuntasi (or even Dholavira discussed in previous chapters), Lothal, and Sutkagen-dor and Sotka-koh. Sutkagen-dor and Sotka-koh were founded by Indus settlers who brought with them basic Harappan goods and situated themselves at strategic locations. At Sutkagen-dor, a massive mudbrick structure served as a rampart or lookout, and at Sotka-koh the site was surrounded by a large enclosure formed by natural rock ridges. George Dales, who discovered Sotka-koh and also excavated at Sutkagen-dor, described the locations of these two sites as "virtually identical – both being in major valleys that provided access from the seacoast to the inland Kej Valley. Neither was presently near enough to the sea to be called a seaport, but both had commanding positions for controlling any movement of people or goods along the valley routes" (Dales and Lipo 1992:110).[5]

To the east of these fortified sites, wedged in between them and the Harappan site of Balakot, are a number of settlements occupied by a people referred to as "Kulli" (Figure 8.1) who lay along an overland route.

The Kulli appear to have been a group having strong local traditions that persisted in the shadow of the Indus civilization untill 2400 B.C., when there is an overlay of Indus materials. Evidence for this culture is distributed over a broad area, inclusive of the area of Las Bela and parts of the Makran. Some aspects of Kulli material culture are distinctive, for example, their sites are constructed of stone. Many human figurine types and pottery shapes and designs are unique, but at the same time they also borrowed design elements and artifacts from the Indus, testifying to contact with the larger culture (Dales 1976). Even though Kulli territory is much smaller than the Indus, they must have been a group with which to reckon. Among the sites discovered are large and small settlement types including Nindowari at fifty hectares. Many are located in "strategic positions" at mountain tops or hills overlooking valleys and controlling plains and passes (Franke-Vogt 2000). The presence of Kulli sites situated in between a more or less continuous line of Harappan settlements appears as a wedge of cultural resistance and one for which the most diplomatic of negotiations had to be exercised (Wright 2002b).

In Mesopotamian texts, references to Magan and Dilmun provide an uneven view of trade because they do not mention contacts specific to the Indus and other cultures on the Arabian Peninsula for which there is significant archaeological evidence. In other words, cultures along the gulf coast were actively engaged in import and export of commodities and relations with the Indus itself. For example, Indus cubical stone weights have been found at gulf sites. In addition some seals referred to as "Persian Gulf" stamp seals appear to have been hybrid Harappan seals. T. Potts (1994) suggests that "the weights and seals have to do with the regulation of trade" (1994:193).

There are many materials from the Indus found at gulf sites, which were apparently not destined for Mesopotamia but were meant for local consumption. For example, etched carnelian beads, finished bronze blade axes of a typical Indus style, carved ivory combs, faience objects, and long cylindrical lapis beads were found at locations along the Arabian coast, stretching from Bahrain to the United Arab Emirates (UAE) and Oman. Also, Indus people very likely exported to the gulf food and fiber products that do not preserve in archaeological contexts, such as textiles, wood, dry foodstuffs, and milk products (yogurt/ghee). Products traded to the Indus may have been perishable supplies, such as cured fishes, spices, dates, and date products.

The presence of a number of distinctive artifacts and pottery types has been well documented by excavations conducted in the UAE and Oman. Gerd Weisgerber (1984) was one of the first to investigate the presence of copper products at the site of Al-Maysar, establishing connections between

Oman and the Indus. Among the artifacts discovered was a prismatic seal similar to others at Mohenjo-daro engraved with bulls and Indus script. Another example was found in Bahrain (Weisgerger 1984:199), establishing a connection between Dilmun and the Indus as well.

Other archaeological research in Oman has involved extensive exploration and excavations at coastal settlements. Indications of contact with the Indus include the occurrence of particular pottery forms, especially the large black storage jars (discussed in Chapter 6) found in Oman and used for carrying products from the Indus (possibly liquid or grain) (Cleuziou and Tosi 1989:40), and perhaps serving as ballast in boats transporting goods from the Indus to the gulf, as amphorae have done throughout antiquity. The jars frequently have Indus signs inscribed on their exteriors. Analytical studies based upon neutron activation analysis of the composition of the clays from which these ceramics were made indicate that at least some in Oman and the UAE were produced in the Indus (Mery and Blackman 2005). These jar types and others are comparable to ceramic types found at Nausharo in Baluchistan (see Chapters 3 and 4), Mohenjo-daro, Harappa, and Lothal during the Urban period and clearly are linked to maritime trade.

The black storage jars are emblematic of the vibrant trade that took place between settlements on the Arabian coast and are one example of the ways in which the material culture of interacting groups became assimilated into local traditions. As described, the storage jars were produced in standardized shapes, constructed efficiently enough to facilitate the containment of liquids or other contents. In addition, because of their "onion-shaped" narrowed lower sections, they could be piled closely in narrow spaces. As Cleuziou and Tosi (2000) point out, Indus

inscriptions frequently stamped or scratched on their shoulder would have been handy reminders of their contents in all operations. Once the jars had reached Oman, they were not sent back but entered the local circuits as an independent resource to be used as containers for all kinds of purposes, not least as containers for shipments within the country. (2000:52)

Finally, from evidence found at sites on the Arabian Peninsula, we can infer that Indus traders traveled there with some frequency. The site of Ras al-Jinz on the coast of Oman may have served as a port for ships from the Indus. In addition to trade, the abundant quantities of shellfish there very likely was an additional attraction. Many aspects of the site suggest that it may even have been built by Indus people who traveled there on a temporary basis during seasons when the fishing would be worthwhile (Cleuziou and Tosi 1994). The presence of inscribed materials, stamp seals, and Indus iconography along with buildings constructed of mudbrick typical of the Indus but unknown in Oman at the time indicate exceptionally close contact with the Indus or the actual presence of Indus people. Perhaps the most spectacular evidence for long-distance contacts is slabs of bitumen interpreted to be remnants of boats. Some slabs are encrusted with barnacles and/or carry mat impressions. Some contain inclusions of crushed reeds and other swamp vegetation. Based on analogy with vessels known in historical periods, they suggest that the boats were produced by lashing together bound bundles (of reeds) that were waterproofed with bitumen (Cleuziou and Tosi 2000:64; Vosmer 2000). Ongoing research projects related to these discoveries involve attempts to determine potential sources for the bitumen using isotopic analyses. Oman has been excluded as the bitumen source; other sources include the Kachi Plain (near Nausharo and Mehrgarh), northern Iraq, and southwestern Iran (Cleuziou and Tosi 2000:66). Indus weights have been discovered elsewhere in the UAE at Tell Abraq (D. Potts 1990b), suggesting that merchants there were emulating Harappan mercantile practices. Archaeological discoveries in Bahrain suggest similar developments there (Carter 2003:40).

Indus Contacts along Overland Routes

Indus forays into the outside world were not confined to the Arabian Peninsula. Based on archaeological evidence, we know overland trade took the Harappans to modern-day Afghanistan, Iran, and Central Asia. In Chapter 7, I discussed the site of Shortugai in northeastern Afghanistan, a fully Indus site.

The expansion of Indus settlements to Shortugai was part of a much larger sphere of contact that Possehl has referred to as a Middle Asian Interaction Sphere (2002:215ff). This "sphere" encompassed non-Indus settlements in central and southern Iran noted on Figure 8.1 (for example, Tepe Yahya, the Jiroft, Shahdad, Shahr-I Sokhta, Siyalk, and Hissar) others in southern Afghanistan (Mundigak and Said Qala), and in central Asia (Altyn Depe and Namazga). Even though all of these settlements were not contemporary, they constituted multiple complex polities during the period 2500–1800 B.C.

Contacts between the Indus and Middle Asia are based on the widespread distribution of artifacts produced in the Indus. They include etched carnelian beads (Mundigak). Distributed over a broad area in Iran, there are etched carnelian and ivory beads, carnelian long-barrel beads, bronze objects and cylinder seals with images, for example, zebus, and Indus script. Of particular interest is the presence of Indus objects at Tepe Hissar along a northern route (the Old Khorasan Road) leading south directly to Tell Asmar in Mesopotamia (where Indus materials have been discovered) and at Susa, traversing a southerly route.

Many of the same Indus materials have been discovered in Central Asia, beginning by the middle of the third millennium B.C. The contact with central Asia accelerated toward the end of the third millennium and beginning of the second, when a material culture associated with people from the Bactrian Margiana region (the general location of Altyn depe and Namazga) is present at a number of Indus settlements. This grouping is referred to as the Bactrian Margiana Archaeological Complex or BMAC, although as Kohl (2007) and others (J.-F. Jarrige 1985) have suggested its origins should be sought over a wider region inclusive of eastern Iran and Baluchistan (2007:237).

Although there is much more research to be done on the presence of the BMAC in the Indus at this time, current evidence indicates, that at a time when the Indus civilization was near its end, it had lost influence in many different areas. In these areas, local groups were establishing contacts with regions even beyond those with whom the Indus had previously interacted.

Contacts with the BMAC includes the presence of stylistic elements and objects associated with Central Asian cultures. At Mohenjo-daro, for example, Alexandra Ardeleanu-Jansen (1991:168ff.) has suggested that although produced in the Indus the style of representation of several Indus stone sculptures (see Figure 1.5 and Chapter 9) bear similarities to images of males seated in the same postures on a BMAC vessel. Elsewhere at the site of Gilund (figure 1.2 in Rajasthan, 30 kilometers from Balathal (discussed in Chapters 3 and 4) recent discoveries include other objects in the BMAC style. At Gilund, occupied between 3000 and 1700 B.C., 100 seal impressions from round seals with design motifs most typical of the BMAC were discovered near the end of Gilund's occupation. Similar seals and seal impressions have been discovered in northern (Nausharo and elsewhere) and southern Baluchistan (Kulli sites), and eastern Iran (Shahdad, Shahr-I Sokhta, Bampur). Their presence at Gilund is the first evidence for the interaction of this culture with settlements "so deep within India, which significantly expands the geographic picture" (Shinde et al. 2005).

In view of this intrusion of new materials so late in the history of the Indus, some scholars have suggested that the BMAC may represent a massive migration of new people into new areas. However, as I discuss in Chapter 9, the shifts in settlement patterns and the founding of new sites described in this chapter and the presence of Kulli materials in Baluchistan and BMAC materials there and elsewhere were not the result of large population migrations. The artifact distributions are based upon small numbers of key objects that alert us to interaction of people over a broad zone. Importantly, there is no biological evidence, based upon continued studies by biological anthropologists of human skeletal remains, for "massive population replacement of Indus Valley populations" by people from the BMAC cultures (Hemphill and Christensen 1994). I will return to the BMAC in Chapter 11.

The Indus and an Interconnected Third – Millennium World

In our modern global society, there is a tendency to think that in earlier times communities were isolated. However, the evidence presented here contradicts that notion and leads us to wonder whether our own fascination with distant lands and cultural influences are that unique. Americans traveling in France, for example, will not be surprised to hear rap music in the streets of Paris. At the same time, they will be captivated by the charm of a Parisian cafe, the essence of which is not easily duplicated outside of the French context. But as we have seen, this curiosity about other cultures and even the desire to emulate them is not an innovation of modern Western society. Some Harappans appear to have shared a curiosity and attraction for distant places, most likely based on practical matters and their geographical proximity, but they also rallied around to "fitting in." In any event, we should not think of Indus people as totally isolated from their contemporaries. In this chapter, I have focused on the economic and political aspects of Indus contact with people beyond their spheres of influence. Mesopotamian textual sources provide a key window into some of the politics involved in external contacts. The archaeological evidence partially confirms the textual sources and brings to light other contacts with the polities in the gulf and Middle Asia. Philip Kohl has suggested that, while it flourished, the Indus (Meluhha) "dominated" maritime long-distance trade along the gulf but that other states – the BMAC and other groups in Middle Asia (Sialk and Hissar) – controlled overland routes in the north while Shahr-I Sokhta, the Jiroft, and Shahdad (see locations on Figure 8.1) may have directed southern routes (Kohl 2007:219).

Unquestionably, trade and other forms of contact (alliances, warfare, and shared ideologies) were significant factors in the Indus economy and its social and political development. In Chapter 7, I broadened our outlook on this question by first addressing the internal (regional and interregional) trade within the Indus itself, a process that was integrally related to the long-distance trade addressed in this chapter.

In fact, there is a long history in the Indus and more generally in the region of wide-ranging exchange networks. As discussed in Chapter 3, materials from great distances – objects made of marine shell and lapis lazuli – were present in burial contexts even in the earliest levels at Mehrgarh. The spread of domesticated plants and animals from southwest Asia are other examples. This trend continued as the number of sites beyond Baluchistan increased. It was in this period, discussed in Chapter 4, that a number of regional polities coexisted and were brought together only later under the single culture of the Indus. The development of internal movements of raw materials and finished products and long-distance trade during the Urban period of the Indus needs to be considered within that context.

It is in that sense that viewing trade and other forms of exchange along this continuum of development provides a basis for evaluating its significance in the consolidation of the Indus. There is much variability with respect to the internal distribution systems present and their organizations. Several types have been advanced, ranging from trader/craftpersons and merchants involved in chert procurement to possible state-sponsored, centralized production and distribution of long-barrel carnelian beads from Chanhu-daro. Trade is especially plausible when the Mesopotamian textual sources are considered. The scale of the distribution systems far outweighs anything known from previous periods and clearly was a catalyst in the growth of urbanism at mid-third millennium B.C.

Most revealing is the expansion of settlement into new territories located in regions strategically placed for long-distance trade linked to maritime routes. Based upon Mesopotamian texts and archaeological evidence, Timothy Potts believes that from the middle of the third millennium B.C., most goods arrived in Mesopotamia by sea. This preference for sea trade differs from previous periods, when Mesopotamians drew on a variety of source areas procured over land. According to Potts, this shift in focus was the result of the lower costs of maritime trade, compared to the use of overland routes, and was based primarily on economic considerations (1994:280). Thinking back now on the installation of settlements at Shortugai, near the lapis source, and the towns at Sutkagen-dor and Sotka-koh, there can be no doubt that these actions were conscious attempts on the parts of traders and merchants to gain control of new avenues for trade over land. In so doing, Indus engagement may have been limited by neighboring groups, as exemplified by the Kulli culture or perhaps as Dales suggested they played a "middleman" role (1976:76). Although boundary cultures like the Kulli seem not to have been fully incorporated into the Indus and remained wedged between its heartland and extended territory, the Harappans devised ways to engage in economic transactions without dominating its trading partners. In addition, by circumventing the Kulli, Sutkagen-dor and Sotka-koh maintained their defensible locations, free from raiding by sea (gulf "pirates") or land (the Kulli).

As discussed, there was an intensification of exchanges between Middle Asia and the Indus when trade among highland groups and others beyond Elam continued throughout the second half of the third millennium B.C. and into the early second. The founding of the Indus site of Shortugai falls within this grouping. Trading relations with groups in Central Asia, Shortugai, and Iran along northerly overland routes leading to the Diyala region and Tell Asmar offered access to additional trading partners and overland trade. On balance, their presence indicates that overland trade remained important even as maritime trade expanded.

The evidence clearly indicates that the organization of trade in the Indus differed from that of Mesopotamia. Although trade arrangements shifted with time in Mesopotamia, it was dominated overall by the temple and palace organizations that directed "traffic in *finished* objects and the transshipment of resources" (Lamberg-Karlovsky 1989:260). Traders were sponsored by these organizations. They obtained goods on consignment and a percentage of profit was paid to them by the temple or palace. In the Indus, trade organization was more varied. There are hints of official control in the presence of Indus standardized weights on the Arabian Pennisula, long-barrel and etched carnelian beads in Mesopotamia (based on the evidence for specialist artisans at Chanhudaro discussed in Chapters 6 and 7), establishment of outposts near source areas specific to long-distance trade (Shortugai, Sotka-koh, Sutkagen-dor), and the presence of Mesopotamian seals in Indus contexts (to be discussed in Chapter 9). In contrast, the evidence for shell working at Kuntasi and Negaswar may indicate that trade was conducted by independent groups, such as merchants or individuals acting on their own on an occasional basis (discussed in Chapter 7). The presence of people of Meluhha (discussed in this chapter) in a former merchant town in Mesopotamia and others taking up seasonal residence in Oman is more suggestive of an independently organized merchant group, though we know little about their status in the Indus community.

In the following chapter, I return to the issues addressed in Chapter 5 with respect to civic authority in Indus cities. Considering the presence of crafts people, merchants, traders, and other individuals who produced and consumed goods discussed in Chapters 6, 7, and 8, I address issues of community identity, social order, and memory by exploring the landscapes of Indus cities.

9 Landscapes of Order and Difference – The Cultural Construction of Space, Place, and Social Difference

> The map [defines a place and] ... geometrically records topographic relationships on a single plane measuring the proximity of one stationary entity to another. The concept of space, on the other hand, undermines the map's static arrangement with phenomenological experience. The "practiced place" is inscribed with the stories of its inhabitants and speaks to the temporality indicative of such movements.
>
> Nichole Wiedemann and Judith Birdsong 2000:8

In Chapters 5 and 6, I described the Indus civilization as a number of urban centers organized into independent city-states (Chapter 5) linked by broad-based production and distribution networks (Chapters 6–8). While the city-states themselves shared certain recognizable cultural traditions, sufficient variation exists in the construction and arrangement of architectural forms, including buildings, public works, wall constructions (see my discussion of differences in city plans at Mohenjo-daro, Harappa, and Dholavira later in this chapter) and "neighborhood" sectors to suggest localized civic authority. Thanks to the results of regional surveys, we also have evidence for hierarchies of rural settlement involving towns and villages associated with the civilization's major cities. People took part in regional production and distribution networks within the city-states, between centers and rural areas and were engaged in diverse occupations. Detailed studies of material culture, technologies, and contexts of work and exchange suggest that many different types of organization coexisted, ranging from the control of finished products and raw materials by individuals, family groups, specialist traders, elite merchants, and possibly state institutions (Chapters 6–8).

These characteristics are expanded on by topics taken up in this chapter. If we assume that an elite class of rulers managed the Indus city-states and that craftspeople, merchants, and other individuals produced and consumed products, there also should be evidence for differences among people in their access to places, spaces, amenities, and material resources. Identifying these differences would provide support for arguments advanced in earlier chapters and would demonstrate the ways in which "practiced places" inscribed a social differentiation that was perceived and visible in day-to-day interactions among the Harappans themselves.

One way in which to examine the archaeological record for social differences is through the study of the creation and use of landscapes. When the term "landscape" comes to mind, our first image may be of the natural environment, but of equal significance is the humanly constructed world. These are the familiar "cultural" landscapes of villages, towns, and cities, where people come to view streets, walkways, and architectural features as common "public" experiences (Crowe 1995). For the Indus civilization, one of our best windows into how the constructed environment reveals social perceptions is in the layout of its cities. We can use information from published data to envision how the Harappans experienced the constructed landscape as they went about their daily lives and how their social positions were actualized.

Studying the constructed landscapes is not new to archaeology. Here, I focus on the social dimensions of landscapes and borrow concepts from recent studies (Crowe 1995, Van Dommelen 1999: 284). These dimensions include studies of landscapes as sites of sociocultural or community identity, social order, and memory (Ashmore and Knapp 1999:14ff.).[1] Each of these will be addressed in this chapter. I address these in order to observe the similarities and differences visible in the spatial relationships of buildings, their size and linkages among households, neighborhoods, and communities. In addition, I examine their interiors and artifact contexts to determine the types of materials consumed in household contexts and identify prestige-related materials. Greater or differential access to materials, goods, services, amenities, and space marks certain people as "different" or "elites". It is in that sense that although Indus cities share common characteristics, they also reveal a consciously created spatial and material order that signaled social hierarchies and "naturalized" a social life that was not equally advantageous for all its members.

In this chapter, then, I argue against the view that perceived homogeneity of the culture reflected unspoken sanctions against public display that concealed inequalities between rulers and other members of the society (D. Miller 1985). What I demonstrate here is that status distinctions and social differences were apparent in the differential value of artifacts, public amenities, and architectural forms.

Landscapes as Community Identity – Mohenjo-daro, Dholavira, and Harappa

Landscapes are inscribed places because in their creation and use they become markers of social and cultural identities. In the Indus, the most visually prominent created landscapes to which we have access were its cities. In large measure, it was in them that community identities were formed and nurtured through the allocation of spaces and resources and the installation of public works. In this chapter, I rely principally on published reports of early twentieth-century excavations at Mohenjo-daro (Marshall 1931; Mackay 1938) and the recent research conducted by the Rheinisch-Westfalischen Technischen Hochschule Aachen (RWTH) and Istituto Italiano per il Medio and Estremo Oriente of Rome (IsMEO). But it is important to note that the early twentieth-century excavations bring with them a host of problems. In these early published accounts only whole objects are illustrated. However, in addition to the materials that actually appear in the reports, others are found curated in museums and repositories. These large numbers of artifacts bear consideration here. The results of recent research at Mohenjo-daro have partially remedied this situation through the use of new mapping and survey strategies and the examination of the original fieldbooks and artifacts stored in museums. The extensive research on building technology at Mohenjo-daro conducted by the RWTH team from Aachen University (Jansen 1993a,b) provides our best starting point for understanding community identity because it specifically addresses issues relating to city planning and other considerations involved in creating a new city.

According to this new research, Mohenjo-daro was built in a short period of time, perhaps "only a few years, equipped from the beginning with vertical water supply systems such as wells, which could hardly have been constructed later than when the city was already flourishing" (Jansen 1984:145). Jansen views the creation of the Mohenjo-daro landscape and especially its extensive water works as "man's attempt to control nature" (Jansen 1993a,b:17). This interpretation is hardly new, as a human desire to tame the natural landscape is an impulse thought to be common in human history. It is exemplified by such constructions as Renaissance garden architecture and "elaborate fountain architecture" known from the Moghul period (Jansen 1993b:17).

His interpretation varies in important ways from the one I offer here. I argue that while humans clearly have attempted to *control* nature in many times and places, the mindset of Indus builders was to *transform* it. I mean by this that a particular set of ideational concepts having to do with the transformation of nature underpin and inform the construction of Indus cites. I further argue that this set of uniquely constructed cultural ideas is also apparent in crafting which was another domain in which artisans manipulated particular elements of the natural and materially constructed world. For the Indus, I view this "transformative" mindset as a technological style, a way of working with materials and restructuring them. In that sense, the creation of city landscapes is closely aligned to some more important, well-established principles adopted by Indus artisans in their production of small-scale objects. In both cases, fundamental aspects of nature were incorporated into the spaces and objects they created, thereby transmitting their ideas *about nature and its relation to "man-made" worlds*, as (Crowe 1995) suggested in other contexts.

In its conception and construction, the city's builders adopted a mindset much like that of the artisans who produced smaller, mobile objects, such as the ornaments discussed in previous chapters. When I speak of actualizing a "transformative" mindset in city building and material artisanry, I mean that the Harappan's applied their intimate knowledge of the transmutational aspects of natural processes to the building materials with which they worked, much like artisans did in the production of their smaller scale, portable objects. As we saw in Chapters 6 and 7, the primary orientation of Indus artisans was to break down and reconstitute raw materials. Grinding down stone (for faience production) and adding mineral pigments to alter its original color or enhancing the color of carnelian by subjecting it to heat to bring out its latent minerals are two examples. As will be discussed, they included large-scale planning that involved the construction of engineering works of a kind unprecedented for their time, evincing the same mindset to transform the natural landscape to one totally humanized by altering and rearranging normal flows of water and a conscious plan to reclaim natural processes for human use. This, then, was a mindset, a technological style, in which Indus artisans appropriated the natural metamorphic processes it took millennia to accomplish in nature. They effected these transformations in a matter of months, as though they had discovered the earth's most intimate secrets long before geologists had done so in the modern era.

Three aspects of city planning and associated technologies – celestial orientations of city layout, platform construction, and the creation of a water management system – demonstrate an orientation to metamorphose natural phenomena and recreate the landscape. First, investigations of the layout of streets at Mohenjo-daro suggest that planners relied on astronomical data of the positions of the sun and fixed stars and integrated them with elements from the physical landscape (Wankze

1984:35). To orient the city's layout, natural landscape elements visible on the Kirthar Mountain Range to the north of the city were combined with observations of the setting sun and the alignments of fixed stars to provide orientation points. Subsequent irregularities in the orientations of buildings at Mohenjo-daro were the result of different building episodes, as new sightings on particular stars were utilized by planners during several hundred years of city building and remodeling (Wanzke 1984:37). These architectural axes to cardinal points and irregularities in these orientations are also observable at other Harappan sites.

A second aspect of centralized planning and another major undertaking was the construction of two massive platforms in the VS and DK-G areas (see Figure 5.2 for locations). They represent a conscious alteration of the landscape that involved the existence of an extraordinary infrastructure for planning and execution (Jansen 1984:13). Given the proximity of the city to flooding (Chapter 2), there likely were practical reasons for constructing platforms. However, similar platforms occur at Indus settlements where flooding does not appear to have been a problem. It remains that, for whatever reasons, the four million cubic meters of clay and sediment plus millions of bricks needed to construct the two platforms at Mohenjo-daro represented a significant labor and material investment. Jansen refers to these constructions as "founding platforms." Although he believes they functioned to protect against flooding, he suggests they may have provided "an iconographic element of elevating specific areas and structures" (1984:15). Conceivably, there was a symbolic connection between the Kirthar Mountains and the founding platforms.

A third aspect of large-scale planning involved the massive engineering works. Over 700 wells (Jansen 1993b:118) distributed throughout Mohenjo-daro, as well as bathing platforms, drainage systems, and refuse disposal arrangements found there were major technological constructions that reclaimed natural processes for human use.

As discussed in Chapter 5, individual houses were equipped with a number of amenities. Bathing and toilet areas were positioned on an outside wall. Like wells, they were made of specially engineered bricks that produced a tight fit, carefully designed and constructed at just above floor level to ensure optimum gravity flow. Facilities were, as in Figure 9.1, sloped toward an outlet that flowed directly into a street drain or cesspit (Jansen 1989:189). A few houses had toilets that were incorporated into the outside wall of the platform (Jansen 1993b: 122) and fitted with seats made of bricks, while others consisted of a hole set over a chute. In addition to the built-in drains, other arrangements were devised to channel water and waste into ceramic soak pits. The pots shown in Figure 9.2 from a house at Harappa were used for that purpose. Solids remained in

Figure 9.1. Interior of residential structure from the SD area, Block 1 at Mohenjo-daro. Courtesy M. Jansen, Aachen Research Project, Mohenjo-daro.

ceramic containers, while water and other liquid waste seeped through the porous walls of vessels or through holes in their bases. Household and street drains, in turn, flowed into a network of drains that channeled water and small waste products out of the city.

Common to each of these public works was the assurance of a constant supply of water and the channeling of waste away from households and pedestrian traffic. All of these processes would have been visible in street drains and bathing areas on a daily basis. As mentioned earlier, great care was taken to set bricks in such a way so as to prevent clogging and to move water and waste as quickly as possible into specially designed drainage outlets.

The best known of these engineering works at Mohenjo-daro is the Great Bath. This large bathing area consists of a deep, watertight pool (12 × 7 × 2.4 meters) deep built of precisely set bricks with joins between them only millimeters wide (after fitting they were plastered with gypsum and sealed with bitumen) (Figure 9.3). At either end, flights of stairs

Figure 9.2. House floor at Harappa with ceramic pots for drainage. Photograph by the Harappa Archaeological Research Project © HARP.

Figure 9.3. Great bath at Mohenjo-daro. Courtesy M. Jansen, Aachen Research Project, Mohenjo-daro.

led down into the pool. Flanking the pool was a pillared gallery, a long corridor, a series of rooms, and a double-walled well, which served as the primary water source for the pool. An outlet at the southwestern corner of the pool directed water flow into a drain roofed over with a corbelled vault 1.8 meters high. Other drains of this type were used to drain off excess water or refuse from inside of the city to outside areas.

As with the founding platforms, there may have been practical reasons for constructing this elaborate system of public works. Studies conducted by physical anthropologists (Hemphill et al. 1991) who have examined skeletal remains at Harappa, where similar arrangements have been discovered, determined that the population was healthier than most urban populations for the period. Conceivably, the water systems afforded protection against disease, since the entire setup provided the assurance of a water supply and the disposal of water and refuse on a day-to-day basis. Mohenjo-daro stood between two parallel river systems (see Chapter 2 for details); shifting of either or both channels by even a few kilometers may have been sufficient to cut off the city from water or to subject it to the danger of flooding. Independent water supplies and drainage outlets, therefore, were desirable. For those in the countryside, the city was a safe haven during flood times when they could seek refuge in it.

Clearly, these qualities of urban form were influenced by an intimate knowledge of nature, the coming and going of monsoon seasons, the danger from flooding, and the properties of soils. Indus builders used this knowledge to master the environment and employ a technological style that imposed a cultural order onto the human landscape not unlike their orientation to stone, clay, and other materials used in the production of portable objects discussed in Chapters 6 and 7. In much the same way, the Great Bath (known only at Mohenjo-daro and therefore, a local innovation) represents a humanized landscape and one that fostered community identity.

Michael Jansen suggests there may have been a "ritual significance" to the Great Bath,[2] an aspect of a general veneration of water given the city's bathroom facilities and wells (1993b:17). In my view, I leave this interpretation aside and am more interested in its function as a communal public place whether for ritual or nonritual bathing. The pool, with its steps leading into the tank, its concentric and colonnaded walkway, associated small rooms, deep well, and drainage system is often interpreted as the site of ritual ablutions. Likewise, it may have served as an earthly/civic experience like the Roman baths of a later period. Whether to purify the body for ritual purposes, simply to cleanse it, or to present oneself to curry favor, all have in common a shared civic experience in which either a restricted group or the community at large met for common purpose.

In the city of Dholavira, the upper town likely functioned to foster communal identity among people in that city, embodying the same quality of humanizing the landscape according to local design (Figure 5.4). In particular, the large open space, sometimes referred to as a stadium and thought to be the site of special ceremonies, had a political or religious function. Whether or not the small tank on the southwest corner of the "castle" was a public bath, as Bisht (2005) has suggested and as discussed in Chapter 5, remains an open question pending ongoing excavations. Clearly, the reservoirs would have been major gathering places as the principal sources of water supply for the city's residents.

At Harappa, the massive gateway, vaulted drain, and adjoining street stood as an impressive entryway to that city. (See location on Figure 4.2.) It was a major alteration of the natural landscape that not only had practical applications but also separated city dweller from outsiders by restricting and monitoring those who entered and exited. Constructed to local specifications, the Harappa gateway in its singularity was a hallmark of that city, uniquely representing the ideals of its citizens.

Finally, common to all of the major cities were structures symbolic of community identity beyond the specifics described previously. They included walls or open spaces between sectors of cities that fostered identification with a "neighborhood" and public amenities constructed according to local tastes that tied citizens to community standards with respect to water and waste management, fostering community identity in that city.

All tolled, urban layouts, material constructions, and creations of architectural forms demonstrate a capacity for planning, an investment of authority, and a manifestation of power. In their conception, major landscape changes provided contexts in which communal identities were formed and upheld. And, by their very nature, given the massive labor efforts required, are indicative of a kind of leadership capable of marshalling and sustaining a substantial infrastructure in their construction. At the same time, the massive infrastructure necessary to maintain layouts, material constructions, architectural forms, and physical manifestations are indicative of the existence of a broad range of social hierarchies, separations between social groups, and differential benefits to the highest levels of society. For the people who eventually inhabited these culturally created landscapes, cities played a major role in the production and reproduction of many aspects of society.

To summarize, in their conception of the city, Indus artisans and builders imposed long-held patterns of thought that incorporated the natural landscape into their built world. Mimicking an orientation to the natural seen in objects of material culture, they restructured the natural landscape on a grand scale into one that metamorphosed the natural into the social. It was a creation of urban form totally consistent with long-held views of the natural and social order of things.

Landscapes as Social Order

Like Indus material culture, the city landscapes in their design and production constituted complex hierarchies, in which social differences were reinforced. Alongside a collective community identity fostered by construction and design, social hierarchies were strengthened and maintained. Embedded within their apparent commonality, underlying differences and complex hierarchies were made and remade on a day-to-day basis. In the following discussion of spatial patterning and the distribution of public works, I provide examples of the ways in which, on closer inspection, images of "sameness" reveal significant difference. At the same time that there was an absence of marked spatial segregation in the compact neighborhoods described, there clearly were preferred spaces and sites of living that reinforced social distance.

Space and Public Works

The form of Indus cities and their amenities had a significant impact on day-to-day life that was felt in households, neighborhoods, and public spaces. At Mohenjo-daro, individual residences were constructed of baked bricks and/or sun-dried mudbricks. The size of the bricks conforms to the same standard utilized for buildings in other Indus cities. The technologies of waste management (e.g., the placement and maintenance of refuse jars for the accumulation of sewage and the disposal of sewage) became part of new standards of hygiene that reached into household contexts. Households, with their special bathing platforms, were dependent upon the community's public works to function properly. In other words, while the technologies very likely improved health standards, their maintenance required cooperation and integration among households, neighborhoods, and community leaders.

At Mohenjo-daro, households typically consisted of several rooms that included sleeping and cooking areas and upper stories. Each had a courtyard located either at the center or on the north side of the house. Access was restricted, as it was necessary to enter other rooms before entering the courtyard (Figure 9.4). Houses typically had few windows on the ground floor except in the latest periods of occupation when some houses opened onto the streets (Figure 9.5). To a limited extent, houses conformed to a restricted number of what A. Sarcina (1979) refers to as

Figure 9.4. Residential structure at Mohenjo-daro, DK-G South, Block 10. Courtesy M. Jansen, Aachen Research Project, Mohenjo-daro.

Figure 9.5. Side street at Mohenjo-daro, long lane in DK-G area. Courtesy M. Jansen, Aachen Research Project, Mohenjo-daro.

"residential models" to which other rooms could be added. This idea of modeling houses along a few standardized lines is reminiscent of the Sears Roebuck pattern-book houses common in early twentieth-century America. Two models are shown on Figure 9.6. The smallest model was on average ninety-seven square meters in size. The large space to the northeast on the plan is the courtyard and the presence of a stairway suggests that living areas upstairs supplemented the space on the small lower floor. Twenty-two examples of this house type were found in the DK-G, and twelve were found in HR areas. Only six residential models were of the largest type also illustrated on Figure 9.6. Five were 183 square meters on average, and one other was 130 square meters (located in HR, V, and DK-G areas).

Within this uniformity of residential models, there also was variability. Although many houses followed the pattern of the smaller model, there were variations in the sizes of houses and in their design. Component parts could be rearranged and stretched to accommodate a more personal choice. In that sense, on closer inspection, the sameness in plan reveals differences.

In a study of the architecture at Mohenjo-daro, Helen Wilkins (2005) provides an important perspective on housing not previously considered by Indus scholars. She notes that house walls were thicker in the earliest buildings at Mohenjo-daro. In later building levels, there was a continuous reduction of wall thicknesses due to structural restrictions imposed by earlier buildings. The diminished thickness of walls

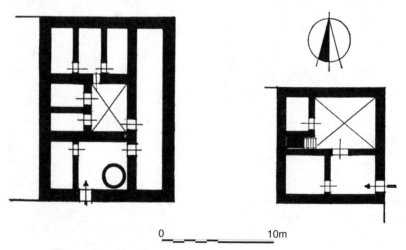

0 _____ 10m

Figure 9.6. Two house models from Mohenjo-daro (Redrawn from Sarcina 1979).

over time suggests they would not have supported upper stories. The ultimate effects of this reduction on living spaces at Mohenjo-daro would be that, lacking separate upstairs and downstairs spaces, the "lighter" buildings would not offer a range of thermal environments and therefore became "less climatically appropriate", a factor that may have made them unsuitable for habitation (2005:144). The interior wall in House IV that runs parallel to a much thicker western exterior wall (Figure 9.7) is an example of the diminished thickness of walls as additions and changes were made.

An individual's identification with a neighborhood community was enhanced by the visual separation afforded by walls and empty areas between individual sectors of the city as noted in Chapter 5. These boundaries are visible on Mohenjo-daro site plans (Figures 5.3a, b). Neighborhoods or streets were places where people engaged in the kind of face-to-face interaction that promotes a sense of community within a large city. Within each neighborhood, residences were densely packed, along wide north–south streets and/or one of the narrow lanes. Though largely for pedestrian traffic, wider streets could accommodate wooden carts drawn by animals. Compact neighborhoods like those at Mohenjo-daro would have provided familiar spaces that its citizens identified as their "place within the city" (Crowe 1995:223).

Public works installations were visible landmarks within Harappan neighborhoods. Water and waste management systems are particularly interesting, especially since in twenty-first-century society we often take them for granted. In fact, scholars of ancient city life tend to avoid technologies associated with human biological functions. When they are mentioned, their practical nature is emphasized, and there is an "aura of necessity … as if the need dictated the shape of the technology" (McGaw 1996:52).

Admittedly, it is risky to use concepts such as cleanliness in our interpretations when we have no direct knowledge of Indus ideas about hygiene. However, it is reasonable to describe the function of the Indus water and waste disposal system using these terms. Since there are no known baths, wells, or toilets in previous periods, a new social order was created in the modifications to nature adopted in city construction. Human biological activities were now subject to different rules and patterns of behavior than previously. In the case of household baths, refuse and bodily excrement and intimate bodily functions were tied to larger neighborhood and community concerns. Drinking water was, after all, shared by households, and bodily excrement disposal was connected to a network of minor and major drainage outlets. It seems likely that rules were imposed about proper places to conduct bodily functions.

These activities and others must have been regulated, at least with respect to scheduling. Thus, though they offered convenience, the creation of household and community spaces specifically allocated for bathing subjected the most intimate of functions to regulation by the larger community.

The system also intruded into the household where scheduling procedures must also have been imposed by the community and new rules and work tasks created to keep the system running smoothly. For example, the placement of kitchen refuse was restricted by the location of interior drains. In addition, the ceramic soak pits used by some households to collect waste were often distant from street drains and needed to be tipped or scooped out regularly if they were fixed to walls. Similarly, cesspits required maintenance, either through municipal collection facilities or individual households, in which case, drains would need to be flushed, cesspits unclogged, and bulk waste eliminated.

This apparent unity of form, however, signified inequalities and social distance in the urban experience. Houses VIII, X, and XI (Figure 9.7 and Figure's 5.3a and b) are examples of differences in space allocation as are the public amenities and drainage arrangements in individual houses. Situated along a lane at the northeast corner of the HR-A area, House VIII is one of the largest dwelling houses at Mohenjo-daro. The house consists of two stories, entrance foyers, interior courtyards, a large well accessible from outside of the house, at least six interior rooms of varying size, and a bathing platform. The floor area of the house is 300 square meters including a courtyard estimated at 100 square meters (Jansen 1993b:64). Its interior terracotta piping, partially built into the east wall of Room 18, passed through Room 9 and then entered a drain at High Lane. Another example is the terracotta drain at House II that wound its way through the house and was connected to a collective street sewer, facilitating the movement of water and waste from interior spaces (Jansen 1993b) to the community at large. Contrast those rather livable conditions to Houses X and XI which were fronted by soak pits that ran along their street-facing exteriors. The major soak pit in which the drain from House II dumped its waste was just a few feet from their entrances. The odors and experience of encountering these pits on a daily basis would have been strong reminders of one's place in society.

It is quite likely that overall such a system promised more than it delivered. One can imagine from the green slime that is apparent around these pits in excavations (and from observations in the streets of modern towns) that offensive materials were not always successfully removed. Waste and odors must have permeated the Harappan city landscape (possibly leaving behind human and animal excrement and foul water). If the systems

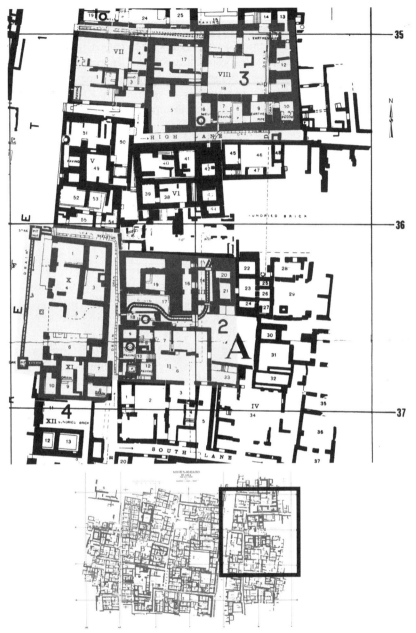

Figure 9.7. Plan of houses at HR-A at Mohenjo-daro. Courtesy M. Jansen, Aachen Research Project, Mohenjo-daro.

were inadequately maintained, rather than freeing people of waste products, they would have been concentrated in city streets. In that event, the full range of human behavior would have been exposed to those who walked and lived in the city, and especially to those entrusted with cleaning and maintaining the waste disposal and drainage system.

Finally, like the complex hierarchies of technological specialization described for the manufacture of material culture objects, an extensive labor pool was necessary to maintain and clean wells and drains. On the outside of houses, the regular cleaning of waste pits required a large workforce that obtained water to flush drains and to clear out deposits (Jansen 1993b:121). Wells also were rebuilt and their shafts extended periodically. It is impossible to know what level of society was employed in the invisible network of infrastructure that made the waste system work.

Interior Spaces and Social Differences

Harappans produced a wide range of artifacts. Investigating the material contents of individual households provides another way in which to assess social differences. My basic assumption is that the quality, quantity and types of material culture found in a given context are proxy measures for differences of status and/or wealth.

In Chapter 7, I discussed the Axes of Relative Value (Figure 7.6) developed by H.M.L. Miller (2008). As a reminder, stoneware bangles as a finished object ranked high on this scale of value because their production involved a highly complex technology; lapis lazuli, on the other hand, was ranked high on the scale in view of the physical distance to its source.[3] In contrast, simple terracotta objects were low on the index of value because materials were locally available and the technology was relatively simple. Miller worked with the assumption that the indices of value would be reflected in consumption patterns. For example, since long beads are produced from both carnelian (high index) and simple terracotta (low index), there would be a relationship between demand and value of material or finished product depending upon one's social and economic status (Miller 2008). Stated differently, like clothing and adornment today (an authentic Ralph Lauren against its "knock-off" counterpart), whether an Harappan wore carnelian long beads or ones of a similar style made of terracotta communicated important information about his or her status and access to wealth. In other words, differences in the end products ranked on the index of value served "to articulate new roles and ranks in urban communities, creating new complex hierarchies but mediating this process with the need to maintain a pervasive social consensus [which was] reflected in the personal ornaments of the

Harappan phase, with status indicated by hierarchies of base materials and social unity by standardized uniform/shape" (Vidale and Miller 2000:153).

The index of value based upon the Axes of Relative Value is an interpretive tool that simplifies complex data. In order to test it against actual consumption patterns, Miller (2008) tabulated the number of beads recovered at Harappa that took place between the 1986–90 and 1993–6 excavations. It is reproduced in Table 9.1.

Vidale (2000) and Miller (Vidale and Miller 2000) suggest that objects of "medium value" produced from faience and paste materials were symbols of status for merchants, traders, and craft producers. Table 9.1 partially confirms the idea that faience and paste materials were less scarce than those produced from other raw materials. In order to test whether these percentages were specific to Harappa, I tabulated published data from the early excavations at Mohenjo-daro using bead counts from the DK-G area (see Figure 5.2 for the general location of DK-G).

Table 9.1. Total Count of Beads, HARP Excavations, Harappa (1986–1990, 1993–1996)

Finished Bead/Pendant (whole and fragments)	1986–90	1993–6	Total Number	Percentage Total
Steatite (talc)/paste[a]	3,850	6,871	10,721	72.31
Terracotta[b]	702	1,661	2,363	15.94
Faience	258	587	845	5.70
Agate/jasper/etc.	164	406	570	3.84
Other stone	40	68	108	0.73
Shell	26	61	87	0.59
Copper	39	63	102	0.69
Gold	20	9	29	0.20
Bone ("amulet")	1	0	1	<0.01
Total	5,100	9,726	14,826	100.00***

Notes: Rough counts are good only for broad comparisons.
[a] These high numbers are deceptive because, in this case, they include hundreds of microbeads used to produce one ornament from the burial of a single individual.
[b] Includes a few spindle whorls and weights.
*** Sum of column is equal to 100.1% due to rounding.
Sources: Meadow et al. (1996: Appendix – tabulation of small finds 1986–90 and 1993–96); H.M.L.Miller (2008).

Each tabulation has its problems. The number of steatite-paste beads listed in Table 9.1 obviously skew results; these beads are exceedingly thin (0.8 millimeters) and many (more than 300) are required to produce a single necklace. At Harappa, steatite-paste beads are ubiquitous and readily collected from the surface as one walks across almost any of the mounds. In addition, the list is only good for broad comparisons because it does not take into account their context. Furthermore, the listed materials are from multiple contexts, involving production, consumption, and discarded materials.

The tabulations in Table 9.2 represent only whole beads and those illustrated in the report of excavations conducted between 1927 and 1931 (Mackay 1938). Therefore, they in no way represent the total numbers of beads recovered.

Archaeologists are confronted with a different set of problems with the data in Table 9.2. The DK-G section, like the other areas at Mohenjo-daro, was divided into blocks that included single houses and open lanes. In some cases, the report notes specific chambers in which an object was found and the depth of the deposit below a datum point. However, the chambers were excavated with poor stratigraphic controls and before the advent of absolute dating methods. In addition, published accounts record only a limited number of objects thought to be "important". Therefore, although the records from which Table 9.2 were drawn provide an indication of some of the block contents, many

Table 9.2. Beads Tabulated from Published Accounts of the DK-G Area

	Total Number	Percentage Total
Steatite/paste[a]	147	47.42
Faience	62	20.00
Shell	30	9.68
Agate/jasper	26	8.38
Other stone[b]	32	10.32
Copper	11	3.55
Gold	2	0.01
Totals	310	

[a] Terracotta beads were not recorded.
[b] 11 carnelian, 8 quartz, 5 limestone, 2 lapis lazuli, 2 green/feldspar, 2 serpentine, 1 onyx, 1 hematite.
Sources: Mackay (1938: 546ff.).

more materials were recovered than reported (see discussion earlier in this chapter).

These problems aside, there remains general correspondence between the percentages of beads at Harappa and Mohenjo-daro when tabulations are compared. Excluding the terracotta beads (not reported for Mohenjo-daro), steatite, faience, and paste beads occur with the greatest frequency at both sites. Mackay (1938) notes that the steatite, whether natural or powdered and fired, along with faience and other vitreous pastes, were the highest "in order of popularity" and distributed throughout the various blocks.

The lack of chronological control in the numbers of recorded beads for both Harappa and Mohenjo-daro leaves open the question of whether demand for beads produced from less rare materials but elaborated technologies changed over time. However, Mackay notes that they were "as frequently found in the lower as in the upper levels" (1938:496), suggesting that (at least in the DK-G area) consumption of materials of medium value did not increase over time.

The tabulations also indicate that beads produced from rare raw materials occurred infrequently. Miller suggested that beads made from exotic materials would be reserved for "the highest elite" (H.M.L. Miller 2008). But would these findings and interpretations hold for other classes of objects beyond beads? If so, which ones and in what contexts were they found? Were particular forms and materials differentially distributed among the wealthy or the elite?

Working with lists of objects published in the excavation reports for the DK-A-F (Marshall 1931) and DK-G (Mackay 1938) areas, I tabulated all nonbead objects and their respective raw materials recorded in the original excavations. In the foregoing tabulations, with rare exceptions, all of the items I listed are from published materials; hence, they do not reflect the actual total of numbers of recovered objects. Of the more than approximately 1,330 objects recorded (omitting 884 seals) 116 of the remaining 446 (less than 26%) were produced from rare raw materials. Of these, approximately 52 (45%) were of shell. The remaining objects were made of (in descending order) ivory, alabaster, limestone, gold, silver, chert, lapis lazuli, chalcedony, and other unidentified stones. These results suggest that rare and difficult-to-access materials and the objects made from them may be considered "luxury" or prestige items.[4]

To further test these ideas I then used published data from Mohenjo-daro to examine the contexts in which some scarce raw materials and objects were distributed. I found statuary to be the most rare objects. Statuary are produced from nonlocal raw materials (including limestone, steatite and alabaster). I discuss statuary and their distributional and material contexts later. Of additional interest are hoards or caches of materials, which though found in poor contexts contain materials that rank high on the index of value. When possible, I make statements concerning the social identity or status of the people who may have been associated with them.

Statuary at Mohenjo-daro. Human and animal statues made of stone and copper are found in small numbers at Mohenjo-daro. (See Figure 9.8 for locations of areas of recovery.) With one exception, all of the stone sculptures representing humans are males and are fragmentary. Interpretations of what these statues represent are varied, but they center on some form of leadership, for example rulers (Ratnagar 1981), ancestral figures, or clan members (Kenoyer 1998). Since all have been discovered in what appear to be residential contexts and no religious

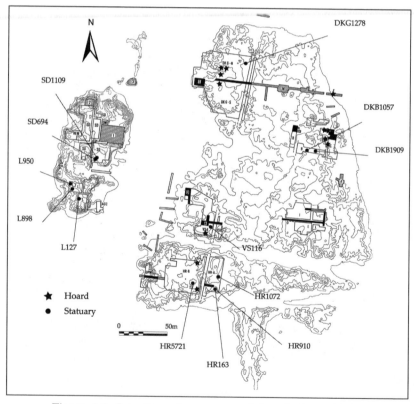

Figure 9.8. Location of statuary and hoards from Mohenjo-daro. © R. P. Wright.

structures have been identified at Indus sites, the attribution of "Priest-King" by the earlier excavators has generally been rejected.

Human representations include two torsos (L-950, SD-694), four heads and upper torso (DK-1909, DK-B-1057, L-898, HR-910), and a male head and torso recovered in three separate pieces (HR-163). A fifth head L-127 in very poor condition was described as female because it appears to have long hair. Two copper-alloy female statuettes (HR-5721, DK-12728) were produced using the lostwax casting technique.

In addition, there are five animal sculptures (VS-116, SD-1109, HR-1072, HR-4952, L-127) of which four are reclining caprids with their legs tucked under their bodies (Ardeleanu-Jansen 1984). Two of the animals are seated on pedestals (HR-1072, SD-1109).

In some cases, the statuary are associated with large buildings with significant amenities or with large quantities of goods. In one, a limestone bearded male head (HR-910) was found in House I in the HR-A sector. The house has more than twenty-five rooms (Figure 5.3b). The statuary fragment was found in an inner courtyard (Room 14) near two symmetrical stairways and a double gateway that provided entry into the building.[5] This head is 17.5 centimeters in height and is stylistically similar to the other male heads recovered at Mohenjo-daro. It features eye sockets (perhaps filled with shell or paste), oval-shaped ears without lobes, high prominent cheekbones, and thick lips (Marshall 1931:177). A second statue, made of alabaster, was recovered in the same house. It was in three pieces. Its torso was found in a courtyard (Courtyard 10) (HR-163); a part of its head, in a nearby street (HR-193); and an additional part (HR-226), in the courtyard of a nearby building. The restored figure is nearly 42 centimeters in height. The treatment of the beard and ear are stylistically similar to the head found in Room 14 (Marshall 1931:178).

House I was excavated by H.R. Hargreaves (Hargteaves 1931; Marshall 1931) and later by Wheeler. The house covers 675 square meters, over a third of which includes walls. It contained more than six hundred artifacts, 98% of which Jansen (1993b:68) classified in the "prestige" category. For Jansen (1993b:68) "prestige" artifacts were "not intended for ordinary, everyday household use" (Jansen 1993b:68). By any measure, this house would rank high on the Axes of Relative Value (Figure 7.6). The original publication lists include an alabaster mace head, small objects of faience and alabaster, an ivory ornament, decorated pottery, and two pointed base goblets impressed with a seal before firing (Marshall 1931:176ff.). (See Figure 5.11 for an example of a similar pottery vessel with a seal impression). The field records listed some unpublished objects, including chert and limestone weights, grinding stones, stoneware bangles, human and animal figurines, shell rings and bangles, copper and various ornaments, including chalcedony, carnelian, white paste beads (steatite), and lapis lazuli (Jansen 1985:191ff., Ardeleanu-Jansen 1984). In addition, the house contained fifteen seals inscribed with the unicorn motif (Figure 9.9). Whatever its function, the size and contents of House I suggest it was occupied by people of high status.

The best-known statue from the Indus civilization is the so-called "Priest-King" depicted in Figure 1.5[6] (DKB-1909) found in the DK-B area (Block 2, Room 1). It was discovered in a large building that contained an elaborate flue system comprised of under floor shafts through which heat circulated. Two of the brick walls in this room were decorated in an ornamental style by alternating brick stretchers and uprights (Marshall 1931:237) to form an attractive pattern. The steatite statue was discovered in a passage below floor level, where it had apparently rolled when the building collapsed.

The "Priest-King" statue has many of the same formal characteristics as other statuary (Marshall 1931:356ff.). It has a characteristic beard. The hair is parted in the middle and pulled to the back in short strands. There is a fillet around the head that is fastened at the back. Perhaps the most distinctive attribute of the statue is the elaborate robe, which contains a trefoil pattern that may have been painted red in the past. Marshall's publication does not include objects recorded for the room in which the statue was discovered, but within Block 2 there is a faience monkey, a terracotta animal mask, numerous seals, a mace head, shell and copper inlay fragments, and knobbed ware ceramics, conceivably associated with the building. The presence of knobbed ware is significant since this ceramic type has been found in southern Mesopotamia. Conceivably, it was considered a prestige item.

Three important statues were found in area L (Figure 9.8). Two were in a building in the northwest corner of the excavated area south of the "stupa" mound. A yellow limestone male head (L-898) was found in a small room (Chamber 77, it was 6.5 meters by 2.3 meters) resting on top of a drain. In a nearby room (Chamber 75 – about the same size), a beautifully sculptured alabaster torso (L-950) was discovered. Ardeleanu-Jansen (1991:167) has suggested that the head of the Priest-King very likely was attached to a torso of this kind, as is shown on Figure 1.5. Debris associated with this block included many terracotta objects, animal and human (male and female) figurines, and pottery (among them seventy-one dishes), and several kilns. The latter may have been installed after the building was abandoned. Several limestone ring door sockets (30 centimeters high and 45 centimeters in diameter with a

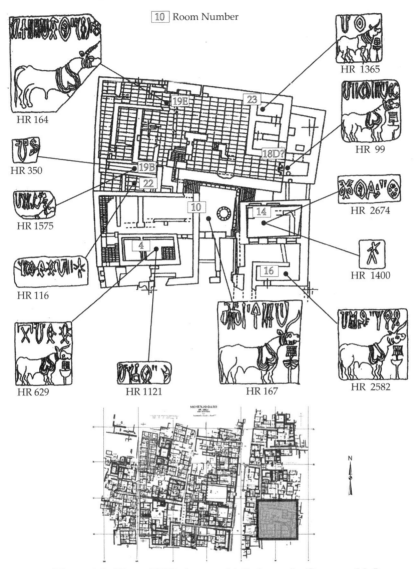

Figure 9.9. House I/HR-A area with Indus seals. Courtesy M. Jansen, Aachen Research Project, Mohenjo-daro.

13.3 centimeter central hole) were discovered. Approximately eighty-five conch shells were found scattered in two locations of this block, some distance away from a possible shellcutter's workshop (Marshall 1931:170ff.). Finally, a third limestone head was designated as female

(L-127) because it appears to have longer hair that is not coiffed in the more common coiled hair style found on many of the male statues. It was located in a large room (12.8 × 4.5 meters) and was in a very poor state of preservation. Various pottery vessels and figurines were associated with these statues.

Human and animal statuary were found in the SD area. The SD area is the location of the Great Bath. The statues were discovered in a complex of buildings that extends along the eastern side of the bath but is separated from it by a street. The torso of one statue (SD-694) was rendered in a style similar to the one found in the L area. Other artifacts found in this area were a faience bangle, steatite seal, and some pottery. In a nearby block (7), a stone of a ram was recovered (SD-1109). It is one of two representations of animals (both probably are rams) on a plinth, where the figure is attached to a cubic pedestal carved out of the same block of stone.

The second animal on a plinth was discovered in HR-A in Block 2 of House III (HR-1072) (Figures 5.3b and 9.8). The house is of medium size but has an upper story and thick walls. There is a vertical drain in the corner of one room that ends up in a street drain. The bricks in this room are carefully laid with gypsum. Other artifacts in House III included a number of jars, balls and beads of faience and alabaster, a shell spoon, ivory fragments, chert flakes, a small steatite object carved with three monkeys, an ivory spatula, and several seals. There also were fifteen unfinished shell bangles found in a large decorated pot.

The two copper lostwax cast female statuettes (HR-5721 and DKG-1278) have been referred to as "dancing girls." The statuette HR-5721 is only 10.8 centimeters high. Her hair is gathered in a coil or bun and she is wearing a large number of bangles on her lower and upper left arm, two on her upper right arm, and one or two others on her lower arm. The house in which the statuette was found is relatively small; other noted artifacts were a copper statuette of an elephant, a copper spoon, and three steatite seals. Statuette DKG-1278 strikes a slightly different pose, but has many of the same characteristics with respect to hair and ornaments. Both are naked and positioned as if about to dance.

Statuary at Other Sites. There are very few stone sculptural objects at other Indus sites. At Harappa, two human statuettes of extraordinary artistic quality have been discovered. And at Dholavira, there is an unpublished (?) torso, reported to resemble the one from Mound L at Mohenjo-daro.

At Harappa, the sculptures were found in public, rather than private spaces. Both are produced from stone and are small. A small male statuette (about ten centimeters in height) produced from grey stone was discovered on Mound F in the area of the Great Granary and described by its early excavators as the torso of a dancer. Its breast nipples, arms, and head were produced separately and it is unclear whether its missing head would have been that of a human or an animal (Vats 1940:22–3). The second statuette (8.6 centimeters high), also from Mound F but south of the Granary near the workmen's platforms (Vats 1940:75), is produced from red sandstone (Vats 1940:75). Like the gray stone statuette, the head, arms, and nipples were made separately.

Given the somewhat different aesthetic of the statues at Harappa, when compared to those at Mohenjo-daro, some scholars have doubted whether those from Harappa were authentic Harappan objects. From my point of view, their differences may simply reflect the implementation of a local style, in the context of the varying artistic conventions of independent city-states. Moreover, as the original excavators pointed out, the stone used for the sculptures was typical of raw materials employed by Indus artisans, though for smaller and different types of objects. It also seems unlikely that those from Harappa were from a later culture, since no statuary of their type has been found in the historic period and thus far non-Indus objects have not been found at any point on the F mound.[7] Finally, the similarities in the pose of the gray stone statue clearly bears comparison to the bronze "dancing girl" statuettes, thereby linking it to the Indus period (Vats 1940:75).

To summarize briefly, limited numbers of statuary have been discovered at Indus sites. Where contextual data are available, statuary was found associated with larger-sized buildings and relatively scarce materials. The combined evidence for rare statuary, greater house size, enhanced architectural details and public amenities, and relatively scarce materials suggest the occupants of these houses had a higher status than other Harappans living at Mohenjo-daro.

Caches, So-Called Hoards. Other groupings of artifacts reveal differential access to materials. Hoards, caches of materials containing precious metals and scarce stone, have been discovered at several sites. Twelve caches are found at Mohenjo-daro, seven are recorded at Harappa, four large hoards and several smaller ones at Chanhu-daro, three are noted at Lothal, one at Allahadino, and one at Manda in Uttar Pradesh (see Figure 1.2 for location of sites). Figure 9.8 plots locations of hoards at Mohenjo-daro. The hoards at Mohenjo-daro were discovered in the DK and HR-B areas in a variety of contexts, including beneath floors, at house floor levels, near blocked-up doorways, and without connection

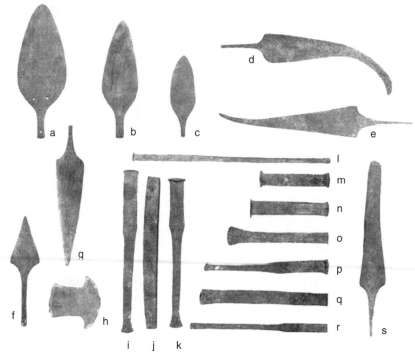

Figure 9.10. Weapons and tools from a hoard at Mohenjo-daro.

to any structures. These collections of artifacts are classified as hoards, either based upon their context (for example, hidden beneath floors) or because they contain artifact types similar to those identified in other hoards found in more secure contexts (Rissman 1988).

The objects found in hoards are either whole or fragmentary but usually all of them are recorded and, often, illustrated in published accounts. The types of objects in the hoards vary, but their contents are fairly uniform. Hoards are typically found in metal or ceramic containers. They include copper/bronze objects and consist of weapons (spearhead, sword), tools (axes, knives, chisels, saw blades, needles, awl, fish hooks), and vessels, examples of which are shown in Figure 9.10. At Chanhu-daro, one of the axes bears an inscription. Other copper includes scale pans, bangles, mirrors, ingots, gold and silver vases, ear ornaments, fillets, finger rings, and terminals or spacers for ornaments. Among scarce stones are agate, amazonite, carnelian, hornblende, jade, jasper, lapis lazuli, onyx, steatite, and turquoise. Other objects include faience and shell ornaments and shell inlay, seals, and a single figurine.

The contents of the hoards can be contrasted with materials listed in Table 9.1 from Harappa and Table 9.2 from Mohenjo-daro. One major difference is that the hoards contain large quantities of precious metals (copper, silver, gold), whereas the assemblages tabulated in Table 9.2 from Mohenjo-daro do not. The quantities and varieties of semiprecious stones ("onyx, lapis, jade, amazonite, turquoise, hornblende, breccia, and jasper") [Rissman 1988:216], agate, steatite, shell, and faience in the hoards also set them apart from other residential contexts.

Tucking goods away in safe places is a reasonable way to secure precious items. In view of the presence of caches with similar materials at several sites, one such practice appears common among Harappans.[8] Like the caches at Mohenjo-daro, others at Harappa, Chanhu-daro, Lothal, Allahadino, and Manda contain precious metals, rare semiprecious stone beads, and large numbers of metal vessels and implements almost exclusively. Unfinished and fragmentary remains of metal, stone and shell also are present. Stone weights, metal ingots, castings, and gold sheets occur in some hoards.

Paul Rissman divided the hoards into three types based on the contents of the Mohenjo-daro corpus. One group contained copper vessels and tools; a second, precious metal and semiprecious stones; and a third, a combination of precious metals, semiprecious stone, and tools. He suggests the first group might represent scrap metal, and the tools and other materials used in the preparation of new objects, most likely by a metal worker. Because of the large numbers of beads produced from semiprecious stones, the second group may also have been stored objects prepared by an artisan and ready for trade. Rissman discounts the possibility that they were curated goods belonging to a consumer, though it remains a distinct possibility. The third group consists of metal, semiprecious stones, and tools. Its meaning is more ambiguous than that of the others, but its contents may be remnants of materials stored by an artisan. The presence of these objects in hoards of whatever types indicates that these items were highly valued and suggests that "gold, silver, copper, semi-precious stone and perhaps shell" (though rare in the hoards when compared to other materials) were the highest forms of material wealth (Rissman 1988:216).

In general the hoards were not found in "highly restrictive contexts," as they were broadly distributed (Rissman 1988:218). Even so, Rissman interpreted the finds as items of "great secular value" (1988:218), an interpretation consistent with the index of scarcity discussed earlier in this chapter. We have very little to go on with respect to good recovery contexts for the hoards. Two houses at Mohenjo-daro were relatively intact. One was in a ten-room dwelling surrounded by a massive wall; another, in a twelve-room house. Both lack the statuary, complex drainage systems, and other items of prestige present in House I, II, or VIII in HR-A, for example. This suggests that the social standing or position of its owners may have been of a different order from the people living in Houses I, II, and VIII.

Rissman has noted the strong association of the caches with artisans or merchants as other scholars have done (Kenoyer 1998). While we know very little about how exchange and trade were managed in the Indus, some merchants traveled far and wide. It seems unreasonable to disregard evidence from this wider world and documents from contemporaneous cultures about merchant activities in early civilizations.

In southern Mesopotamia, written accounts of merchant activities from the mid to late third millennium B.C. include evidence for the kinds of materials routinely used in exchange transactions. These materials cannot be considered "money," but they are referred to in lists involving "prices" (Powell 1996), and "monies" is a term used as a convenience. We are better at understanding what "monies" were not, than what they were. They were not backed by bullion or institutions as in a modern context, they were not coinage, and with rare exceptions (to be discussed later) they were not "symbolic or representational monies" (Powell 1996:227). Based on Mesopotamian texts, the materials that did function in exchanges were "barley, lead, copper or bronze, tin, silver, gold....Barley, lead and copper or bronze ... [were] ... cheaper monies, tin was mid-range, silver and the much rarer gold were high-range monies" (Powell 1996:227ff.). Other texts use words interpreted as cakes, loaves, ingots, or coils and there are references to silver cups and jewelry as circulating forms of money. What distinguishes silver and barley from the materials listed, along with "cows, sheep, asses, slaves, household utensils" and other useful items, is that they possessed a common denominator for value based on systems of weighing, measuring, and possibly quality (Powell 1996:234; see also Garfinkle 2002, Widell 2005 who calculates the relative value of barley to silver in the late third millennium B.C. as 0.028 grams of silver per liter of grain, see Snell 1988 for other details of value and use). Dates also may have been used as a form of monies during the last centuries of the third millennium B.C. (Widdell 2005).

A key issue raised in the context of monies in Mesopotamia is that we know something about them from texts, but the recovery of monies is more elusive in archaeological contexts. How do we recognize monies? An assumption can be made that metals most likely were recycled, certainly not thrown away (Powell 1996:235). Some forms that have been recognized as used in exchange are "'ring' silver," that is, continuous circular bands, coils, or spirals. Several of these items examined by Powell had what he described as a "beaten off character" or were "hacked" (1996:236).

The only form of representational money in Mesopotamia was axes. Though textual references to actual transactions involving axes are rare, axe hordes are "ubiquitous" in Mesopotamian archaeological contexts. The relationship of the axe to monies is based on the Sumerian sign for shekel, "a stylized picture of an axe" and the word *gin* used for "shekel" is also the word for "axe." As Powell notes, "This can hardly be accidental" (1996:238). He regards the axe as a possible early form of monies in Mesopotamia.

It is also worth noting that in Mesopotamia some of the texts from the late third millennium B.C., again contemporaneous with the Indus Urban period, were from archives involving individual merchants. These trader/merchants (in Sumerian *damgar*) were organized into professional communities, frequently linked by family ties (Garfinkle 2002:32). This form of organization is also known among artisans in Mesopotamia. A Mesopotamian merchant named Turam-Ili, for example, used silver as a medium of exchange as well as plant and animal resources (garlic seeds, grown garlic, ox-hides, onions) and utilitarian goods (grinding stones) (Garfinkle 2002:32ff.).

The contents of the hoards provide a window into Harappan systems of value. In a barter system, we assume that many of their contents would have had a high value in line with the Axes of Relative Value. Copper and precious metals and the technological complexities of the production process would rank many of the objects kept in the hoards at a high value, thereby according their owners high status.

Still, there may be more to the hoards beyond these indices of value in light of the evidence from Mesopotamia and its system of "monies". The large quantities of metal, semi-precious stones and the occasional presence of weights in the Indus hoards take on a significance beyond simple caches of materials stored by artisans for future use in manufacture. Hoards contained many of the same materials used in exchange transactions in Mesopotamia, for example, gold, various bits of foil, sheets and coils of wire, a silver bar with chisel marks, thirty copper axes, one of which was inscribed and quantities of semi-precious stones. The differential values accorded materials in Mesopotamian transactions may have affected the value of these materials in the Indus. Moreover, Indus merchants who dealt in foreign trade, admittedly few in number, would have been cognizant of the use of common denominators of value in transactions. Finally, the uniformity of the Indus system of weights as a standard of measurement that was widely employed within the Indus and among the cultures with which it engaged in international trade lends support to the idea that common denominators of value existed in the Indus. It is a possibility that warrants additional study.

In any event, I would agree with Rissman (1988) that the contents of the hoards were used in commercial transactions and that they reflect a status hierarchy. Here, I am suggesting that they may have had a greater significance to the economy and the status of the individuals who possessed them than simply as hidden objects waiting to be recycled into new products (Wright n.d.).

One final context in which aspects of status and wealth often can be inferred are from burial or grave goods. Although there are cemeteries at Harappa, Lothal, Kalibangan, Ropar, and Chandigarh, my discussion is confined to those at Harappa and Kalibangan. Skeletal remains at Mohenjo-daro also are discussed.

Landscapes and Memory

Wendy Ashmore and Bernard Knapp speak of landscapes as places in which memory is materialized, "fixing social and individual histories in space" (1999:13). In fact, the most poignant sites of memory invested in by people are burials, the revered spaces of ritual and memory of past generations. In this section, I discuss burials at three Indus sites, although I focus on cemeteries at Harappa and Kalibangan. I do this to demonstrate the similarities and differences in burial practices on the western and eastern boundaries of the civilization. Even though burial practices varied within and between the two sites, it is clear that at both settlements people set aside special places for burial, as opposed to burying family members in house floors for which there are many examples in other early societies. Finally, I include a short section on Mohenjo-daro, in view of a number of so-called "tragic" burials described in the published literature.

My primary interest in landscapes, burials, and memory is to introduce additional evidence from which aspects of identity and social differences can be inferred. Cemetery sites are not only integral to the cultural construction of landscape but they also contribute to social and group identity. They are landscapes of memory in the sense that the "long-term placement of the dead creates living identity" (Silverman and Small 2002:4) between past and present. In terms of practiced places, they are inscribed with the stories of its dead inhabitants and the day-to-day pursuits of an individual's social group. These social groups can vary with respect to family, kinship, ethnicity, class, occupation, or other affiliations.

Analyses of burials and associated rituals, therefore, involve more than a dead body. They must include the location of burials within a settlement, kinds of physical spaces selected, construction of the grave site, associated material culture, and orientation of the individuals interred, all of which represent symbolic cultural traditions. Analyses of skeletal remains provide critical information with which to reconstruct demographic factors within the society. As discussed in Chapter 3 for the burials at Mehrgarh, they provide information on health factors, insights into the types of work in which people engaged during their lives, and, as discussed in this chapter, genetic affiliations.

The R37 Cemetery and Cemetery H at Harappa

There are two known cemetery areas at Harappa. Both (designated R37 and Cemetery H) are located in low-lying areas in the southwest corner of the city. Thus far, no wall has been found enclosing these cemetery areas. For the present, we have to assume the cemetery was outside of the city's walled and gated sectors. There are no tombstones or other commemorative devices to mark individual burial places, but, conceivably, objects were placed there or perishable items may have provided identifying markers, though there is no archaeological evidence for this practice. Nevertheless, people entering the city from the southwest would have routinely passed around or through the cemeteries, and the local population would have been well aware that the ancestors of some of the city's inhabitants rested there.

The R37 cemetery was used by a restricted population of the city. To date, four separate teams of archaeologists have excavated this cemetery which held an estimated total of two hundred individuals. This number is obviously too small to represent the large number of people who lived at Harappa during the Urban period.

The most recent analysis of the physical remains has been by a team of physical anthropologists led by Kenneth Kennedy in 2000 (Hemphill et al. 1991). The focus of their research was on the excavations at R37 and recent findings of the Harappa Archaeological Research Project. It involved the examination of the population for age and sex ratios, genetic affinities, and paleopathologies. These data, along with analyses of the artifacts buried with the individuals, are providing new understandings of the social relationships among the interred, their health conditions, and their burial practices.

The team's analyses indicate that the Harappans buried in the R37 cemetery were indeed from a restricted segment of the population living in the city. This interpretation is based upon the strong genetic affinities among the female (n = 84) (Hemphill et al. 1991) population. Females also have a high degree of affinity with females in the earliest burials in Cemetery H (Stratum II), suggesting that the people at Harappa practiced matrilocality, a system in which couples move to the village or town where the bride's kin group resides after marriage.

The general health of the burial population was judged to have been good, especially for people who were relying on cultivated foods. Data from New World populations suggest that intensification of agriculture often leads to deterioration of dentition. However, the diversified diet of the Harappans included domesticated, as well as hunted and foraged, foods. They also consumed a variety of grains (Chapters 6 and 7), which may have led to overall better health (Hemphill et al. 1991:170). As discussed earlier, the public works in its cities may also have contributed to a healthier population.

Yet, some paleopathologies were discovered. They included spinal arthritis, which was common among both sexes, perhaps due to biomechanical stress related to carrying large amounts of weight on the top of the head (Lovell 1994). Bearing loads in this manner is a common practice in many parts of the world, where wheeled transport is scarce and not available to everyone. The team also noted significant differences between males and females with respect to disease-related factors. Females had higher incidences of cavities than males, and lines on their canine teeth suggested they had experienced periodic disruptions in growth. These disruptions could be due to nutritional differences, resulting from access to certain types of foods. Among the possible causes for these nutritional differences are preferential treatment of sons (Lukacs and Joshi 1992) or "food preparation practices, frequencies of eating times, and even differences in ratios of nutrients with high protein content and those within the starchy carbohydrate group" (Kennedy 2000:306). Consumption of roots, tubers, and grains rather than "flesh foods" derived from animals could explain the higher incidence of cavities among women. In any event, Kennedy suggests that the types of dental pathologies noted for the men and women at Harappa are "similar to that encountered in other ancient farming-herding communities" (2000:306).

Some individuals in the cemetery were interred in brick-lined pits and others in wooden coffins. Although the coffin itself is not preserved, visible wood stains are indicative of their presence. Still others were buried in simple rectangular pits that varied in size. With rare exceptions, bodies were placed in the graves in an extended position. Their heads were positioned to the north (between northwest and northeast). Any grave goods buried with the dead were usually placed near the head, though occasionally others were found at the feet and to the side of the body (Wheeler 1947).

Figure 9.11. Pottery from burial lot 145 at Harappa. Photograph by
the Harappa Archaeological Research Project © HARP.

As a general rule, the principal grave good buried with the dead was
pottery. The number of vessels deposited ranged from zero to forty per
grave though occasionally more are encountered. There is some variability in the types of pottery recovered, but in general, vessels consisted
of a limited number of shapes produced in different sizes. (The pottery
shown in Figure 9.11 is from burial lot 145 at Harappa.) The uniformity in their shape and the technology and standardization of decorative
motifs among the painted pots suggests that pots in several burials may
have been prepared by the same potter, perhaps as gifts for the burial
itself. Some of the most highly-crafted pottery discovered at Harappa
is from these grave contexts, such as the two large painted pots shown
in Figure 9.11. The interiors of large vessels were devoid of food or any
other remains. Large quantities of plates were found in some graves. For
example, Wheeler (1947) reported fifteen flat plates in one grave. Many
of the plates that I examined from the R37 cemetery, though newly constructed, had deep cut marks on them, suggesting that they may have
been used for feasts conducted during a funerary ritual and then placed
with the dead person as an offering or in commemoration. A distinctive
pottery type, the pointed-base goblet, referred to in previous chapters
(though none are seal impressed), was scattered over parts of the cemetery ground surface and suggests that feasting took place at the R37
cemetery, either at the time of burial or later.

Other grave goods are sparse. Personal ornaments were found on men and women and included shell bangles, steatite disc beads, copper items, and lapis lazuli, carnelian, and jasper beads. With the exception of steatite beads, shell and small stone amulets were simply placed at the throats of females. Another ornament associated with females is shell bangles which were worn on the lower and upper left arm. One interment contained as many as fourteen such objects. Others had seven, five, and two bangles, respectively. Copper/bronze mirrors were found in several female burials (Kenoyer 1998:123). Neither male nor female burials included seals or figurines.

An older male was found wrapped in a shroud and placed in a coffin. Among the pottery was a large jar and more than ten smaller jars, pots, and dishes. Like some other males, he was adorned with personal ornaments. While it is not unusual for steatite disc beads to be found in graves, this individual wore 340 steatite beads and three rare beads, (one each of onyx, banded jasper, and turquoise); and three gold beads (Kenoyer 1998:124).

The other cemetery at Harappa, Cemetery H, is to the northeast of R37. The cemetery has two strata, one of which is Late Harappan (Stratum II) and the other post-Harappan (Stratum I). In Stratum I, bodies are interred in pots. In Stratum II, the lower or older stratum, they are buried in the earth. The earth burials are comprised of complete (eastern section) and fractional (western section) remains. Archaeologists believe that fractional burials may occur when an individual dies away from home. After the body has decomposed, the skeletal remains are brought home for appropriate burial and ritual. In the context of Harappan burials, the latter type is unusual.

There is continuity between the pottery and main grave goods found in the later HII burials and the R37 cemetery, but that is where the comparison ends. In Stratum II, the orientation of the bodies was from east to west. M. S. Vats, the excavator of this section of the cemetery, describes a typical position: "The head was turned on the left cheek, the left arm was bent up and placed over the shoulder, and the right forearm was bent so as to place the hand between the left arm and pelvis. The feet were also turned to the left". (Vats 1940:220). In another grave, the pottery was placed at the feet and the dismembered carcass of a sheep or goat was placed alongside the body of the person interred. Pottery is the main burial offering.

The burials in Stratum I are potburials, in which skeletal remains were placed in large jars painted with geometric and figurative designs. The pot burials contain remains of single and sometimes several individuals. One multiple interment consisted of an adult female and children. The pots are small and the method of placing bodies into the vessels seems a bit unpleasant. Wheeler (1994:47) noted that in one case, the pot had to be sawn in half to properly extract the bones in order to excavate it.

Another pot contained two skulls but the postcranial remains were from a single individual!

Our data from the examination of the skeletal remains by the physical anthropologists help us to address some of our questions about the social relations among the people interred in the Harappa cemeteries. The strong genetic affinities among the women in the R37 cemetery and those in HII demonstrate continuity of segments of the population over time. Males in the R37 cemetery differed genetically from rural males, and rural males aligned more directly with the R37 females. This evidence indicates that females in R37 "constituted a regionally stable genetic pattern with closer affinities to post-Harappan cemetery H females than did cemetery R37 males" (Kennedy 2000:306). R37 males, on the other hand, revealed "a higher degree of biological affinities to males from outside Harappa. These data may reflect a greater degree of one-way gene flow by cemetery R37 males into the sedentary population of cemetery R37 females" (2000:306).

The Cemetery at Kalibangan

To follow this regional perspective, I turn now to the cemeteries at Kalibangan (see Figure 1.2 for location of the site) where three types of contemporary burials (see Figure 9.12 for cemetery layout) have been excavated (Sharma 1999). Type 1 is similar to the R37 practices. The individual is placed in a supine position in a rectangular or oval pit, sometimes brick lined. Grave goods largely consist of pottery. Two other burial types were symbolic in the sense that the individual's skeletal remains were not interred. Type 2 at Kalibangan involved pot burials in circular pits. Type 3 consisted of a large pot with grave goods placed in a rectangular or oval pit without skeletal remains.

Unlike the R37 and the HII cemeteries at Harappa, the three burial traditions were practiced contemporaneously at Kalibangan. All were found in the same general area but were segregated into three different parts of the cemetery. The excavator, A. K. Sharma (1999), indicates that the interments of the first type were placed in groups, suggesting to him that locations were set aside for families or related kin. The three different types of burials, located in close proximity, but forming separate sectors of the cemetery, brings to mind differences in treatment of the dead, according to affiliation with a particular family or membership in a larger kin or ethnic group.

The goods in the Kalibangan burials are similar to objects placed in Harappan graves. They include quantities of pottery; shell ornaments (bangle fragments with a female and earring with a male); carnelian, steatite, agate, and gold beads; an agate gamesman or amulet; and a copper

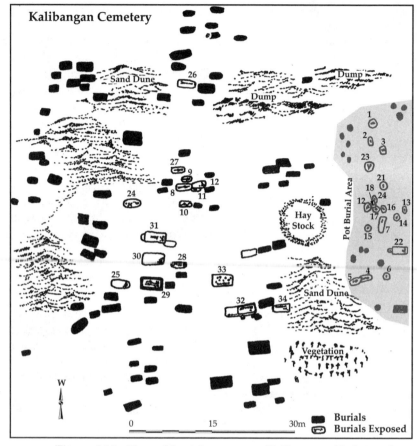

Figure 9.12. Plan of burial sectors at Kalibangan. Redrawn from Sharma (1999).

mirror. According to Sharma (1999:87), the most important individual in the cemetery is an older male. He was interred in a mudbrick chamber along with seventy pottery vessels. Like the individuals buried at Harappa, most of the interred were "middle-aged" (between 35 and 55 years).

Human Remains at Mohenjo-daro

No cemetery has as yet been found at Mohenjo-daro. In the main, the potential "burial" sites are scattered throughout the city and are in significant disarray. Materials include skeletal remains found in streets or in ruined chambers (Marshall 1931: 83ff.). For example, a human skull was found in the corner of a room along with some postcranial remains (thought to have been thrust down a deep hole possibly at a later date; Mackay 1938:49). Urn "burials" were erroneously reported (Marshall 1931) and are actually pots holding trash. They do not contain bodies, but materials such as terracotta balls and animal figurines, bangles, and an occasional copper nail indicative of trash deposits found at Harappa and elsewhere.

There are several other situations in which skeletons were found scattered on stairways of houses. One of these might qualify as evidence for a traumatic end to a family. It includes the remains of male and female skeletons and one child. Thirteen individuals appear to have died simultaneously (Marshall 1931:79). They are wearing ornaments typical of the Urban period. What makes their traumatic death plausible is the following description: "With them were found a variety of personal ornaments, some of which still encircled the bones, viz. shell and copper bracelets, copper finger rings, copper and faience beads and seal" (Marshall 1931:79). Seals have not been found in any other Indus cemetery.

The burials at Mohenjo-daro are worth reviewing in view of some of the conclusions from the analysis of the skeletal remains. The results indicate that of all the Harappan samples (from the various cemetery sites at Harappa, Kalibangan, and others not discussed in this chapter; see Hemphill et al. 1991), the Mohenjo-daro remains "exhibit a unique pattern of regional phenotypic variability with striking differences setting them apart from skeletal series at other Harappan sites" (Kennedy 2000:304). Another difference in the Mohenjo-daro biological data is evidence for a "high frequency of abnormal hemoglobins," a mutation that is commonly associated with malaria areas and a natural prophylaxis against malaria. Strikingly, there was only one case of anemia or malaria-related disease at Harappa. As Kennedy suggests, however, the data from Mohenjo-daro need to be regarded with caution in view of the disarray of the skeletal remains (2000:304). With the exception of the burial described previously by Marshall, many of the skeletal remains at Mohenjo-daro most likely were from a time period long past when the Harappans had abandoned the city.

Death and Memory in the Indus

When the data from the studies of the skeletal remains are taken together, they provide important genetic information. As discussed, the R37 burials have their closest affinities with the HII cemetery. There is no discontinuity, therefore, in the people at Harappa between the Urban and Late Harappan periods. When the Harappa specimens were compared to later Iron Age populations from Timargarha (800 B.C.) in northern Pakistan that postdate the Indus civilization by 1,000 years, they show close genetic affinities. The physical anthropologists put these data together with their studies from the site of Mehrgarh (Chapter 3). At Mehrgarh, genetic evidence indicates that there was a disruption in the population between Periods I and II (see Chapter 3) and Period III, ca. 4500 B.C. But there were no demographic disruptions before or after the Urban period of the Indus civilization. After the disruption at Mehrgarh in Period III, the population was stable, and there is continuity between 4500 and 1750 B.C. (Kennedy 2000:304). Although the Kalibangan remains were not examined by Kennedy's team, based on limited available evidence, he believes they may represent a "pattern of regional phenotypic variability," suggesting that the Harappans were not a biologically homogenous population throughout the region they occupied (2000:304).

With respect to grave goods, there is more homogeneity than difference. The Type 1 burials at Kalibangan and R37 are sufficiently similar to reflect broadly held ideologies on death and the afterlife. Both at Kalibangan and Harappa, based on biological data for R37 and the distribution of the burials at Kalibangan, people most likely were interred with family members or a larger kinship group. At Harappa, although we cannot match the R37 population to any specific group in the city, the burial groupings suggest that the city's walled neighborhoods (Chapter 5) may have been occupied by closely related individuals who were later interred together. The only significant status-related differences are the two older males at Harappa and Kalibangan, each conceivably heads of the lineages represented in the two cemeteries.

The people who buried their dead in the R37 and HI and II cemeteries had different ideas about appropriate burial practices. There is often a mutual understanding and highly charged symbolic meaning to the standardized placement of the body in east–west or north–south facing directions. Whether a body is supine or flexed or turned on its side, much less crammed into a pot, reveal differences in the meaning of death. These (right and wrong) ways of burying the dead, often a beloved member of a family or kinship group, become embedded in a group's social identity or, importantly, in remembering who that person or those persons were in life. They may also imply religious ideologies and ideas about the afterlife or lack thereof. The placement of goods in graves with a particular individual may reflect the idea that a person needs to be provisioned in another world, beyond that of the living. On the other hand, grave goods may simply be gifts offered on behalf of the deceased. They may also simply be the individual's personal possessions.

The rationale behind the specificities of burial practices in R37 and HI and II and Kalibangan can never be known with any certainty. Even if written documents were present in the Indus, they likely would not account for the many different social groups in the society. But even so, it would be unreasonable to assume that one or multiple sets of practices can be applied to all members of what probably were multiethnic, stratified societies.

Community Identity, Social Order, and Memory

In this chapter, I reviewed evidence from various Indus sites to discuss aspects of social differences within Indus society. My focus was on landscapes as practiced places in which community identity, social order, status, and wealth were formed, recognized, and maintained. In many earlier works, researchers considered the Indus civilization to be a homogeneous society that was socially undifferentiated or one in which differences were masked. In that view, the argument was advanced that the Indus was at best a two-tiered society dominated by a single individual who ruled an undifferentiated mass of nonelites. The Priest-King statute is the idealized signature for this idea.

These interpretations no longer seem tenable, considering the recent research on artisanship, craft specialization, advances in agriculture and husbandry, extensive internal exchange systems, and relations over a broad territory involving the founding of new settlements and trade with neighboring cultures.

As a consequence, in Indus studies, many recent discussions have turned away from the homogeneity model to a more complex understanding of the civilization. Throughout this book, I have focused on identifying the infrastructure of a complex and diverse society inhabited by farmers, pastoralists, craft producers, traders, merchants, rulers, planners, and others involved in maintaining extensive public works.

My focus on Mohenjo-daro drew from our best evidence available for Harappan conceptions of cities, in which I stressed aspects of its plan that suggest the city was built by a civic authority. They included the planned nature of the settlement, now better understood based on the recent research at the site; the construction of major building projects, including substantial structures like the Great Bath; the erection of the "founding platforms"; and its uniquely complex public works. These community projects argue for an investment of authority and a multi-tiered social structure that permits some level of access by most citizens, simultaneously creating harmony and difference.

At the same time, the layout of the city and its public works forged a community identity that reached into neighborhoods and households. The orderly nature of Mohenjo-daro and its layout provided numerous spaces that served as markers on the landscape. Individual neighborhoods, walled and made distinct from others by empty spaces, served as practiced places in which social identities were formed. Public amenities drew neighborhoods together, providing links between household, neighborhood, and communities and their leaders.

These linkages by no means imply that people living within blocks and houses of various sectors of the city were homogeneous. In fact, the evidence discussed in this chapter demonstrates significant variation in wealth and status based upon house size, types of amenities, and possessions. House I in the HR-A area, in which rare stone statuary and large numbers of seals of the same type were discovered, provides convincing evidence for these differences.

Speaking more generally, these differences were encountered throughout the city. Many would undoubtedly have been perceptible to people living in the city as they moved about its neighborhood streets, taking full account of the odors and debris visible in certain locations (Jansen 1993b:120). Material goods were displayed, at least on certain occasions, and perhaps worn only at celebratory times. Otherwise, they were stored and virtually hidden. The scarcity of metals, especially gold, and semiprecious stones argues for a society in which there was a differential access to wealth and status.

There is, therefore, spatial variation in the loci of the various materials discussed. When the locations of different objects – rare statuary, seals, scarce and highly valued ornaments and raw materials, and those less-valued items – have been identified, we see differences in their spatial contexts. In households, the presence of rare statuary, seals, and ornaments correlate with the size of structures, the level of amenities such as public works, and/or the building design elements with which they were constructed. Hoards also occur in these private spaces. Some of these may contain the materials of craftspeople in the process of reshaping previously used, discarded materials, in view of the presence of lapidary tools and sheet metal in some. Others appear to signal the storage of items of value that conceivably were used in public contexts at appropriate occasions and/or for exchange purposes.

The fact that few of these differences are visible at burial sites makes sense from a number of perspectives. Our best available evidence is from the R37 cemetery, where analysis of skeletal remains suggests that the burial ground housed a limited segment of the population. Outside of quantities of pottery, few rare objects are present. An exception is the case of an older male individual who is wrapped in a shroud and placed in a coffin. Like some interred males, he wore personal ornaments, including steatite beads, which are found in other graves, but he was also adorned with beads made of onyx, jasper, turquoise, and gold (Kenoyer 1998:124) that single him out when compared to others. The presence of an older male at Kalibangan accompanied by elaborate grave goods may be indicative of status differences with respect to age or leadership. In either event, special interment of elderly males in cemeteries of related individuals would serve to cement transgenerational affiliations and solidify family and kinship relations. Whether a society buries vast quantities of wealth, essentially taking materials out of circulation, requires a basic understanding of general conceptions about life and death. Taking material out of circulation has economic and political implications, but it also reflects on people's understanding of the meaning of "goods" and materials in their lives.

A final aspect of the built environment and the goods identified in its spaces are the symbolic associations that metamorphosed natural landscape elements. The creation of the Harappan landscape emphasized the relationships between the mindset employed in the creation of small objects which I have referred to as its technological style and the structures and amenities built into Harappan cities. Aspects of this mindset can also be perceived in Indus imagery, where the natural and the human, along with supernatural beings, are viewed as part of a single realm as will be discussed in Chapter 10. Collapsing these three features of human experience is not uncommon in the ancient world, though it is not universally applicable to material culture forms and technologies in the ways I have described for the Harappans. In the chapter that follows, I turn to Indus imagery in an attempt to find a link between the mindset adopted by the artisans and city builders and the fragmentary hints of similar intentions to intrude into the world of nature in its world views.

10   Models for Indus Religious Ideologies

In this chapter, we enter into one of the most complex and poorly understood aspects of the Indus civilization. So far, we have been able to reconstruct Harappan economies, technologies, and built landscapes and to decipher features of its political economy, urban form, and city-state/hinterland relations. However, it is much more difficult to construct plausible models for its religious ideology. In the absence of decipherable written texts, access to this largely mental world is (frustratingly) indirect. To enter it, we must rely on interpreting those architectural features and material culture believed to be devoted to religious practices, for example ritual objects, and imagery in which gods, goddesses, and mythological beings are depicted. Even so, these interpretations still require a "bridging framework" to take us with greater confidence from the material world into the world of the Indus ideological system. Such frameworks are varied. They include the *direct historical approach*, in which better-known historical imagery and texts from present-day South Asian religions are applied to ancient remains from the Indus. This method has been employed by archaeologists since the earliest Indus discoveries. Other effective interpretations involve comparative analyses from a relatively large sample of early complex civilizations in order to identify regularities in selected aspects of social behavior that might shed light on the Harappan case. A final approach is comparisons with more thoroughly studied contemporaries (in this case Mesopotamia and Iran) that are brought to bear on that of the less well known Indus to provide insights into the latter's religious views.

In this chapter, I invoke each of these approaches toward constructing the spiritual side of Indus life and its religious institutions in different ways. I begin by reviewing and critiquing the use of direct historical analogies previously applied to the study of Indus religious views. I illustrate problems with the use of the method in my discussion of the shortcomings inherent in "religious" interpretations of architecture and figurines. I then build a new, alternative framework by using a comparative approach to the study of early civilizations based on the recent

274

research of Bruce Trigger (2003). Applying this comparative approach to the Indus is a strategy not previously undertaken by Indus scholars. In doing so, I examine Indus masks, figurines, and narrative imagery (seals and tablets) as media that I believe bring us closer to understanding Indus conceptions of the cosmos and the roles of their deities. I then combine this by weighing these results against studies of imagery from neighboring Mesopotamia and Iran. This serves to integrate interpretations from the comparative approach into the broader world of intercultural contact discussed in Chapter 8. Finally, I bring these findings together with a portrayal of a complex mental and symbolic world in which the Harappans fashioned their place *in nature*, a place configured amongst an Indus pantheon that conveyed conceptions of hierarchy, order, balance, and an interdependence between the human and natural world.

These multiple approaches and converging lines of evidence provide powerful new tools with which to approach Indus symbolism, ideology, and religion and to draw us more deeply into its systems of thought. Still, whether based on direct historical analogies or cross-cultural and comparative ones, each is only a vehicle through which we may come to approximate the religious practices of a long-dead culture.

Direct Historical Analogies and the Study of Indus Religion

Views of Indus religion in which historical South Asian religious practices are linked directly to its ancient past have a long history. In this section, I review and critique interpretations (often unsubstantiated) by early excavators that were based on their initial discoveries of the Indus civilization. These interpretations began with attempts to identify ceremonial structures, such as temples. In the absence of solid evidence for this type of architecture, other studies concentrated on identifying the ideologies behind so-called religious or ritual objects, such as terracotta masks, figurines, and "narrative" imagery on seals and tablets (Marshall 1931). These early works have made a lasting impact on Indus scholarship and provide a baseline for understanding present-day debates concerning Indus religion.

Identifying Ceremonial Places

As I discussed in Chapter 1, M.S. Vats was the first archaeologist to recognize that the architecture and materials that had been unearthed at Mohenjo-daro and Harappa came from a previously unknown culture

(Lahiri 2005:248ff.). Later, Sir John Marshall announced the discovery of the civilization to a wider world, presenting some of the key artifacts that were characteristic of its culture. As he familiarized himself with Indus architectural plans, imagery, and artifacts, Marshall made it clear that the civilization had developed indigenously. (Lahiri 2005:264). For Marshall, it was therefore necessary to come to an understanding of the civilization based on Indus materials alone. So, he worked to reconstruct the geographical setting and aspects of the climate and river systems and to describe the sites, buildings, and artifacts discovered. Reconstructing systems of thought without benefit of deciphered texts was another matter; however, Marshall did not shy away from discussing it.

In two key chapters of his "official" account of the excavations at Mohenjo-daro, Marshall (1931) identified buildings he thought were constructed for religious purposes (1931: Chapter III). In a subsequent chapter (1931: Chapter V), he discussed the civilization's "religious character."

In his attempts to identify buildings that were built for religious purposes, I believe that Marshall had in mind to locate a "state" religion. After all, it was well known that other ancient civilizations possessed strong religious institutions. In Mesopotamia two great institutions, represented by monumental architecture, the temple and the state, were the primary ruling bodies; in Egypt, political and religious leadership was inseparable. What role did religion play and what architectural forms were associated with it in the Indus?

Marshall's identifications of "religious" buildings at Mohenjo-daro were based on interior features and relative sizes of structures. Two houses – one in the HR-A area, House V (Figure 5.3b), and the other in the HR-B area, House XVIII (Figure 5.3a) – were large and contained many courtyards and rooms. For Marshall, these could have functioned as temples. Other buildings, such as House L, were thought to be possible shrines (Figure 5.3a). House L contained two rooms with a corridor on the side. Chapels or shrines with this ground plan were known from Minoan palaces and from contemporary Hindu houses where shrines were kept (1931:23). Marshall's attention was also drawn to a pillared hall. In this case, he drew his analogy from Buddhist temples. Based on the presence of an impressive hall and the broken brick and debris discovered in it, he suggested the bricks had been benches that lined the corridor for the seating of "monks" during assemblies. For Marshall, the Great Bath, with its large well-constructed pool, called to mind modern Hindu practices. He stated that the construction of such an elaborate structure for the purpose of bathing must have indicated that the Harappans regarded bathing as "a religious duty" (1931:75) given Hindu reverence for water.

Marshall also expected to find statues representing deities and other artifacts suggestive of religious practices in the sacred spaces he had identified. In the end, he was not wholly satisfied with his analyses of the function of these buildings because they lacked "any object at all to suggest that they possessed a religious character" (Marshall (1931:23).

In spite of the absence of good contextual data, other scholars built on Marshall's interpretations, as did Ernest Mackay (1938) for one, who also conducted research at Mohenjo-daro. Mackay (1938:20) described the Great Bath as a "priestly community". Later, as noted in Chapter 9, Wheeler identified House I in HR-A (Figure 5.3b) as a potential temple because of its massive architecture and stairways. He thought a nearby circular enclosure might have been constructed for protecting a "tree or other object" (Wheeler 1968:53) of sacred significance.

In summary, even though structures at Mohenjo-daro have been identified as possible religious buildings, each lacks the necessary contextual data to verify their functions. Using the same criteria, no religious structures have been identified at Harappa and Dholavira or any other Indus sites. Verardi's study of the so-called stupa discussed in Chapter 5 (Box 5.3) has excited great interest in renewed excavations of the structure. If permission to excavate is granted, results should clarify whether it was contemporary with the Indus Urban period and whether it served a religious function.

Terracotta Masks, Figurines, and Narrative Imagery

Three minor Indus arts – terracotta masks (Figure 10.1), figurines (Figure 10.2), and narrative seals and tablets (Figure 10.3) – are among the most frequently cited artifacts associated with Indus ritual and cultic practices. (See Box 6.2 for a discussion of seals and sealing devices.) Marshall referred to these in the same chapter on religion in which he searched for religious buildings.

Terracotta Masks. Several terracotta masks depicting faces were discovered at Mohenjo-daro and Harappa. The masks were produced in molds, are hollow, and contain holes on each side for fastening (Figure 10.1). Their faces combine human and animal-like features evoking a supernatural creature. They also possess horns (Marshall 1931, pls. XCV 1, 2, 3; XCV 1, 5, 6, and 341), an element present on some narrative seals and tablets. Horned imagery is common among cultures in the Near East and appears on various Indus media, including painted designs on ceramics (Srinivasan 1975–76). Marshall thought the masks were attached to some form of drapery and used for ceremonies.

Figure 10.1. Terracotta mask from Harappa. Photograph by the Harappa Archaeological Research Project © HARP.

Figure 10.2. Animal and human figurines from Harappa. Photograph by the Harappa Archaeological Research Project © HARP.

Figure 10.3. Narrative image of seated deity. Courtesy Ute Franke-Vogt.

Terracotta Figurines. Marshall was very taken with what he viewed as the similarity of Indus female figurines to cultic images used in household shrines in the modern Indian villages with which he had become familiar. His view complemented a widespread nineteenth- and early twentieth-century belief that a "Mother or Nature Goddess" cult spread from present-day Turkey to western Asia in antiquity (Marshall 1931:50). This idea was based on so-called stage theories in which societies were believed to have "progressed" from matriarchal societies in which women led and dominated societies to male-dominated, patriarchal societies (for example, Bachofen 1861).[1] The discovery of female terracotta figurines in many cultures throughout Europe and

Asia seemed to confirm these notions, and they were collectively interpreted as fertility goddesses. Similarly, the Indus figurines "were credited with the function of 'sacred images' in some kind of mother goddess cult" (Ardeleanu-Jansen 1992:6).

Narrative Imagery. Marshall's views of the meanings of terracotta figurines were complemented by his interpretations of a selection of narrative seals and tablets. As an illustration of his thinking, I focus on one of the most provocative seals in the Indus corpus (Figure 10.3), a seated human figure in a "yogic" position that Marshall identified as a Hindu god Siva. Although he also identified some of the male figurines and terracotta masks with the god, he considered the particular image on this seal and those that were reproduced on several others as primary examples of a "proto-Siva." Four attributes led him to this interpretation. First, he thought that the yogic posture, feet drawn under the body and hands extended above the knees signified Siva as the prince of yogis. Second, the figure appears to have three faces, which he interpreted as a representation of Siva's several characteristics as a three-faced god (Klostermaier 1994:139). Third, Siva was Lord of the animals, and the four animals depicted with him (the elephant, tiger, rhinoceros, and water buffalo) were interpreted by Marshall as representations of that attribute. Fourth, the figure's horned headdress, an artistic convention used to represent divinity on Mesopotamian seals, provided what Marshall referred to as "another link in a chain that connects" Siva to the Indus and "later days, when the form of a trident was a special attribute of Siva" (Marshall 1931:55). In Figure 10.3, the figure wears a headdress of buffalo horns with a fan-shaped projection at its center; on other seals the same figure wears animal horns that are combined with plant elements, thought to be a tree branch of pipal leaves (Marshall 1931:55) or "twig of pipal" (Mackay 1938:335).[2]

Marshall used other attributes present on the seals to draw direct historical analogies with modern Hindu and Buddhist practices. For example, the pipal tree, schematically represented on numerous seals, is of special significance in Hinduism and Buddhism. He specifically linked some of the animals portrayed on the seals (Figure 10.3) to aspects of Hinduism and Siva, such as water buffalo with the god of death and dark demons of water, tigers with the Mother Goddess in her destructive aspects, elephants as the vehicle of the goddess Indra or the embodiment of good luck, and the gharial, a crocodile worshiped in certain Indian localities (1931:72ff.).

What is most significant about Marshall's interpretations is the attribution of specific meanings of Indus artifacts to gods known in contemporary South Asian religions. Although he stated that the seals, figurines, and masks only provided evidence for the most popular side of Hindu religious practices and not its philosophical concepts, his analogy reached deeply into its philosophical basis. Posing what seems like a rhetorical question, he asked whether it was not "reasonable to presume that the peoples [of the Indus] who contributed so much to the cultural and material side of Hinduism, contributed also some of the essential metaphysical and theological ideas so intimately associated with it?" (Marshall 1931:78).

Interpretations linking Indus imagery to Hinduism and Buddhism have had a sustained impact on Indus scholarship. They continue to stimulate varied interpretations. Piggott and Wheeler were in general agreement regarding associations of the proto-Siva figure on seals and Great Mother Goddess figurines (Piggott 1950:202; Wheeler 1968:109). Regarding their relationship to the development of Indus indentity, Piggott flatly declared that old faiths died hard and that the "Indus was essentially Indian from the start" (Piggott 1950:203). Wheeler was more equivocal, suggesting the imagery represented a mélange of religions in which particular mythological deities known from Mesopotamia were augmented by "specific anticipations of the later Hinduism" (Wheeler 1968:110).

Numerous scholars have either rejected these interpretations outright or elaborated on specific aspects. Doris Srinivasan (1984) rejects the identification of the seated figure as a proto-Siva, based on the inconsistency of features Marshall had considered attributes of the historic god. For example, she notes that (with the possible exception of the water buffalo), the animals depicted on the seals are wild and the historic god did not protect wild animals (1984:83). J. M. Koller (2006) finds similar discrepancies between philosophical foundations of later Indian culture and the Indus. They include Indus urbanism versus the pastoral and village character of later traditions, emphasis on bulls and other male animals in the Indus as opposed to cows; the worship of religious images versus the fact that the sacred is "not worshipped through images" (2006:23). He does, however, suggest that yoga "may have been practiced by the Indus people," based on the seated posture shown on the proto-Siva seal. Possehl also views the posture of the image on Figure 10.3 as consistent with the yoga that emerged as a "physical and mental discipline" in the first millennium B.C. (2003:144). In distinction, A. L. Basham (1989) argues strongly against Marshall's interpretation, stating that "the evidence for any kind of continuity between this prehistoric god and Siva is rather weak" (1989:4)

In summary, several lines of evidence have been used to identify depictions of gods, goddesses (discussed earlier), and animals as symbols of practices known from historic South Asian religions, principally Buddhism and Hinduism. The figurines and narratives depicted on seals continue to be central to arguments for and against these interpretations. Their direct relationship to modern South Asian religions remains ambiguous in view of the great time depth between the last vestiges of the Indus civilization and the emergence of Hinduism and Buddhism in the mid to late first millennium B.C. Even if later religions were to have borrowed and /or revived imagery from the Indus culture, the meanings attached to them are unlikely to have remained the same, since the meanings inherent in borrowed images typically are transformed in a new cultural context (Collon 1995:212ff.).

My principal objections to these interpretations center on the lack of evidence for continuity through time. In order to establish the plausibility of a prototypical Hinduism or Buddhism in the Indus between 2600 and 1800 B.C., scholars will need to identify the specific mechanisms by which these ideas were transmitted and sustained across time and space, and explain how they reflected identical ideals after over a thousand years of intervening history.

New Approaches to Uncovering Indus Ideologies

Are there reasonable alternatives to direct historical analogs that advance our understanding of Indus religious ideologies?

As I said at the beginning of this chapter, I believe there is a more fruitful way to illuminate Indus ideologies. The approach presented here combines both the broad-ranging comparative analysis drawn from Bruce Trigger's (2003) study of early civilizations with cross-cultural comparisons of Mesopotamian and Iranian imagery. The regularities Trigger observed in his analysis of comparative religious systems serve as a foundation and as a baseline from which to look anew at the kinds of materials – masks, figurines, narrative imagery – that had been used previously in direct historic interpretations of Indus religion. I then compare these findings to interpretations of imagery drawn from studies of Mesopotamia and Iranian seals. I begin by outlining the methods and results of Trigger's comparative research (which did not include the Indus).

Comparative Study of Early Civilizations

The comparative study of early civilizations involves the examination of a relatively large sample of cultures in order to determine whether there are regularities in selected features of social behavior among them.

Although these regularities cannot be applied uncritically, they provide an entry point for further inquiries and more in-depth study of materials from a specific culture.

Bruce Trigger's (2003) comparative sample involved examination of a relatively large sample of cultures that possessed textual sources and had been subjected to intensive archaeological study. Trigger sought to identify regularities in select cultural patterns, including religion.[3] His results demonstrated robust patterns of commonality in many aspects of religion. Although the religions of each of these societies developed independently, they nevertheless reflected many common concerns and aspirations.

All of the civilizations Trigger studied were craft-producing, agrarian or pastoral societies. In each he found that people's close association with nature may explain aspects of their religious views. In all of the cultures studied, people viewed themselves as a part of the natural order of things and they made no distinctions between natural, supernatural, and social realms. They believed that the universe was "animated by powerful forces that possessed human-like personalities" (Trigger 2003:412).

None of the civilizations studied was found to be monotheistic. As a way of surmounting their fears and uncertainties in such a world, people in these early societies created rich pantheons of deities who represented natural phenomena, such as gods of water or sun. In myths and legends about their deities, gods and goddesses engaged in activities in which they attempted to control unpredictable aspects of nature, for example, ensuring adequate rainfall for the cultivation of crops and the rising and setting of the sun at appropriate times of day. The power of the gods and the ability of people to appeal to them preserved the natural order of things.

Ancient peoples used a highly symbolic vocabulary in both literature and imagery to represent this association of gods with specific natural phenomena. Because people viewed humans, nature, and supernatural beings as part of a single universe (in contrast to a dichotomous one in which humans and animals were opposites), gods and goddesses, were often represented as half human and half animal or were associated with specific plants and animals. Given that humans and the supernatural were inseparable, gods, goddesses, and heroes portrayed in myth and image engaged in the ordinary difficulties people encountered in the real world while at the same time being challenged by supernatural forces. Many readers will be familiar with the well-known Mesopotamian Gilgamesh epic, in which the hero struggled with his own mortality. Along with his companion and friend, Enkidu, Gilgamesh killed the Bull of Heaven who had set out to punish him because he rejected the affections of the goddess Inanna (Collon 1987:178).

The fact that ancient people viewed the social, natural, and super-natural as part of a single realm is not a reflection of their intellectual development. It does not suggest that they were at a prelogical stage of evolution, as some early scholars had thought.[4] Rather, their views were based upon rationalities that differed from those of many present-day religions. They did, in fact, understand causality, i.e., that water flowed downhill and that particular materials worked better for specific products. As Trigger points out, "People felt less cut off from nature by a massive intervening technology than we do but actively sought to insert themselves, as individuals and societies, into a natural order which they believed was simultaneously a supernatural one" (Trigger 2003:442).

Speaking of religion in the context of early societies, Thorkild Jacobsen (1976) defined the qualities basic to many early religions that help us understand the mindset Trigger describes. For Jacobsen, religion is a means of communication for describing and controlling those "other worldly" (or "Wholly Other") occurrences humans encounter that are poorly understood. The response to these events can be

terrifying, ranging from sheer demonic dread through awe to sublime majesty; and fascinating, with irresistible attraction, demanding unconditional allegiance. It is the positive human response to this experience in thought (myth and theology) and action (cult and worship) that constitutes religion. (1976:3)

Even though there is always the possibility that the Harappans might indeed be unique among all the civilizations to which Trigger referred, the broad geographical and temporal scope of his study provides us with some guidelines for examining Indus material imagery within the contexts of the kinds of ideological realms and religious worlds he describes for other civilizations, both neighboring and farther afield.

Alternative Visions – Masks and Figurines

While few scholars currently hold the precise views expressed earlier in the section on direct historical approaches, there is general agreement that the masks, figurines, and narrative imagery provide windows into Indus cultic practices and conceptions of spirituality. Since stylistic conventions, like language, are vehicles for communication, the images and their individual characteristics are cultural signs of historical ideals that would have been familiar to the Harappans. For example, composite representations of humans and animals convey a "tacit collective agreement" as to the ways in which natural and human phenomena are intertwined and human characteristics are transformed. These are culturally constructed ideologies of significance in ritual or religious contexts.

Terracotta Masks

With a single exception, the poor contexts of the masks discovered by Marshall's excavations at Mohenjo-daro make it difficult to assign their function. Two were found in a test trench, the provenance of a third is not recorded, and the room in which a fourth was discovered is not described. The fifth locus was a room in the L area (Figure 5.1 for general location), where one of the few examples of limestone statuary, discussed in Chapter 9, was discovered. It included a feline mask with elongated eyes. The remaining finds in the room, beads and a pottery jar cover, are unremarkable.

There is general agreement that these masks were used in performances. Kenoyer (1998:83) interprets them as finger puppets or amulets used to illustrate myths and legends in "dramatic enactments [that] covered both religious and possibly political themes," as similar objects are used in the region today. Other scholars associate them with magical rituals (During-Caspers 1992), deities (Parpola 1994:234) or interpret them as ritual paraphernalia, such as "talismans on shamans' costumes" (Clark 2007:508), a topic to which I will return.

Terracotta Figurines

The most common terracotta figurines represent domesticated animals, especially zebu (bulls), water buffalo, and caprids (sheep and goat). Other representations include dogs, deer, rhinoceros, elephants, large felines, rabbits, turtles, bears, monkeys, gharials (a fish-eating alligator), and birds, which are less frequent. Human figurines consist of males, females, and others with ambiguous gender traits (Clark 2007:127ff.) (see Figure 10.2 for examples).

The forms of animal and human figurines are rendered schematically. Animal figurines consist of quadruped and bipedal forms (the legs are joined in the back and front) and have few details. A few examples have movable parts (Clark 2007:139ff.), such as changeable heads, holes for movable appendages or wheels, suggesting they could be suitable for animated performances.

Human figurines are produced using a standard procedure.[5] Figurines are not made in molds, a technique known from other crafts. They are hand-built and are either solid or hollow. Human figurines are made from two pieces joined together or vertically rolled pieces of clay that make up the head, upper and lower body, and legs. Arms are applied separately (Dales 1991a and b: 66; Clark 2007:130). They are produced from refined clays and temper inclusions with mineral compositions that are similar to those used to produce vessels (Clark 2007).

The stylized and formulaic renderings of human figurines make it possible to distinguish between females and males (Clark 2007). The upper torsos of female figurines have prominent breasts and headdresses, while their lower torsos and genitalia are covered either by a belt and/or cloth wrapped below the waist. Female headdresses most often are fan-shaped (Clark 2007:526). Male figurines occasionally are decorated with headdresses that may carry widely curled, V-shaped, or rounded horns (2007:527). They are nude, and their genitalia are articulated. Other decorative elements were added to basic male and female forms. Most include ornaments; for example, several strands of beads are draped over the torsos of females, whereas males may be adorned by a single ornament.

Another important distinction (besides sexual attributes) between male and female figurines is the styles of the headdresses or hairdos they exhibit. A common form of female headgear is a fan-shaped form that projects vertically above the head, most likely either a headdress or a hairdo greased and stiffened. Some headgear is ornamented with rosettes or flowers or hair that is twirled or looped. The latter are held in place with the figurine's hand. Some males and females have bun hairstyles, in which female buns are rounded or pinched, while male hairdos have doubled buns that are wrapped with an appliquéd band. Braids or ponytails, appliquéd locks, and painted hair are found on males and females (Clark 2007).

A very few figurines either do not have female or male attributes or their sexes are ambiguous. Among a corpus of figurines at Harappa, one such figurine not only had a beard but also breasts and a fan-shaped headdress (Clark 2003:319), while others had nipples and wore belts normally associated with females. These apparent males in female dress may represent a physiological androgyny or cross-dressing.

These new looks by Sharri Clark (2003, 2007) at several aspects of Harappan figurines have advanced our knowledge about them and have provided important clues to their potential roles in religious and ideological expressions as varied categories as sexuality, fertility, shamanistic practice, life-force, household cults, and the mythical world are illuminated.

In order to assess whether the human figurines were fertility gods or goddesses, in response to earlier assumptions, Clark (2003) examined them for indications of sexuality. Although the female figurines represented youthful bodies, they were rendered in appropriate proportions in which no features were overemphasized (2003:309). Only small percentages were females holding infants. Male figurines were easily distinguished by the presence of genitalia and beards; some represent adults while others may be immature males. Based on these mixed characteristics, Clark concluded that neither the males nor the females had physical characteristics suggestive of fertility (2007).

Two human figurine types may provide a window into Indus cosmology and ritual. Several human figurines with male attributes wear headdresses that have animal horns or ears. Another small group is depicted sitting in characteristic positions. These lack sexual attributes (Figure 10.2 at the center of the photograph). They have their hands raised and pressed together and are assumed to be males or possibly eunuchs. According to Clark (2003), taken together these figurine types can be seen as communicating ideas related to shamanistic transcendence and transformative practice, since shamans are "associated with transcendence and harnessing both male and female sexual potential" (2003:319).

Another significant characteristic is the white and black body paint found on the headgear and hair of some figurines. Clark (2007:166ff.) conducted laboratory analyses of the pigments used to produce these colors. She found that the pigments were created by heating the bone to 800 degrees centigrade (about the same temperature as most pottery at Harappa). As the carbon in bone burns off, the bone white or ash is retained on the surface. Bone black is a mixture of bone, minerals, and organic materials and was used for stripes or geometric patterns, most commonly on headdresses of female figurines and heads of males, usually the hair. Clark suggests the use of bone to decorate some figurines is suggestive of a type of "life force" (Clark 2007), which I believe is another example of the transformative technological style that is consistent with the mindset of Indus artisans. In this instance, natural bone was transformed into a human substance, adding power to the figurine.

One of the missing components in understanding the potential religious and ideological function of the figurines is their poor contexts of discovery. Many are from excavations in which artifacts were not quantified and recording procedures were poor (Sinopoli 2007). At Mohenjo-daro, Ardeleanu-Jansen (1992) examined field records of the early excavations for contexts of the terracotta figurines. Even though Marshall and Mackay gave the impression that there were female figurines in every household at Mohenjo-daro, she found that the number of human and animal figurines was actually small, amounting to less than 500. The majority of the terracotta figurines were found in "terminal rooms" in houses. These rooms are places with a single entrance, some of which were directly accessible from "public" rooms. A very few terminal rooms were accessible through rooms with more than one entrance. The overwhelming majority, therefore, were concentrated in "the least public rooms, that is, those with the highest potential degree of privacy" (Ardeleanu-Jansen 1992:11).

In her study of human figurines at Harappa, Clark found higher percentages of female figurines than their male counterparts. Of the 2,527 whole figurines and fragments studied, 1,143 were identified as probable females and 407 were males (Clark 2007:203). The remainder were indeterminate with respect to sex (2007:526). All were found in normal household debris such as the sump pots described in Chapter 5 and 9. One possible explanation for this behavior is that figurines were discarded "at the end of their social lives" (Clark 2003:309) or were meant for other types of short-term use (Ardeleanu-Jansen 1991:172).

In summary, the most recent studies of human and animal figurines have overturned previous interpretations, and several new types have been identified. Their attributes have been reevaluated, opening fresh interpretive possibilities. The association of female figurines with a Great Mother Goddess cult can be dismissed, though in view of their contexts of recovery at Mohenjo daro, their association with folkloristic rituals remains a possibility. A small subset of gender variants may be related to ritual or cultic practices, possibly shamanistic ones. The use of burned bone to decorate some figurines, which is never used as a colorant on pottery, may be suggestive of the application of some sort of "life force" (Clark 2007). It further recalls the Indus technological style to intrude into the world of nature by transforming natural materials (here biological) through heat into a humanly constructed substance. Applying heated bone on the figurines conceivably imbued them with supernatural powers.

These interpretations are in accord with Trigger's findings, in which he noted that household and local cults may communicate directly with gods and/or through shamans or ritual intermediaries who are conduits between the human and supernatural powers. Finally, the identifications of stylized conventions specific to male and female representation and gender variants provides an as yet undeciphered "vocabularly" of attributes that may be useful in interpreting aspects of the symbolism represented on the narrative imagery (Wright 1997).

Alternative Visions – Seal and Tablet Narrative Imagery

In Box 6.2, I discussed the seals and tablets produced by Indus artisans. The majority of the intaglio seals are square and are largely formulaic in design. They combine an animal image with Indus script and a small icon. Many of the faience and terracotta molded tablets and some intaglio seals portray narrative scenes that appear to convey stories or myths.

Unlike the relatively static figures on the standard square stamp seals, narrative imagery depicts active poses. Included are fantastic animals, such as tigers with horns, two- or three-headed bulls and others in which animal and human bodies are combined. A small number are depicted performing actions that evoke myths, tell stories or act out what appear to be ritual performances. For example humans play instruments and/or dance in the presence of a tiger (see Franke-Vogt 1991a, Tafel XXX–XL, for examples).

As Frenez and Tosi (2005) have noted (Box 6.2), the Indus seals and tablets are part of a conceptually related grouping of objects that was widely employed throughout the Near East in the third millennium B.C. We have seen in Chapter 8 the references to Meluhha gleaned from Mesopotamian texts and noted the presence of artifacts and seals with Indus affinities in Mesopotamia and elsewhere. Here I explore common iconographic and stylistic features on a selection of seals and tablets from the Indus, Mesopotamia, and the Jiroft culture in Iran. (See Figure 8.1 for locations.) The motifs and images on Mesopotamian and Iranian seals complement Indus themes and offer additional support for Trigger's comparative analyses of early civilizations and their religious practices and world views.

A number of other scholars have drawn parallels among the Mesopotamian, Iranian, and Indus visual imagery (Amiet 1986; Parpola 1994; During-Caspers 1992), but their analyses differ from those I offer in this chapter. Pierre Amiet viewed the shared iconographic features of Mesopotamia and Iran as evidence for exchange over a broad geographic area, which he linked to the trade. Elizabeth During-Caspers also focused on the relations between trade, exchange, and Indus imagery, suggesting they represented a "commercial alliance"(1992:122). Asko Parpola, in contrast, employed the seal imagery toward developing a systematic catalog of signs and decipherment by examining comparable representations of motifs better known in Mesopotamia as clues to their meaning in the Indus (1994). For example, he associates the gharial (a fish-eating alligator) depicted on many Indus narrative seals with a "sign" he interprets as fish that, in turn, is associated with a star sign. In Mesopotamia, the star sign signifies divinity (1994:183). Based on the presence of the star and fish on some proto-Siva seals, he considers them "an emblem" of proto-Siva and Enki (the Mesopotamian water god).

Two themes shared in Mesopotamian and Iranian imagery during the second half of the third millennium are contests and rituals involving presentations or offerings. The contest theme involves a struggle with wild and domesticated animals in which humans or supernatural beings intervene. The principal focus of the scene is a hero. No real identity can be ascribed to the hero, as it varies in different contexts, even though the style of presentation is conventionalized. The focal point of the ritual theme is a deity or several in which an offering is being made in what appears to be a sacred rite. I begin with a discussion of the themes and motifs in Indus imagery.

Themes and Motifs in Indus Narrative Imagery

The imagery on the Indus seals and sealings presents a complex array of characteristics involving humans, composite beasts with human and animal attributes, and supernatural beings. They appear in different guises though often aligned with specific animals or vegetation. Striking active poses, they participate in processions, kneel and gesture toward another figure, present offerings, restrain animals, sit on trees and stools, and stand in trees. A quick look at some specific actions situates these "characters" within the context of the two themes described here.

Most, though not all, of the narrative images contain at least one human (Figure 10.4c), supernatural (Figure 10.4a), or animal image (Figure 10.4b) as the focus of some aspect of the scene. All motifs are drawn directly from nature, such as the wild tiger (Figure 10.4d) or apparently tame animal (Figure 10.4b). Two trees are represented, the acacia tree (Figure 10.4a, 10.4c, 10.4e, Franke-Vogt 1991b; 184) and the pipal (Figure 10.4b).

Although themes often are combined, the number of activities is restricted. In figures 10.4a, 10.4d, and 10.5a a human or supernatural figure is engaged in a "contest" scene in which the figure restrains a "real" or supernatural animal. In Figure 10.4a, a supernatural being has a human face an upper torso with female breasts and a lower torso of a bovid with hoofs and tail, wears a horned headdress. She is flanked by an acacia and a tiger with bared teeth, projecting claws, and horns. In Figure 10.4c the contest theme is shown in a different form, in which the figure restrains humans uprooting acacia trees. In Figure 10.5a, a human restrains tigers, and on the reverse side of the tablet (Figure 10.5b) another spears a water buffalo. The figure, seated in the yogic position, gazes toward the scene, simply observing or commanding the action. Another variation on the contest theme is the depiction on the cylinder seal impression shown in Figure 10.4f in which the action is reversed. Here, the central figure is flanked by two humans who grasp his/her hands and envelop the figure by crossing their spears. This act could be interpreted as one of restraint or solidarity. Standing to the side is a supernatural creature who attends the performance either as an observer or in command of the action. He/she wears a headdress with animal horns and a floral sprig extending upward from its

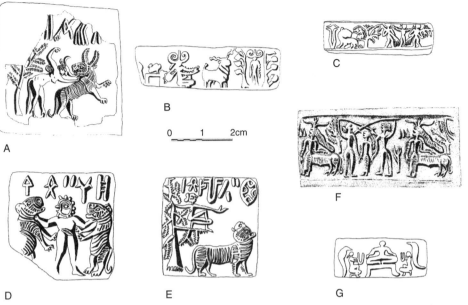

Figure 10.4. Narrative image from Mohenjo-daro (A–E, G) and Kalibangan (F). Courtesy Ute Franke-Vogt.

center. The acacias have some significance, as they float throughout the narrative.

The second theme shows an offering either to a central figure or one toward which all other figures are facing. In Figure 10.4b, a kneeling figure (bangle laden) offers an animal to a human, also wearing multiple bangles, standing in the pipal tree. The significance of the duck on a stool behind the human kneeling figure is unclear. In Figure 10.4g the kneeling humans hold containers (possibly votive) and gesture toward a person seated on a stool in a position that mirrors Figure 10.3. Snakes, rare in Indus narratives, frame the scene.

The procession in Figure 10.6 is one of the most evocative narratives in Indus imagery. I show it in two aspects, as in the original square seal and in which I have separated its registers into a single procession. The original seal was carved in two registers and depicts an elaborate presentation scene. In the top register, a human figure with a horned headdress is symbolically represented in or under a pipal tree/arbor and gazes towards a kneeling human wearing a horned headdress adorned with a spray of foliage. The kneeling figure appears to be presenting a rather unusual animal, with its apparent half human/half animal face and the

Figure 10.5. Narrative imagery from Harappa. Photograph by the Harappa Archaeological Research Project © HARP.

horns of a markhor goat to the standing deity. Seven figures wearing single-horned headdresses walk or stand in an orderly row. Viewed as a continuous sequence of actions, the image preserves an aspect of the seal that I believe was the intended vision of the event, in which the seven figures process or ascend toward the animal and the kneeling and standing figures. In that view, the standing figure is the focus and the action is pointed in its direction.

Figure 10.6. A narrative image of processing deities from Mohenjo-daro. Courtesy Ute Franke-Vogt.

Decoding Indus Narratives

The actions performed on the seals and sealings carry a widely shared symbolic vocabulary and underlying structure of presentation. The symbolism is explicit. Deities wear headdresses consisting of the horns of powerful animals and vegetation known from the Indus landscape which have taken on sacred meaning. Equally explicit is the representation of supernatural beings, powerful animals, and vegetation in which natural forces are suppressed or harnessed. In some instances, figures are aligned with specific animals or vegetation. They are shown in different scenes and can be identified by the vegetation or animals that accompany them. The underlying structure of representation includes symmetry of representations, juxtapositions of the tamed and untamed, specific acts associated with heroes and heroines and forceful presentation of challenging conflicts among destructive and nurturing forces, superhuman qualities and performance of great feats and devotion and the exaltation of deities.

These motifs and themes are reformulated in multiple instances in which an Indus pantheon of gods and goddesses, heroes and humans together engage in actions in a natural and supernatural world, much as Trigger has shown in his comparative study of religion and worldviews

in other early civilizations. Examples are the tiger that has taken prominence in this group of images and is symbolically laden. In Figure 10.4a,
the tiger appears as a powerful animal wearing a homed headdress, while
in another (Figure 10.4d) is restrained, and finally in Figures 10.4c, e
appears to be dominated by the gesturing human in the tree, thereby
creating a more ordered world. Other examples are the seals in which an
offering is depicted. The most evocative is the procession in Figure 10.6.
All of the figures wear headdresses with unique characteristics that may
symbolize such differences as stages in the life cycle, gender distinctions
or hierarchies of deities. In this and two other seals, representations of
humans (10.4g) and deities (104b) are indicative of embedded conceptions of hierarchy.

Details of representation mark the presence of major and minor deities. The most obvious are the headdresses. They include several types:
buffalo horns (Figure 10.4a) and buffalo horns with a floral center
(Figure 10.5b), a curled horn with a center projecting upward (Figure
10.4b and 10.6), a curled horn with a pipal floral center (Figure 10.6), a
horn of a markhor goat with an acacia sprig at the center (Figure 10.4f), a
wide and curved horn with a fan-like center (Figure 10.3), and the single
horns of the processing figures in Figure 10.6.

The presence of headdresses is explicit, adding significance to whether
the figures who wear them are human or supernatural. In this small
sample of the thirteen figures with horns, two are supernatural beings
and the eleven remaining are human. They either stand and observe a
scene (Figure 10.4f) or engage in combat with a tiger (Figure 10.4a).
The humans wearing horned headdresses present offerings to a standing human wearing a headdress (Figures 10.4b and 10.6). The standing
human figures with hair locks (Figures 10.4d and 10.5a) flanked by tigers
and the horned supernatural Figure 10.4a engage in a closely related
scene, possibly suggesting variants of myths that involve sequences of
action or humans and supernaturals in transitional states, conceivably
at different stages of the life cycle (Box 10.1). There is no basis on which
to determine whether the human figures represent deities, though in
view of the extra human feats they perform, they clearly enjoy a special
status.

Box 10.1 Rituals, Performance, and Stories

Some of the seals appear to represent a still frame or snapshot of
rituals or story telling. The cylinder seal from Kalibangan (Figure
10.4f) is one example of what could be interpreted as a rite of passage,

Box 10.1 *(Cont.)*

possibly involving a life cycle change or achievement of membership in a cult (Wright 1997). The ritual itself is a performance that marks a transitional phase in which an individual takes on a new social identity. In this image, the central figure is a composite being with animal and human characteristics (the lower torso bears hoofs and the stripes represent a tiger). He/she is rendered at a smaller scale than the two humans with spears. The standing deity is shown at an even larger scale and is flanked by an acacia on one side and two signs of the Indus script, one of which could represent an acacia. It is tempting to identify both the small figure and the larger deity as females, largely based upon their long braids, and the presence of the acacia, associated with females in other narrative seals. In any case, the small figure is a miniature version of the deity, with the single exception of the deity's elaborate headdress that combines animal horns and vegetation. Viewed in this way, the deity appears as a supernatural creature (part human, part tiger based on the body, though the hoofed feet are suggestive of a bovid). She wears bangles (as does the smaller figure) associated with deities in several seals and directs the performance. The two figures standing on either side of the smaller figure grasp or hold its hands as they place their spears over her. This gesture may convey status, thus acquiring the symbolic trappings of power, in which the smaller figure is in the process of crossing that transition point between youth or adolescence and maturity as she enters the cult of the goddess.

Seals also may have been used for story-telling. On Figure 10.5a a female engages with two tigers and is accompanied by an elephant. On the reverse side of the seal (Figure 10.5b), a human spears a wild water buffalo with a barbed spear. The figure has hair locks, but unlike the heroine on the reverse of the seal wears a double-bun hairdo, perhaps suggesting the "hunter" is a male. A gharial is drawn at the top of the seal over the water buffalo. The motifs on this seal are replete with symbols of power – all powerful animals, humans engaged with natural forces, and the presence of a deity. It is easy to imagine the retelling of a myth in which the imagery on this seal and others were used as devices to recall the adventures of a single or several deities engaged in heroic deeds, meeting formidable challenges. One attempts to dominate the water buffalo, an animal indigenous to the Indus and domesticated there, and the other, a female tames rather than destroys the wildest of animals, the tiger. The seated figure personifies the sacred power of these acts.

Another status marker of religious significance are the bracelets worn by many of the central figures. There are a high number of deities with horned headdresses who also wear bracelets in both presentation (Figures 10.4b and 10.6) and contest scenes (Figures 10.4c and 10.4f). The thousands of bangles produced from simple low-fired terracotta and the technically sophisticated stoneware types in small quantities, as well as others of shell and copper, attest to their popularity. Moreover, as Kenoyer suggests, bangles may have been emblematic of identities that conferred social status and ritual power (1998:107) and carry specific religious meanings.

Additional insights can be gained by comparing styles and attributes of human figurines to those on the narrative seals in order to determine consistency and/or overlap (Wright 1997). On both narrative seals and figurines, the female breast, but not the vulva, is an explicit reference to females. Breasts on the seals and tablets are shown in profile on the human and supernatural figures on several seals in which they engage with tigers. In an unusual scene, a female human stands between two people uprooting trees. In distinction, a principal marker of males on figurines is the presence of genitalia, which is rare in the narrative seals.

While some gender-based attributes on figurines complement imagery on narrative seals and tablets, others are less clear or point in different directions. The curled locks of hair on Figures 10.4d and 10.5a are associated with female figurines, and although male figurines also wear this hairstyle, the breasts in profile clearly signify the presence of a female. The double bun hairstyle associated with male figurines and depicted on the humans flanking the central figure in Figures 10.4f and 10.4c may represent males, but the central figure in Figure 10.4c, given the trace of a female breast, suggests possible gender ambiguity in view of the double bun he/she wears. Braid hairstyles are present on both male and female figurines, leaving open whether the kneeling figures in Figure 10.4b and others in Figures 10.4f and 10.4g are males or females. Clark (2007) attributes headdresses as signifiers of female identity (2007:548) but the widely curled horned headdresses, though rare, are exclusively associated with male figurines. Using that indicator, both figures in Figure 10.4b could be male. On the other hand, the curled headdress with a floral sprig (associated with female figurines and never with males) worn by the kneeling figure in Figure 10.6 and the figure in the yogic posture in Figure 10.5b, and possibly the figure in Figure 10.3 whose curled horn headdress carries a fan-shaped center associated with female figurines is a graphic example of the merging of male and female attributes. One possibility is that gender lacked significance in the actions presented or that the absence of specificity is an explicit reference to gender variance, possibly representing beings with special powers or a reference to different aspects of a single deity.

Cross-Cultural Comparisons

The narrative imagery below from Mesopotamia and Iran represents a small sample of seals that have been more extensively studied than the Indus narratives. They complement the analyses offered here as they provide additional visualizations of systems of thought that are closely aligned with Trigger's comparative analyses.

Mesopotamian Seal Imagery

The illustrations on Figures 10.7a,b are impressions of an engraved Mesopotamian Cylinder Seal when it is rolled on a pliable surface. If rolled continuously multiple images of the same scene would result. The repetition of the small figure to the extreme left and right of the image is an example. The contest theme was popular in Mesopotamia during the third millennium (and earlier) and is illustrated on many Mesopotamian seals beginning in the late fourth millennium B.C. It continued to be popular in Mesopotamia and elsewhere, well beyond the point at which the Indus civilization had come to an end. In the classic scene, the action involves a hero holding a "halter" about the neck of the animal. Dominique Collon interprets this action (Figure 10.7a) as a "gesture of protection" (1995:73, 1987). The figures on either side of the hero are the so-called bull-man who wears a horned headdress. He is the hero's ally. In some analyses, the bull-man is erroneously identified as Enkidu (Collon 1987:197). The image also includes lions, who are opponents in the scenes, and in some cases (not shown here) have wings. Others are various monsters, bulls, human-headed bulls, water buffalo, and a variety of wild and tame animals, including horned animals (1987:197).

An offering scene is shown on Figure 10.7b. This theme is an adaptation of a banquet scene in which humans acted as celebrants to deities. In the later adaptation, the theme shifted to an offering or presentation that was made directly to a deity, when there was a "reorganization" of deities in Mesopotamia. Deities, recognized by their horned headdresses and floral sprigs at their centers, are shown standing or seated, receiving an offering from a single worshipper or several. Figure 10.7b is typical. Deities wear ears of wheat sprouting from their shoulders and present a major female deity (recognized by her horned headdress, costume and long braid) with vegetation and the contents of a vessel. The three minor standing deities wear horned headdresses and vegetation sprouts from their shoulders. Standing deities processing toward a seated deity

B

A

Figure 10.7. Cylinder seal impressions from Mesopotamia. Courtesy
British Museum.

was a common image on seals during the last centuries of the third
millennium (Collon 1995:81).

The imagery on the two Mesopotamian seals discussed here reproduces elements on the Indus seals and their symbolic vocabulary. They
include animal and plant motifs on headdresses bearing either a horn
or plant or in combination. Supernatural, human and animal forms
represent heroes or deities. On Mesopotamian seals different types of
stools, astral signs, natural elements (water, wind), weaponry (quivers
and bows), vessels, clothing and shoes are associated with specific deities
or royal persons known from Mesopotamia texts. Gender distinctions
are represented by hairstyles, beards and clothing.

The same underlying structure is rendered in the Mesopotamian seals
in which symbols appear in multiple contexts of action. Representations
of horned animals, human-headed bulls, humans with or without headdresses, and animals perform a variety of actions though all are recognized as a contest scene (see Collon 1987:29–33). In offering scenes the
female goddess shown in Figure 10.7b is replaced with other deities and
the context of action differs. In seals not reproduced here, a sun god is

shown with attendants who hold open "the gates of dawn" or a water god is accompanied by attendants who hold flowing vases (Collon 1987: Figures 847–9). In another scene the water god (Ea/Enki) is shown with a captured bird and is accompanied by his vizier (an attendant) named Usmu, who is represented with a double face. This representation of a double face conveys Usmu's ability to look forward and backward simultaneously facing the water god and the captured "zu-bird". Conceivably the seated figure in the Indus "proto-Siva" seal (Figure 10.3) with three faces is meant to convey the same idea, a useful device that would allow the figure (Figure 10.3) to observe the animals to its left and right and the viewer of the seal simultaneously!

Iranian Seal Imagery

To judge from comparisons with recently excavated material, the Iranian seals illustrated here belong to the "Jiroft culture" centered on the region of the Halil Basin (see Figure 8.1 for location) and share many of the same themes and imagery with cultures further to the west. While these similarities may be due to the strong early ties of this region to cultures to the west (Pittman 2001:234–6), this changed in the late third millennium when the stylistic features indicate "a reorientation among the communities on the Iranian plateau [and especially in the Halil River Basin the Jiroft culture] away from the urban centers in the west, and toward the communities of the north, south and east." (Pittman 2001:236). All of the Iranian seals discussed in this chapter are from this period of reorientation.

The motifs and imagery on the Iranian seals carry a similar symbolic vocabulary structure of presentation reminiscent of both Indus and Mesopotamian imagery. They include the representation of natural phenomena, principally plants and animals as well as supernatural beings. Further, there is a focus either on human or animal figures identified as divine on the basis of the presence of horned headdresses, wings, and emerging vegetation (Figures 10.8a, 10.8b, 10.8f, 10.8g). Headdresses include bull horns and vegetation, while vegetation, wings, and snakes may be directly attached to the bodies of deities (Figure 10.8e). Deities often are depicted in pairs (Figures 10.8b and 10.8g) (Pittman 2001b:237).

Many of the Iranian deities are considered female because of specific attributes including the presence of breasts (Figure 10.8g, standing; Figure 10.8f, seated and kneeling) and featured elements such as the figure holding "wands" at the left (Figure 10.8f). Male figures are identified by their posture and bun hairstyle (Pittman 2001b:237), although human males are often shown with long hair falling over the front of the

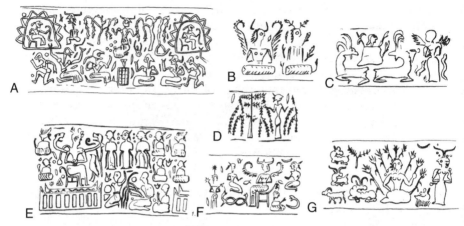

Figure 10.8. Narrative imagery from Southeastern Iran and Tepe Yahya.

shoulder. All of the cylinder seals that Holly Pittman examined from the site of Shahdad in south-central Iran, and others from Tepe Yahya (see Figure 8.1 for locations) depict female deities (Pittman 2002:223). But others found in excavations at Konar Sandal in the Jiroft clearly depict male as well as female deities. The gendered transposition in the contest scenes when compared to Mesopotamian examples clearly reflects on the underlying meaning of the narratives and possible differences in gender ideologies in the Indus (Wright 1997) and Iran.

The Iranian seals include the contest theme. Though the "stories represented differ from the Mesopotamian and Indus narratives," they carry the same symmetry as in Figure 10.8c in which a seated goddess rests on the backs of two large horned caprids (Pittman 2001b:223), animals that may be more reflective of life on the Iranian plateau, and a common Iranian theme. To the right, a standing goddess is winged and is flanked by snakes, a variation on the contest theme. Another Iranian image (Figure 10.8d) shows a figure flanked by vegetation, possibly an acacia, a variation on Indus symbolism (Figure 10.4c).

Ritual or festival scenes differ from the Mesopotamian seals but provide a link to certain depictions in the Indus corpus. Ritual or festival scenes show a pantheon of deities on many Iranian seals. One depicts standing and/or kneeling figures processing toward or facing a deity (Figure 10.8e), evoking Indus Figure 10.6. In others a pantheon is most strongly depicted (Figures 10.8c, 10.8f, and 10.8g) (Pittman 2001b) either with vegetation sprouting from their shoulders or wearing horned headdresses. Figure 10.8f includes many relevant themes, in which a seated deity wears a garment, a headdress, and wings or vegetation emerging from her shoulders. To her right, a standing deity holds what appear to be "wands." The seated deity is attended by three kneeling figures, one of whom faces a snake. Two intertwined snakes separate the principal deity from the standing deity.

The motifs on the seal share common elements with Figure 10.8g, in which a seated deity, legs under its body, has vegetation emanating from its shoulders and a headdress comprised of plant or tree branches. A second standing female deity holds its arms in the same position as the sitting and standing deity in Figure 10.8f (described earlier) but wears a horned headdress. To the right of the seated deity (Figure 10.8g), a tree branch (an acacia?) floats in space and four horned caprids (sheep or goat) complete the scene.

Finally the imagery on eastern Iranian seals is sometimes composed in two registers (Figures 10.8a, and 10.8e) a convention known from the Indus (Figure 10.6) and on occasional seals in Mesopotamia (Collon 1987:35). On Figure 10.8e, the female (based on the placement of the arms and palms) is seated on a chair on top of a building or terrace of a large structure. She wears a hairstyle of curly locks and snakes emanate from her shoulders. She is flanked on the left by what appears to be the same pair of deities (minor?) shown in Figure 10.8b. On the right, a bird faces her, perhaps an offering to a snake goddess. In a separate frame to the left of the seated deity, three humans process toward her (interpreted as female because of their clothing, Pittman 2001b). Other kneeling figures complete the procession. In the lower register, in addition to the kneeling figure, two others, one of whom plays a harp and another with its hands raised, incorporate elements of Mesopotamian banquet scenes, where musical instruments often are shown. Figure 10.8a is a complex scene. In the lower register, seated and kneeling figures participate in a festival or banquet of a different sort from Figure 10.8e. Here, the figures face a table with offerings or provisions. In the top register, at its center a kneeling horned deity is flanked by trees, possibly acacia. In a second scene a deity with a horned headdress kneels before a seated deity positioned within or under a trellis or perhaps stylized tree, reminiscent of the deity in the pipal tree in the Indus Figure 10.6.

Rethinking Indus Religion and World Views. Shared Vocabularies, Modes of Presentation and Systems of Thought

My goal in this chapter has been to examine the imagery on Indus narrative seals in order to understand Indus systems of thought. Through the investigation of a selective sample of seals, I have offered a new view of the meaning of this imagery that lends support to the notion of a society that conceived of an undifferentiated natural/human/supernatural world inhabited by a pantheon of gods and dominating elements of the natural world and the cosmos. According to the symbolism represented, gods and goddesses are aligned with powerful aspects of nature in the form of animals and vegetation. These interpretations are very much in line with the comparative analyses of systems of thought in early civilizations.

As additional modes of inquiry, I have drawn together multiple lines of evidence as a bridging framework to establish ways in which to reconceptualize an Indus world based on commonalities with Trigger's comparative studies and narratives known cross-culturally throughout the broad region with which the Indus interacted. Working through this process, I have bridged image and meaning by revealing a symbolic vocabulary and underlying structure of ideas and presentation that is present in the Indus, and that appears also to be common in Mesopotamian and Iranian narrative imagery. To demonstrate these ideas, I have presented contexts of common presentation in the use of specific kinds of motifs and artistic conventions that underlay particular renderings. These references include identification of deities based on the appearance of horns and horned and vegetal headdresses, supernatural beings and presumed linkages of those images to an Indus mythology.

I have suggested that throughout Mesopotamia, south central Iran, and the Indus the symbolic content of seal imagery complements Trigger's observations based on his comparative studies. Embedded in the symbolic vocabulary of the seals and the depiction of anthropomorphized deities, there is an expression of a belief in a natural order that was simultaneously human and supernatural, lending support to the idea of a society that conceived of a world inhabited by a pantheon of gods and goddesses, humans and composite animal beings that dominate or are dominated by elements of the natural world and the cosmos. According to the symbolism represented, the pantheon and beings are aligned with powerful aspects of nature in the form of animals and vegetation. Interestingly (and importantly), there is a lack of distinction between humans and supernatural beings. All of the supernatural beings are identifiable as at least partially human and where humans and mythical beings are present, they appear to interact with each other.

While I have described a consistency of motifs and underlying structure of thought, we also have seen cultural modifications that transform the narratives to uniquely local styles. Whatever the content of shared ideas and representation, they were manipulated to conform to local concerns. Most obvious are the substitution of animals of equal power and ferocity to ones more at home in an Indus landscape and local plants that took on a symbolic significance. Also visible are devices of ornamentation, such as bangles ubiquitous in Indus artifact assemblages and an emphasis on hairstyle and headdresses that falls in line with conceptions for terracotta female figurines. The occurrence of androgynous characters, with their absence of overt sexuality and the predominance of female deities is striking on both Indus and Iranian seals. In the Indus, their presence is most explicit in the depiction of females as masters of animals or vegetation.

As we have seen in the above sections, the motifs and imagery on Indus seals and tablets provide powerful insights into Indus ideology. Indus artisans rendered motifs and imagery that reflected a symbolic vocabulary that when viewed as a whole related culturally meaningful narratives that expressed particular sets of ideologies. The overall images, while visual in nature, carried important messages that were conveyed repeatedly through the use of recurring and modifiable motifs. We have seen many examples of new or recombined versions modeled on previous ones.

Other classes of material in the form of masks and figurines, especially the latter, served as important transmitters of symbolism, ideology, and religion. New interpretations of these objects introduce notions of sexuality, shamanistic practice, transcendent experiences, life force, and household cults to the body of Indus belief. From a technological perspective, the transformation of natural bone into a humanly constructed substance through heating and applied to the bodies of figurines as a colorant, likely imbued them with supernatural powers.

These interpretations are in accord with Trigger's findings, in which he noted that household and local cults and individuals could communicate directly with gods and/or through shamans or ritual intermediaries who are conduits between the human and supernatural powers. Finally, the identification of stylized conventions employed on figurines that are specific to male and female representation and gender variants is yet another component of the symbolic vocabulary of attributes that prove useful in interpreting aspects of the symbolism represented on the narrative imagery (Wright 1997).

An Indus Pantheon, Elements of Order, and
Conceptions of Power and Hierarchy.

When Sir Mortimer Wheeler published a major book on the Indus civilization, he devoted a little more than three paragraphs to a section entitled "The Indus Religions" (1968:108). Embedded in his text, however, under discussions of Indus art, he spoke of almost nude female Great Mother Goddesses (1968:91), statuettes representing "gods" one of whom was a legendary priest-king like those in Mesopotamia and the seated Siva, "replete with the brooding, minatory power of the great god of historic India" (1968:109), nude gods or goddesses standing in a pipal tree "with seven clothed ministrants engaged in a ritual dance," (1968:105) and figures holding back tigers characteristic of the Sumerian "Gilgamesh and his lions" (1968:110). In a section describing the city plan at Mohenjo-daro, he referred to the Great Bath as the site of public ritual ablutions known from Hinduism, describing the entire complex of the "citadel" as the seat of religious life

for the city or its rulers. In modern Hinduism, and indeed in other religious systems, ceremonial cleansings are an important feature, and the elaboration and prominent position of the bathing establishments on the Mohenjo-daro citadel proclaim their official status (1968:43).

Although Wheeler referred to the Indus religion as a mélange of influences, it was to Hinduism that he returned in his conclusion, suggesting that an "Harappan mentality" anticipated its later religions (1968:136).

This image of a substrate philosophy linking the Indus to Hinduism and Buddhism has been pervasive in reconstructions of the Indus civilization and have contrived a political authority intertwined with a philosophy at once Hindu and Buddhist (D.Miller 1985). Such interpretations have consigned the civilization to a homogeneous caste-like society in which political authority was vested in a reclusive priest king. In these analyses, systems of authority were based upon an ideology in which ones social class or stage of life was the moral order, each individual fulfilling "the purpose for which one was given that place originally" (Fairservis 1971:301). In such a society, power lies masked behind a veil of tradition that lends the moral base (Ibid.:301).

These long-held ideas about a highly organized society in which images of gods and goddesses and a legendary priest-king (like those in Mesopotamia) presage the evolution of Hindu and Buddhist India have been challenged here. As a more robust alternative, the interpretations I have offered provide plausible interpretations to the meanings represented on Indus imagery. They conform well with the evidence Trigger gleaned from the several civilizations he studied (but did not include the Indus or Iran) and provide insight into the ways in which Indus people experienced their world. In line with Trigger's findings, the focus of the narrative imagery is on natural phenomena, and supernatural forms are presented as proxies for the powerful forces with which Indus people had to contend, the 'Wholly Other' that lie outside of normal experience (Jacobsen 1976:3).

The images also suggest that the deities may have possessed personal characteristics that resembled powerful human beings, as Trigger (2003:246) noted for other early civilizations and as is known from studies of contemporary imagery in Mesopotamia. Of special relevance are the relations of specific actions and the exaltations of recognizable heroes or deities, the forceful presentation of superhuman qualities and performance of great feats and devotion, and the expression of an underlying structure of oppositions of tamed and untamed.

Additionally, the notion that this imagery communicates an essential cognitive theme of humans making a place for themselves in nature is very much in line with the principles that I outlined in Chapters 6, 7 and 9 concerning motivations and inspirations for the technological style of Indus artisans in creating objects and cultural landscapes. As many examples demonstrated, Indus artisans appropriated natural processes by remaking natural materials through grinding, heating and manipulating mineral pigments, thus rendering them suitable for production into cultural products. It is in that same sense that the builders of Indus cities were master crafters of landscape and architecture, refashioning nature to a material form that took its place *in* nature. Similarly, this same vision is repeated in the narrative imagery.

But has the material presented in this chapter taken us closer to identifying the structure of religion or its leadership? As indicated earlier, the lack of contextual evidence to confirm the use of specific buildings as temples or shrines leaves identification of religious structures in doubt. Moreover, none of the ritual or cult scenes depicted are represented within structures. We must conclude that on the basis of lack of evidence, it is not possible to say anything about an Indus "state" religion at this time nor identify an institutionalized "officiant" in organized ceremonies. Indeed, most of the materials discussed, especially the terracotta figurines, masks and seals are more likely to be objects owned and deployed by individuals.

Still, there are aspects of seal imagery that provide windows into the potential insinuation of rulers into the world of myth that reinforced worldly authority. Barry Kemp, discussing central elements in Egyptian imagery, views the use of wild and fierce animals "as an allegory of the forces of life" with political implications (1989:47). In Indus imagery, humans and supernatural creatures similarly master natural forces. They present powerful stories that demonstrate the human ability to incorporate moments of order and potential resolution in their engagement with natural forces. For example, the uprooting of the acacias, a tree repeated in this imagery with sufficient regularity to suggest its sacred nature, is balanced against a scene on the same seal (Figure 10.4c) in which the tiger standing on the ground and human figure seated in the firmly rooted acacia appear reconciled. The tiger looks back with a quizzical gaze (not rage in any event) at the individual gesturing in the tree.

Box 10.2 An Imagined Performance and Ritual Space

I end this chapter with a venture into an imagined performance and ritual space. I turn to the spaces identified at Dholavira for an "imagined" space in which rituals and ceremony might have been performed. The terracotta mask shown in Figure 10.1 is hollow and contains holes on each side for fastening. It is a human- and animal-like face that recalls the tiger viewed in many of the images on the narrative seals. Some masks possess horns (Marshall 1931:pls. XCV 1-3 XCV1 5, 6, and 341), which we have seen in much of the imagery discussed. Horned imagery is common among cultures of the Near East and appears on various Indus media. The masks are too small to be viewed at a distance, but may have been models for larger ones produced from perishable materials such as animal skins. The imagined space I have in mind at Dholavira is one of the two ceremonial grounds described by its excavator as "two 'stadia' - one wide and extensive, the other much smaller and compact" (Bisht 2005:12). Situated adjacent to the two largest buildings (Bisht's castle; see Figure 5.4), we can envision a procession through the lower and middle towns toward a ceremonial area. Perhaps a sovereign or shaman was present, standing at the apex under a sacred pipal tree, or simply there, reminding others of his/her unique relationship with the deity. In any event, the notion of hierarchy and preferred access would not be missed by those present or others viewing this high scene from afar in the lower city.

I like Stephen Houston's vision of such events: "divine essences came to visit, briefly, and were made animate by human flesh and motion" (Houston 2006:149), to which I would add in the Indus case imagined here, and established a relation with supernatural powers that ensured continued well-being, justifying a created social order.

Of additional significance is the presentation scene in Figure 10.6 in its depiction of the epitome of a universe in which conceptions of hierarchy and order are firmly embedded. The seven "ministrants" or initiates process in an orderly row in an image that is not static. On the original seal, the kneeling deity is shown in the top register, the initiates below, as they process to a higher plane. The collapsing of the two registers into a single image, preserves another aspect of the intended vision of the event. An ascending deity kneels before what clearly is a major deity encircled by or standing under a pipal tree and is the focal point of the image. The minor deity presents a magnificent (its size and its strange, almost human, face), animal to the major deity. Thus a minor and major deity and others, perhaps transitioning to divine states, process toward the higher plane, promoting and sustaining a social order that reproduces hierarchy and a "practiced place" in which status and hierarchies are prescribed (Box 10.2).

In the absence of texts to complement the view presented in this chapter, we cannot know whether this presumed system of thought represents a true reality. However, the results of this investigation using cross-cultural analogies and models derived from comparative analysis present plausible scenarios that move us away from direct historical approaches and forward in gaining a richer understanding of Indus narrative themes and mental life. We have found that the association of gods and goddesses with natural phenomena and references to supernatural and animistic beings fall closely in line with Indus imagery and a deeply expressed impulse to break down and transform the natural world into a built world. What also seems clear is that Indus people had formulated ideas of the supernatural in ways that appear similar to the larger world with which they interacted and Trigger's interpretations based on comparative analyses. Yet the symbolism and underlying systems of thought proposed here remain an elusive "truth" that can only approximate the ideals that lingered in the minds of the people who created and preserved them.

11 The Decline and Transformation and the Comparative Study of Early States

When Sir Mortimer Wheeler described the end of the Indus civilization, he did so in the comprehensive manner characteristic of his writing, citing various possibilities for its demise. His comments set the stage for this chapter and the various controversies that continue to plague Indus scholars. Wheeler's research on Mohenjo-daro influenced his understanding of the end of the society. Using a decidedly local view of "collapse," he concentrated on aspects of Mohenjo-daro that he believed forecast the degeneration of political authority. He described the city as "slowly dying." Maintenance of its public works and buildings had fallen behind. New constructions were shoddy, bricks were reused, larger houses were carved up into "warrens for a swarming lower-grade population" and the city "was becoming a slum" (Wheeler 1968:127). He believed this decline was caused by an eroding economy brought about by the overcultivation of land, overuse of wood for producing baked bricks that deforested the land, and steady wearing out of the landscape due to overgrazing. Other causes involved periodic flooding, disruption of its maritime trade, and a "massacre" evidenced by the skeletal remains discovered at Mohenjo-daro (Wheeler 1968:131) (see Chapter 9).

As an urban society, the Indus civilization at its height lasted less than a thousand years. Sometime around 1900 B.C. major transformations began to occur. The circumstances leading to its final days and the importance of many of the factors cited by Wheeler and others continue to be debated. New evidence indicates the process was uneven and involved changes that were gradual and others that were more abrupt. They included the abandonment of some settlements, the expansion of others, and the retention of a few lingering vestiges of the material culture that we identify with its major periods of urbanization.

When a civilization ends, archaeologists want to know what happened and why. By developing research projects to answer specific questions, the "what happened" part often can be determined. As I discussed in Chapter 2, an investigation of environmental indicators can lead us to understand whether there were adverse changes that coincided with decline. More

difficult to determine is whether environmental changes were sufficiently abrupt and devastating, like the "tsunami" that hit Southeast
and South Asia in the winter of 2004 that caused massive loss of life and
destruction of the people's way of life, that little could be done to restore
former social conditions. Or were the changes gradual so that adjustments could be made? With growing populations, was there an overuse of resources, an inability or lack of incentive in rural communities
to stay linked to centers? Or were the political and economic systems
flawed and unable to make the adjustments necessary to maintain a
viable society?

   In the first part of this chapter, I will review ideas that scholars have put
forth concerning the general decline of the Indus, then move on to review
local causes across regions. In my discussion, I evaluate Wheeler's views
in the context of more recent evidence for cultural collapse. In the final
section, I will return to the Urban period and review the significant factors in its political economy and the infrastructural elements that made it
a viable network of interacting city states. I also will synthesize evidence
discussed in earlier chapters and what it reveals about Indus urbanism,
economy, and society and its place in the comparative study of early
civilizations.

The Decline and Transformation of the Indus

Studies of the "collapse" of civilizations have shown that it is important
to differentiate among "general" and "local" causes when attempting to
explain their demise. Disruptions of a general nature potentially affect
the civilization as a whole. In the Indus, archaeologists have proposed
general causes that include environmental shifts, the invasion of foreign
peoples (the "massacre" to which Wheeler referred), and disruptions in
maritime trade. In contrast, the deterioration of public works and architecture due to the degeneration of civic authority at Mohenjo-daro may
have been specific to that city and "local" changes. Conditions in each
region need to be assessed individually and our view needs to encompass
regions that stretch beyond the alluvial plain to contemporary settlements on its borderlands in Afghanistan and Baluchistan.

   The way that archaeologists refer to the final periods of the Indus
is derived from chronologies built from region-specific evidence.
These chronologies are related to spatial and temporal phases and are
named for the specific sites or regions they represent. Each is presented
in Table 11.1.

   As the chronologies indicate, the archaeological evidence for occupation in the Post-urban period varies regionally. Diagnostic markers are

Table 11.1.[a] Post-urban Chronologies

Post-urban chronologies	Approximate Temporal Range
Cemetery H/Late Harappan (Upper Indus/ Harappa)	1900–1700 B.C.
Post-urban/Jhukar (Lower Indus)	1900–1700 B.C.
Post-urban/Late Harappan (Cholistan)	1900–1700/1500 B.C.
Post-urban/Late Harappan (northwest India)	1900–1500 B.C.
Post-urban/Late Harappan (Sorath Harappan)	1900–1700 B.C.

[a] The absolute dates cited in this table are from Meadow et al. (2001) for Harappa, Mughal (1992a) for Jhukar and Cholistan, and Possehl and Rissman (1992) for northwest India and Sorath. Shaffer's 1992 article in the most recent *Chronologies in Old World Archaeology* is a basic reference.

largely based on pottery types. In some regions, the terminal dates are based on a limited number of radiocarbon dates, while in others, larger numbers are available. There also are disagreements on the appropriate designations to apply to specific regions. For example, Mughal (1990) prefers the term, "Late Harappan" instead of "Post-urban" because of the presence of the large settlement of Kudwala (38 hectares) in Cholistan during this period. While it is the case that even some of the urban settlements traditionally associated with the Indus, for example Harappa, remain occupied, I am persuaded by their diminished size that urbanism was severely curtailed in the Post-urban period. Diagnostic pottery types for the Post-urban/Late Harappan in Cholistan and northwest India (the combined area of the Ghaggar-Hakra Rivers) and the Upper Indus are derived from the Cemetery H pottery from the cemetery at Harappa (see Chapter 9). The Jhukar terminology is based on excavations at the site for which it is named. I have used Possehl's term, Sorath Harappan, because the region has produced a good absolute chronology based on excavations at Rojdi (Possehl and Raval 1989) and elsewhere. Figure 11.1 shows the approximate locations of all of the areas to be discussed including regions on the western edge of the Indus alluvial plain, labeled borderlands.

In the following I discuss several factors that contribute to collapse. They include potential causes of a general nature and a region by region assessment of local factors. In so doing, I examine the factors that Wheeler had raised as potential causes and introduce others based

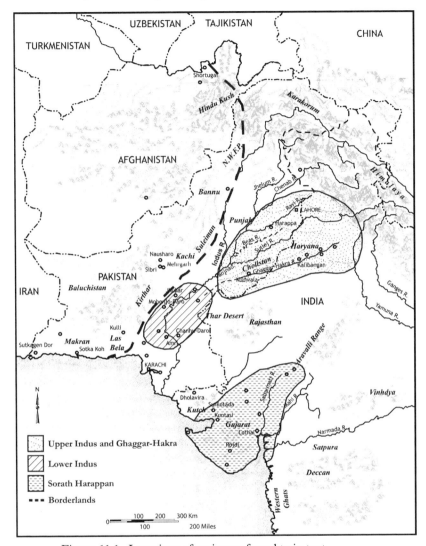

Figure 11.1. Locations of regions referred to in text.

on more recent research. Whether any of them caused a fundamental breakdown of the political and cultural conditions that characterized the Indus Urban period will be addressed. I also evaluate current debates on the relationship between the Indus civilization and later periods.

Causes of a General Nature

For the Indus, general causes that may have contributed to the decline and transformation of the civilization include environmental shifts, alterations of river courses, intrusion of new populations, and disruptions of trade relations. These changes are considered general in the sense that they may have had overarching consequences for the civilization as a whole.

Environmental Changes – Climate, Precipitation, and River Courses

Episodes of environmental change are often cited as causes of the "collapse" of civilizations. These fluctuations can be particularly devastating to the agropastoral economies practiced by many early civilizations. For the Indus, I addressed this issue in Chapter 2 by drawing on several types of evidence indicative of a general pattern of instability in climate and disruptions in river regimes that began in the terminal phases of the Urban period. These fluctuations included changes in precipitation levels and the rapid or gradual shifting of river courses that may have caused flooding, disruptions of settlements, and potential loss of grazing and farm land.

Ambiguities in the paleo-environmental data for the Indus as a whole preclude us from understanding the full extent of its overall effects over the vast expanse of the civilization. As I suggested in Chapter 2, their effects need to be assessed based on more comprehensive regional data-bases than currently exist. Along the Beas and at Harappa I described changes in river discharge patterns and fluctuations in precipitation levels that necessitated adjustments in order to adapt to these changing conditions. In the Lower Indus, as discussed in Chapter 2, studies by Flam (1993a), Shroder (1993), and Jorgensen et al. (1993) have documented dramatic shifts in river courses that resulted in significant differences between the present course of the Indus and the level of the coastline in Harappan times. Sometime between 4000 and 2000 B.C., the Indus shifted eastward from the Jacobabad course to the Sindhu Nadi (Figure 2.3). The course of the Nara Nadi remained the same, until it reached toward the south and joined the Sindhu Nadi, just to the north of the coastline, then approximately 153 kilometers north of its present location (Flam 1993a). Abrupt channel displacements may have placed the city of Mohenjo-daro in an imperiled position.

Changes documented in the Ghaggar-Hakra system complement those for the Lower Indus. Significantly reduced seasonal flooding and reduction in flow lines of the Hakra northward was part of a larger change that occurred in the Ghaggar-Hakra River system as a whole. Based on Courty's (1995) studies of paleosols in northwest India on the Ghaggar Plain between 4000 and 2500 B.P. (ca. 2,000 – 500 B.C.), drying conditions there disrupted a predictable seasonal flooding cycle. In Cholistan, on the Hakra side, Wilhemy (1969), working with historical texts and extant maps, also documented reduced flooding cycles in several historical periods but was unable to determine when that process began. Additional geoarchaeological research and the collection of samples for absolute dating would provide a stronger basis with which to interpret the timing of settlement shifts at Ghaggar-Hakra sites.

Changes in the natural drainage of the Ghaggar-Hakra system may have been the result of tectonic shifts. Under such conditions, land contours may change, causing divergence of water flow, drainage modification, and adoption of new river channels. This process may have occurred when the Yamuna River, part of the Ganges system, captured the waters of the Ghaggar (Allchin et al. 1997b). The Ghaggar either "dried into a lake-like depression" or met the eastern Nara Nadi (see Figure 2.3) (Agrawal and Sood 1982:226). Although a firm chronology based upon absolute dates such as radiocarbon or AMS analyses does not exist, there clearly were dramatic changes in settlement locations in the Post-urban period along the Ghaggar-Hakra to be discussed in more detail later.

Massacres and Aryan Invasions

When Wheeler wrote about the massacre, he was referring to the skeletal remains found at Mohenjo-daro. His interpretation, now largely discredited, focused on what he believed to be the remains of "vestiges of a final massacre, after which Mohenjo-daro ceased to exist" (Wheeler 1968:131). This explanation fit neatly into the concept of an Aryan invasion. As discussed in Chapter 1, this view is related to legendary sources in the hymns of the Rigveda (which Wheeler attributed to the second half of the second millennium) stating that Aryan-speaking peoples had invaded "the Land of the Seven Rivers, the Punjab and its neighbouring region" (Wheeler 1968:131).

While the evidence cited by Wheeler came from Mohenjo-daro, the alleged Aryan invasion was believed to have occurred throughout the region. There now is good evidence with which to interpret the human remains at Mohenjo-daro based upon a scientific analysis by a team of physical anthropologists (Kennedy 2000) to refute this process. As discussed in Chapter 9, the skeletal remains do not show marks of trauma, as would be expected at a "massacre." Results of a discrete trait analysis and multivariate measures determined that the Mohenjo-daro skeletal series showed significant phenotypic differences from other Indus populations. These differences, however, were not due to the invasion of Aryans, but could be accounted for by the general regional variability found among the skeletal remains at other Indus sites, for example at Lothal and possibly Kalibangan. In that case, it would mean that the Harappans were not a homogeneous population but biologically heterogeneous. As Kennedy points out, "Had an Aryan presence been coincident with the decline of the Harappan civilization ... then the period immediately after 2000 B.C. would have been marked by the introduction of a novel phenotypic pattern. Such is not the case. There is no evidence of demographic disruptions either immediately before or after the period of Harappan cultural decline" (2000:304).

Disruptions and Changes in Intercultural Trade

Two types of evidence can be brought to bear on the circumstances under which external trade between the Harappans and other cultures was disrupted. A primary source is the textual evidence from southern Mesopotamia. Textual references to Meluhha diminish near the end of the third millennium. At that time, the area of Magan (Figure 8.1 for location) is referred to most frequently, after which Dilmun (after 2000 B.C.) is almost exclusively mentioned and there are no references to Meluhha (T. Potts 1994:290).

A second source is the archaeological evidence. Viewed from the vantage point of maritime trade, Indus exports such as objects and raw materials of gold, carnelian, and ivory, and Indus-like seals, shell and bone inlay, cubical weights, and ceramics are present in southern Mesopotamia and at sites along the coast of the Arabian peninsula until about 1900 B.C. After that time, contacts are between coastal settlements in Oman at Ras al-Jinz, Bahrain, and Gujarat (Cleuziou and Tosi 2000:60), suggesting that Indus trade with the Arabian Gulf settlements continued even though Indus contact with Mesopotamia may have diminished.

Roughly coincident with these shifts during the Post-urban/Late Harappan (as discussed in Chapter 8), there is mounting evidence for increased contacts with Central Asian cultures, represented by the BMAC (Bactrian Margiana Archaeological Complex). Although this interaction occurs over a broad zone, the artifact distributions are small in number and are not the result of massive migration replacements (see Chapter 8 and Hemphill, in press; Hemphill et al., in press; Hemphill and Christensen 1994). Other changes involving the BMAC will be discussed below.

Shifting Regional Histories, Transformations,
and Decline – Causes of a Local Nature

In addition to these large-scale changes, with their potential effects throughout the civilization, other causes were specific to individual regions. Most significant among these was abandonment of settlements. In some cases, this process took place over a period of several hundred years, while in other locations it appears to have occurred abruptly.

Upper Indus (Cemetery H/Late Harappan)

Harappa is one of the few settlements for which there is documentation of continuity from the Urban to Post-urban/Late Harappan periods of occupation. Evidence for this last period is present in four areas at Harappa (Cemetery H, Mounds AB, E, and F on Figure 4.2). In the 1930s, Vats discovered Cemetery H northeast of the R37 burial area (R37 is dated to the Urban period.) As I discussed in Chapter 9, there were some differences between the burial practices in Cemetery H and those in R37. Cemetery H has two strata, one in which bodies are interred in pots (Stratum I) (see Chapter 9 for details) and an older stratum (Stratum II) of earth burials with complete and fractional remains.

In spite of these changes in burial practices and modifications in pottery styles and other artifacts, archaeologists see continuity between the Post-urban/Late Harappan and Urban period at Harappa. In excavations on the north side of Mound AB, the Harappa team found in situ hearths, intact walls, charred grain deposits, and ceramic vessels, some of which contained inscriptions. The hearth has been radiocarbon dated to approximately 1700 B.C. A cache of typical Harappan materials, including 133 beads and other objects, produced from copper alloy, agate, carnelian, and faience, attest to the continuation of the technological style employed during the Urban period.

This evidence indicates that settlement at Harappa had undergone some changes at the intersection between the Urban and Post-urban periods, but there is no evidence for a massive and abrupt exodus from the city or intrusion of new people. New structures did encroach onto streets and public spaces, suggestive of a general disruption of orderliness. The changes give the impression that some, though not all, neighborhoods continued to be populated, although arrangements took somewhat altered form (Meadow et al. 2001). The site was ultimately abandoned at the end of the Post-urban period and not reoccupied until several thousand

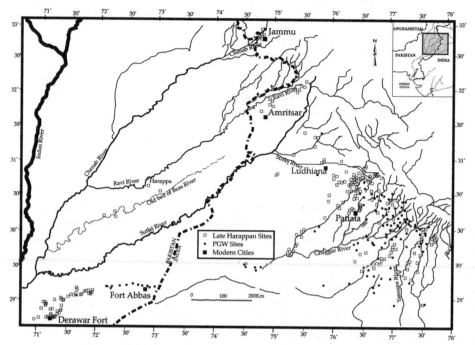

Figure 11.2. Post-urban Late Harappan settlement pattern. Left to right: Chenab, Ravi, and Beas sites; Cholistan and Northwest Indian sites. © R. P. Wright.

years later, when a caravanserai was built to the south of Mound E and ET (Figure 4.2 labeled Mughal serai).

Regionally, the pattern at Harappa is mirrored by its rural settlements. Of the eighteen settlements including Harappa that had been occupied during the Urban period, all but three of the original Beas sites remained and a new one is established, as shown on Figure 11.2 (see Chapter 5 and Figure 5.9 for the Urban period). In each instance, they were diminished in size. For example, at Vainiwal, only small quantities of archaeological materials were recovered from our surface surveys and they were restricted to limited areas of the settlement. All of the sites near the Indus, Chenab, and Ravi, with the exception of Harappa, were abandoned at this time.

Lower Indus – Late Harappan and Jhukar Styles

The disruptions of architectural forms and the city plan at Harappa are much like what Wheeler had described for Mohenjo-daro, except that decline there appears to have culminated in a fairly rapid abandonment of the city. Significant encroachment and carving up of housing began in the city in the latter part of the Urban period, after which it was abandoned and possibly reoccupied in the later Buddhist period.

The term, Jhukar, refers to a pottery style that marks the end of the Post-urban habitation on the Lower Indus. The shapes and motifs on the Jhukar pottery differ from the Urban styles and there are innovative technical changes in the use of new pigments to produce different color effects on the pottery designs. However, there is enough continuity that the new Jhukar style does not appear to signal a break in the sequence, as Ernest Mackay had thought when he discovered Jhukar pots in the 1930s at Chanhu-daro (Mackay 1938).[1] Jhukar pottery also is present at the site of Jhukar, Mohenjo-daro and Amri. Thus far continuity has been documented by Rafique Mughal (1992a:215) at Mohenjo-daro and at the site of Jhukar. In the most recent reanalysis of the site plan and artifacts at Chanhu-daro by Heidi Miller (2005:255–6), she found a similar continiuty. There are changes, however. At Chanhu-daro, Miller describes the settlement as "haphazard and less focused" during this transitional phase that marks the end of occupation of many sites in the Lower Indus. The square stamp seals are replaced with circular ones bearing new motifs and the terracotta female figurines associated with Indus ideologies and cubical stone weights, both signature artifacts of the civilization, are rare. The Indus script also disappears, save for examples incised on pottery (Mughal 1992a:215), perhaps signaling the end of an administrative system.

After this period, the sites in the Lower Indus were abandoned and not reoccupied until several hundred years later, constituting a clear break with the Indus civilization. The Shah Abdul Latif, Khairpur University team did not find any Post-urban/Late Harappan settlements among the sites described in Chapters 4 and 5.

Post-urban/Late Harappan: The Ghaggar-Hakra
(Cholistan and Northwest India)

The principal evidence for the Post-urban/Late Harappan. In this region is from the regional settlement studies conducted by M. R. Mughal (1997), Sir Aurel Stein (1931, 1937), and the Archaeological Survey of India (Nath 1998, 1999; Bala and Kant 2000) in northwest India. Many sites in Cholistan were abandoned during this period and new settlements were founded (see Figure 11.2). Fifty sites are documented in the Post-urban/Late Harappan, nine of which are industrial settlements, fourteen are settlements with kilns, and fourteen are settlements without kilns. Ten are campsites and three remain unclassified. Although there are no radiocarbon dates from Cholistan, Mughal uses calibrated dates from several Post-urban sites elsewhere as approximate benchmarks. He proposes that the period ended in Cholistan between 1700 and 1500 B.C., a date that is consistent with the chronology in northwest India.

Sites in Cholistan labeled PGW (Painted Gray Ware) (see Figure 11.2) are from a period that follows the Post-urban. PGW sites appear to the north of the more densely populated southern area in the Post-urban period. In the PGW period, the number of settlements in Cholistan is reduced to fourteen with a total settled area of 36 hectares. (compared to 255 hectares). One of the most vexing problems in Indus studies is the relationship between the Post-urban/Late Harappan and the Painted Gray Ware (PGW) sites. In Cholistan and in northwest India, PGW sites follow the Post-urban period. Excavations at a few sites in northwest India suggest there may be a stratigraphic continuity between the Post-urban/Late Harappan and PGW sites (Shaffer and Lichtenstein 1999). Whether the PGW Cholistan settlements, where excavations have not been conducted, represent continuous occupation between the Post-urban and PGW is uncertain. Absolute dates for the PGW are variously reported as 1100–500 B.C. (Possehl 2002), 1200–800 B.C. (Kenoyer 1998), and 1700–1400 B.C. (Bisht 1982:122).

These reduced numbers and a geographical shift toward northwest India signal an important change in the focus of settlement. In northwestern India (including settlements in the Indian Punjab, Haryana, northern Rajasthan and western Uttar Pradesh) to the east of Cholistan, 563 sites have been recorded in the Post-urban/Late Harappan (Mughal 1990:2). In some parts of the region, (see Figure 11.2 for site distributions), there is a significant increase in the number of occupied sites between the Urban and Post-urban/Late Harappan.

Post-urban/LateHarappan – Kutch, Gujarat, and Sorath Harappan

The evidence from this region provides two very different trajectories for the decline of the Indus and a continued occupation in these regions. One set of evidence shows a clear breakdown of settlement in which sites are abandoned after a disruptive period. Other evidence is more suggestive of a transformative process in which there is a continuation of settlement. In the latter, some elements of "the civilization" are present, while many of its defining characteristics are absent. Each of these is discussed below.

In Kutch, one of the most important changes was the abandonment of Dholavira, whose monumental upper town, castle, and bailey, and other aspects were described in Chapters 5 and 9. Excavators at Dholavira documented erosion and cracks in the walls of some of its large structures that occurred near the end of the Urban period and may have been due to an earthquake. Various makeshift repairs were made to its eastern gate and other walled enclosures. During this period or soon after, circular houses were constructed, disrupting the layout of this well-planned city and its architectural features. These changes have been interpreted as a breakdown in civic authority.

At Kuntasi and Lothal, there are similar indications of hasty repairs and eventual abandonment. The decline of Kuntasi began at around 1900 B.C., when its industrial center was abandoned and new houses were built of stone rubble. By 1700 B.C. it had been reduced to a small rural village, described by its excavator as a "jejune shadow of the once flourishing urbanites" (Dhavalikar 1992:81) who had lived there. At Lothal a similar breakdown in settlement, production, and trade occurred (Rao 1985).

Unlike Kuntasi, Dholavira or Lothal, some settlements continued to be occupied. There are a number of settlements that share a material assemblage referred to as Sorath Harappan (Possehl 1991). During the Urban period, the region appears to have lain outside of the Harappan central core. Ceramics there were somewhat different from the "standard" Harappan style, but at the same time, the assemblage included typical Indus chert weights, etched carnelian beads, and graffiti resembling the Indus script on pottery sherds. Based on these factors, Possehl (2002) believes the Sorath region had a degree of independence from the major centers throughout the Urban period. Rojdi, for example, was an agropastoral settlement occupied during the Urban period. It continued to be occupied long after many other Indus sites had been abandoned. Even though it was a small village, major parts of the main mound were rebuilt in the Post-urban period.

Unlike other areas where there was a general depopulation, there are 231 Post-urban sites (Mughal 1992a:217). Survey data indicate that between the Urban period and Post-urban, many settlements were abandoned and new ones were founded in the region. According to Shaffer and Lichtenstein (1999) "96% of the settlements change occupation status with 93% being new settlements [suggestive of] ... considerable settlement mobility and influx of human populations" (1999:254). Based on studies of faunal remains at Rojdi and Oriyo Timbo (near Rojdi), Rissman suggests there was a "normalization" or adaptation already in place during the Urban period (Rissman 1985). Later, the Sorath sites remained viable at a time when their neighbors at Kuntasi and Dholavira had abandoned their settlements (Possehl 1997).

Borderland Regions – Afghanistan and Baluchistan (West and Southern Margins)

While this region lies outside of the core areas of Indus settlement, changes also were occurring on its western borderlands. Baluchistan was populated throughout the Pre-urban and Urban periods. Mehrgarh (the site to which Chapter 3 was devoted) is our earliest evidence for a settlement with a long-term sequence in which animal and plant domestication have been documented during the Early Food Producing and Pre-Urban periods. The terminal phases at Mehrgarh (Period VII) have been placed at approximately 2600 B.C. (Chapter 3). After period VII, there is a break in settlement and new forms of material culture associated with the BMAC are present in cenotaphs (tombs with grave goods but without skeletal remains), designated Period VIII. Coincident with these burials there is evidence for BMAC materials at the site of Nausharo (discussed in Chapter 4 and 7) and the new site of Sibri, 6 kilometers south of Mehrgarh.

In addition to BMAC materials, at Nausharo in Period IV (radiocarbon dated to approximately to 2200–2000 B.C.), there are pottery styles (designs and vessel shapes) and female terracotta figurines associated with the Kulli culture (see Figure 8.1 for location) from southern Baluchistan (J.-F. Jarrige 1994), a politically independent cultural group, contemporary with the Indus and possibly a political rival (as discussed in Chapter 8).

The archaeological evidence from Afghanistan, in periods coincident with the end of the Urban period, indicates that important changes were taking place there. At Shortugai in Afghanistan (discussed in Chapters 5 and 8), Indus materials are replaced by a typical BMAC material culture (Francfort 1989 et al.:337ff.). The sites of Sutkagen-dor and Sotka-koh in southern Baluchistan, two fortified trading outposts (see Chapter 8), were abandoned (Dales and Lipo 1992:157).

Collapse, Transition, or Transformation – Culture Traits and Political Structure

The preceding discussion outlines some of the factors that may have contributed to the final days of the Indus civilization, its decline and transformation. Although our understanding of its end is by no means resolved, the process clearly was not uniform. I structured this chapter by first examining causes of a general nature that included environmental changes, invasions, and trade disruptions. This section was followed by a region-by-region discussion of local changes affecting single sites and transformations that were occurring in neighboring regions. Below I assess the validity of the various factors discussed.

The possibility of an Aryan invasion is an idea that now can be put to rest. There neither is on-the-ground evidence for militarism and volatile destruction nor genetic changes in regional populations suggestive of new groups migrating into the region.

Whether there were environmental changes that affected the entire region will continue to be debated. However, it is certain that environmentally related shifts in river courses and changes in precipitation did have an impact on specific regions. Survey data confirms that changes in the Beas and Ghaggar-Hakra Rivers resulted in severe dislocation of settlements. The Cholistan evidence is the most compelling, as it shows a falloff in population, the abandonment of the major city of Ganweriwala and a diminished number of settlements in the Post-urban/Late Harappan. Along the Ghaggar, survey data and observations of satellite imagery show major dislocations in the region to the east of Cholistan in northwest India. Although northwest India was inhabited in earlier periods, there was an increase in the number of settlements during the Post-urban/Late Harappan. In the Lower Indus there were major disruptions in the river system and abandonment of settlements.

These changes in river systems and climate most likely did cause major disruptions in the civilization as a whole. It would be a mistake, however, to consider them as ultimate "causes" of the "collapse" or "decline" of the Indus. A more compelling approach is to consider the responses taken in individual regions and to examine their effects on the Harappan infrastructure with respect to agricultural and pastoral strategies, as well as craft production and social changes.

Several strategic shifts in agriculture and pastoralism occurred in the Post-urban period. As discussed in previous chapters, crop diversity had increased throughout the Urban period, a pattern that continued in the Post-urban. Wheat and barley remained the principal crops grown, although barley, a drought-resistant crop, became dominant (Weber 2003:181). While summer millets and rice were grown in the Urban period at Harappa, they became more widespread. Madella and Fuller (2006:1298) argue that these crops would be "most feasibly grown on the eastern distribution zone" (northwest India), where we find the greatest continuity of settlement and founding of new settlements.

Of great significance is a shift in crop processing. At Harappa and Rojdi, seed remains from the Post-urban period contain large densities of by-products such as chaff and weeds, residues from "threshing, winnowing, grinding and cleaning of grains." These data indicate that in the Post-urban period, crop processing was now taking place in households. This change from the centralized or communal processing of the Urban period (discussed in Chapter 7) (Weber 1999, 2003:181; Fuller and Madella 2000) reflects a political and social reorganization rather than an environmental crisis.

In addition to these changes in the agricultural base, others occurred among pastoralists. Although the sample of animal remains at Harappa is small for the Post-urban, there is limited evidence for changes in the exploitation of cattle for traction and possibly dairying (L. Miller 2004:618). Whereas in the Urban period, the most distinctive pattern is the use of cattle for meat and secondary products (Miller 2004:618), in the Post-urban, animal husbandry strategies reverted to patterns previously known in the Pre-urban period, when sheep and possibly goats were present in significant quantities (L. Miller 2004:618) as opposed to cattle. This shift may signal a reorientation of pastoralism and possibly a reduced demand for traction animals, due to the less intensified agricultural system described above. An additional factor was a reduction in the need for transport to rural networks, interregional and intercultural exchanges of raw materials, craft objects or food products. By the time the Post-urban period had ended, three new species, camels, donkeys and horses, were introduced into the region. At the post-Indus site of Pirak in northern Baluchistan, there are figurines of "two-humped camels, horses and riders beginning between 1,800 and 1,500 cal B.C."; faunal remains come from the first millennium cal B.C. (Meadow and Patel 2003:82). These animals brought advantages for local and long-distance movement of people and goods, and for work animals, but they appear too late to have made an impact on the Indus civilization.

Related to these changes are signs that all was not well with craft producers. This is evidenced by the diminished presence of high-status objects produced from technologically elaborated crafts. In the Post-urban period, many, though not all of the elaborated craft objects disappear, along with the specialized tools used in their production. The diminished presence of these status markers, statuary, chert weights, seals and tablets, not only signals a fall-off in the presence of status objects but also of the material hierarchies apparent in the Urban period. The changes also signal the reduced presence of artisans and managers who controlled and derived prestige from the control of these more salient symbols of status.

Intercultural trade reached a fragile stage near the end of the Urban Period and during the Post-urban/Late Harappan. The maritime trade with Mesopotamia came to an end and the settlements of Sutkagendor and Sotka-koh were abandoned. Of additional importance is the interaction with the BMAC culture. This contact was widespread throughout the Indus at its major cities during the Post-urban period. Although BMAC materials are found in small quantities, they are present at Mohenjo-daro, Harappa, in Baluchistan[2], and as far afield as Rajasthan. Finally, at the Indus site of Shortugai, Afghanistan, discussed in earlier chapters, once critical to the trade in lapis and other products (Chapter 7), a major shift occurred around 2200 B.C. Although the site continues to be occupied, the Indus materials diminish and are replaced by the Central Asian BMAC materials (Francfort 1989 et al.:174). These are strong indications that as the core areas of the Indus civilization and its urban centers were near their end, other groups were establishing contacts with regions even beyond those with which the Indus had previously interacted. In Baluchistan, Nausharo continues to be occupied, but its Indus elements virtually disappear only to be replaced by evidence for increased interactions with the nearby Kulli culture. This change may signal an extension of Kulli influence into northern Baluchistan that is wholly in keeping with the smaller-scale exchanges and affiliations described in Chapter 7 (Wright 2001).

When we turn to Indus city plans and landscapes, we find significant evidence for a general breakdown in major settlements at Dholavira, Mohenjo-daro, and Harappa that fall squarely within a category of change reflecting political and economic problems and a breakdown in civic order. City structures are not maintained and there is squatting in formerly orderly neighborhoods. These widespread encroachments and alterations of structures at major centers appear to signal shifts in leadership, while they as well could be construed as acts of defiance in the midst of social conflicts, though not militaristic ones.

As was discussed in Chapter 10, the founders who built Indus cities and the people who lived in them conceived of their cities as humanly created manifestations of nature. Although individual cities differed, their underlying structure and even those at many smaller towns and villages were shaped to conform to a particular vision of a properly ordered society. The degradation of structured city plans, hierarchical orderliness, and remade natural landscapes may signal an intentional rejection of a once integrated society and the leadership that promoted it and maintained order.

The settlements that survived appear to have been less dependent on an urban way of life. For example, the Sorath Harappan persisted for several hundred years after the major centers of the Indus had been abandoned. Settlements like Rojdi and others in Gujarat appear in altered form. Missing there are the central elements of the Indus bureaucracy and important elements such as a writing system, systems of weights and measures, the technologically elaborated crafts, human and animal figurines, and narratives on seal imagery. What did survive was in a sufficiently altered form so as to appear as vestiges of the civilization at its urban peak.

The Indus city-states and the leadership that sustained them came to an end. Left behind were rural settlements inhabited by people who preserved in memory some remnants of the civilization's former glory. They moved into another era where only some elements of Indus material culture were retained. Even at the edge zones of the Indus among the Sorath Harappan, the political, economic, and social relations that once characterized the Indus civilization were not reproduced.

Cycles of Change or Breakdown of Society

As civilizations go, the Indus was short lived when compared to many other ancient states. For example, Mesopotamian and Egyptian cultures persisted (through several millennia) despite periods of political change involving upheavals and disruptions in their histories. In the New World, vestiges of the Maya culture, which may have appeared as early as 400 B.C. (Demarest 2004), still endure today, though in a significantly altered form. This despite the fact that the days of the great Maya lords are gone and many social and political shifts and struggles have occurred in the interim.

Some Indus scholars believe that a cultural continuity can be traced from the Post-urban to the early historic period, when a second urbanism occurred in the Ganges Valley at around 800 to 600 B.C. Jim Shaffer and Diane Lichtenstein (1999) have most strongly expressed this view based upon several factors. One centers on how the expansion of settlement eastward toward the Ganges in the Post-urban/Late Harappan and continuing in the PGW is interpreted. Since the PGW complex is a direct predecessor to the early historic period, they propose that "It is possible now to discern cultural continuities linking specific social entities in South Asia into one cultural tradition" (Shaffer and Lichtenstein 1999:255–6). In their view, the discontinuities that did occur, for example the shift of settlement from the Upper Indus to the east and southeast in the Post-urban, were regional population shifts. What appear as discontinuities (introduction of the PGW complex, for example), therefore, are the result of ecological factors, such as adjustments in agriculture and pastoralism, as populations moved into new regions.

My assessments of these data differ from Shaffer and Lichtenstein in my basic assumption that establishing continuity with the Indus past rests on identifying an unbroken chain of evidence for those elements with which we define the *basic character* of the civilization. These include its planned cities, technical virtuosity, systems of weights, seals and sealings, narrative imagery, and Indus script, all of which came to an end in the Post-urban period. Without such evidence, I await the results of continued investigations of the PGW that clarify its connections to the early historic and provide evidence for vestiges of an Indus presence.

In this chapter, I have outlined a process of change that began in the later phases of the Urban period and continued into the Post-urban. By the end, however, there are clear indications that leadership in the city-states, in individual cities and rural areas, and the hegemony that once held was severely diminished. The absence of the essential elements that defined the political, economic, and social relationships within the society argues against a continuous sequence beyond the Post-urban period. Judging by differences in the civilization between the Urban period and the Post-urban, the final phases of the Indus are marked by changes and disruptions that were not wholly ecological. The disruptions in city plans, abandonment of settlements, shifts to household cropping patterns, and changes in animal preferences represent a collapsed infrastructure. What remained were village-based societies some of which pursued a more diminished and less complex agropastoral and craft producing economy, while others forged new cultural connections and avenues of interaction.

The Indus Civilization in Comparative Perspective

The evidence brought to bear on the Indus represents a little less than a hundred years of field research on the civilization's major cities and regional surveys of smaller settlements. Of no less importance have been the fine-grained laboratory analyses of the objects produced and consumed by the Harappans and the raw materials procured from sources within and beyond the regions in which they settled. These studies of craft production and technologies are complemented by archaeobotanical and zooarchaeological studies that are providing new evidence for a diverse agropastoral economy. Textual sources and imagery from the greater Near East and the results of cross-cultural studies offer a broadened framework from which to establish an Harappan place in interactions with neighboring third millennium cultures. In addition, they afford a comparative context from which to gain insight into Indus religious ideologies and worldviews.

Perhaps more importantly, the interpretations offered here have benefited from the comparative study of early state societies and the reexamination of previously held evolutionary views that emphasized a top-down approach focused on centralized authority (McIntosh's ex-astra model in Chapter 1). Comparative studies of early states now discredit the widely held view that "class displaced kinship and ethnicity as the main organizing principle of society" (Trigger 2003:47). As a "counterweight" to these longstanding elite-centered views in studies of early states (Adams 2008), scholars now seek to understand how diverse social and economic groups interacted in production, consumption, and exchange contexts. Below, I briefly review the salient aspects of the Harappan infrastructure, i.e., the fundamental technologies, land and labor requirements, economic system, and diversity of social groups that maintained the civilization during its fluorescence. As I have discussed in several earlier chapters, they include the intensification, diversification, and specialization of the Harappan agropastoral and craft producing economy; significant development of the natural and cultural landscape and the growth of Harappan urban centers, rural communities, and outlying settlements; interregional exchange of raw materials, craft, and plant and animal products; and wide-ranging contact with neighboring cultures. In a later section, I discuss Indus urbanism and city state-development.

The Harappan Economy and Society

Beginning in the Pre-urban but accelerating in the Urban period, the agropastoral economy underwent fundamental changes. These changes included the adoption of winter and summer cultivars and the development of a multicropping strategy. As new crops were introduced, preexisting taxa continued to be exploited. This diversified strategy increased output per unit of land and the opportunity for generating a surplus. In addition to the cultivation of seasonal fields for harvests of staple foods, however, lands were also set aside for the growth of perennial crops such as cotton, grapes and dates. This kind of production required sustained and dedicated specialists with the technical knowledge required to properly nurture the plants and process them into food, fiber, and beverages.

Indus cities were at the center of the civilization's agropastoral and craft-producing economies. Archaeobotanical evidence from Harappa, the only major center for which we have extensive evidence, suggests it was at the center of "storage, trade, and the centralization and control of the food supply" (Weber 2003:194) in the Upper Indus. This interpretation is based on analyses of botanical remains that indicate processing of crops (winnowing, threshing, harvesting) was carried out in fields. In distinction, as discussed above in the context of the Post-urban period, when plants are processed in households, chaff and other by-products of cereal grains will be present. "In field" processing would have been carried out within the context of communities, perhaps by neighborhood or kinship groups or a centralized authority (Weber 2003; Fuller and Madella 2000; Madella and Fuller 2006).

In pace with agriculture are shifts in pastoral practices that began in the Pre-urban and accelerated during the Urban period. These changes involved the development of special cattle breeds for dairying, for traction, and for ploughing agricultural fields. Plow agriculture promotes modifications of soil structure that may increase crop production per unit of land. Of additional importance was the use of draft animals for the transport of goods between rural and urban centers and possibly beyond. As with agriculture, the development and nurturance of new breeds required specialists to maintain them leading to the emergence of an elaborated system of pastoral specialists.

Specialized pastoral economies also served to establish linkages among urban, rural, and more marginal settlements. Full-time and semisedentary pastoralists were either based in urban centers or rural areas. Semisedentary pastoralists moved about seasonally, taking their animals to grazing lands at higher elevations in the summer months and bringing them back to lowland areas in winter. In addition, nomadic specialists were present on the margins of some urban centers, as Mughal has noted based on his settlement studies in Cholistan.

Large numbers of craft producers provided an infrastructural base for the production of a range of diversified and highly specialized goods and commodities. These included large-scale and small-scale production of finished objects produced from exotic resources and locally available materials. Craft producers used a broad range of techniques to create an array of ornamental styles, such as the stoneware bangles discussed in earlier chapters. Many other crafts involved the implementation of complex technologies and highly standardized production procedures. Judging by the standardization we see in the production of square engraved seals, they were produced by a limited number of specialist artisans who may have been linked together in guildlike arrangements. The production of tablets also falls into this category, given the redundancy of motifs depicted on some and the Indus script represented on others. Both the technical knowledge and ideological representations reflect production processes that set their producers apart from other artisans.

Another example of specialized production lies in the manufacture of the standardized system of weights used by Indus artisans and in merchant trade with Arabian Gulf settlements. Kenoyer (1991) suggests that the technical skill required in the selection of appropriate chert sources and the production of the weights themselves may have been closely monitored and controlled by merchants. In any event, the uniformity of the Indus weights and their dissemination over a vast area suggest "an extremely strong overarching authority, considering how variable weights and measures were within European states until the adoption of the metric system" (Cowgill 2008:966).

Important innovations in the conversion of raw materials into finished products went hand and hand with the emergence of new kinds of artisanal and technological specializations. One primary example is the invention of artificial materials using methods of vitrification known from the site of Mehrgarh in Baluchistan as early as 4500 B.C. At Harappan centers in the Urban period, these new artificial materials and the methods used to create them were elaborated upon to produce objects of social and economic significance. I have referred to this technological style in various contexts throughout this book. Production of small, movable objects, manufactured as ornaments, signaled differences in and among social groups depending on the degree of elaboration involved in the production process and raw material chosen. As discussed in earlier chapters, a major way to see these differences is to look at the range of technological styles chosen by Indus artisans in the production of small-scale objects at various levels of relative value.

The well-established "transformative" technological style that was applied by artisans in the production of small-scale objects was also employed in the creation of city landscapes. City building involved the construction of engineering works of a kind unprecedented for their time in which the natural landscape was altered and reclaimed for human use. At Mohenjo-daro, the city's founders constructed a well-planned city and built massive platforms in which the physical landscape was integrated with landscape elements visible on the Kirthar range and orientation points aligned with fixed stars. Impressive engineering innovations in the form of public works, particular architectural styles and platform constructions were positioned in and among the streets and narrow lanes of the city and distributed throughout neighborhoods. Less elaborate structures with poor quality amenities took their places side-by-side with more sophisticated structures. These features served as highly visible reminders of social differences among the city's residents, much like the objects of varying relative value produced using the same technological style. In Chapter 9, I tested the idea that these landscape features were correlated with social differences by comparing consumption patterns in the form of access to wealth and status objects using evidence from a sample of residential structures at Mohenjo-daro. The comparisons showed a good correlation when the presence of rare statuary, valued ornaments, seals, and raw materials were set against the size of structures, architectural details, and types of public amenities. These differences suggest the presence of a diversity of social groups, possibly farmers, pastoralists, traders, merchants, artisans, and others at higher, and lower ranks that did not participate in the society in a field of equal status but that lived together within the city's neighborhoods.

Is it possible now to further break down ranks of social status and differentiation or to identify major governing institutions? As discussed in previous chapters, there are no architectural structures in the Indus that can be positively identified as temples or administrative centers of the type known in other early states. Yet there are hints that the idea of a ranked hierarchy or higher orders was not alien to the Harappans. One example of this is the representation of shamans among the corpus of Indus figurines. Shamans are individuals with specialized knowledge and powers and in many societies achieve high status as healers and religious specialists. Among the Maya, for example, rulers and priests played important roles in communicating with supernatural forces for "divination and prophecy" (Demarest 2004:184). Additionally, the presence of burials of older males at Harappa and Kalibangan whose interments are accompanied by grave goods that included a proportionally higher number of prestige objects than other burials indicate that these individuals were accorded high status. Elders often possess a high status in their roles as representatives of ancestors, for example. At the least, these better-provisioned elders suggest that the Harappans accorded transgenerational esteem for some of the males interred.

Beyond the evidence gleaned from individuals, we have no basis on which to determine the specifics of who the founders of Indus cities and the groups in better-provisioned residences may have been. Were they merchants, artisans, ritual specialists, kings? Several of the residences at Mohenjo-daro indicate that persons of substantial authority and status lived in them. House I in HR-A area, for example (Figure 5.3b), has often been cited as a possible residence of a person of high status or a religious authority. The large number of high prestige items, for example the unicorn seals discovered in the same house (Figure 9.9), are suggestive of economic or political authority, but thus far, there is no basis on which to proclaim kingship. With the exception of the limited numbers of small statuary that may represent men of political or religious authority, the kind of self-glorifying leadership known in other early states seems to be totally lacking in the Indus.

Still, there are aspects of seal and tablet imagery that suggest a belief in higher-order individuals that reinforced worldly authority. The various images of heroes or deities dominating animals and representations of multiple deities are ever-present in Indus iconography. It is the presence of minor and major deities, however, that may signify a thought process in which social order is sustained by prescribed social hierarchies.

This broad reconstruction of the Indus economy and society conjures a picture of a vibrant and integrated civilization. Principally situated on the alluvial plains of the Indus and the Ghaggar-Hakra Rivers but encompassing an extensive area beyond the plains, the economic foundation of the civilization was a complex agropastoral and craft producing economy. In spite of the apparent uniformity of its landscape vision and material culture, there now are clear indications of social differences based on access to prestige goods and other forms of wealth.

Indus Urbanism and City-States

I have stressed throughout this book that the core or heartland of the Indus civilization lies in its natural and cultural landscape, and in the development and growth of its urban centers, rural communities and outlying settlements. That Indus cities were central to the civilization's identity has been well known since Marshall's announcement of its discovery in the 1920s. Excavations of broad exposures at Mohenjo-daro, Harappa, and Dholavira and the results of current research have provided us with evidence for well-planned urban layouts and engineering works that, although they varied from city to city, were a hallmark of a Harappan view of a city landscape. Even though the builders of Indus cities shared a vision of how their cities should be designed, each put their own stamp on the cities they constructed. I consider buildings like Mohenjo-daro's Great Bath, Harappa's granary or great hall and extensive platform constructions, walled enclosures, and gateway and Dholavira's castle and bailey emblematic of each of those cities as comparable to the type of monumentality associated with other civilizations both in their scale and in their signaling of social differences.

It is interesting to note that there are important differences in the timing of the emergence of Harappan cities. For example, the city of Harappa developed gradually as a small village starting with its early Ravi levels, ultimately becoming an extensive urban complex in the Urban period. In contrast, as the Aachen University team discovered, Mohenjo-daro's growth was more rapid. Our evidence from Dholavira and Ganweriwala suggest a similar rapid rise. In each case, however, as George Cowgill has noted for the early Teotihuacan state, the scale and orderly layouts of these cities suggest that their founders "possessed great ambition and strong power" (Cowgill 2008:966).

Urbanism in the Indus continues to have broad implications for assessing the civilization's place in ongoing dialogs about city-states. As discussed in Chapter 5, the concept of a city-state, among other features, is linked to a particular settlement pattern and type of political organization. In contrast to other state systems that govern over a vast territory, city-states are culturally unified but politically independent.

Adoption of the city-state concept and cross-cultural studies of early states by Bruce Trigger (1989, 2003) and Deborah Nichols and Thomas Charlton (1997) have significantly refined our understanding of the internal workings of early states and their systems of authority. Charlton and Nichols (1997) define city-states as systems that are centered on a capital city that is integrated with a hinterland or rural area of small and large settlements. Although city-states are politically independent and relatively self-sufficient economically, they remain part of a network of neighboring city-states with which they interact and share cultural traditions. Kenoyer (1997a) was the first to use the city-state concept in the context of the Indus civilization. He emphasized features common to Indus cities and introduced textual evidence from early historic city-states in South Asia as potential models for the Harappan city-state. Here, I have followed Kenoyer in adopting the city-state model for the Indus, although my points of comparison are largely outside of South Asian historical contexts.

Comparative and cross-cultural studies of city-states indicate that they developed complex forms of political organization. Of the early states studied by Trigger (2003), all of them "probably had monarchs, even if kingship was defined somewhat differently and the actual power exercised by such rulers varied" (Trigger 2003:73). Still, there are exceptions; for example, classical Athens and possibly Teotihuacan (Cowgill 2008:966) appear to have lacked a monarch. Where kings did exist their principal role was to promote their own social and political interests, but they left self-government to local groups. So-called councils consisted of individuals from important lineages, merchant associations, temple organizations, and various other influential groups who "shared power with or organized their activities around a king" (Trigger 2003:269). This system of rule was practiced in Mesopotamia, at least between the Early Dynastic and Old Babylonian periods. Decisions by local councils were based on consensus among council members (Stone 1997; see my Chapter 1). Stone and Morris (1997) "propose a continuum of political forms" for the administration of city-states, at one end of which a small minority of elites controls state institutions, whereas at the other, there exists "segmentation and fragmentation, consensual arrangements [and] an ideology of citizen participation in government" (Charlton and

Nichols 1997:11). Ideologies based on consensus are dependent upon "vertical structures of integration" (i.e., where members of local councils are drawn from the many different groups and share power on an equal footing) (Stone 1997; Sinopoli 2003).

The spatial layouts at Harappa and Mohenjo-daro and the diversity of social groups in Indus cities suggest that the kind of vertical integration and local councils about which Morris, Stone, and Sinopoli speak may be operant in the Indus. The clear division of the residential areas within Indus cities into neighborhoods and the differences in house sizes, types of public amenities, and material goods within them reveal a mix of socioeconomic groups and offer potential loci for councils of the type proposed for other early city-states. As Stone notes for Mesopotamia, a key feature of the consensual basis of city-state administration there was the structuring of habitation in which "both elites and manufacturing [i.e., artisan workshops] were firmly embedded in residential neighborhoods" (1997:20).

Vertically integrated systems of authority in city states are dependent upon shared values and notions of commonality. The symbolic association of Mohenjo-daro and its landscape with distinctive, identifiable features such as its massive engineering works and public gathering places would have been strong reminders of Harappan loyalties to that city. The open spaces at Dholavira, the gateway at Harappa, and the colonnaded buildings of the upper town at Mohenjo-daro with its Great Bath and founding platforms are examples of the kinds of symbolic landscapes that foster community identity.

As I have already noted, the city-state concept rests on the notion that urban centers and their outlying rural settlements form an integrated network that engages in reciprocal flows of resources. Such networks have been documented for several Indus cities and their respective outlying areas. In the Upper and Lower Indus and in the Ghaggar-Hakra, evidence coming from rural settlements is sufficiently extensive to propose that a strong agropastoral base provided the raw materials for at least some of the products consumed in Indus cities at the same time that rural areas drew on urban resources. Especially in Cholistan where preservation of settlements is greater than elsewhere, there is good evidence for a diversity of settlement types and potential inflow of resources. While craft production was an important element in each city's infrastructure, evidence indicates that some crafts flowed from rural areas to centers. Evidence for rural craft production has been found at the numerous workshops at Dubi and the Veesar Valley, (see Figure 5.12) in the Lower Indus near Mohenjo-daro and at rural settlements in Cholistan and the Beas near Harappa.

This is not to suggest that rural settlements were dominated by urban centers. For example, unlike many other civilizations dependent on major river systems, there is no evidence for a centrally controlled irrigation system of the type proposed by Wittfogel (1957) for early states. Based on the current evidence, the only water management technologies constructed for agropastoral purposes are the gabarbands discovered by Flam (1999). These gabarbands are known from Urban period settlements that lie outside of the alluvial plain. Even there, this relatively simple technology could have been managed on a local level.

The settlements associated with each city extended over an area that was greater than that of early city-states in other civilizations. Kenoyer (1997a) has estimated the sizes of hinterland areas of the five Indus cities. His results are rough estimates calculated by placing borders at halfway marks "between two or three cities and eliminating uninhabitable areas" (Kenoyer 1997:54). He found that the geographical extent of Indus city-states ranged from 100,000 to 170,000 square kilometers. The closest distance between two Indus cities was 280 kilometers, which was the distance between Harappa and Ganweriwala. In contrast, Mesopotamian cities were situated between twenty and twenty-five kilometers from each other (Stone 1997) and the largest territory of a Late Aztec city-state was 900 square kilometers. The territories of other Late Aztec city-states ranged between 20 and 228 square kilometers (Hodge 1997:218).

In the Indus, rural areas included vast expanses of diverse ecological zones that offered opportunities for extraction of naturally occurring resources. Cultivation occurred within reasonable distances of waterways, on terraces, oxbow lakes, and backwater swamps. However, outside of these areas, there were forested areas useful for hunting, collecting plants, and woodcutting. Marginal areas of scrub vegetation could serve as grazing lands. Thus the diversity of resources and distances separating Indus cities suggests that whatever loyalties existed between hinterland settlements and centers were fluid and, at least in the case of the most distant rural settlements, thrived well outside of the gaze of an urban center.

Having examined the structure of Indus city-states and the relationships between cities and their hinterlands, we can now turn our attention to asking what mechanisms held this civilization and its city-states together. In his comparative study of city-states Trigger noted that those featuring vertical structures of integration and administration based on local consensus may experience difficulties sustaining external cohesion with other city states on an interregional level (Trigger 2003:117). In spite of efforts toward consensus, conflicts and competition among different interest groups may exist. Various policies are employed in order to maintain long-term political and economic integration. These vary when viewed cross-culturally. One means of political integration is through warfare (Stone 1997; Yoffee 1997) while others include public festivals or funeral celebrations (Small 1997:114), alliances and treaties (Yoffee 1997:259), establishment of "social or political connections with" leaders in other cities (Kenoyer 1997a), and intercity trade for raw materials or prestige products (Trigger 2003). How did the Indus maintain political integration, especially given the great distances between its city-states?

In the case of the Indus, the appearance and distribution of a suite of homogeneous material culture items, styles and features across the civilization as a whole provides a valuable clue to understanding the ways in which city-states remained politically integrated, while sustaining the infrastructures that were so central to their individual viability. These include a standardized system of weights and measures, and uniformity of seal and tablet designs with common iconographic imagery, signs etched on a variety of media, pottery form and design, and style of representation of figurines. Viewed in this light, evidence for trade and interregional exchanges among city-states is the most compelling means by which political integration was maintained. Raw materials of various types were broadly distributed throughout the Indus. Carnelian, lapis lazuli, shell, limestone, and precious metals are found in limited geographical locations and were brought to centers from various parts of the civilization (see their distribution on Figure 7.2). Artisan produced finished products were sent to other Indus cities and smaller settlements. We have seen that shell production areas at Kuntasi, Nageswar, and Balakot were situated near raw material sources. Finished and semi-finished bangles were prepared in workshops and exported to other locales. Similarly, chert principally procured at Rohri left the quarry either unmodified or prepared into chert cores and blades. The prepared cores made their way to Harappa and the Beas, where they were modified further, while the prepared blades were ready for use when they arrived at Balakot and where chert cores are absent.

We also have seen that in order to procure finished and unfinished materials from more distant locations, Harappans ventured far beyond the alluvial plains to found settlements such as Shortugai in Afghanistan. The production of lapis beads in a workshop at Shortugai attests to their manufacture there but lapis also was shipped directly to producers elsewhere, such as Ghazi Shah in the Lower Indus where reworked lumps of lapis have been discovered. The founding of the settlements at Sotka-koh and Sutkagen-dor as entrepots for intercultural trade are other examples.

Harappan interregional trade involving city-states was not confined to the above items. The Harappans exploited the region's ecological diversity, and engaged in interregional exchanges that included exotic plant and animal products like ivory, birds, marine fish, and woods, such as teak and night jasmine. Dispersed throughout the civilization were various "agricultural packages" comprised of different plant resources. Wheat, barley, millets, and other crops were diffused over long distances, often ending up in ecological zones that may have been unsuitable for their cultivation, such as the wheat that appears at Balathal. Still others, such as dates, have good preservative qualities. The presence of date seeds at Harappa, where they are unlikely to have been grown, suggest they may have been a trade item. Exchanges of this sort most likely were influenced by the prestige derived through trade and the desire for new cuisines (Fuller 2003:377). Similarly, Meadow and Patel (2003:82), taking stock of the most recent evidence for distributions of animal breeds across the civilization, cite the presence of domesticated water buffalo at Dholavira (Bisht 2000a, 2005; Patel 1997), preferential breeding of goats in Baluchistan at Naushara (Meadow and Patel 2003), and the specialized breeds of cattle for traction and dairying documented by L. Miller (2003, 2004) at Harappa. The by-products of specialized breeds supplied dairy foods, such as milk and yogurt, cattle for meat and traction, and sheep for wool for internal consumption became important commodities for exchanges among city-states.

The transportation of commodities was critical to the maintenance of interregional exchange and the political unity it fostered. One method of transport was along the civilization's extensive river systems that served as major conduits connecting city-states. The representation of a flat-bottomed boat incised on steatite at Mohenjo-daro and a clay boat model from Harappa support this possibility. Perhaps the two most important innovations that captured the potential for engaging in inter-regional exchanges and strengthening ties among the city-states were the invention of carts and the development of specialized breeds to pull them. When taken together, these developments allowed for movement of higher volumes of goods than would have been possible by human transport alone and effectively "shortening" the distances between regions (L. Miller 2004) and promoting cultural cohesion.

While the advantages of using draft animals in agricultural and pastoral pursuits has been discussed at many points in this book, their importance is underscored when considering their additional role in conveyance of bulk raw materials on overland tracks that brought together a vast land of resources and people that maintained interregional and intercultural networks over long distances. The two-wheeled carts they pulled no longer exist in the archaeological record. However, carts appear at many Indus sites in the form of clay "toys," thought to be models of their life-size counterparts, which were produced from more substantial models of wood (see Figure 7.7 for a modern version of an oxcart). While there were many variations of cart design, two are especially relevant here. One type had a hollow, rectangular frame into which several holes were pierced on each side. Ernest Mackay suggested that the hollow floor of the frame may have been lined with matting or a rope-work net and that the pierced holes on each side would have held stakes of wood to hold in cargo such as agricultural produce, possibly straw, dung, fodder, or cloth (Mackay 1943, plate LVIII, for examples; L. Miller 2004). Miller refers to the hollow box carts as the "Ford truck" of the Indus, since they most likely were used for regular, day-to-day transport work (L. Miller 2004:646). A second cart type had a rectangular frame with a solid base and built-in side bars which would have made it suitable for long-distance transport of heavier loads such as raw materials, plant, animal, and small and large craft products.

Finally, the Indus city-states should not be viewed in isolation but as part of what Philip Kohl (2007) describes as an "interconnected" world in which people and ideas circulated (2007:259). A significant aspect of Indus trade was its outreach to distant lands on the Arabian Peninsula and the Greater Near East where political and social ties were forged on a more global and intercultural scale. The presence of Indus traders in a Mesopotamian village referred to in Mesopotamian textual sources and frequent references to interaction with Meluhha identify the Indus as one of the major players in an active intercultural trade in objects and raw materials. All indications are that Indus trading relations by sea and overland were played out as an interaction among peer cultures that included Mesopotamia, Iran, Central Asia, and the Arabian Peninsula.

Archaeological evidence in the form of Indus material culture distributed throughout the region complements the evidence gleaned from texts. Major markers are its standardized weights and the seals and sealings that represent a widespread use of a transcultural administrative system that effectively tied the Indus into this interconnected world and a global sphere of influence. As in later times, "goods, knowledge, technologies and belief systems flowed out of and into South Asia through many ports and routes" (Sinopoli 2003:61).

The intercultural connections that the Harappans maintained with this greater world were not only limited to material things but also extended to the transmission of meaningful ideas. My discussion of systems of thought represented by the iconographic representations on seals and tablets reveals a symbolic vocabulary, structured modes of presentation, and visualizations of ideologies that the Harappans shared with the cultures with which it interacted. In the Indus, these ideologies revolved around a view in which humans coexisted in an animated world of deities and supernatural beings that were set within familiar Indus landscapes. In the sample of images discussed in Chapter 10, the tiger gains prominence, certain trees (the acacia and pipal) are represented in the company of humans, and supernatural beings wear horned headdresses and/or are engaged in heroic feats. Presented in different guises and in a world inhabited by a pantheon of gods and goddesses, they appear to engage in actions designed to preserve a social order.

This comparative and cross-cultural analysis of city-states combined with the results of archaeological research from the Indus has revealed many points of commonality that the Indus shared with other early civilizations. Of course, none of the city-states cited replicate Indus society; they only provide observation points from which we can compose "properly qualified observations" (Yoffee 1997:262). Throughout this book, I have tried not to stray beyond what the archaeological evidence will support.

In the end, though the Harappans shared much with other city-states, the Indus provides us with its own unique features with which to renew our thinking about early states. If Egypt was the gift of the Nile, then the gift of the Indus was a unique geographical setting that its leaders brought together into an integrated society. With its core situated among rich alluvial plains and ecologically diverse zones, Indus farmers, pastoralists, artisans and merchants developed and sustained a complex agropastoral and craft-producing economy. Irradiating out from the plains was a resource rich environment. To its north, west, and east were mountains and deserts from which the Harappans drew an abundance of raw materials. From these the Harappans fashioned elaborated crafts and developed a complex administrative system of standardized weights and inscribed devices which were used to good effect in establishing political and social networks that enhanced the civilization's vertical integration. To its south were the oceans and seas and port locations that provided outlets to contemporary complex societies that grew and flourished throughout the Greater Near East and through which it established an active intercultural trade. In this, the Indus established a place as an important player on a world stage. Importantly, these interactions brought the Meluhhans into contact with cultures bearing different ideas and ways of life that to a greater or lesser extent, cross-fertilized with their own.

Throughout this book, I have described the key features that gave rise to the fluorescence and demise of a complex, multidimensional civilization. Starting from a virtually unknown and undefined body of ruins and artifacts, our understanding of the civilization has now emerged as an ordered world of ideas and activities that is coming into sharper focus. Here, I have drawn together aspects of the civilization's political economy toward creating a perspective that places the Indus within the broadened framework of what is now known about the nature and character of early state societies.

Notes

1. A Long-Forgotten Civilization

[1] A slightly altered version of this tale has been relayed to me during my research at Harappa.

[2] Research on the Indus has become an increasingly collaborative venture between foreign and local scholars. Our team at Harappa is a collaborative effort between American and Pakistani archaeologists, as well as others from many European and Asian countries.

[3] The absolute dates are derived from radiocarbon analysis of excavated materials from Harappa and other sites.

3. From Foraging to Farming and Pastoralism

[1] The plant remains from Mehrgarh are from seeds and imprints on bricks, plasters, and floors (Costantini 1984).

[2] In some instances the ocher lined the grave floor. The use of ocher may have been an attempt at preserving the body, a practice known ethnographically (Cucina et al. 2005:81).

[3] Ouch!

4. An Era of Expansion and Transformation

[1] Chronologies for the Pre-urban and Urban periods for the Indus are based on the excavations at Harappa. The absolute dates cited for phases of occupation are based upon the most recent radiocarbon analyses.

[2] Paint/slips are pigments mixed with clay slurries. They are not glazes, but under microscopic examination, paint/slips have a more glassy texture than slips (de Atley 1985).

[3] The exploitation of microenvironments is a pattern known in other Pre-urban contexts. In southern Mesopotamia during the Uruk period, Adams interprets patterns of specialist exploitation of different ecosystems as an infrastructural basis for a later establishment of urban centers (Adams 1981).

[4] In 1941, Sir Aurel Stein conducted a brief survey along the dry bed of the Ghaggar-Hakra River in both India and Pakistan. His unpublished report, along with subsequent investigations by other archaeologists, was the basis on which Mughal conducted his survey of Cholistan in Pakistan in the 1970s. Stein had discovered fifty-eight sites, and approximately thirty-six are related to the Indus civilization (Mughal 2001:2ff., Mughal 2005.)

[5] Figure 4.5 is a synthesis of published data on the three regional surveys. The map key reflects the categories assigned to settlement phases in each area. In the Upper Indus,

Ravi and Kot Diji are used; in Cholistan, Hakra and Kot Diji; in northwest India, Early Harappan. The latter includes what are referred to as Ravi, Hakra, and Kot Diji in the Upper Indus and Cholistan.

[6] Periano wet ware is a type of pottery in which a clay slurry is applied to the surface of a pot. They are also decorated with painted, usually black and red, horizontal bands on their rims or necks (Fairservis 1975). This type is found in northern Baluchistan at numerous sites.

[7] Alexander Burnes, who visited Harappa and was discussed in Chapter 1, also visited Amri. Burnes sailed the length of the Indus River. While in the Lower Indus he spotted Amri, and his writings include details about the site.

[8] For an important discussion on the imperfect nature of establishing systems of value for different cultures, see an early essay by Lloyd Fallers (1967) on the complex nature of the cultural construction of systems of value.

5. Urbanism and States: Cities, Regions, and Edge Zones

[1] These designations and others (C, D, E) were made by Cunningham (see Chapter 1), in 1872 when he conducted a survey of the site (Lahiri 2005:23ff.).

[2] One possibility currently being explored (based on the analysis of the clay and silt layers) is the use of the platforms for dyeing or processing plant materials, such as indigo. Dye preparation of indigo takes place in pits and in closed rooms absent of light during which the dye is a dark green color (reminiscent of the dark green color noted in the sediment of the Harappa working platforms). Upon exposure to light it turns a vibrant blue (Kenoyer et al. 1999).

[3] Excavations were undertaken at Ganweriwala by the Department of Archaeology of the University of the Punjab in winter 2007.

[4] These data are available through the generosity of Dr. Nilofer Shaikh.

[5] For example, during the early periods in Egypt (Early Dynastic and Old Kingdom), a single center, Memphis, was the administrative center of government.

[6] Other settlements on the Kachi Plain and in Quetta, Zhob, and Loralai have many features typical of contemporary Indus sites.

6. Agropastoral and Craft-Producing Economies I – Intensification and Specialization

[1] Double-chambered kilns have been found at Harappa, Lal Shah, Nausharo, Amri, Balakot, Kot Diji, Lothal, Chanhu-daro, and Cholistan (see H.M.L. Miller 1997 for references), as well as Vainiwal (Wright et al. 2005).

[2] The term "stoneware" refers to a ceramic in which firing temperatures range from 1,200 to 1,400 degrees centigrade, causing the clay to fuse until it is nonporous. In that sense, the stoneware bangles are not stoneware at all, since they were probably not fired beyond 1,000 degrees centigrade. True stoneware did not reappear until 1300–1400 B.C. in another part of the world.

[3] For an extensive discussion of the introduction of millets and other crops to various areas, see Fuller and Madella (2000) and Madella and Fuller (2006).

7. Agropastoral and Craft-Producing Economies II – Diversification, Organization of Production, and Distribution

[1] In contrast, the lords of the ancient Maya appear not to have concerned themselves with agricultural production. They left those aspects of the economy to local farming

communities. The primary interests of the Maya lords lay with trading networks (Demarest 2004).

2 Chert came from several sources; for example, a dark to reddish brown chert found at Indus sites did not come from the Rohri source. Deposits along the Kirthar range in Sindh and pebbles in riverbeds in Baluchistan may have been exploited (Kenoyer 1991, Vidale 2000:36).

3 These indices of value for raw materials correspond to the identification of source areas for the materials listed (Figure 7.1).

4 In other contexts (e.g., in Pre-urban occupations at the small village of Tarakai Qila in the NWFP), on-site crop processing has been interpreted as evidence for household production (i.e., growing and harvesting by the inhabitants of households) (Thomas 2003:422). According to Hillman (1984) under modern cultivation practices in Turkey, bulk processing takes place in fields, but light chaff, spikelets, coarse waste, and other semiclean grain may make their way to household storage for a variety of reasons.

5 Belcher's model is based on Melinda Zeder's study of zooarchaeological and related evidence from the site of Malyan in southwestern Iran (Zeder 1991).

8. The Lure of Distant Lands

1 The identifications of Bahrain, Oman, and the Indus are based on the research of Assyriologists, experts in translating Mesopotamian texts. They have pieced together these locations based upon geographical landmarks such as references to mountains and other features (for example, see Steinkeller 2006). The translation of the text on page 216 is from Kramer (1963:178) and Kramer and Maier (1989:46ff) and cited in Parpola (1994:14).

2 *Mesu* refers to wood and *haia* bird to peacocks. Enki is the Mesopotamian water god identified with the city of Uruk.

3 The texts are dated to between 2062 and 2028 B.C. (S. Parpola et al. 1977:150).

4 Textual sources from the end of the third millennium B.C. indicate Mesopotamian trade was carried out by a class of merchants. One of them, Lu-Enlilla, is well-known. He and others "were employed as seafaring merchants, and went directly to Makkan in order to purchase copper in exchange for great quantities of wool and garments" (Potts 1978:40).

5 For a firsthand account of the conditions under which George Dales and his wife Barbara explored the Makran coast by boat, camel, truck, and on foot, see George F. Dales and Carl P. Lipo (1992). Their many diary entries provide vivid accounts of their experiences.

9. Landscapes of Order and Difference – The Cultural Construction of Space, Place, and Social Difference

1 For an important discussion of landscape studies, see Ashmore and Knapp (1999).

2 The structure was built in four phases. The first included two-meter-thick enclosure walls and a concentric layout around the tank. There were twin staircases and transit rooms. In a second phase, the northern staircase was blocked, a room was sealed off, and a portion of outer streets built around the structure were destroyed. In a third phase, the tank was filled with debris and pillar rows were destroyed. They were partially used as a production area. In the final phase, a drain was constructed near the surface "traversing" one entrance. The structure underneath was completely buried (Ardeleanu-Jansen 1984:54). This reconstruction coupled with an analysis of secondary debris found associated with the complex may indicate that the Great Bath was abandoned

"as such while the Harppans were still in occupation of the site" (Ardeleanu-Jansen et al. 1983:54). Associated debris was broken down based on clusters at the floor level and clusters on the surface. Ardeleanu-Jansen (1984) found that prestige and ideology related artifacts constituted the largest percentages of materials (34%). This percentage dropped to 12% at the surface level.

3 The indices of value for raw materials correspond to identifications of source areas for the materials listed (Figure 7.2).

4 The argument presented by Miller provides an excellent starting point for making the assessments discussed. Her papers and others by colleagues (Kenoyer 1992; Barthelemy de Saizieu and Bouquillon 1994; Vidale 2000) should be consulted, and the complexity of the technologies involved should be considered.

5 The "grand" entrance and the courtyard's proximity to a small circular enclosure with rings of brickwork led the archaeologist, Sir Mortimer Wheeler, to identify this building as a temple. He was impressed by the double stairway at the buildings entrance and believed the ring of brickwork was an enclosure for a "sacred" tree (1968:52).

6 The Priest-King got his name because of the pattern on his cloak, which is similar to trefoil inlay ornaments known from contemporary cultures in Mesopotamia and Egypt (Ardeleanu-Jansen 1991:167).

7 As Marshall (1931:44) noted, the two statues were found at different locations and both were well below the surface, at two to three meters deep.

8 At Manda in western Uttar Pradesh, India, a newly discovered hoard is an example of the richness of materials found in hoards and their similarities to objects found at distant sites. The cache has a poor context, since it was recovered in a field under cultivation but nevertheless demonstrates that objects of value were present and kept in caches throughout the civilization. The find spot of the cache is a small mound, where remnants of burnt brick had been sighted by local villagers. It was discovered by chance as a farmer was leveling a field and after some of the materials had been looted. Still, the pottery at Manda and style of objects leave no doubt it is contemporary with the Urban period. The cache included extraordinary quantities of materials, including gold bracelets now on display at the National Museum. The materials were placed in a large copper vessel and included bead types, such as gold spacers, gold circular wafer beads, D-shaped beads, banded agate, and onyx similar to others at Allahadino, Harappa, and Mohenjo-daro. Sharma et al. (2000:39) believe a rectangular box may have been for gold fillets such as those found at Mohenjo-daro and Harappa.

10. Models for Indus Religious Ideologies

1 Years later, Maria Gimbutas, an archaeologist whose primary research was in Europe, elaborated on this theme. She believed that female images of goddesses in Europe and elsewhere were symbolic of an ancient "matriarchy," a society in which females were the dominant leaders. For Gimbutas, it had been a peaceful world that came to be dominated by destructive patriarchal and war-loving males (Tringham 1991:96). According to a more recent interpretation of Gimbutas's work (see Sanday 2002 for views on the topic), she did not view females as "rulers." Instead, she envisioned a "matristic" society, in which the sexes were linked in a partnership model. A principal criticism is that it is simply impossible to state what form of social organization prevailed in the prehistoric periods on which Gimbutas based her studies. A more general criticism relates to the unproven assumption that a particular psychology (rather than a socially constructed definition of female) can be aligned with some universal, natural, static, inevitable, and predictable female mode of being. Although discredited, the idea of an ancient

matriarchy continues to fascinate the general public, particularly eco-feminists. It is doubtful that Marshall viewed the Indus as a matriarchical society.

[2] Possehl cites sixteen seals in which a seated individual is depicted in this seated posture (Possehl 2002:145), though only a few have the multiple faces Marshall noted.

[3] They are Old and Middle Kingdom Egypt, southern Mesopotamia from the late Early Dynastic to Old Babylonian period, northern China in late Shang and early western Zhou, Valley of Mexico Aztec society, Classic Maya, the Inca Kingdom, and Yoruba and Benin peoples of west Africa, mid-eighteenth century to the colonial era. Trigger did not include the Indus civilization since there are "so few written documents" (2003:33).

[4] Countless examples could be offered for just this sort of error in judgment. When sixteenth-century Spanish missionaries were faced with systems of thought that were similar to those described in the text and foreign to their own Christian views, they considered them profane. Studies of the religious views of the Maya, Aztec, and Inca peoples have shown they were as complex and logical as the Christian beliefs held by Europeans.

[5] The Harappan figurines differ in their manufacture and stylistic attributes from the much earlier Mehrgarh figurines described in Chapter 3.

11. The Decline and Transformation and the Comparative Study of Early States

[1] Mackay believed that certain changes in architecture indicated the presence of squatters. These changes included the presence of poor quality rectangular huts and floors paved with broken bricks that were unlike the urban architecture of the Urban period.

[2] A black steatite wig found at Harappa is stylistically similar to others known in greater numbers in Central Asia and may be from the BMAC (Meadow 2002).

Bibliography

Abdi, Kamyar. 2003. The Early Development of Pastoralism in the Central Zagros Mountains. *Journal of World Prehistory* 17(4) 395–443.

Adams, R. McC. 1981. *Heartland of Cities*. University of Chicago Press, Chicago.

1992. Ideologies: Unity and Diversity. In *Ideology and pre-Columbian Civilizations*, edited by. A. A. Demarest and G. W. Conrad, pp. 205–21. School of American Research Press, Santa Fe.

2006. Sheperds at Umma in the Third Dynasty of Ur: Interlocutors with a World Beyond the Scribal Field of Vision. *Journal of the Economic and Social History of the Orient.* 49(2): 133–69.

2008. An Interdisciplinary Overview of a Mesopotamian City and its Hinterlands. Cuneiform *Digital Libary Journal* 1:1–23.

Agrawal, D. P. 1971. *Copper Bronze Age in India: An Integrated Archaeological Study of the Copper Bronze Age in India in the Light of Chronological, Technological, and Ecological Factors, ca. 3000–500 B.C.* Munshiram Manoharlal, New Delhi.

1982. *The Archeology of India*. Curzon Press, London.

1984. Paleoenvironment and Prehistoric Studies in the Kashmir Valley. In *Studies in the Archaeology and Paleoanthropology of South Asia*, edited by K. A. R. Kennedy and G. L. Possehl, pp. 33–40. Oxford and IBH and the American Institute of Indian Studies, New Delhi.

2000. *Ancient Metal Technology and Archaeology of South Asia: A Pan-Asian Perspective*. Aryan Books International, New Delhi.

Agrawal, D. P. and A. Ghosh. 1973. *Radiocarbon and Indian Archaeology*. Tata Institute of Fundamental Research, Bombay.

Agrawal, D. P. and S. Kusumgar. 1974. *Prehistoric Chronology and Radiocarbon Dating in India*. Munshiram Manoharlar, New Delhi.

Agrawal, D. P. and R. K. Sood. 1982. Ecological Factors and the Harappan Civilization. In *Harappan Civilization: A Contemporary Perspective*, edited by G. L. Possehl, pp. 223–31. Oxford and IBH and the American Institute of Indian Studies, New Delhi.

Agrawal, O. P., H. Narain, J. Prakash, and S. K. Bhatia. 1990. Lamination Technique in Iron from Artifacts in Ancient India. *Journal of the Historical Metallurgy Society* 24(1): 12–26.

Aitken, E. H. 1907. *Gazetteer of the Province of Sind*. Government of Bombay, Karachi.

Allchin, B. 1976. The Discovery of Paleolithic Sites in the Plains of Sindh and Their Implications. *The Geographic Journal* 142(3): 471–89.

Allchin, B. and F. R. Allchin. 1968. *The Birth of Indian Civilization*. Penguin Books, Baltimore.

1982. *The Rise of Civilization in India and Pakistan*. Cambridge: Cambridge University Press.

1997. *Origins of a Civilization*. Viking, New Delhi.

Allchin, F. R. 1984. The Northern Limits of the Harappan Culture Zone. In *Frontiers of the Indus Civilization*, edited by B. B. Lal and S. P. Gupta, pp. 51–4. Books and Books, New Delhi.

1985. The Interpretation of a Seal from Chanhu-daro and Its Significance for the Religion of the Indus Valley. In *South Asian Archaeology 1983*, edited by J. Schotsmans and M. Taddei, pp. 369–84. Istituto Universitario Orientale, Naples.

1990. Indo-Aryan and Aryan: Language, Culture and Ethnicity. *Ancient Ceylon* 10: 13–23.

1992. An Indus Ram: A Hitherto Unrecorded Stone Sculpture from the Indus Civilization. *South Asian Studies* 8: 52–4.

1995. *The Archaeology of Early Historic South Asia: The Emergence of Cities and States*. Cambridge University Press, Cambridge.

Alden, J. 1982. Trade and Politics in Proto-Elamite Iran. *Current Anthropology*. 23: 613–40.

Amiet, J. 1979a. Les sceaux de Shahr-I Sokhta. In *South Asian Archaeology 1975*, edited by Lohuizen-deLeeuw, pp. 3–6. Brill Academic Publishers, Leiden.

1979b. Archaeological Discontinuity and Ethnic Duality in Elam. *Antiquity* LIII: 195–204.

Amiet, P. 1986. *L'Age des Echanges Inter-Iraniens*. Editions de la Reunion des Musees Nationaux, Paris.

1995. La glyptique transelamite. In *De Chypre a la Bactriane, les sceaux du Proche – Orient ancien*, edited by A. Caubet, pp. 121–6. Actes du colloque international organize au Musee du Louvre par le Service Culturel le 18 Mars 1995.

Amundson, R. and E. Pendall. 1991. Pedology and Late Quaternary Environments Surrounding Harappa: A Review and Synthesis. In *Harappa Excavations 1986–1990*, edited by R. H. Meadow, pp. 13–27. Prehistory Press, Madison.

Anderson, B. 1991. *Imagined Communities*. Verso, New York.

Ardeleanu-Jansen, A. 1984. Stone Sculptures from Mohenjo-daro. In *Interim Reports*, Vol. 1, edited by M. Jansen and G. Urban, pp. 139–58. Forschungsprojekt, Mohenjo-daro, Schinkelstrasse 1, Aachen.

1991. The Sculptural Art of the Harappa Culture. In *Forgotten Cities on the Indus: Early Civilization in Pakistan from the 8th to the 2nd Millennium B.C.*, edited by M. Jansen et al., pp. 167–78. Verlag Philipp von Zabern, Mainz.

1992. New Evidence on the Distribution of Artifacts: An Approach Towards a Qualitative-Quantitative Assessment of the Terracotta Figures of Mohenjo-daro. In *South Asian Archaeology 1989*, edited by C. Jarrige, pp. 5–14. Prehistory Press, Madison.

Arnold, D. E. 1985. *Ceramic Theory and Culture Process.* Cambridge University Press, Cambridge.

Aruz, Joan. 2003. *Art of the First Cities: The Third Millennium B.C. from the Mediterranean to the Indus.* The Metropolitan Museum of Art, New York.

Ashmore, W. and B. A. Knapp, eds. 1999. *Archaeologies of Landscape: Contemporary Perspectives.* Blackwell Publishers, Malden, Mass.

Atre, S. 1989. Toward an Economico-Religious Model for Harappan Urbanism. *South Asian Studies* 5: 49–58.

Bachofen, J. J. 1861. *Des Mutterecht. Eine Untersuchung über die Gynaikokratic der alten Welt nach ihrer Religiösen und Rechtliclen Natur.* Kraus and Hoffmann, Stuttgart.

Baker, A. Sandler. 1999. High-Resolution Holocene Environmental Changes in the Thar Desert, Northwestern India. *Science* 284: 125–8.

Bala, M. and V. Kant. 2000. Dhalewan: An Early Harappan Site in Punjab. *Puratattva* 30: 42–4.

Banerji, N. R. 1965. *The Iron Age in India.* Munshiram Manoharlal, Delhi.

1973. Amirthamangalam 1955: A Megalithic Urn-burial Site in District Chingleput, Tamilnadu. *Ancient India* 22: 3–36.

Barfield, T. J. 1989. *The Perilous Frontier: Nomadic Empires and China.* Blackwell, London.

Barthelemy de Saizieu, B. and A. Bouquillon. 1994. Steatite Working at Mehrgarh during the Neolithic and Chalcolithic Periods: Quantitative Distribution, Characterization of Material and Manufacturing Process. In *South Asian Archaeology 1993*, Vol. 1, edited by A. Parpola and P. Koskikallio, pp. 47–59. Suomalainen Tiedakatemia, Helsinki.

1997. Evolution of the Glazing Techniques from the Chalcolithic to the Indus Periods from the Data of Mehrgarh and Nausharo. In *South Asian Archaeology 1995*, edited by B. Allchin, pp. 63–76. Oxford and IBH, New Delhi.

Bar-Yosef, O. and R. H. Meadow. 1995. The Origins of Agriculture in the Near East. In *Last Hunters, First Farmers: New Perspectives on the Prehistoric Transition to Agriculture*, edited by T. D. Price and A. B. Gebauer, pp. 39–95. School of American Research, Santa Fe.

2001. Emergence et Evolution des Matériaux Vitrifiés dans la Région de L'Indus au 3e Millénaire (Mehrgarh-Nausharo). *Paléorient* 26(2): 93–111.

Basham, A. L. 1989. *The Origins and Development of Classical Hinduism.* Beacon Press, Boston.

Belcher, W. R. 2003. Fish Exploitation of the Indus Valley Tradition. In *Indus Ethnobiology*, edited by S. A. Weber and W. R. Belcher, 95–174. Lexington Books, New York.

Belcher, W. R. and W. R. Belcher. 2000. Geologic Constraints on the Harappa Archaeological Site, Punjab Province, Pakistan. *Geoarchaeology* 15(7): 679–713.

Besenval, Roland. 1997. Entré le Sud-est Iranien et la plaine de l'Indus: le Kech-Makran. Recherches archéologiques fur le peuplement ancient d'une marche des confines indo-iraniens. *Arts Asiatiques* 52: 5–38.

Besenval, R. and P. Sanlaville. 1990. Settlements in Pakistani Makran. *Mesopotamia* XXV: 79–146.

Bhan, K. K. 1986. Recent Explorations in the Jamnagar District of Saurashtra. *Man and Environment*, X: 1–21.

    1992. Late Harappan Gujarat. *Eastern Anthropologist*, Indus Civilization Special no. 45(1–2): 173–92.

    2005. The Water Structures and Engineering of the Harappans at Dholavira (India). In *South Asian Archaeology, Vol. 1, Prehistory*, edited by C. Jarrige and V. Lefevre, pp. 11–26. Editions recherché sur les civilizations, Paris.

Bhan, K. and J. M. Kenoyer. 1983. Nageswar, an Industrial Centre of Chalcolithic Period. *Puratattva* 1980–81: 115–19.

Bhardwaj, H. C. 1973. Aspects of these Early Iron Technology in India. In *Radiocarbon and Indian Archaeology*, edited by D. P. Agrawal and A. Ghosh, pp. 391–9. Tata Institute of Fundamental Research, Bombay.

Bhatia, S. B. and Singh, N. 1988. Middle Holocene Palaeoclimatic and Palaeoenvironmental Events in Southern Haryana. In *Palaeoclimatic and Palaeoenvironmental Changes in Asia; During the Last 4 Million Years*, edited by D. P. Agrawal, P. Shanna, and S. K. Gupta, pp. 236–46. Indian National Science Academy, New Delhi.

Biagi, P. and M. Cremaschi. 1991. The Harappan Flint Quarries of the Rohri Hills (Sind, Pakistan). *Antiquity* 65: 97–102.

Biagi, P., C. Ottomano, A. Pessina, and N. Shaikh. 1995. The 1994 Campaign on the Rohri Hills (Sindh-Pakistan): a Preliminary Report. *Ancient Sindh* 1: 1–6.

Bisht, R. S. n. d. Harappans and the Rgveda: Points of Convergence. In *The Dawn of Indian Civilization (up to c. 600 B.C.)* edited by G. C. Pande, pp. 391–440. Munshiram Manoharlal Publishers Pvt Ltd., Delhi.

    1982. Excavations at Banawali: 1974–77. In *Harappan Civilization: A Contemporary Perspective*, edited by G. L. Possehl, pp. 113–24. Oxford and IBH, Publishing Company, New Delhi.

    1987. Further Excavations at Banawali: 1983–84. In *Archaeology and History: Essays in Memory of Shri A. Ghosh*, vol. 1, edited by B. M. Pande and B. D. Chattopadhyaya, pp. 135–56. Agam Kala, Delhi.

    1991. Dholavira: New Horizons of the Indus Civilization. *Puratattva* 20: 71–81.

    1995. Recent Research at Dholavira. Paper read at the 13th Conference of South Asian Archaeology, Cambridge March 7, 1995.

    1996. The Harappan Colonization of the Kutch: An Ergonomic Study with Reference to Dholavira and Surkotada. In *History and Art*, edited by K. Deva, L. Gopal, and S. B. Singh, pp. 265–72. Ramanad Vidya Bhawan, New Delhi.

    2000a. Indus Civilization, The Last Fifty Years of the Study in India. In *Exhibitions of the World's Four Great Civilizations: The Indus Exhibition*, pp. 26–8. NHK, Tokyo.

    2000b. Urban Planning at Dholavira. In *Ancient Cities, Sacred Skies, Cosmic Geometries and City Planning*. In Ancient India, J. McKim Malville and L. M. Gujral, eds., pp. 11–23. Aryan Books International for Indira Gandhi National Centre for the Arts, New Delhi.

    2005. The Water Structures and Engineering of the Harappans at Dholavira (India). In *South Asian Archaeology 2001*, Vol. 1, edited by C. Jarrige and V. Lefevre, pp. 11–26. CNRS, Paris.

Biswas, S. 1993. Dholavira Harappan Treasure Trove. *India Today*. pp. 90–2.

Blackman, J. M. and M. Vidale. 1992. The Production and Distribution of Stoneware Bangles at Mohenjo-daro and Harappa as Monitored by Chemical Characterization Studies. In *South Asian Archaeology 1989*, edited by C. Jarrige, pp. 37–44. Monographs in World Archaeology, no. 14. Prehistory Press, Madison.

Boehmer, R. M. 1965. *Die Entwicklung der Glyptik wahrend der akkad-zeid*. Untersuchungen zur Assyriologie and vorderasiatischen archaologie, 4. Walter der Gruyter, Berlin.

Bokonyi, S. 1997. Horse Remains from the Prehistoric Site of Surkotada, Kutch, Late 3rd millennium B.C. *South Asian Studies* 13: 297–307.

Boserup, E. 1965. *The Conditions of Agricultural Growth*. Aldine De Gruyter, Chicago.

Bouquillon, A. and B. Barthelemy de Saizieu. 1995. Decouverte de nouveau matérieu dans les parunes de la période pre-Indus de Mehrgarh (Balochistan): la 'faience' de steatite. *Techne* 2: 50–5.

Bradley, R. 2004. Domestication, Sedentism, Property, and Time: Materiality and the Beginnings of Agriculture in Northern Europe. In *Rethinking Materiality: The Engagement of Mind with the Material World*, edited By E. DeMarrais, C. Gosden, and C. Renfrew. Monograph:107.114. McDonald Institute, Cambridge.

Brady, J. E., A. Scott, A. Cobb, I. Rodas, J. Fogarty, and R. V. Sanchez. 1997. Glimpses of the Dark Side of the Petexbatun Project: The Petexbation Regional Cave Survey. *Ancient Mesoamerica* 8: 353–64.

Braudel, F. 1993. *A History of Civilization*. Penguin Books, New York.

Bryson, R. A. 2005. Archaeoclimatology. In *The Encyclopedia of World Climatology*, edited by J. E. Oliver, p. 68. Springer, Dordrecht.

Bryson, R. A. and K. M. DeWall, eds. 2007. *A Paleo Climate Workbook: High Resolution Site Specific Macrophysical Climate Modeling and CD*. Mammoth Springs Publication, Hot Springs, SD.

Bryson, R. A. and A. M. Swain. 1981. Holocene Variations of Monsoon Rainfall in Rajasthan. *Quaternary Research* 16: 135–45.

Bryson, R. A., R. P. Wright, and J. Schuldenrein. 2007. Modeling Holocene Climates and Rivers in the Harappa Vicinity. In *A Paleoclimatology Workbook: High Resolution, Site Specific, Macrophysical Climate Modeling*, edited by R. A. Bryson and K. M. DeWall, pp. 123–8. Mammoth Springs Publication, Hot Springs, SD.

Burnes, A. 1834. *Travels into Bokhara Together with a Narrative of a Voyage on the Indus*, 3 vols. Oxford University Press, Karachi.

Butzer, K. 1964. *Environment and Archaeology. An Introduction to Pleistocene Geography*. Aldine Publishing, Chicago.

1982. *Archaeology as Human Ecology*. Cambridge University Press, Cambridge.

Carter, R. 2003. Restructuring Bronze Age Trade: Bahrain, Southeast Asia, and the Copper Question. In *The Archaeology of Bahrain*, edited by H. Crawford, BAR International Series 1189, pp. 31–42.

Casal, J. 1964. *Fouilles d'Amri*, 2 vols. Librarie C. Klincksieck, Paris.

Casanova, M. 1992. The Sources of Lapis-Lazuli Found in Iran. In *South Asian Archaeology 1989*, edited by C. Jarrige. pp. 49–56. Prehistory Press, Madison.

350 Bibliography

Chakrabarti, D. K. 1973. Concept of Urban Revolution and the Indian Context. *Puratattva* 6: 27–32.

1977. India and West Asia – An Alternative Approach. *Man and Environment* 1: 25–38.

1988. *A History of Indian Archaeology: From the Beginning to 1947.* Munshiram Manoharlal, New Delhi.

1990. *The External Trade of the Indus Civilization.* Munshiram Manoharlal, New Delhi.

1991. Aspects of Continuity in Indian Metal-working Technology: A Study of Geological and Ethnographic Sources. In *Cultural Heritage of the Indian Village.* Occasional Papers No. 47. British Museum, London.

1997. *Colonial Indology: Sociopolitics of the Ancient Indian Past.* Munshiram Manoharlal, New Delhi.

1999. Documenting Heritage – Some Observations on the Indian Situation. In *Our Fragile Heritage: Documenting the Past and the Future*, edited by H. J. Hansen and Y. Quine. The Danish Museum, Copenhagen.

Chakrabarti, D. K. and P. Moghadam. 1977. Some Unpublished Indus Beads from Iran. *Iran* 15: 192–4.

Charles, J. A. 1980. The Coming of Copper and Copper-base Alloys and Iron: A Metallurgical Sequence. In *The Coming of the Age of Iron*, edited by T. A. Wertime and J. D. Muhly, pp. 151–81. Yale University Press, New Haven.

Charlton, T. H. and D. L. Nichols. 1997. The city-state concept: Development and applications. In D. L. Nichols and T. H. Charlton, eds. *The Archaeology of City-states: Cross-Cultural Approaches.* pp. 1–14. Smithsonian Institution Press, Washington D.C.

Childe, V. Gordon. 1950. The Urban Revolution. *Town Planning Review* 21: 3–17.

Christaller, W. 1966. *Central Places in Southern Germany*, translated from Die zentralen orte in Suddeutschland by C. W. Baskin. Prentice-Hall, Englewood Cliffs.

Clark, Sharri R. 2003. Representing the Indus Body: Sex, Gender, Sexuality, and the Anthropomorphic Terracotta Figurines from Harappa. *Asian Perspectives* 42(2): 304–28.

2007. *The Social Lives of Figurines: Reconsidering the Third Millennium B.C. Terracotta Figures from Harappa (Pakistan).* University Microfilms (UMI).

Clark, J. D. and M. A. J. Williams. 1989. Paleoenvironments and Prehistory in North Central India: A Preliminary Report. In *Studies in the Archaeology of India and Pakistan*, edited by J. Jacobson, pp. 19–41. Oxford and IBH, New Delhi.

Clemens, S. C. and W. L. Prell. 1990. Late Pleistocene Variability of Arabian Sea Summer Monsoon Winds and Continental Aridity: Eolian Records from the Lithographic Component of Deep Sea Cores. *Paleoceanography* 5:109–45.

Cleuziou S. and M. Tosi 1989. The Southeastern Frontier of the Near East. In *South Asian Archaeology, Aarhus 1985*, Scandinavian Institute of Asian Studies Occasional Papers No. 4, edited by K. Frifelt and P. Soerensen, pp. 15–47. Curzon Press, London.

1994. Black Boats of Magan. Some Thoughts on Bronze-Age Water Transport in Oman and Beyond from the Impressed Bitumen Slabs of Ra's al-Junayz. In *South Asian Archaeology, Helsinki* 1993, Vol. II, edited by A. Parpola and P. Koskikallio, pp. 645–761. Soumalainen Tiedakatemia, Helsinki.

2000. Ras al-Jinz and the Prehistoric Coastal Cultures of the Ja'alan. *The Journal of Oman Studies* 11: 19–73.

Cohen, B. S. 1996. *Colonialism and Its Forms of Knowledge: The British in India*. Princeton University Press, Princeton.

Collon, D. 1987. *First Impressions: Cylinder Seals in the Ancient Near East*. University of Chicago Press, Chicago.

1995. *Ancient Near Eastern Art*. University of California Press, Berkley.

Coppa, A., L. Donioli, A. Cucina, D. W. Frayers, C. Jarrige, J.-F. Jarrige, G. Quivron, M. Rossi, M. Vidale, and R. Macchiarelli. 2006. Early Neolithic Tradition of Dentistry. *Nature*. 44 (April 6): 755–6.

Costantini, L. 1984. The Beginning of Agriculture in the Kachi Plain: The Evidence of Mehrgarh. In *South Asian Archaeology 1981*, edited by B. Allchin, pp. 29–33. Cambridge University Press, Cambridge.

1990. Harappan Agriculture in Pakistan: The Evidence of Nausharo. In *South Asian Archaeology 1987*, edited by M. Taddei, pp. 321–32. Istituto Italiano per il Medio ed Estremo Oriente, Rome.

Costin, C. L. and R. P. Wright, eds. 1998. Craft and Social Identity. *American Anthropological Association*, Archaeology Division Monograph 8.

Courty, M.-A. 1989. Integration of Sediment and Soil Formation in the Reconstruction of Proto-historic and Historic Landscapes of the Ghaggar Plain, North-west India. In *South Asian Archaeology 1985*, edited by K. Frifelt and P. Sorenson, pp. 255–9. Curzon Press, London.

1990. Pedogenesis of Holocene Calcareous Parent-Materials under Semi-arid Conditions (Ghaggar Plain, NW India). In *Soil Micromorphology: A Basic and Applied Science. Developments in Soil Science 19*, edited by L. A. Douglas, pp. 361–6. Elsevier, Amsterdam.

1995. Late Quaternary Environmental Changes and Natural Constraints to Ancient Land Use (Northwest India). In *Ancient Peoples and Landscapes*, edited by Eilleen Johnson, pp. 105–26. Museum of Texas Tech University, Lubbock.

Courty, M.-A. and N. Fedoroff. 1985. Micromorphology of Recent and Buried Soils in Northwestern India. *Geoderma* 35: 287–332.

Courty, M-A., P. Goldberg, and R. I. Macphail. 1989. Soils and Micromor-phology in Archaeology. *Cambridge Manuals in Archaeology*. Cambridge University Press, Cambridge.

Cowgill, G. L., 2008. An Update on Teotihuacan. *Antiquity* 82:962–75.

Crawford, H. E. W. 1973. Mesopotamia's Invisible Exports in the Third Millennium B.C. *World Archaeology* 6: 242–71.

Crowe, Norman. 1995. *Nature and the Idea of a Man-Made World: An Investigation into the Evolutionary Roots of Form and Order in the Built Environment*. The MIT Press, Cambridge.

Cucina, A. and P. Petrone. 2005. The 1997–2000 Field Seasons at Mehrgarh: Preliminary Anthropological and Taphonomic Evidence. In *South Asian*

Archaeology 2001, pp. 79–84, edited by C. Jarrige and V. Lefevre, Editions Recherche sur les Civilisations, Paris.

Cucarzi, M. 1987. A Model of Morphogenesis for Mohenjodero. In *Interim Reports* Vol 2. edited by M. Jansen and G. Urban, ISMEO-Aachen University Mission, Aachen.

Cunningham, A. 1864–5. *Archaeological Survey of India Report III.* Delhi.

1875. Harappa. *Annual Report of the Archaeological Survey of India.* 5: 105–8.

Cunningham, R. and R. Young. 1999. The Archaeological Visibility of Caste: An Introduction. In *Case Studies in Archaeology and World Religions: The Proceedings of the Cambridge Conference,* edited by T. Insoll. BAR International Series, Oxford.

Dales, G.F. 1962. Harappan Outposts on the Makran Coast. *Antiquity* 36:86–92.

1976. Shifting Trade Patterns between the Iranian Plateau and the Indus Valley in the Third Millennium B.C. In *Le Plateau Iranien et L 'Asie Central des Origines a la Conquete Islamique,* No. 567, pp. 67–78. Colloques Internationaux du Centre National de la Recherche Scientifique, Paris.

1979. The Balakot Project: Summary of Four Years of Excavations in Pakistan. *Man and Environment* 3:45–53.

1982. Adaptation and Exploitation at Harappan Coastal Settlements. In *Anthropology in Pakistan: Recent Socio-Cultural and Archaeological Perspectives,* edited by S. Pastner and L. Flam. Cornell University, Cornell.

1991a. The Phenomenon of The Indus Civilization. In *Forgotten Cities on the Indus: Early Civilization in Pakistan from the 8th to the 2nd millennium B.C.,* edited by Michael Jansen, Maire Mulloy, and Gunter Urban, pp. 129–144. Verlag Philipp von Zabern, Mainz.

1991b. Some specialized ceramic studies at Harappa. In *Harappa Excavations 1986–1990. A Multidisciplinary Approach to the Third Millennium Urbanism,* Monographs in World Archaeology No. 3, edited by Richard H. Meadow, pp. 61–9. Prehistory Press, Madison.

1992. Harappa 1989: Summary of the Fourth Season. In *South Asian Archaeology 1989,* edited by C. Jarrige, pp. 57–68. Prehistory Press, Madison.

Dales, George F. and Carl P. Lipo. 1992. *Explorations on the Makran Coast, Pakistan. A Search for Paradise.* Contributions of the Archaeological Research Facility, University of California, Berkeley.

Dales, G.F. and J.M. Kenoyer. 1986. *Excavations at Mohenjo-Daro, Pakistan: The Pottery.* University Museum, Monograph 53. University Museum, University of Pennsylvania, Philadelphia.

1989. Excavations at Harappa – 1988. *Pakistan Archaeology* 24: 88–176.

Dales, G. and J.M. Kenoyer. 1992. Excavations at Harappa 1991. *Pakistan Archaeology* 27: 31–88.

Dames, M.L. 1886. Old Seals Found at Harappa. *The Indian Antiquary* 15:1.

Dani, A.H. 1963. *Indian Palaeography.* Clarendon Press, Oxford.

1970–1. Excavations in the Gomal Valley. *Ancient Pakistan* 5: 1–177.

1978. Gandhara Grave Culture and the Aryan Problem. *Journal of Central Asia* 1(1): 42–56.

Dani, A.H., ed. 1967. Timargarha and the Gandharan Grave Complex. *Ancient Pakistan* 3: 1–407.

Dani, A. H. and F. A. Durrani. 1964. A New Grave Complex in West Pakistan. *Asian Perspectives* 8: 164–5.

De Atley, S. P. 1985. Mix and Match: Traditions of Glaze Paint Preparation at Four Mile Ruin, Arizona. In *Ceramics and Civilization: Ancient Technology to Modern Science*, vol. 1, edited by W. D. Kingery, pp. 297–330. American Ceramic Society, Columbus, OH.

de Cardi, B. 1965. Excavations and Reconnaissance in Kalat West Pakistan. The Prehistoric Sequence in the Surab Region. *Pakistan Archaeology* 2:861–82.

1970. Excavations at Bampur, A Third Millennium Settlement in Persian Baluchistan, 1966. *Anthropological Papers for the American Museum of Natural History* 51(3):231–355.

1983. *Archaeological Surveys in Baluchistan 1948 and 1957*. Occasional Publication No. 8, Institute of Archaeology London.

Demange, Francoise. 2003. Cylinder Seal of Shu-ilishu, interpreter for Meluhha. In *Art of the First Cities: The Third Millennium B.C. from the Mediterranean to the Indus*, edited by J. Aruz, p. 413. The Metropolitan Museum of Art, New York.

Demarest, A. A. 1992. Archaeology, Ideology and Pre-Columbian Cultural Evolution: The Search for an Approach. In *Ideology and Pre-Columbian Civilizations*, edited by A. A. Demarest and G. W. Conrad, pp. 1–4. School of American Research, Santa Fe.

2004. *The Ancient Maya: The Rise and Fall of a Rain Forest Civilization*. Cambridge University Press, Cambridge.

Deotare, B. C. and M. D. Kajale. 1996. Quaternary Pollen Analysis and Paleoenvironmental Studies of the Salt Basins at Panchpadra and Thob, Western Rajasthan, India: Preliminary Observations. *Man and Environment* 21: 24–31.

Deshpandi-Mukherjee, A. 1998. Shell Fishing and Shell Crafts during the Harappan Period in Gujarat. *Man and Environment* XXIII: 63–80.

Dhavalikar, M. K. 1989. Human Ecology in Western India in the Second Millennium B. C. *Man and Environment* 14: 83–90.

1992. Kuntasi: A Harappan Port in Western India. In *South Asian Archaeology 1989*, edited by C. Jarrige, pp. 73–82. Prehistory Press, Madison.

Dhavalikar, M. K. and G. L. Possehl. 1974. Settlement and Subsistence Patterns of an Early Farming Community in Western India. *Puratattva* 7: 39–46.

Dikshit, K. N. 1924–5. Explorations, Western Circle, Sind, Mohenjo-daro. *Annual Report of the Archaeological Survey of India*, 1924–25, pp. 63–73. Archaeological Survey of India, Delhi.

1925–6. Exploration, Western Circle, Upper Sind Frontier District. *Annual Report of the Archaeological Survey of India*, 1925–26, pp. 98–100. *Archaeological Survey of India*. Delhi.

1984. The Harappan Levels at Hulas. *Man and Environment* 8: 99–102.

Dorsey, B. 1999. Agricultural Intensification, Diversification, and Commercial Production among Smallholder Coffee Growers in Central Kenya. *Economic Geography* 75(2): 178–95.

Dupree, L. P. 1963. Deh Morasi Ghundai: a Chalcolithic Site in South-Central Afghanistan. *Anthropological Papers of the American Museum of Natural History* 50(2): 59–135.

Dupree, L., P. Gouin, and N. Omer. 1971. The Kosh Tapa Hoard from North Afghanistan. *Afghanistan* 24(1): 44–54.

During-Caspers, E. C. L. 1992. Intercultural/Mercantile Contacts between the Arabian Gulf and South Asia at the Close of the Third Millennium B.C. *Proceedings of the Seminar for Arabian Studies*, Vol. 22.

Durrani, Farzand. 1988. Excavations in the Gomal Valley: Rehman Dheri Excavation Report No. 1. *Ancient Pakistan* VI, pp. 1–232. Department of Archaeology Peshawar University, Peshawar.

Dutta, P. C. 1983. *The Bronze Age Harappans: A Bio-anthropological Study of the Skeletons Discovered at Harappa.* Anthropological Survey of India, Calcutta.

Enzel, Y., L. L. Ely, S. Mishra, R. Ramesh, R. Amit, B. Lazar, S. N. Rajaguru, V. R. Baker, and A. Sandler. 1999. High-Resolution Holocene Environmental Changes in the Thar Desert, Northwestern India. *Science* 284: 125–8.

Fairservis, W. A. 1956. Excavations in the Quetta Valley, West Pakistan. *Anthropological Papers of the American Museum of Natural History* 45(2): 167–402.

1959. Archaeological Surveys in the Zhob and Loralai Districts, West Pakistan. *Anthropological Papers of the American Museum of Natural History* 47(2): 277–448.

1967. The Origin, Character, and Decline of an Early Civilization. In *American Museum Novitiates 2302.* American Museum of Natural History, New York.

1971. *The Roots of Ancient India.* University of Chicago Press, Chicago.

Fallers, Lloyd. 1967. Social Stratification and Economic Processes. In *Economic Transition in Africa*, edited by M. J. Herskovits and M. Harwitz, pp. 113–30. Northwestern University Press, Chicago.

Fentress, M. A. 1985. Water Resources and Double-Cropping in Harappan Food Production. In *Recent Advances in Indo-Pacific Prehistory*, edited by V. N. Misra and P. Bellwood, pp. 359–68. Oxford and IBH, New Delhi.

Flam, L. 1981. *The Paleogeography and Prehistoric Settlement Patterns in Sind, Pakistan (4000–2000 B.C.).* PhD. Diss. University of Pennsylvania, Philadelphia.

1986. Recent Explorations in Sind: Paleogeography, Regional Ecology, and Prehistoric Settlement Patterns (ca. 4000–2000 B.C.). In *Studies in the Archaeology of India and Pakistan*, edited by J. Jacobson, pp. 65–89. Oxford and IBH Publishing, New Delhi.

1993a. Fluvial Geomorphology of the Lower Indus Basin (Sindh, Pakistan) and the Indus Civilization. In *Himalayas to the Sea: Geology, Geomorphology and the Quaternary*, edited by J. F. Shroder, Jr., pp. 265–87. Routledge, New York.

1993b. Excavations at Ghazi Shah, Sindh, Pakistan. In *Harappan Civilization: A Recent Perspective*, 2nd ed, edited by G. Possehl, pp. 457–67. Oxford and IBH and American Institute of Indian Studies, Oxford.

1996. Excavations at Ghazi Shah 1985–87, an Interim Report. *Pakistan Archaeology* 28: 131–58.

1998. The Other Side of the Mountains: Explorations in the Kirthar Mountains Region of Western Sindh, Pakistan. In *Arabia and Its Neighbors*, Vol. II, edited by C.S. Phillips, D.T. Potts, and S. Searight, pp. 315–26. ABIEL, Brussels.

1999. Ecology and Population Mobility in the Prehistoric Settlement of the Lower Indus Valley, Sindh, Pakistan. In *The Indus River: Biodiversity, Resources, Humankind*, edited by Azra Meadows and Peter S. Meadows, pp. 313–23. Oxford University, Oxford.

Fontugne, M.R. and J.-C. Duplessy. 1986. Variations of the Monsoon Regime during the Upper Quaternary: Evidence from the Carbon Isotopic Record of Organic Matter in North Indian Ocean Sediment Cores. *Paleogeography, Paleoclimatology, Paleoecology* 56: 69–88.

Foster, B. 1995. *From Distant Days: Myths, Tales, and Poetry of Ancient Mesopotamia*. Capital Decisions Ltd., Bethesda, MD.

Francfort, H.-P. 1986. Preliminary Report (1983–1984): Archaeological and Environmental Researches in the Ghaggar (Saraswati) Plains. *Man and Environment* 10: 97–100.

1992. New Data Illustrating the Early Contacts between Central Asia and the North-West of the Subcontinent. In *South Asian Archaeology 1989*, edited by C. Jarrige, pp. 97–102. Prehistory Press, Madison.

Francfort, H-P., Ch. Boisset, L. Buchet, J. Desse, J. Echallier, A. Kermorvant, and G. Willcox. 1989. *Fouilles de Shortughai: Recherches sur l'Asie Centrale Protohistorique*. 2 vols. Diffusion de Boccard, Paris.

Franke-Vogt, U. 1989. Inscribed Bangles: An Enquiry into Their Relevance. In *South Asian Archaeology 1985*, edited by K. Frifelt and P. Sorensen, pp. 237–46. Scandinavian Institute of Asian Studies, Occasional Papers No. 4. Curzon Press, London.

1991a. *Die Glyptik aus Mohenjo-Daro: Uniformitat und Fariabilitat in der Induskultur, untersuchungen zur Typologie, Iknonographie und Raumlichen Verteilung*. 2 vols. Verlag Philipp von Zabern, Mainz.

1991b. The Glyptic Art of the Harappa Culture. In *Forgotten Cities on the Indus*, edited by M. Jansen et al. pp. 179–87. Verlag Philipp Von Zabern, Mainz.

1992. Inscribed Objects from Mohenjo-daro: Some Remarks on Stylistic Variability and Distribution Patterns. In *South Asian Archaeology 1989*, edited by C. Jarrige, pp. 103–12. Prehistory Press, Madison.

2000. The Archaeology of Southeastern Balochistan. Internet publication with 121 photographs. http://www.harappa.com/baluch.

2005a. Excavations at Sohr Damb/Nal: Results of the 2002 and 2004 Seasons. In *South Asian Archaeology 2003*, edited by U. Franke-Vogt and H.-J. Weisshaar, pp. 62–76. Linden Soft, Aachen.

2005b. Balakot Period I: A Review of Its Stratigraphy, Cultural Sequence and Date. In *South Asian Archaeology 2001*, Vol. 1, edited by C. Jarrige and V. Lefevre, pp. 95–103. Editions Recherche sur Les Civilizations, Paris.

Frankfort, H. 1933. *Tell Asmar, Khafaje and Khorsabad: Second Preliminary Report of the Iraq Expedition.* Studies in Ancient Oriental Civilization No. 16. The Oriental Institute of the University of Chicago, Chicago.

1936. A New Site in Mesopotamia: Tell Agrab, Temples Deserted 5000 Years Ago and a Wealth of Art Relics, Including Fresh Proof of Indo-Sumerian Cultural Association. *Illustrated London News*, September 12, pp. 432–6.

Frenez D. and M. Tosi. 2005. The Lothal Sealings: Records from an Indus Civilization Port Town at the Eastern End of the Maritime Trade Network across the Arabian Sea. *Studi in onore di Enrica Fiandra, Contributi di Archeologia Egea e Vicinorientale*, edited by Massimo Pernaa, pp. 65–103. Diffusion de Boccard, Paris.

Fried, M. H. 1967. *The Evolution of Political Society.* Random House, New York.

Fuller, D. Q. 2002a. An Agricultural Perspective on Dravidian Historical Linguistics: Archaeological Crop Packages, Livestock and Dravidian Crop Vocabulary. In *Examining the Farming/Language Dispersal Hypothesis*, edited by P. Bellwood and C. Renfrew, pp. 191–213. McDonald Institute Monographs, Cambridge.

2002b. Fifty Years of Archaeobotanical Studies in India: Laying a Solid Foundation. In *Indian Archaeology in Retrospect, Vol. III. Archaeology and Interactive Disciplines*, edited by S. Settar and R. Korisettar, pp. 247–364. Indian Council of Historical Research, Manohar.

2003. Indus and Non-Indus Agricultural Traditions: Local Developments and Crop Adoptions on the Indian Peninsula. In *Indus Ethnobiology*, edited by S. Weber and W. R. Belcher, pp. 243–396. Lexington Books, Lanham.

Fuller, D. Q. and M. Madella. 2000. Issues in Harappan Archaeobotany: Retrospect and Prospect. In *Indian Archaeology in Retrospect, Vol. II, Protohistory, Publications of the Indian Council for Historical Research*, edited by S. Settar and R. Korisettar, pp. 391–408. Manohar, New Dehli.

Fuller, D., R. Korisetta, P. C. Venkatasubbaiah, and M. K. Jones. 2004. Early Plant Domestications in Southern India: Some Preliminary Archaeobotanical Results. *Veget Hist Archaeobot* 13: 115–29.

Gadd, C. J. and S. Smith. 1924. The New Links between India and Babylonian Civilizations. *Illustrated London News*, October 4, pp. 614–16.

Garfinkle, S. J. 2002. Turan-ili and the Community of Merchants in the Ur III Period. *Journal of Cuneiform Studies* 54: 29–48.

Gaur, R. C. 1983. *Excavations at Atranjikhera: Early Civilization of the Upper Ganga Basin.* Motilal Banarsidass and Center of Advanced Study, Department of History, Aligarh Muslim University, Delhi.

Gaur, R. C. ed. 1994. *Painted Grey Ware.* Publication Scheme, Jaipur.

Ghosh, A. 1952. The Rajputana Desert: Its Archaeological Aspect. *Bulletin of the National Institute of Sciences in India* 1: 37–42.

1953a. Exploration in Bikanir. *East and West* 4(1): 31–4.

1953b. Fifty Years of the Archaeological Survey of India. *Ancient India* 9: 29–52.

1962. The Archaeological Background. In *Human Skeletal Remains from Harappa*, edited by P. Gupta, P. C. Dutta, and A. Basu, pp. 1–5. *Memoirs of* the *Anthropological Survey of India no. 9*. Anthropological Survey of India, Calcutta.

1965. The Indus Civilization: Its Origins, Authors, Extent and Chronology. In *Indian Prehistory: 1964*, edited by V. N. Misra and M. S. Mate, pp. 113–24. Deccan College Postgraduate and Research Institute, Poona.

Gibson, M. 1977. An Indus Valley Stamp Seal from Nippur, Iraq. *Man and Environment* 1: 67.

Gimbutas, M. 1973. The Beginning of the Bronze Age in Europe and the Indo-Europeans: 3500- 2500 B.C. *The Journal of Indo-European Studies* 3: 163–214.

1999. *The Living Goddess*. University of California Press, Berkeley.

Gordon, D. H. *The Prehistoric Background of Indian Culture*. Bhulabhai Memorial Trust, Bombay.

Griffith, R. T. G., trans. 1896. *The Hymns of the Rigveda*, 2nd ed. 2 vols. 1987 reprint. Munshiram Manoharlal, Delhi.

Grigson, C. 1984. Some Thoughts on Unicorns and Other Cattle Depicted at Mohenjo-daro and Harappa. In *South Asian Archaeology 1981*, edited by B. Allchin, pp. 166–9. Cambridge University Press, Cambridge.

Guha, B. S. and P. C. Basu. 1938. Report on the Human Remains Excavated at Mohenjo-Daro in 1928–29. In *Further Excavations at Mohenjo-Daro*, edited by E. J. H. Mackay, pp. 613–38. Government of India, Delhi.

Gupta, P., P. C. Dutta, and P. C. Basu. 1962. *Human Skeletal Remains from Harappa. Memoirs of the Anthropological Survey of India no. 9*. Anthropological Survey of India, Calcutta.

Gupta, S. P. 1978. Origin of the Form of Harappa Culture: A New Proposition. *Puratattva* 8: 141–6.

ed. 1989. *An archaeological tour along the Ghaggar-Hakra River*. Kusumanjali Prakashan, Meerut, India.

Halim, M. A. and M. Vidale. 1984. Kilns, Bangles and Coated Vessels. Ceramic Production in Closed Containers at Mohenjo-daro. *In Interim Reports*, vol. 1, edited by M. Jansen and G. Urban, pp. 63–98. IsMEO-Aachen University Mission, Forschungsprojekt Mohenjo-Daro.

Hallo, W. W. 1996. Bilingualism and the Beginnings of Translation. In *Texts Temples and Traditions*, edited by M. V. Fox, V. A. Hurowitz, A. Hurvitz, M. L. Klein, B. J. Schwartz, and N. Shupak, pp. 345–57. Eisenbrauns, Winona Lake, IN.

Hargreaves, H. 1929. Excavations at Baluchistan in 1925, Sampur Mound, Mastung, and Sohr Damb Nal. In *Memioins of the Archaeological Survey of India*, no. 35. Antiquity Publications, Calcutta.

1931. HR Area. In *Mohenjo-daro and the Indus Civilization*, edited by J. Marshall. Arthur Probsthain, London.

Harvey M. and L. Flam. 1993. Prehistoric Soil and Water Retention Structures (Gabarbands), Sindh Kohistan, Pakistan: An adaptation to environmental change? *Geoarchaeology* 8(2): 1097–126.

1999. The Prehistoric Indus River System and the Indus Civilization in Sindh. Man and Environment XXIV (2): 35–62.

Heimpel, W. 1982. A First Step in the Diorite Question. *Revue d'Assyoiologie et Archéologie Orientale* 76(1): 65–67.

Helms, M. W. 1988. *Ulysses Sail*. Princeton University Press, Princeton.

1993. *Craft and the Kingly Idea: Art, Trade, and Power*. University of Texas Press, Austin.

Hemphil, B. E. In Press. A View to the North: Biological Interactions across the Intermontane Borderlands during the Last Two Millennia B.C. In *South Asian Archaeology 2007*, edited by M. Tosi and D. Frenez, BAR-Archaeopress, Oxford.

Hemphill, B. E. and A. F. Christensen. 1994. The Oxus Civilization as a Link between East and West: A Non-metric Analysis of Bronze Age Bactrian Biological Affinities. Paper presented at the South Asia Conference 1994, Madison, Wisconsin.

Hemphill, B. E., I. Ali, S. Blaylock, and S. Willits. In Press. Are the Kho an Indigenous Population of the Hindu Kush? A Dental Morphometric Approach. In *South Asian Archaeology 2007*, edited by M. Tosi and D. Frenez, BAR-Archaeopress, Oxford.

Hemphill, B. E., J. R. Lukacs, and K. A. R. Kennedy. 1991. Biological Adaptations and Affinities of Bronze Age Harappans. In *Harappan Excavations 1986–1990: A Multidisciplinary Approach to Third Millennium Urbanism*, edited by R. H. Meadow, pp. 137–82. Prehistory Press, Madison.

Hiebert, F. T. 1994a. Production Evidence for the Origins of the Oxus Civilization. *Antiquity* 68: 372–87.

1994b. *Origins of the Bronze Age Oasis Civilization in Central Asia*. Peabody Museum of Archaeology and Ethnology, American School of Prehistoric Research, Bulletin No. 42. Cambridge: Peabody Museum of Archaeology and Ethnology, Harvard University, Cambridge, Mass.

1995. South Asia from a Central Asian Perspective. In *The Indo-Aryans of Ancient South Asia: Language, Material Culture, and Ethnicity*, edited by George Erdosy, pp. 191–204. Walter de Gruyter, New York.

Hillman, G. 1984. Traditional Husbandry and Processing of Archaic Cereals in Modern Times: Part I, the Glume-Wheats, *Bulletin of Sumerian Agriculture*, Vol. I: 114–52.

Hiltebeitl, A. 1978. The Indus Valley "Proto-Siva," Reexamined Through Reflections of the Goddess, the Buffalo, and the Symbolism of Vahanas. *Anthropos* 73: 767–97.

Hodge, M. G. 1997. When Is a City-state? Archaeological Measures of Aztec City-states and Aztec City-state Systems. In D. L. Nichols and T. H. Charlton, eds. *The Archaeology of City-states: Cross-Cultural Approaches*, pp. 209–228. Smithsonian Institution Press, Washington, D.C.

Holmes, D. A. 1968. The Recent History of the Indus. *Geographic Journal* 134(3): 367–82.

Hooja, R. 1988. *The Ahar Culture*. BAR International Series 412. B.A.R. Company, Oxford.

1996. Expressing Ethnicity and Identity: Frontiers and Boundaries in Prehistory, *The Indian Journal of Social Work* 57(1): 91–114.

Houston, S. D. 2006. Impersonation, Dance, and the Problem of Spectacle among the Classic Maya. In *Archaeology of Performance: Theaters of Power, Community, and Politics*, edited by Takeshi Inomata and Lawrence S. Coben, pp. 135–55. Rowman Altamira Press, Walnut Creek.

Hunter, G. R. 1932. Mohenjo-Daro—Indus Epigraphy. *Journal of the Royal Asiatic Society of Great Britain and Ireland*, 64:466–503.

1934. *The Script of Harappa and Mohenjo-Daro and Its Connection with Other Scripts*. Kegan Paul, London.

Huntington, S. L. 1985. *The Art of Ancient India*. Weatherhill, New York.

Hussain, M. 1989. Salvage excavation at Moenjodaro. *Journal of the Pakistan Historical Society* 37(1): 89–98.

Inden, R. 1990. *Imagining India*. Blackwell, Basil.

Inomata, T. and L. S. Coben, eds. *Archaeology of Performance: Theatre of Power, Community, and Politics*. Rowman Altimira Press, Walnut Creek.

Jacobsen, T. 1976. *The Treasures of Darkness*. Yale University Press, New Haven.

Jansen, M. 1984. Preliminary results on the "forma urbis" research at Mohenjo-daro. In *Interim Reports*, Vol. 2, edited by M. Jansen and G. Urban, pp. 9–22.

1985. Mohenjo-daro, HR-A House I, a Temple? In *South Asia Archaoelogy 1983*: 157–206.

1986. *Die Indus Civilization: Widerentdeckung einer Fruhen Hochkultur*. DuMont Buchverlag, Kolm.

1989. Water Supply and Sewage Disposal at Mohenjo-daro. *World Archaeology* 21(2): 172–92.

1993a. Mohenjo-Daro: Type Site of the Earliest Urbanization Process in South Asia. In *Urban Form and Meaning in South Asia*, edited by H. Spodek and D. M. Srinivasan, pp. 33–51. Studies in the History of Art, 31. Center for Advanced Study in the Visual Arts Symposium Papers 15. National Gallery of Art, Washington, D.C.

1993b. *Mohenjo-daro: City of Wells and Drains, Water Splendour 4500 years ago*. Bergisch Gladbach Frontinus-Gesellschaft, Bonn.

Jansen, M. and G. Urban, eds. 1987. *Reports on Field Work Carried out at Mohenjo-Daro, Pakistan, 1983–1984*. Interim Reports, Vol. 2. IsMEO Aachen–University Mission, Aachen.

Jarrige, C. 1991. The Terracotta Figurines from Mehrgarh. In *Forgotten Cities of the Indus*, pp. 87–93. Verlag Philipp von Zabern: Mainz.

1992. *South Asian Archaeology 1989*. Prehistory Press, Madison.

2005. Human Figurines from the Neolithic Levels at Mehrgarh (Balochistan, Pakistan). In *South Asian Archaeology 2003* edited by U. Franke-Vogt and H-J Weisshaar, Aachen:Forschungen zur Archaeologie, Band 1: 27:38.

Jarrige, C., J.-F. Jarrige, R. H. Meadow, and G. Quivron. 1995. *Mehrgarh: Field Reports 1974–1985. From Neolithic Times to the Indus Civilization*. The Department of Culture and Tourism, Government of Sindh, Karachi.

Jarrige, J.-F. 1985. Continuity and Change in the North Kachi Plain (Baluchistan, Pakistan) at the Beginning of the Second Millennium B.C. In *South Asian Archaeology 1983*, edited by J. Schotsmans and M. Taddei, pp. 35–68. Rome.

1994. The Final Phase of the Indus Occupation at Nausharo and Its Connection with the Following Cultural Complex of Mehrgarh VIII. In *South Asian Archaeology 1993*, Vol. 1, edited by A. Parpola and P. Koski-kallio, pp. 295–313. Suomalainen Tiedeakatemia, Helsinki.

1995. Introduction. In *Mehrgarh Field Reports 1974–1985, from Neolithic Times to the Indus Civilization*, edited by C. Jarrige, J.-F. Jarrige, R. H. Meadow, and G. Quivron, pp. 1–95. The Department of Culture and Tourism, Government of Sindh, Karachi.

2000. Mehrgarh Neolithic: New Excavations. *South Asian Archaeology 1997*, edited by M. Taddei and G. De Marco, pp. 259–83. Rome.

Jarrige, J.-F. and M. U. Hassan. 1989. Funerary Complexes in Baluchistan at the End of the Third Millennium in the Light of Recent Discoveries at Mehrgarh and Quetta. In *South Asian Archaeology 1985*, Occasional Papers no. 4, edited by K. Frifelt and P. Sorensen, pp. 150–66. Scandinavian Institute of Asian Studies, Copenhagen.

Jarrige, J.-F. and Lechevallier, M. 1979. Excavations at Mehrgarh, Baluchistan: Their Significance in the Prehistorical Context of the Indo-Pakistani Borderlands. In *South Asian Archaeology 1977*, edited by M. Taddei, pp. 463–535. Istituto Universitario Orientale, Seminario di Studi Asiatici, Naples.

Jarrige, J.-F. and R. H. Meadow. 1980. The Antecedents of Civilization in the Indus Valley. *Scientific American* 243:122–33.

Jarrige, J.-F., C. Jarrige, and G. Quivron. 2005. Mehrgarh Neolithic: The Updated Sequence. In *South Asian Archaeology 2001, Vol. 1 Prehistory*, edited by C. Jarrige and V. Lefevre, pp. 128–141. Editions Recherce sur les Civilisations, Paris.

Jayaswal, V. 1989. Socio-Ritual Significance of Ancient Terracottas in the Gangetic Plains: The Ethnoarchaeological and Literary Evidence. In *Old Problems and New Perspectives in the Archaeology of South Asia*, edited by J. M. Kenoyer, pp. 253–62. University of Wisconsin, Madison.

Jorgensen, D. W., M. D. Harvey, S. A. Schumm, and L. Flam. 1993. Morphology and Dynamics of the Indus River: Implications for the Mohenjo-Daro Site. In *Himalayas to the Sea: Geology, Geomorphology and the Quaternary*, edited by J. F. Schroder, Jr., pp. 288–326. Routledge, New York.

Joshi, J. P. 1976. Excavations at Bhagwanpura. In *Mahabharata: Myth and Reality, Differing Views*, edited by S. P. Gupta and K. S. Ramachandran, pp. 238–9. Agam Prakashan, Delhi.

1977. *Overlap of Late Harappan Culture and Painted Grey Ware Culture in Light of Recent Excavations in Haryana, Punjab, and Jammu.* Paper presented at Seminar: Indus Civilization: Problems and Issues. Simla: Indian Institute of Advanced Study.

1978. A note on the excavations at Bhagwanpura. Puratattva 8:178–80.

1993. Excavation at Bhagwanpura 1975–76 and Other Explorations and Excavations 1975–81 in Haryana, Kashmir and Punjab. *Memoirs of the Archaeological Survey of India*, No. 89. Archaeological Survey of India, New Delhi.

Joshi, J. P. and M. Bala. 1982. Mandi: A Harappan Site in Jammu and Kashmir. In *Harappan Civilization: A Contemporary Perspective*, edited by G. L. Possehl, pp. 185–95. Oxford & IBH and the American Institute of Indian Studies, New Delhi.

Joshi, J. P. and A. Parpola 1987. *Corpus of Indus Seals and Inscriptions. Vol. 1. Collections in India.* Annales Academiae Scientiarum Fennicae, B239. Helsinki and Memoirs of the Archaeological Society of India, Calcutta and Delhi.

Joshi, J. P., M. Bala, and J. Ram, 1984. The Indus Civilization: A Reconsideration on the Basis of Distribution Maps. In *Frontiers of the Indus Civilization*, edited by B. B. Lal and S. P. Gupta, pp. 511–31. Books and Books, New Delhi.

Joshi, S. D. 1970. *History of Metal Founding on the Indian Sub-Continent Since Ancient Times (4000 B.C.–1970 A.D.)*. Sushila S. Joshi, Ranch.

Kaiser, T. and Voytek, B. 1983. Sedentism and Economic Change in the Balkan Neolithic. *Journal of Anthropological Research* 2: 323–53.

Kemp, Barry J. 1989. *Ancient Egypt. Anatomy of a Civilization*. Routledge. London.

Kennedy, K. A. 2000. *God-Apes and Fossil Men. Paleoanthropology in South Asia*. University of Michigan Press, Ann Arbor.

Kennedy, K. A. R. and P. C. Caldwell. 1984. South Asian Prehistoric Human Skeletal Remains and Burial Practices. In *The People of South Asia: The Biological Anthropology of India, Pakistan and Nepal*, edited by J. R. Lukacs, pp. 159–97. Plenum Press, New York.

Kenoyer, J. M. 1984a. Shell Working Industries of the Indus Civilization: A Summary. *Paleorient* 10: 49–63.

1984b. Chipped Stone Tools from Mohenjo-daro. In *Frontiers of the Indus Civilization*, edited by B. B. Lal and S. P. Gupta, pp. 118–131. Books and Books, New Delhi.

1989. Socio-Economic Structures of the Indus Civilization as Reflected in Specialized Crafts and the Question of Ritual Segregation. In *Old Problems and New Perspectives in the Archaeology of South Asia*, edited by J. M. Kenoyer, pp. 183–92. University of Wisconsin, Madison.

1991. The Indus Valley Tradition of Pakistan and Western India. *Journal of World Prehistory* 5(4):331–85.

1992. Harappan Craft Specialization and the Question of Urban Segregation and Stratification. *Eastern Anthropologist*. Indus Civilization Special Number 45(1–2):39–54.

1993. Lithic Studies. In *Harappan Civilization: A Recent Perspective*, 2d ed., edited by Gregory L. Possehl, p. 512. Oxford & IHH and the American Institute of Indian Studies, Delhi.

1995a. Shell Trade and Shell Working during the Neolithic and early Chalcolithic at Mehrgarh, Pakistan. In *Mehrgarh: Field Reports 1974–1985 from Neolithic Times to the Indus Civilization*, edited by C. Jarrige et al., pp. 566–82. The Department of Culture and Tourism, Government of Sindh, Karachi.

1995b. Interaction Systems, Specialized Crafts and Culture Change: The Indus Valley Tradition and the Indo-Gangetic Tradition in South Asia. In *The Indo-Aryans of Ancient South Asia: Language, Material Culture, and Ethnicity*, edited by G. Erdosy, pp. 213–57. De Gruyter, Berlin.

1997a. Early City-states in South Asia. In *The Archaeology of City-states: Cross-Cultural Approaches*, edited by D. L. Nichols and T. H. Charlton, pp. 51–70. Smithsonian Institution, Washington, DC.

1997b. Trade and Technology of the Indus Valley: New Insights from Harappa, Pakistan. *World Archaeology* 29(2): 262–80.

1998. *Ancient Cities of the Indus Valley Civilization*. Oxford University Press, Oxford.

2004. Die Karren der Induskulture Pakistans und Indians. In *Rad und Wagen: Der Urspringe Einer Innovation Wagen in Verderen Orient and Europa*, edited by M. Fansa and S. Burmeister, pp. 87–106. Verlagg Philipp van Zabern, Mainz an Rhein.

Kenoyer, J.M. and R.H. Meadow. 2000. The Ravi Phase: A New Cultural Manifestation at Harappa, Pakistan. In *South Asian Archaeology 1997*, edited by M. Taddei and G. De Marco. pp. 55–76. Istituto Italiano per l'Africa e l'Oriente and Istituto Universitario Orientale, Roma.

Kenoyer, J.M. and H.M.-L. Miller. 1999. Metal Technologies of the Indus Valley Tradition in Pakistan and Western India. In *The Archaeometallurgy of the Asian Old World*, edited by V.C. Pigott, pp. 107–51. University Museum Monograph No. 89, MASCA Research Papers in Science and Archaeology, vol. 16. University Museum, University of Pennsylvania, Philadelphia.

Kenoyer, J.M., M. Vidale, and K.K. Bhan. 1991. Contemporary Stone Bead Making in Khambhat, India: Patterns of Craft Specialization and Organization of Production as Reflected in the Archaeological Record. *World Archaeology* 23(1): 44–63.

1994. Carnelian Bead Production in Khambhat, India: An Ethnoarchaeological Study. In *Living Traditions. Studies in the Ethnoarchaeology of South Asia*, edited by B. Allchin. Oxford Books, Oxford

Khan, F.A. 1965. Excavations at Kot Diji. *Pakistan Archaeology* 2:11–85.

Khatri, J.S. 2000. Excavations at Kunal District, Hissar. In *Indian Archaeology 1993–4: A Review*, pp. 47–50. Archaeological Survey of India.

Khatri, J.S. and M. Acharya. 1994. Kunal: A New Indus–Sarasvati Site. *Puratattva* 25: 84–6.

Khazanov, A.M. 1984. *Nomads and the Outside World*. Cambridge Studies in Social Anthropology. Cambridge University Press, Cambridge.

Klostermaier, K.K. 1994. *A Survey of Hinduism*. 2nd ed. State University of New York Press, Albany.

Kohl, P.L. 1978. Archaeological Reconnaissances in Eastern Afghanistan, 1975–1976. *Estratto da ANNALI dell'Istituto Orientale di Napoli*, vol. 38 (N.S.XXVIII): 64–74.

1979. The "World Economy" of West Asia in the Third Millennium B.C. In *South Asia Archaeology 1977*, edited by M. Taddei, pp. 55–85. Istituto Universitario Orientale, Naples.

2007. *The Making of Bronze Age Eurasia*. Cambridge University Press, Cambridge.

Kohl, P.L. and C. Fawcett. 1995. Archaeology in the Service of the State: Theoretical Considerations. In *Nationalism, Politics and the Practice of Archaeology*, edited by P.L. Kohl and C. Fawcett, pp. 3–18. Cambridge University Press, Cambridge.

Koller, J.M. 2006. *The Indian Way*. Pearson/Prentice Hall, Upper Saddle River, NJ.

Kosambi, D.D. 1963. The Beginnings of the Iron Age in India. *Journal of the Economic and Social History of the Orient* 6: 309–18.

Koskenniemi, K. and A. Parpola. 1982. *A Concordance to the Texts in the Indus Script*. Research Reports No. 3. Department of Asian and African Studies, University of Helsinki, Helsinki.

Koskenniemi, S., A. Parpola, and S. Parpola. 1973. *Materials for the Study of the Indus Script, Vol. I: A Concordance to the Indus Inscriptions.* Acta Academiae Scientarium Fennicae, Helsinki.

Kramer, S. N. 1963. *The Sumerians: Their History, Culture and Character.* University of Chicago Press, Chicago.

Kramer, S. N. and J. Maier. 1989. *Myths of Enki, the Crafty God.* Oxford University Press, New York.

Krishnamurthy, R. V. M., J. Deniro, and R. K. Pant. 1982. Isotope Evidence for Pleistocene Climatic Change in Kashmir, India. *Nature* 298(5875): 640–1.

Kutzbach, J. E. and COHMAP Members. 1988. Climatic Changes of the Last 18,000 Years: Observations and Model Simulations. *Science* 241 (August): 1043–52.

Laghari, M. H. 1996. Gharo Bhiro: An Archaeological and Environmental Analysis of the Site. *Ancient Sindh* 3:117–24.

Lahiri, N., ed. 2000. *The Decline and Fall of the Indus Civilization.* Permanent Black, Delhi.

2005. *Finding Forgotten Cities: How the Indus Civilization Was Discovered.* Permanent Black, Delhi.

Lal, B. B. 1954–5. Excavations at Hastinapura and Other Explorations in the Upper Ganges and Sutlej Basins. *Ancient India* 10: 115–155.

1968. Iron Tools, Forest Clearance and Urbanization in the Gangetic Plains. 1968. *Man and Environment* X: 83–90.

1970–1. Perhaps the Earliest Ploughed Field so far Excavated Anywhere in the World. *Puratattva* 4: 1–3.

1979. Kalibangan and Indus Civilization. In *Essays in Indian Protohistory*, edited by D. P. Agrawal and D. Chakrabarti, pp. 65–97. B. R. Publishing Corporation, Delhi.

1981. Some Reflections on the Structural Remains at Kalibangan. In *Indus Civilization: New Perspectives*, edited by A. H. Dani, pp. 47–54. Quaid-i-Azam University, Islamabad.

1989. Faience. In *An Encyclopedia of Indian archaeology*, Vol. I, edited by A. Ghosh, p. 321. Munshiram Manoharlal, Delhi.

1992. Antecedents of the Signs Used in the Indus Script: A Discussion. In *South Asian Archaeology Studies*, edited by G. L. Possehl, pp. 54–6. Oxford & IBH, Delhi.

Lal, M. 1984a. *Settlement History and the Rise of Civilization in the Ganga-Yamuna Doab.* B. R. Pub. Corp., New Delhi.

1984b. Summary of Four Seasons of Explorations in Kanput District, Uttar Pradesh. *Man and Environment* 8: 61–80.

1986. Iron Tools, Forest Clearance and Urbanisation in the Gangetic Plains. *Man and Environment* 10: 83–90.

1987–8. Iron at Ahar: A Comment. *Puratattva* 18:109–12.

1997. *The Earliest Civilization of South Asia.* Aryan Books International, New Delhi.

Lamberg-Karlovsky, C. C. 1986a. Death in Dilmun. In *Bahrain through the Ages, the Archaeology*, edited by S. H. A. A. Khalifa and M. Rice, pp. 157–64. KPI Limited, New York.

1986b. Third Millennium Structure and Process: From the Euphrates to the Indus and the Oxus to the Indian Ocean. *Orients Antiquus* XXV: 189–219.

1988. Indo-Europeans: a Near-Eastern perspective. *Quarterly Review of Archaeology* 9(1): 8–10.

1989. Introduction. In *Archaeological Thought in America*, edited by C. C. Lamberg-Karlovsky. Cambridge University Press, Cambridge.

1994. Foreword. Initiating an Archaeological Dialogue: The USA-USSR Archaeological Exchange. In *Origins of the Bronze Age Oasis Civilization in Central Asia*, American School of Prehistoric Research, Bulletin 42, pp. XVII–XXX. Peabody Museum of Archaeology and Ethnology, Harvard University, Cambridge, MA.

Lambrick, H. T. 1964. Sind: A General Introduction. *History of Sind series*, Vol. 1. Sindhi Adabi Board, Hyderabad, Pakistan.

Langdon, S. H. 1931a. The Indus script. In *Mohenjo-daro and the Indus Civilization*, edited by J. Marshall, pp. 423–55. 3 vols. Arthur Probsthain, London.

Law, Randall. 2005. Regional Interaction in the Prehistoric Indus Valley: Initial Results of Rock and Mineral Sourcing Studies at Harappa. In *South Asian Archaeology 2001*, Vol. 1, edited by C. Jarrige and V. Lefevrre, pp. 179–90. CNRS, Paris.

2008. *Interregional Interaction and Urbanism in the Ancient Indus Valley: A Geologic Provenance Study of Harappa's Rock and Mineral Assemblage*. PhD Diss. University of Wisconsin, Madison.

Lemonnier, P. 1992. *Elements for an Anthropology of Technology*. University of Michigan Museum of Anthropology, Ann Arbor.

Leshnik, L. S. 1968. Prehistoric Explorations in North Gujarat and Parts of Rajasthan. *East and West* 18(3–4): 295–310.

Littlefield, A., L. Lieberman, and L. T. Reynolds 1982. Redefining Race: The Potential Demise of a Concept in Physical Anthropology. *Current Anthropology* 23: 641–55.

Livingstone, F. B. 1964. On the Nonexistence of Human Races. In *The Concept of Race*, edited by A. Mongatu, pp. 46–60. Free Press, New York.

Loftus, R. T., D. E. MacHugh, D. G. Bradley and P. M. Sharp. 1994. Evidence for Two Independent Domestications of Cattle. *Proceedings of the National Academy of Science* (USA) 91: 2757–61.

Lovell, N. C. 1997. Anemia in the Ancient Indus Valley. *International Journal of Osteoarchaeology* 7: 115–23.

1994. Spinal Arthritis and Physical Stress at Bronze Age Harappa. *American Journal of Physical Anthropology* 93:149–54.

Lukacs, J. R. 2002. Hunting and Gathering Strategies in Prehistoric India: A Biocultural Perspective on Trade and Subsistence. In *Forager-Traders in South and Southeast Asia*, edited by K. D. Morrison and L. L. Junker, pp. 41–61. Cambridge University Press, Cambridge.

Lukacs, J. R. and J. P. Joshi 1992. Enamel Hypoplasia Prevalence in Three Ethnic Groups of Northwest India: A Test of Daughter Neglect and a Framework for the Past. *Journal of Paleo-Pathology Monographic Publications*, no. 2. 359–72.

Lukacs, J.R. and S.R. Walimbe. 1986. *Excavations at Inamgaon: The Physical Anthropology of Human Skeletal Remains*. Vol. 2, Part 1: An Osteobiographic Analysis. Deccan College, Pune.

1998. Physiological Stress in Prehistoric India: New Data on Localized Hypoplasia of Primary Canines Linked to Climate and Subsistence Change. *Journal of Archaeological Science* 25: 571–85.

Lycett, M. 1995. Non-architectural Sites of the Vijayanagara Metropolitan Region: Searching for Patterns in Ambiguous Categories. In *South Asian Archaeology 1993*, Vol. 271, edited by A. Parpola and P. Koskikallio, pp. 413–24. Academiae Scientarium Fennica, Helsinki.

Lynch, Kevin, 1961. *The Image of the City*. MIT Press, Cambridge.

1981. *A Theory of a Good City*. MIT Press, Cambridge.

1984. *Good City Form*. MIT Press, Cambridge.

Mackay, D. 1945. Ancient River Beds and Dead Cities. *Antiquity* 19: 35–44.

Mackay, E.J.H. 1931. DK Area. In *Mohenjo-daro and the Indus Civilization*, 3 vols., edited by Sir John Marshall, pp. 233–61. Arthur Probsthain.

1933. An Important Link Between Ancient India and Elam. *Antiquity* 6: 356–7. London.

1938. *Further Excavations at Mohenjo-Daro, Being an Official Account of Archaeology Excavations Carried Out by the Government of India between the Years of 1927 and 1931*, Vols. I and II. Government Press, New Delhi.

1943. *Chanhu-daro excavations, 1935–1936*. American Oriental Society, New Haven.

Madella, M. 2003. Investigating Agriculture and Environment in South Asia: Present and Future Contributions of Opal Phytoliths. In *Indus Ethnobiology*. edited by S. Weber and W.R. Belcher, pp. 199–250. Lexington Books, Lanham.

Madella, M. and D.Q. Fuller. 2006. Paleoecology and the Harappan Civilisation of South Asia: A Reconsideration. *Quaternary Science Reviews* 25(11–12): 1283–1301.

Majumdar, N.G. 1934. *Explorations in Sind. Memoirs of the Archaeological Survey of India No. 48*. Archaeological Survey of India, New Delhi.

Malik, S.C. 1968. Indian Civilization: The Formative Period. *A Study of Archaeology as Anthropology*. Indian Institute of Advanced Study, Simla.

1973. The Role of Theory in the Study of Archaeology in India. *Puratattva* 6: 1–11.

1975. *Understanding Indian Civilization: A Framework of Inquiry*. Indian Institute of Advanced Study, Simla.

1979. Changing Perspectives of Archaeology and Interpreting Harappan Society. In Essays in Indian Protohistory, edited by D.P. Agrawal and D.K. Chakrabarti, pp. 187–204. B.R. Publishing Corporation, Delhi.

Mandal, D. 1993. *Ayodhya: Archaeology After Demolition*. Orient Longman, New Delhi.

Marshall, J. 1924. First Light on a Long-Forgotten Civilization: New Discoveries of an Unknown Prehistoric Past in India. *Illustrated London News*, September 20, pp. 428–32 and 548 ff.

1931. *Mohenjo-Daro and the Indus Civilization, Being an Official Account of Archaeological Excavations at Mohenjo-Daro Carried Out by the Government of India Between the Years 1922 and 1927.* 3 vols. Arthur Probsthain, London.

Masson, C. 1842. *Narrative of Various Journeys in Balochistan, Afghanistan and the Punjab,* 3 vols. Oxford University Press, Karachi.

Masson, V. M. 1988. *Altyn Depe,* University Museum Monograph 55, translated by Henry Michael. University of Pennsylvania Museum, Philadelphia.

Masson, V. M. and V. I. Sarianidi 1972. *Central Asia: Turkmenia before the Achaemenids.* Praeger, New York.

Maula, Erikka. 1984. The Calendar Stones from Mohenjo-daro. In *Interim Reports vol. 1. Reports on Field Work Carried Out at Mohenjo-daro, Pakistan, 1982–83,* edited by M. Jansen and G. Urban, pp. 159–70. IsMEO-Aachen-University Mission, Aachen.

McAlpin, D. W. 1975. Elamite and Dravidian: Further Evidence of Relationship. *Current Anthropology* 16: 93–104.

1981. Proto-Elamo-Dravidian: The Evidence and Its Implications. *Transactions of the American Philosophical Society* 71(3): 3–155.

McGaw, Judith. 1996. Reconceiving Technology: Why Feminine Technologies Matter. In *Gender and Archaeology,* edited by R. Wright, pp. 52–78. University of Pennsylvania Press, Philadelphia.

McIntosh, R. J. 2005. *Ancient Middle Niger. Urbanism and the Self-Organizing Landscape.* Cambridge University Press, Cambridge.

McKean, M. B. 1983. *The Palynology of Balakot, a Pre-Harappan and Harappan Age Site in Last Bela, Pakistan.* Ph.D. Dissertation. Southern Methodist University, Dallas, University Microfilms, Ann Arbor.

Meadow, R. H. 1984. Notes on the Faunal Remains from Mehrgarh, Pakistan with a Focus on Cattle (Bos). In *South Asian Archaeology 1981,* edited by B. Allchin, pp. 34–40. Cambridge University Press, Cambridge.

1987. Faunal Exploitation Patterns in Eastern Iran and Baluchistan. In *Orientalia Josephi Tucci Memoriae Dicata,* edited by G. Gnoli and L. Lanciotti, pp. 881–916. Istituto Italiano peril Medio ed Estremo Oriente, Rome.

1989a. Prehistoric Wild Sheep and Sheep Domestication on the Eastern Margin of the Middle East. In *Animal Domestication and its Cultural Context,* edited by P. J. Crabtree, D. V. Campana, and K. Ryan, pp. 24–36. University Museum, University of Pennsylvania, Philadelphia.

1989b. Osteological Evidence for the Process of Animal Domestication. In *The Walking Larder: Patterns of Domestication, Pastoralism, and Predation,* edited by J. Clutton-Brock, pp. 80–90. Unwin Hyman, London.

1993. Animal Domestication in the Middle East: A Revised View from the Eastern Margin. In *Harappan Civilization,* 2nd ed., edited by G. L. Possehl, pp. 295–320. Oxford and IBH, New Delhi.

1996. The Origins and Spread of Agriculture and Pastoralism in Northwestern South Asia. In *The Origins and Spread of Agriculture and Pastoralism in Eurasia,* edited by D. R. Harris, pp. 390–412. Smithsonian Institution Press, Washington, D.C.

1998. Pre- and Proto-Historic Agricultural and Pastoral Transformations in Northwestern and South Asia, *The Review of Archaeology* 19(2): 12–21.

Meadow, R. H. and J. M. Kenoyer. 2000. The "Tiny" Steatite Seals (Incised Steatite Tablets) of Harappa: Some Observations on Their Context and Dating. In *South Asian Archaeology 1971*, edited by M. Taddei and G. De Marco, pp. 321–40. Istituto Italiano per I 'Africa E' L'Oriente, Rome.

Meadow, R. H. and A. Patel. 1997. A Comment on "Horse Remains from the Prehistoric Site of Surkotada, Kutch, Late 3rd Millennium B.C." by Sandor Bokonyi. *South Asian Studies* 13: 308–15.

2003. Prehistoric Pastoralism in Northwestern South Asia from the Neolithic through the Harappan Period. In *Indus Ethnobiology*, edited by S. Weber and W. R. Belcher, pp. 65–94. Lexington Books, Lanham.

Meadow, R. H., J. M. Kenoyer, and R. P. Wright. 1996. *Harappa Archaeological Research Project.* Harappa Excavations 1996. Report Submitted to the Department of Archaeology, Government of Pakistan.

2001. *Harappa Archaeological Research Project.* Harappa Excavations 2000 and 2001. Report Submitted to the Department of Archaeology, Government of Pakistan.

Mehta, R. N. 1995. Indigenous Perceptions of the Past. *Man and Environment* XX(1): 1–5.

Mehta, R. N., K. N. Momin, and D. R. Shah. 1980. *Excavation at Kanewal.* Archaeology Series, no. 17. Maharaja Sayajirao University, Baroda.

Mery, S. 1994. Ceramics and Patterns of Exchange across the Arabian Sea and the Persian Gulf in the Early Bronze Age. In *The Prehistory of Asia and Oceania*, edited by G. Afanas'ev, S. Cleuziou, R. Lukacs, and M. Tosi, pp. 167–79. XIII International Congress of Prehistoric and Protohistoric Sciences, Flori, Colloquium 16, Abaco, Forli.

2000. *Les Ceramiques d'Oman et l'Asie Moyenne: Une archeologii des exchanges à l'Age du Bronze.* CRA Monographies 23. CNRS Editions, Paris.

Mery, S. and M. James Blackman 2005. Socio-economical Patterns of a Ceramic Container: The Harappan Black Slipped Jar. In *South Asian Archaeology 2001*, Vol. 1, edited by C. Jarrige and V. Lefevre, pp. 227–35. Editions recherché sur les civilizations, Paris.

Miller, D. 1985. Ideology and the Harappan Civilization. *Journal of Anthropological Archaeology* 4: 34–71.

Miller, Heather M.-L. 1994. Metal Processing at Harappa and Mohenjo-Daro: Information from Non-Metal Remains. In *South Asian Archaeology 1993*, Vol. II, edited by A. Parpola and P. Koskikallio. Helsinki.

1997. Pottery Firing Structures (Kilns) of the Indus Civilization during the Third Millennium B.C. In *Prehistory and History of Ceramic Kilns*, edited by P. M. Rice and D. W. Kingery, Ceramics and Civilization, Vol. VII, pp. 41–71. American Ceramic Society, Columbus, OH.

1999a. The Indus Talc-Faience Complex: Types of Materials, Clues to Production. In *South Asian Archaeology 1999*, edited by K. R. van Kooij and E. M. Raven, eds. Mackay, Leiden.

1999b. *Pyrotechnology and Society in the Cities of the Indus Valley.* PhD diss. University of Wisconsin, Madison. Ann Arbor: University Microfilms.

2005. Investigating Copper Production at Harappa: Surveys, Excavations, and Finds. In *South Asian Archaeology 2005*, pp. 245–52.

2007. *Archaeological Approaches to Technology*. Academic Press, Elsevier, Burlington, MA.

2008. Issues in the Determination of Ancient Value Systems: The Role of Talc (Steatite) and Faience in the Indus Civilization. In *Intercultural Relations Between South and Southwest Asia. Studies in Commemoration of E.C.L During Caspers (1934–1996)*, edited by E. Olijdam and R. H. Spoor. BAR International Series, Archaeopress, Oxford.

Miller, Heidi. 2005. A New Interpretation of the Stratigraphy at Chanhudaro. In *South Asian Archaeology 2001*, edited by C. Jarrige and V. Lefevre, pp. 253–6. Editions Recherché Sur les Civilizations, Paris.

Miller, Laura J. 2003. Secondary Products and Urbanism in South Asia: The Evidence for Traction at Harappa. In *Indus Ethnobiology*, edited by S. Weber and W. R. Belcher, pp. 251–326.

2004. Urban Economies in Early States: The Secondary Products Revolution in the Indus Civilization. PhD diss. New York University.

Miller, N. and W. Wetterstrom. 2000. The Beginnings of Agriculture: The Ancient Near East and North Africa. In *The Cambridge World History of Food*, edited by K. F. Kiple and K. C. Ornelas, Vol. 2: pp. 1123–39, Cambridge University Press.

Misra, V. N. 1984. Climate, a Factor in the Rise and Fall of the Indus Civilization – Evidence from Rajasthan and Beyond. In *Frontiers of the Indus Civilization*, edited by B. B. Lal and S. P. Gupta, pp. 461–89. Books and Books, Delhi.

Misra, V. N. and Rajaguru. 1989. Paleoenvironment and Prehistory of the Thar Desert. Rajasthan, India. In *South Asian Archaeology 1985*, edited by K. Frifelt and P. Sorenson, pp. 296–320. Curzon Press, London.

Mockler, E., Major. 1877. On Ruins in Makran. *Journal of the Royal Asiatic Society of Great Britain and Ireland* 9: 121–34.

Moore, H. 1990. *Feminism and Anthropology*. University of Minnesota Press, Minneapolis.

Morris, I. An Archaeology of Equalities? The Greek City-States. In *The Archaeology of City States*, edited by D. L. Nichols and T. H. Charlton, pp. 91–106. Smithsonian Institution Press, Washington, DC.

Morrison, K. D. 1994. The Intensification of Production: Archaeological Approaches. *Journal of Archaeological Method and Theory* 1(2): 111–59.

1996. Typological Schemes and Agricultural Change: Beyond Boserup in Precolonial South India. *Current Anthropology* 37(4): 583–608.

2002a. Introduction. In *Forager-Traders in South and Southeast Asia*, edited by K. D. Morrison and L. L. Junker, pp. 21–40. Cambridge University Press, Cambridge.

2002b. Pepper in the Hills: Upland-Lowland Exchange and the Intensification of the Spice Trade. In *Forager-Traders in South and Southeast Asia*, edited by K. D. Morrison and L. L. Junker, pp. 105–130. Cambridge University Press, Cambridge.

2006. Historicizing Foraging in South Asia: Power, History, and Ecology of Holocene Hunting and Gathering. In *Archaeology of Asia*, edited by Miriam T. Stark, pp. 279–302. Blackwell Publishing, Oxford.

2008. Daroji Valley: Landscape History, Place, and the Making of a Dryland Reservoir System. *Vijayanagara Research Project Monograph Series 18*. Manohar Press, Delhi.

Morrison, K. D. and L. L. Junker, eds. 2002. *Forager-Traders in South and Southeast Asia*. Cambridge University Press, Cambridge.

Morrison, K. D. and M. T. Lycett. 1997. Inscriptions as Artifacts: Precolonial South India and the Analysis of Texts. *Journal of Archaeological Method and Theory 4(3/4)*: 215–37.

Mughal, M. R. 1970. *The Early Harappan period in the Greater Indus Valley and Baluchistan*. PhD. Diss. Department of Anthropology, University of Pennsylvania, Philadelphia.

1972. Excavation at Jalilpur. *Pakistan Archaeology* 8:117–24.

1981. New Archaeological Evidence from Bahawalpur. In *Indus Civilization: A New Perspective*, edited by A. H. Dani, 33–41. Center for the Study of the Civilizations of Central Asia, Quaid-e-Azam University, Islamabad.

1982. Recent Archaeological Research in the Cholistan Desert. In *Harappan Civilization: A Contemporary Perspective*, edited by G. L. Possehl. Oxford & IBH and the American Institute of Indian Studies, Delhi.

1990. The Harappan Settlement Systems and Patterns in the Greater Indus Valley (circa 3500–1500 B.C.). *Pakistan Archaeology* 25: 1–72.

1992a. Jhukar and the Late Harappan Cultural Mosaic of the Greater Indus Valley. In *South Asian Archaeology 1989*, edited by C. Jarrige, pp. 213–276. Prehistory Press, Madison.

1992b. The Consequences of River Changes for the Harappan Settlements in Cholistan. *The Eastern Anthropologist* 45: 105–16.

1994. Ancient Cities of the Indus. *Lahore Museum Bulletin* VII: 53–7.

1997. *Ancient Cholistan: Archaeology and Architecture*. Ferozsons (Pvt.) Ltd., Lahore.

2001. Resurrecting Sir Aurel Stein from the Cholistan Desert. *Context* 15(2): 1–4.

2005. Sir Aurel Stein's Papers on the Survey of the Ghaggar-Hakra River, 1940–1942. In *South Asian Archaeology 2001*, Vol. 1, edited by C. Jarrige and V. Lefevre, pp. 263–7. Editions Recherché sur les Civilizations, Paris.

Mughal, M. R., G. M. Khan, F. Iqbal, M. Hassan, and M. Afzal Khan. 1997. Archaeological Sites and Monuments in Punjab. Preliminary Results of Explorations: 1992–6. *AM Survey Report*.

Nath, A. 1998. Rakhigarhi: A Harappan Metropolis in the Sarasvati-Drishadvati Divide. *Puratattva* 28: 39–45.

1999. Further Excavations at Rakhigarhi. *Puratattva* 29: 46–9.

Negrino, F., C. Ottomano, E. Starnini, and G. M. Veesar. 1996. Excavations at Site 862 (Rohri Hills, Sind, Pakistan): A Preliminary Report of the 1995 and 1997 Campaigns. *Ancient Sindh* 3: 67–104.

Nichols, D. L. and T. H. Charlton, eds. 1997. *The Archaeology of City-States: Cross-cultural Approaches*. Smithsonian Institution Press, Washington, D.C.

O'Flaherty, W.D. 1978. The Clash between Relative and Absolute Duty: The Dharma of Demons. In *The Concept of Duty in South Asia*, edited by W.D. O'Flaherty, J. Duncan and M. Derrett, pp. 96–106. South Asia Books, Vikas Publication House, Delhi.

Paddayya, K. 1978–9. Palaeoethnography vis-á-vis the Stone Age Cultures of India: Some Methodological Considerations. *Bulletin of Deccan College Research Institute* 38: 63–90.

    1995. Theoretical Perspectives in Indian Archaeology. In *Theory in Archaeology: A World Perspective*, edited by P.J. Ucko, pp. 110–49. Routledge, London.

Pande, B.M. and B.D. Chattopadhyaya. 1987. *Archaeology and History*. RAJ Press, New Delhi.

Panja. S. 1996. Strategies, Site Structure and Settlement Organization: An Actualistic Perspective. *Man and Environment* XXI(1): 58–73.

Parpola, Asko. 1986. The Indus Script. A Challenging Puzzle. *World Archaeology. Early Writing Systems*: 399–419.

    1994. *Deciphering the Indus Script*. Cambridge University Press, Cambridge.

    2000. *Deciphering the Indus Script: Basic Methodology and Some Sample Interpretations*, pp. 1–16. Indian Archaeological Society, Tokyo.

    2005. Administrative Contact and Acculturation between Harappans and Bactrians: Evidence of Sealings and Seals. In *South Asian Archaeology 2001*, edited by C. Jarrige and V. Lefevre, pp. 267–74. Editions Recherce sur les Civilizations, Paris.

Parpola, A., S. Koskenniemi, S. Parpola, and P. Aalto. 1969. *Decipherment of the Proto-Dravidian Inscriptions of the Indus Civilization: A First Announcement*. Special Publications, No. 1. Scandinavian Institute of Asian Studies, Copenhagen.

Parpola, S., A. Parpola, and R.H. Brunswig, Jr. 1977. The Meluhha Village: Evidence of Acculturation of Harappan Traders in Late Third Millennium Mesopotamia? JESHO 20(2): 129–65.

Patel, A. 1997. The Pastoral Economy of Dholavira: A First Look at Animals and Urban life in Third Millennnium Kutch. In *South Asian Archaeology 1995*, Vol. 1, edited by R. Allchin and B. Allchin, pp. 101–13. The Ancient India and Iran Trust, Cambridge.

Pedde, F. 1993. Pottery from Northern Baluchistan–the Noetling Collection in the Museum of Indian Art, Berlin. In *South Asian Archaeology 1991*, edited by A.J. Gail and G.J.R. Mevissen, pp. 215–30. Franz Steiner Verlag, Stuttgart.

Pendall, E. and R. Amundson. 1990. The stable isotope chemistry of pedogenic carbonate in an alluvial soil from the Punjab, Pakistan. *Soil Science* 149: 199–211.

Pfaffenberger, B. 1992. Social Anthropology of Technology. *Annual Review of Anthropology* 21: 491–516.

Phadtre, N.R. 2000. Sharp Decrease in Summer Monsoon Strength 4000–3500 ca. yr. B.P. In the Central Higher Himalaya of India Based on Pollen Evidence from Alpine Peat. *Quaternary Research* 53: 122–9.

Piggott, S. 1950. *Prehistoric India to 1000 B.C.* Penguin Books, Baltimore.

Pittman, H. 1984. *The Art of the Bronze Age: Southeastern Iran, Western Central Asia, and the Indus Valley.* The Metropolitan Museum of Art, New York.

1994a. *The Glazed Steatite Glyptic Style: The Structure and Function of an Image System.* Berlinger Beitrage zum Vorderen Orient Vol. 16. Dietrich Reimer Verlag, Berlin.

1994b. Towards an Understanding of the Role of Glyptic Imagery in the Administrative Systems of Proto-Literate Greater Mesopotamia. In *Archives before Writing*, edited by P. Ferioli, E. Fiandra, G. G. Fissori, and M. Frangipane. Minstero per I beni culturali e ambientali, Turin.

1997. The Administrative Function of Glyptic Art in Proto-Elamite Iran. *Res Orientales* 10:133–53.

2001. Glyptic Art of Period IV. In *Excavations at Tepe Yahya, Iran 1967–1975*, edited by D. Potts, 231–68. Peabody Museum of Archaeology and Ethnology.

2002a. The "Jeweler's" Seal from Susa and the Art of Awan. In *Leaving No Stones Unturned: Essays on the ANE and Egypt in Honor of Donald P. Hansen*, edited by E. Ehrenberg, pp. 209–34. Eisenbrauns, Winona Lake, IN.

Poliakov, L. 1974. *The Aryan Myth.* Basic Books, New York.

Pollock, S. 1999. *Ancient Mesopotamia.* Cambridge University Press, Cambridge.

Popenoe, Paul. 1973. The Date Palm. Field Research Projects, Coconut Grove FL.

Possehl, G. 1976. Lothal: A Gateway Settlement of the Harappan Civilization. In *Ecological Backgrounds of South Asian Prehistory*, edited by K. A. R. Kennedy and G. L. Possehl, pp. 118–31. Occasional Papers and Theses, No. 4 Cornell University South Asia Program, Ithaca, NY.

1979. Pastoral Nomadism in the Indus Civilization: A Hypothesis. In *South Asian Archaeology 1977*, edited by M. Taddei, pp. 537–51. Series Minor 6. Istituto Universitario Orientale, Seminario di Studi Asiatici, Naples.

1980. *Indus Civilization in Saurashtra.* B. R. Publishing Corporation, Delhi.

1990. Revolution in the Urban Revolution: The Emergence of Indus Urbanization. *Annual Review of Anthropology* 19: 261–82.

1991. The Harappan Civilization in Gujarat: The Sorath and Sindhi Harappans. *Eastern Anthropologist*, 45(1–2): 117–54.

1996a. *Indus Age: The Writing System.* University of Pennsylvania Press, Philadelphia.

1996b. Meluhha. In *The Indian Ocean in Antiquity*, edited by Julian Reade. Kegan Paul International Association with the British Museum, London.

1997. Seafaring Merchants of Meluhha. *South Asian Archaeology* 1995, edited by R. and B. Allchin. Oxford and IBH, Delhi, pp. 87–100.

1998. *Indus Age: The Beginnings.* University of Pennsylvania Press, Philadelphia.

2002. Harappans and Hunters: Economic Interaction and Specialization in Prehistoric India. In *Forager-Traders in South and Southeast Asia*, edited by K. D. Morrison and L. L. Junker, pp. 62–76. Cambridge University Press, Cambridge.

2003. *The Indus Civilization: A Contemporary Perspective.* Alta Mira Press, New York.

Possehl, G. and P. Gullapalli. 1999. The Early Iron Age in South Asia. In *The Archaeometallurgy of the Asian Old World*, edited by V. Pigott, pp. 153–175. University Museum Monograph 89, Vol. 16. The University Museum, Philadelphia.

Possehl, G. L. and M. H. Raval. 1989. *Harappan Civilization and Rojdi*. Oxford and UBH and the American Institue of Indian Studies, Delhi.

Possehl, G. L. and P. C. Rissman. 1992. The Chronology of Pre-historic India: From Earliest Times to the Iron Age. In *Chronologies in Old World Archaeology*, 3rd ed., edited by R. W. Ehrich. Chicago: Univ. of Chicago Press: 447–74.

Postgate, N. 1990. Excavations at Abu Salabikh, 1988–89. *Iraq* 52: 95–106.

Postgate, N. 1992. *Early Mesopotamia: Society and Economy at the Dawn of History*. Routledge, London.

Potts, D. 1978. Towards an Integrated History of Culture Change in the Arabian Gulf Area: Notes on Dilmun, Makkan and the Economy of Ancient Sumer. *Journal of Oman Studies* 4: 29–51.

1990a. The Arabian Gulf in Antiquity I: From Prehistory to the Fall of the Achaemenid Empire. Clarendon Press, Oxford.

1990b. *A Prehistoric Mound in the Emirate of Umm al Quwain. U.A.E. Excavations at Tell Abraq in 1989*. Munsgaard, Aarhus.

2005. In the Beginning: Marhasi and the Origins of Magan's Ceramic Industry in the Third Millennium B.C. *Arabian Archaeology and Epigraphy* 16: 67–78.

Potts, T. 1994. *Mesopotamia and the East. An Archaeological and Historical Study of Foreign Relations ca. 3400–2000 B.C.* Oxford University Committee for Archaeology, Monograph 37. Oxbow Books, Oxford.

Powell, M. A. 1996. Money in Mesopotamia. *Journal of the Economic and Social History of the Orient*, 39(3): 224–42.

Poyck, A. P. G. 1962. Farm Studies in Iraq. *Medelingen van de Landbouwhogeschool, Te Wageningen*, Nederland 62(1): 1–99.

Pracchia, S. and M. Vidale. 1993. The Archaeological Context of Stoneware Firing at Mohenjo-Daro. *East and West*, 43: 23–68.

Pringle, H. 1998. Neolithic Agriculture: Reading the Signs of Ancient Animal Domestication. *Science* 282(5393): 1448.

Quivron, G. 1987. Die neolithische Siedlung von Mehrgarh. In *Vergessene Städte am Indus*: 67–73. Verlag Philipp von Zabern, Mainz am Rhein.

1988. L'Architecture néolithique de Mehrgarh. In *Les Cités oubliées de l'Indus*, pp. 47–51. Association Française d'Action Artistique, Paris.

2000. The Evolution on the Mature Indus Pottery Style in the Light of the Excavations at Nausharo, Pakistan. *East and West* 50(1–4): 147–90.

Raikes, R. L. 1964. The End of the Ancient Cities of the Indus. *American Anthropologist* 66(2): 284–99.

Raikes, R. L. and G. F. Dales. 1986. Reposte to Wasson's Sedimentological Basis of the Mohenjo-Daro Food Hypothesis. *Man and Environment* 10: 33–44.

Raikes, R. L. and R. H. J. Dyson. 1961. The Prehistoric Climate of Baluchistan and the Indus Valley. *American Anthropologist* 63: 265–81.

Rao, S. R. 1963a. Excavations at Rangpur and Other Explorations in Gujarat. *Ancient India* 18–19: 5–207.

1963b. A "Persian Gulf" seal from Lothal. *Antiquity* 37: 96–9.

1973. *Lothal and the Indus Civilization.* Bombay: Asia Publishing House.

1979. Lothal: A Harappan Port Town, 1955–62. *Memoirs of the Archaeological Survey of India* 1(78). Archaeological Survey of India, New Delhi.

Rasool, N. ed. 1996. Archaeological Sites and Monuments in Punjab. *Pakistan Archaeology*, Special issue no. 29 (1994–1996). Department of Archaeology, Karachi.

Ratnagar, S. 1981. *Encounters. The Westerly Trade of the Harappan Civilization.* Oxford University Press, Delhi.

Ratnagar, S., K. Abdi, C. Brosius, R. Coningham, M. Dietler, R. Friedland, A. Gupta, M. Herzfeld, S. Srinivas, J. Heitzman, and S. Ratnagar. 2004. Archaeology at the Heart of a Political Confrontation. *Current Anthropology* 45: 239–59.

Ray, H. P. 2003. *The Archeology of Seafaring in Ancient South Asia.* Cambridge University Press, Cambridge.

Reddy, S. N. 1997. If the Threshing Floor Could Talk: Integration of Agriculture and Pastoralism during the Late Harappan in Gujarat, India. *Journal of Anthropological Archaeology* 16: 162–87.

2003. Food and Fodder: Plant Usage and Changing Socio-cultural Landscapes during the Harappan Phase in Gujarat, India. In *Indus Ethnobiology*, edited by S. Weber and W. R. Belcher, pp. 327–42. Lexington Books, Lanham.

Rendell, H. 1981. A Preliminary Investigation of the Sedimentary History of the Bannu Basin in the Late Holocene. In *South Asian Archaeology 1979*, edited by H. Hartel, pp. 219–25. Curzon Press, London.

Renfrew, C. 1986. *Peer Polity Interaction and Socio-political Change.* Cambridge University Press, Cambridge.

1987. *Archaeology and Language: The Puzzle of Indo-European Origins.* Cambridge University Press, New York.

Revelle, R. 1964. A Report on Land and Water Development in the Indus Plain. Prepared for the Worldbank.

Rissman, P. C. 1985. The Oriyo Timbo Excavations and the End of the Harappan Tradition in Gryarat. In *South Asian Archaeology 1983*, edited by J. Schotsman and M. Todder. Naples: Instituto Universitario Orieintale, Dipartimento di Studi Asiatice, Series Minor XXIII: 345–6.

1988. Public Displays and Private Values: A Guide to Buried Wealth in Harappan Archaeology. *World Archaeology* 20(2): 200–28.

1989. The Organization of Seal Production in the Harappan Civilization. In *Old Problems and New Perspectives in the Archaeology of South Asia*, edited by J. M. Kenoyer, pp. 159–70, no. 2, Wisconsin Archaeological Reports, Madison.

Rissman, P. C. and Y. M. Chitalwala. 1990. *Harappan Civilization and Oriyo Timbo.* Oxford and IBH, New Delhi.

Robb, J. E. 1998. The Archaeology of Symbols. *Annual Review of Anthropology* 27: 329–46.

Rosen, A. and S.A. Rosen. 2001. Determinist or not Determinist. Climate, Environment, and Archaeological Explanation in the Levant. In *Studies in the Archaeology of Israel and Neighboring Lands in Memory of Douglas L. Esse*, edited by S. Wolff, pp. 535–9. Studies in Ancient Oriental Civilization 59, Oriental Institute, Chicago.

Roy, T. N. 1961. *The Story of Indian Archaeology: 1784–1947*. Government of India, Delhi.

Russell, N. 1995. The Bone Tool Industry at Mehrgarh and Sibri. In *Mehrgarh: Field Reports 1974–1985 from Neolithic Times to the Indus Civilization*, edited by C. Jarrige et al., pp. 583–591. The Department of Culture and Tourism, Government of Sindh, Karachi.

Rybcynzki, W. 1995. *City Life*. Scribner, New York.

Sahi, M. D. N. 1979. Iron at Ahar. In *Essays in Indian Protohistory*, edited by D. P. Agrawal and D. Chakrabarti, pp. 365–8. B. R. Publishing Corporation, Delhi.

Sahni, D. R. 1926–7. Mohenjo-Daro. *Annual Report of the Archaeological Survey of India*, pp. 60–88. Archaeological Survey of India, Delhi.

  1931a. HR area Section B. In *Mohenjo-Daro and the Indus Civilization*, edited by J. Marshall, pp. 187–213. 3 vols. Arthur Probsthain, London.

  1931b. VS area. In *Mohenjo-Daro and the Indus Civilization*, edited by J. Marshall, pp. 214–32. 3 vols. Arthur Probsthain, London.

Sahni, M. R. 1956. Biological Evidence Bearing on the Decline of the Indus Valley Civilization. *Journal of the Paleontological Society of India* 1(1): 101–7.

Salim, M. 1991a. Painted Grey Ware Sites around Islamabad. *Pakistan Archaeology* 26(1): 144–55.

  1991b. Dhok Gangaal: A Painted Grey Ware Site in Islamabad. *Ancient Pakistan* 27: 27–33.

Samzun, A. 1992. Observations on the Characteristics of the Pre-Harappan Remains, Pottery and Artifacts at Nausharo, Pakistan (2700–2500 B.C.). In *South Asian Archaeology 1989*, edited by C. Jarrige, pp. 245–252. Prehistory Press, Madison.

Samzun, A. and P. Sellier. 1985. The First Anthropological and Cultural Evidence for the Funerary Practice of the Chalcolithic Population of Mehrgarh Pakistan. In *South Asian Archaeology 1983*. edited by J. Schotsmanns and M. Taddei, pp. 91–119. Istituto Universitario Orientale, Naples.

Sanday, P. R. 2002. *Women at the Center: Life in the Modern Matriarchy*. Cornell University Press, Ithaca.

Sankalia, H. D. 1964. Traditional Indian Chronology and C-14 Dates of Excavated Sites. *Journal of Indian History* 13: 635–50.

  1973. Prehistoric Colonization in India. In *World Archaeology* 5: 86–91.

  1974. *The Prehistory and Protohistory of India and Pakistan*. 2nd ed. Deccan College Postgraduate and Research Institute, Poona.

Sankalia, H. D., S. B. Deo, and Z. D. Ansari. 1969. *Excavations at Ahar (Timbavati) 1961–62*. Deccan College Post-graduate and Research Institute, Poona.

  1971. *Chalcolithic Navdatoli: The Excavations at Navdatoli 1957–59*. Publication no. 2. Deccan College Postgraduate and Research Institute/Maharaja Sayajiro University, Poona/Baroda.

Santoni, M. 1984. Sibri and South Cemetery at Mehrgarh: Third Millennium Connections between the Northern Kachi Plain (Pakistan) and Central Asia. In *South Asian Archaeology 1981*, edited by B. Allchin., pp. 52–60. Cambridge University Press, Cambridge.

1989. Potters and Pottery at Mehrgarh during the Third Millennium B.C. (Periods VI and VII). In *South Asian Archaeology 1985*, edited by K. Frifelt and P. Sørensen, pp. 176–85. Curzon Press, London.

Sarcina, A. 1979. A Statistical Assessment of House Patterns at Mohenjo-Daro. In *Mesopotamia XIII–XIV*, pp. 155–99. IsMEO, Rome.

Sarianidi, V. I. 1993. Margiana in the Ancient Orient. *International Association for the Study of the Cultures of Central Asia, Information Bulletin* 19: 5–28.

1998. *Margiana and Protozoroastrism*. Kapon Editions, Athens.

Sarkar, S. S. 1985. Human Skeletal Remains from Lothal. In *Lothal: A Harappan Port Town, 1955–62*, edited by S. R. Rao, pp. 269–304. *Memoirs of the Archaeological Survey of India* 2(78).

Sastri, K. N. 1965. *New Light on the Indus Civilization*. Vol. 2. Atma Ram & Sons, Delhi.

Sayce, A. H. 1924. Remarkable discoveries in India. *Illustrated London News*, September 27, pp. 525, 566.

Scheil, V. E. 1925. Un nouveau sceau pseudo-Sumerian. *Revue d'Assyriologie et d'Archéologie Orientale* 22(2): 55–66.

Schimmel, A. 1999. The Indus River of Poetry. In *The Indus River: Biodiversity, Resources, Humankind*, edited by A. Meadows and P. S. Meadows, pp. 409–15. Oxford University Press, Karachi.

Schmandt-Besserat, D. 1979. Reckoning before Writing. *Archaeology* 32(3): 22–31.

Scholz, F. 1982\83. Baluchistan: A Brief Introduction to the Geography of Pakistan's Mountainous Province. *Newsletter of Baluchistan Studies* 1: 13–18.

Schuldenrein, J., R. P. Wright, and M. A. Khan. 2007. Harappan Geoarchaeology Reconsidered: Holocene Landscapes and Environments of the Greater Indus Plain. In *Settlement and Society*, edited by E. Stone, p. 86–116. UCLA, Cotsen Institute of Archaeology, Los Angeles.

Schuldenrein, J., R. P. Wright, M. A. Khan, and M. R. Mughal. 2004. Geoarchaeological Explorations on the Upper Beas Drainage: Landscape and Settlement in the Upper Indus Valley, Punjab. Pakistan. *Journal of Archaeological Sciences*, 31: 777–92.

Schwab, R. 1984. *The Oriental Renaissance: Europe's Rediscovery of India and the East, 1680–1880*. Columbia University Press, New York.

Sellier, P. 1991. Mehrgarh: Funerary Rites and the Archaeology of Death. In *Forgotten Cities on the Indus: Early Civilization in Pakistan from the 8th to the 2nd Millennium B.C.*, edited by M. Jansen et al. Verlag Philipp von Zabern, Mainz.

Sewell, R. B. S. and B. S. Guha. 1931. Zoological remains. In *Mohenjo-Daro and the Indus Civilization*, edited by J. Marshall, pp. 649–73. 3 vols. Arthur Probsthain, London.

Shaffer, J. G. 1992. Indus Valley, Baluchistan and the Helmand Drainage (Afghanistan). In *Chronologies in Old World Archaeology*, 3rd ed., edited by R. W. Ehrich. University of Chicago Press, Chicago.

1993. Reurbanization: The Eastern Punjab and Beyond. In *Urban Form and Meaning in South Asia*, edited by H. Spodek and D. Srinivasan, pp. 53–67. National Gallery of Art, Washington, DC.

Shaffer, J. G. and D. Lichtenstein. 1999. Migration, Philology and South Asian Archaeology. In *Aryan and non-Aryan in South Asia*, edited by J. Bronkhorst and M. Deshanpande, pp. 239–60 Harvard Oriental Series, Cambridge.

Shaikh, Nilofer. 1996. Mohenjo-daro, A Challenge in Conservation. *Ancient Sindh* 3: 49–66.

Shar, G. M. 1987. The Mohanna–An Unknown Life on the Indus River. *Reports on Field Work Carried Out at Mohenjo-daro, Pakistan, 1983–1984*, Interim Reports, Vol. 2, edited by M. Jansen and G. Urban, p. 169–83. IsMEO-Aachen-University Mission, Aachen.

Shar, G. M., F. Negrino, and E. Starnini. 1996. The Archaeological Finds from Duhbi (Thar Desert, Sindh, Pakistan). *Ancient Sindh* 3: 39–47.

Sharma, A. K. 1974. Evidence of a Horse from the Harappan Settlement at Surkotada. *Puratattva* 7: 75–6.

1999. *The Departed Harappans of Kalibangan*. Sundeep Prakashan, New Delhi.

Sharma, D. V., V. N. Prabhakar, R. Tewari, and R. K. Srivastava. 2000. Harappan Jewelry Hoard from Manda. *Puratattva: Bulletin of the Indian Archaeological Society*, 30: 36–41.

Sharma, R. S. 1983. *Material Culture and Social Formations in Ancient India*. Macmillan, Delhi.

Sherratt, A. G. 1983. The Secondary Exploitation of Animals in the Old World. *World Archaeology* 75: 90–104.

Shinde, V. 1991. A Horn-Headed Human Figure on a Harappan Jar from Padri, Gujarat. *Man and Environment* 16(2): 87–9.

1992. Padri and the Indus Civilization. *South Asian Studies* 8: 55–66.

Shinde, V., G. L. Possehl, and M. Ameri. 2005. Excavations at Gilund 2001–2003: The Seal Impressions and Other Finds. In *South Asian Archaeology 2003*, edited by U. Franke-Vogt and H-J Weisshaar, pp. 159–70. Forschungen zur Archäologie Aussereuropaischer Kulturen, Band 1, Bonn.

Shroder, J. 1993. *Himalayas to the Sea: Geology, Geomorphology and the Quaternary*. Routledge, London and New York.

Silverman, H. and D. B. Small eds. 2002. *The Space and Place of Death*, Archaeological Papers, Vol. II, pp. 1–12. American Anthropological Association, Washington, DC.

Singh, Upinder. 2004. *The Discovery of Ancient India: Early Archaeologists and the Beginnings of Archaeology*. Permanent Black, Delhi.

Singh, G., R. D. Joshi, S. K. Chopra, and A. B. Singh. 1974. Late Quaternary History of Vegetation and Climate of the Rajasthan Desert, India. *Philosophical Transactions of the Royal Society of London* 267: 467–501.

Singh, G., R. J. Wasson, and D. P. Agrawal. 1990. Vegetational and Seasonal Climatic Changes since the Last Full Glacial in the Thar Desert, Northwestern India. *Review of Paleobotany and Palynology* 64: 351–8.

Sinopoli, C. M. 2003. *The Political Economy of Craft Production: Crafting Empire in South India, c. 1350–1650*. Cambridge University Press, Cambridge.

Sinopoli, C. M. 2007. Gender and Archaeology in South and Southwest Asia. In S. M. Nelson, ed. *Worlds of Gender*, Altamira Press, 73–96.

Small, David. 1997. City-state Dynamics through a Greek Lens. In *The Archaeology of City States*, edited by D. L. Nichols and T. H. Charlton, pp. 107–18. Smithsonian Institution Press, Washington, DC.

Snell, D. C. 1988. The Allocation of Resources in the Umma Silver Account System. *Journal of the Economic and Social History of the Orient*. 31(1): 1–13.

Somayajulu, B. L. K. 1990. Geoarchaeology and Geochemical Approaches to the Study of Quaternary Climates. *Man and Environment* 15(1): 1–11.

Sonawane, V. H. 1992. Fresh Light on the Specialized Crafts of the Harappans in Gujarat. *The Eastern Anthropologist*, 45(1–2): 155–72.

Sorley, H. T. 1959. The Former Province of Sind Including Khairpur State. *Gazetteer of West Pakistan*. Government of West Pakistan, Karachi.

Southworth, F. C. 1990. The Reconstruction of Prehistoric South Asian Language Contact. In *The Uses of Linguistics*, edited by E. H. Benedict, p. 583, Annals of the New York Academy of Sciences, New York.

1992. Linguistics and Archaeology: Prehistoric Implications of Some South Asian Plant Names. In *South Asian Archeology Studies*, edited by G. L. Possehl, pp. 81 6. Oxford & IBH, Delhi.

Srinivasan, D. 1975–6. The so-called proto-Siva seal from Mohenjo-Daro: An Iconographical Assessment. *Archives of Asian Art* 29: 47–58.

1984. Unhinging Siva from the Indus Civilization. *Journal of the Royal Asiatic Society of Great Britain and Ireland*, 77–89.

Staubwasser, M., F. Sirocko, P. M. Grootes, Mc. Segl. 2003. Climate Change at the 4.2 ka BP Termination of the Indus Valley Civilization and Holocene South Asian Monsoon variability. *Geophysical Research Letters*, 30(8): 1425–31.

Stein, A. 1928. *Innermost Asia*. 4 vols. Clarendon Press, Oxford.

1931. An Archaeological Tour in Gedrosia. No. 43. *Memoirs of the Archaeological Survey of India*, Delhi.

1937. *Archaeological Reconnaissances in Northwestern India and Southeastern Iran*. London.

1943a. On Alexander's Route into Gedrosia: An Archaeological Tour in Las Bela. *Geographical Journal* 102(5–6): 193–227.

1943b. An Archaeological Tour along the Ghaggar-Hakra River, 1940–42. Microfilm ADI-481. Library of Congress, Washington, DC.

Steinkeller, P. 1982. The Question of Marhasi: A Contribution to the Historical Geography of Iran in the Third Millennium B.C. *Zeitschrift fur assyriologie und verderasiatische Archaologic* 72: 237–65.

1987. The Foresters of Umma: Toward a Definition of the Labor in the Ur III. In *Labor in the Ancient Near East*, edited by M. Powell, American Oriental Society, New Haven.

2006. New Light on Marhasi and Its Contacts with Makkan and Babylonia. *Journal of Magan Studies* 1: 1–17.

Steward, J. 1949. *Irrigation Civilizations: A Comparative Study. A Symposium on Method and Result of Cross-Cultural Regularities*. Washington Social Science Section, Department of Cultural Affairs, Pan-American Union, Washington, DC.

Stone, E. 1997. City States and Their Centers: The Mesopotamian Example. In *The Archaeology of City-States: Cross-cultural Approaches*, edited by D. L. Nichols and T. H. Charlton, pp. 15–26. Smithsonian Institution Press, Washington, D.C.

2007. The Mesopotamian Urban Experience. In *Settlement and Society*, edited by E. Stone, pp. 213–34. UCLA, Cotsen Institute of Archaeology, Los Angeles.

Stone, E. C. and P. Zimansky. 1992. Mashkan-shapir and the Anatomy of an Old Babylonian City. *Biblical Archaeologist* 55: 212–18.

1994. The Second and Third Seasons at Tell Abu Duwari, Iraq. *The Journal of Field Archaeology* 21:437–55.

Subramanian V. and R. A. Dalavai. 1978. Denudation by Indian Rivers. *Man and Environment* II: 14–17.

Tandon, O. P. 1967–8. Alamgirpur and the Iron Age in India. *Puratattva* 1: 54–60.

Tengberg, M. and S. Thiebault. 2003. Vegetation History and Wood Exploitation in Pakistani Baluchistan from the Neolithic to the Harappan Period: The Evidence from Charcoal Analysis. In *Indus Ethnobiology*, edited by S. Weber and W. R. Belcher, pp. 21–64. Lexington Books, Lanham.

Tessitori, L. P. 1918–19. *Exploration, Bikaner. Annual Report of the Archaeological Survey of India*, 1918–19, pp. 22–3. Archaeological Survey of India, Delhi.

Thapar, B. K. 1970. The Aryans: A Reappraisal of the Problem. In *India's Contribution to World Thought and Culture*, edited by L. Chandra, S. P. Gupta, D. Swarup, and S. Goel, pp. 147–64. Vivikananda Rock Memorial Committee, Madras.

1973. New Traits of the Indus Civilization at Kalibangan: An Appraisal. In *South Asian Archaeology*, edited by N. Hammond, pp. 85–104. Noyes Press, Park Ridge.

1975. Kalibangan: A Harappan Metropolis beyond the Indus Valley. *Expedition* 17(2): 19–32.

1977. Climate during the Period of Indian Civilization: Evidence from Kalibangan. In *Ecology and Archaeology of Western India*, edited by D. P. Agrawal and B. M. Pande, pp. 67–73. Concept Publishing Company, Delhi.

1989. Kalibangan. In *An Encyclopedia of Indian Archaeology*, Vol. 2, edited by A. Ghosh, pp. 194–6. Munshiram Manoharlal, Delhi.

Thapar, R. 1966. *A History of India*. Vol. I. Penguin, Harmondsworth.

Thiebault, S. 1988a. Paleoenvironment and Ancient Vegetation of Baluchistan Based on Charcoal Analysis of Archaeological Sites. *Proceedings of the Indian National Science Academy* 54A: 501–9.

1988b. L'evolution de La Vegetation a Mehrgarh. In *Les Cites Oubliees de l'Indus*, p. 45. Musee National des Artes Asiatiques, Guimet, Paris.

1989. A Note on the Ancient Vegetation of Baluchistan Based on Charcoal Analysis of the Latest Periods from Mehrgarh, Pakistan. In *South Asian Archaeology 1985*, edited by K. Frifelt and P. Sorensen, pp. 186–8. Curzon Press, London.

1992. Complementary Results in Anthracological Analysis from Sites in Baluchistan. In *South Asian Archaeology 1989*, edited by C. Jarrige, pp. 271–6. Prehistory Press, Madison.

1995. First Results of the Ancient Vegetation of Mehrgarh through Anthracological Analysis. In *Mehrgarh Field Reports 1974–1985 – from Neolithic Times to the Indus Civilization*, edited by C. Jarrige, J. F. Jarrige, R. H. Meadow and G. Quivron, pp. 524. Department of Culture and Tourism, in Collaboration with French Ministry of Foreign Affairs, Karachi.

Thomas, K. D. 2003. Minimizing Risk? Approaches to Pre-Harappan Human Ecology on the Northwest Margin of the Greater Indus System. In *Indus Ethnobiology*, edited by S. Weber and W. R. Belcher, pp. 397–430. Lexington Books, Lanham.

Tosi, Maurizio. 1974. *The Problem of Turquoise in Protohistoric Trade on the Iranian Plateau*. Vol. 2, pp. 148–62. Memorie dell'Istituto Italiano di Paleontologia, Umana.

1991. The Indus Civilization beyond the Indian Subcontinent. In *Forgotten Cities on the Indus*, edited by M. Jansen, M. Mulloy and G. Urban, pp. 111–28. Verlag Philipp von Zabern, Mainz.

Tosi, M. L. Bondioli, and M. Vidale. 1983. Craft Activity Areas and Surface Survey at Mohenjodaro. In *Interim Reports*, Vol. 1, edited by M. Jansen and G. Urban, pp. 9–38. Forschungsprojekt, Aachen.

Trautmann, Thomas R. 1971. *Kautilya and the Arthasastra*. Brill, Leiden.

1997. *Aryans and British India*. University of California Press Berkeley, Los Angeles, London.

Trautmann, T. R. and C. M. Sinopoli. 2002. In the Beginning Was the Word: Excavating the Relations between History and Archaeology in South Asia. *Journal of Economic and Social History of the Orient* 45(4): 492–523.

Trigger, B. G. 1989. *A History of Archaeological Thought*. Cambridge University Press, Cambridge.

2003. *Understanding Early Civilizations*. Cambridge University Press, Cambridge.

Tringham, R. E. 1991. Households with Faces: The Challenge of Gender in Prehistoric Architectural Remains. In *Engendering Archaeology: Women and Pre-History*, edited by Joan Gero and Margaret Conkey, pp. 93–131. Basil Blackwell, Oxford.

Tripathi, V. 1976. *The Painted Grey Ware: An Iron Age Culture of Northern India*. Concept Publishing Company, Delhi.

Vandiver, P. B. The Production Technology of Early Pottery at Mehrgarh. In *Mehrgarh: Field Reports 1974–1985 from Neolithic Times to the Indus Civilization*, edited by C. Jarrige et al., pp. 648–61. The Department of Culture and Tourism, Government of Sindh, Karachi.

Van Dommelen. 1999. Exploring Everyday Places and Cosmologies. In *Archaeologies of Landscape: Contemporary Perspectives*, edited by W. Ashmore and A. B. Knapp, pp. 277–87 Blackwell Publishers, Malden, MA.

Varma, R. 1997. Prehistoric Research in India: An Assessment. *Man and Environment* XXII(1): 1–7.

Vats, M. S. 1937. *Annual Report of the Archaeological Survey of India 1934–1935*. Government of India, Calcutta.

1940. *Excavations at Harappa*. Government of India, Delhi.

Vaughan, P. C. 1995. Functional Analysis of Samples of Neolithic, Chalcolithic, and Bronze Age Flints from Mehrgarh (Balochistan,

Pakistan). In *Mehrgarh: Field Reports 1974–1985 from Neolithic Times to the Indus Civilization*, edited by C. Jarrige et al., pp. 614–25. The Department of Culture and Tourism, Government of Sindh, Karachi.

Verardi, G. 1987. Preliminary Reports on the Stupa and Monastery of Mohenjo-daro. In *Interim Reports*, Vol. 2, edited by M. Jansen and G. Urban, pp. 44–58. IsMEO-Aachen University Mission, Aachen.

Vidale, M. 1989. Specialized Producers and Urban Elites on the Role of Craft Production in Mature Harappan Urban Contexts. In *Old Problems and New Perspectives in the Archaeology of South Asia*, edited by J. M. Kenoyer. University of Wisconsin, Madison.

1990. On the Structure and the Relative Chronology of an Harappan Industrial Site. In *South Asian Archaeology 1987*, edited by M. Taddei and P. Callieri, Part I, pp. 203–44. Istituto Italiano per il Medi ed Estremo Oriente, Rome.

1992. *Produzione Artigianale Protostorica: Ethnoarchacologia e Archeologia*. Universita degli Studi di padova, Padua.

2000. *The Archaeology of Indus Crafts: Indus Craftspeople and Why We Study Them*. IsIAO, Italiano per l'Oriente, Rome.

2005. The Short-horned Bull on the Indus Seals: A Symbol of the Families in the Western Trade?. In *South Asian Archaeology 2003*, edited by U. Franke-Vogt and H-J Weisshaar, Aachen: Forschungen zur Archaeologie, Band 1: 147–158.

Vidale, M. and P. Bianchetti. 1997. Mineralogical Identification of Green Semiprecious Stones From Pakistan. In *South Asian Archaeology 1995*, edited by R. Allchin and B. Allchin, vol. 2, pp. 947–53. New Delhi.

Vidale, M. and H. M. L. Miller. 2000. The General Case Through Time. In M. Vidale, *The Archaeology of Indus Craft*, Appendix 143, p. 150. IsIAO, Rome.

2005. The Short-Horned Bull on the Indus Seals: A Symbol of the Families in the Western Trade? In *South Asian Archaeology 2003*, edited by U. Franke-Vogt and H. J. Weisshaar, pp. 147–58. Lindensoft, Aachen.

Von Rad, U., M. Schaaf, K. H. Michels, H. Schulz, W. H. Berger, and F. Sirocko. 1999. A 5,000-yr Record of Climate Change in Varved Sediments from the Oxygen Minimum Zone off Pakistan, Northeastern Arabian Sea. *Quaternary Research* 51: 39–53.

Vidale, and G. M. Shar. 1991. Zahr Muhra: Soapstone Cutting in Contemporary Baluchistan and Sind. *Annali Estrattoda Annal, dell'Istituto Universitario Orientale, Napoli*, 50: 61–78.

Vosmer, Tom. 2000. Ships in the Ancient Arabian Sea: The Development of a Hypothetical Reed-Boat Model. *Proceeding of the Seminar for Arabian Studies* 30: 235–42.

Wankze, H. 1984. Axis Systems and Orientation at Mohenjo-Daro. In *Interim Reports Vol. 2. Reports on Field Work Carried out at Mohenjo-Daro, Pakistan 1983–84 by the IsMEO-Aachen-University Mission*, edited by M. Jansen and G. Urban, pp. 23–32. Forschungsprojekt "Mohenjo-Daro," Aachen.

Waters, M. R. 1992. *Principles of Geoarchaeology: A North American Perspective*. The University of Arizona Press, Tucson.

Weber, S. A. 1990. Millets in South Asia: Rojdi as a Case Study. In *South Asian Archaeology 1987*, Serie Orientale Roma, Vol. 3, edited by M. Taddei, pp. 333–48. Istituto Italiano per il Medio ed Estremo Oriente, Roma.

1991. *Plants and Harappan Subsistence: An Example of Stability and Change from Rojdi*. Delhi: Oxford & IBH and American Institute of Indian Studies.

1999. Seeds of Urbanism: Paleoethnobotany and the Indus Civilization. *Antiquity* 73(282): 813–26.

2003. Archaeobotany at Harappa: Indications for Change. In *Indus Ethnobiology*, edited by S. Weber and W. R. Belcher, pp. 175–98. Lexington Books, Lanham.

Weber, S. A. and W. R. Belcher. 2003. *Indus Ethnobiology. New Perspectives from the Field*. Lexington Books, Lanham.

Weisgerber, G. 1984. Makan and Meluhha–Third Millennium B.C. Copper Production in Oman and the Evidence of Contact with the Indus Valley. *South Asian Archaeology 1981*, edited by B. Allchin, pp. 196–201. Cambridge University Press, Cambridge.

Wheeler, M. 1947 [1994]. Harappa 1946: the Defenses and Cemetery R37. *Ancient India*. 3: 58–130.

1968. *The Indus Civilization*. 3rd ed. Supplement volume to the Cambridge History of India. Cambridge University Press, Cambridge.

Widell, M. 2005. Some Reflections on Babylonian Exchange during the End of the Third Millennium B.C. 48(3): 288–400.

Wiedemann, N. and J. Birdsong. 2000. Drawing Cities. *Platform*, Spring 2000: 7–9.

Wigley, T. M. L., M. J. Ingram, and G. Farmer. 1981. *Climate and History: Studies in Past Climates and Their Impact on Man*. Cambridge University Press, Cambridge.

Wilhemy, H. 1969. Das Urstromtal am Ostrand der Indusebene und das Saraswati Problem. *Zeitschrift fur Geomorphologie* 8: 76–83.

Wilkins, H. 2005. From Massive to Flimsy: The Declining Structural Fabric at Mohenjo-daro. In *South Asian Archaeology 2003*, edited by U. Franke-Vogt and H. J. Wersshaar, pp. 123–36. Linden Soft, Aachen.

Williams, M. A. J., D. L. Dunkerley, P. De Deckker, A. P. Kershaw, and T. Stokes. 1993. *Quaternary Environments*. Edward Arnold, London, Museum/University Museum, London/Philadelphia.

Wiseman, D. J. 1959. *Cylinder Seals of Western Asia*. Bathworth Press, London.

Wittfogel, K. A. 1957. *Oriental Despotism: A Comparative Study in Total Power*. Yale University Press, New Haven.

Wright, H. E. 1993. Environmental Determinism in Near Eastern Prehistory. *Current Anthropology* 34(4): 458–69.

Wright, R. P. 1980. The Agricultural System and Agrarian Structure of Sumer. Paper on File, Harvard University, Tozzer Library.

1984. *Technology, Style and Craft Specialization: Patterns of Interaction and Exchange on the Indo-Iranian Borderlands, Third Millennium B.C.* PhD. Diss. Harvard University and University Microfilms.

1985. Technology and Style in Ancient Ceramics. In *Ceramics and Civilization: Ancient Technology to Modern Science*, Vol. 1, edited by W. D. Kingery, pp. 5–25. American Ceramic Society, Columbus, OH.

1989. Production and Exchange of Ceramics on the Oman Peninsula from the Perspective of Hili (with M. J. Blackman and S. Mery). *Journal of Field Archaeology* 1691: 61–77.

1991. Women's Labor and Pottery Production in Prehistory. In *Engendering Archaeology: Women and Pre-History*, edited by Joan Gero and Margaret Conkey, pp. 194–223. Basil Blackwell, Oxford.

1993. Technological Styles: Transforming a Natural Material into a Cultural Object. In *History from Things: Essays on Material Culture*, edited by S. Lubar and W. D. Kingery, pp. 242–69. Smithsonian Institution Press, Washington, DC.

1995. Fine Ware Traditions at Mehrgarh. In *Mehrgarh: Field Reports 1974– 1985 from Neolithic Times to the Indus Civilization*, edited by C. Jarrige et al., pp. 662–71. The Department of Culture and Tourism, Government of Sindh, Karachi.

1996. Technology, Gender, and Class: Worlds of Difference in Ur III Mesopotamia. In *Gender and Archaeology*, edited by R. P. Wright. University of Pennsylvania Press, Philadelphia.

1997. Images of Women in the Art of the Indus Valley. *Female and Male from Amarna to Middle Asia*. The Charles K. Wilkinson Lecturer for Ancient Near Eastern Art Department, Metropolitan Museum of Art.

2001. Edge Zones, Cores and Peripheries: Defining the Margins of the Indus Valley-Civilization. Paper presented at the American Anthropological Association Meetings, November 2001.

2002a. The Origin of Cities. In *Encyclopedia of Urban Cultures: Cities and Cultures Around the World*, Vol. 1, edited by M. Ember and C. R. Ember. A Scholastic Company, Danburt.

2002b. Revisiting Interaction Spheres – Social Boundaries and Technologies on Inner and Outermost Frontiers. *Iranica Antiqua* XXXVII: 403–17.

2008. Gendered Relations and the Ur III Dynasty, Kinship, Property, and Labor. In *Gender Through Time in The Ancient Near East.*, edited by D. Bolger, pp. 247–870. Altamira Press, Lanham.

n.d. "Monies and the Indus."

In Press. Marking Landscapes: The Tungabhadra Project from History to Prehistory. In *States and the Landscape*, edited by S. E. Falconer and C. L. Redman.

Wright, R. P. and C. Hritz. In Press. Satellite Remote Sensing Imagery: New Evidence for Site Distributions and Ecologies in the Upper Indus. In *South Asian Archaeology 2007*, edited by M. Tosi and D. Frenez, Ravenna.

Wright, Rita P., M. Afzal Khan, and J. Schuldenrein. 2002. Urbanism in the Indus Valley: Environment and Settlement on the Beas River. *Indus Valley Civilization. Dialogue among Civilizations*, edited by M. A. Halim and Abdul Ghafoor, pp. 102–13. Crystal Printers, Islamabad.

Wright, R. P., R. Bryson, and J. Schuldenrein. 2008. Water Supply and History: Harappa and the Beas Regional Survey. *Antiquity* 82: 37–48.

Wright, R. P., J. Schuldenrein, M. A. Khan, and S. Malin-Boyce. 2005a. The Beas River Landscape and Settlement Survey: Preliminary Results from the Site of Vainiwal. In *South Asian Archaeology 2003*, edited by U. Franke-Vogt and H-J. Weisshaar, pp. 101–11. Linden Soft, Aachen.

Wright, R. P., J. Schuldenrein, M. A., and M. R. Mughal. 2005b. The Emergence of Satellite Communities along the Beas Drainage: Preliminary, Results from Lahoma Lal Tibba and Chak Purbane Syal. *South Asian Archaeology 2001*, Vol. 1, pp. 327–36. CNRS, Paris.

Yoffee, N. 1997. The Obvious and the Chimerical: City-states in Archaeological Perspective. In *The Archaeology of City-States*, edited by D. L. Nichols and T. H. Charlton, pp. 255–64. Smithsonian Institution Press, Washington, DC.

Yoffee, N. and G. L. Cowgill. 1988. *The Collapse of Ancient States and Civilizations*. Univ. of Arizona Press, Tucson.

Zagarell, A. 1997. The Megalithic Graves of the Nilgiri Hills and the Moyar Ditch. In *Blue Mountains Revisited: Cultural Studies in the Nilgiri Hills*, edited by P. Bockings, pp. 23–73. Oxford University Press, New Delhi.

n.d. Collapse of Civilization and the Potential for Multi-linear Evolution.

Zeder, M. 1991. *Feeding Cities*. Smithsonian Institution Press, Washington DC.

Index

385